Spiritual Recovery From Addiction

A Daily Devotional

Pastor Blaine MacNeil

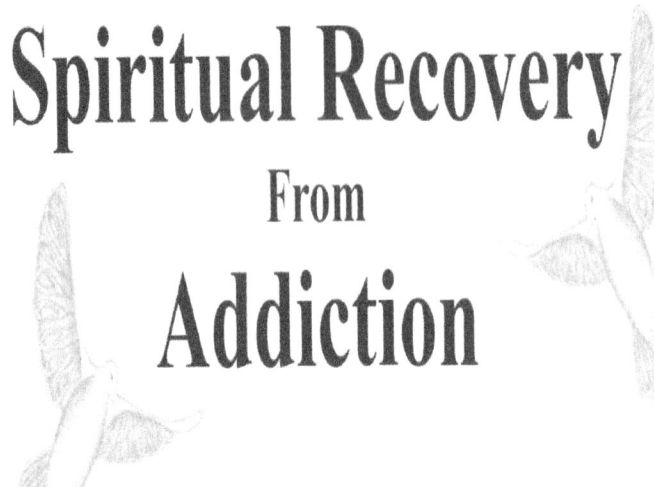

Spiritual Recovery From Addiction

A Daily Devotional

Pastor Blaine MacNeil

Meet Me on Facebook

Copyright 2020 by Pastor Blaine MacNeil. All rights reserved. No part of this book may be used or reproduced in any manner whatsoever without the written permission of the publisher or the author.

Cover and artwork by Blaine MacNeil Copyright 2020

The Twelve Steps of Alcoholics Anonymous are adapted and includes biblical scriptures with permission of Alcoholics Anonymous World Services, Inc. ("A.A.W.S.") Permission to reprint this adaptation of the Twelve Steps does not mean that A.A.W.S. has reviewed or approved the contents of this publication, or that A.A.W.S. necessarily agrees with the views expressed herein. A.A. is a program of recovery from alcoholism only - use of the Twelve Steps in connection with programs and activities which are patterned after A.A., but which address other problems, or in any other non-A.A. context, does not imply otherwise. Additionally, while A.A. is a spiritual program, A.A. is not a religious program. Thus, A.A. is not affiliated or allied with any sect, denomination, or specific religious belief.

Unless otherwise noted all the scripture quotations are from the English Standard Version of the Bible: The Holy Bible, English Standard Version® (ESV®), Copyright © 2001 by Crossway, a publishing ministry of Good News Publishers. All rights reserved. ESV Text Edition: 2016.

NRSV - New Revised Standard Version Bible, copyright © 1989 National Council of the Churches of Christ in the United States of America. Used by permission. All rights reserved worldwide.

NASB - Scripture quotations taken from the New American Standard Bible® (NASB), Copyright © 1960, 1962, 1963, 1968, 1971, 1972, 1973, 1975, 1977, 1995 by The Lockman Foundation. Used by permission. www.Lockman.org.

KJ21 - Scripture quotations taken from the 21st Century King James Version®, copyright © 1994. Used by permission of Deuel Enterprises, Inc., Gary, SD 57237. All rights reserved.

There are a few case studies and examples that that I mention in my book. In keeping with our tradition of anonymity these fictious people and their case studies are simply composites based on the experiences of many people and their experiences. All of these have been mixed and matched together. Any similarities between the names or events I used are merely coincidental and unintentional.

Religion / Christian Life / Recovery / Inspirational
Printed and bound in the USA
Cover art Pastor Blaine MacNeil

Table of Contents

Dedication
Bio
Preface
Introduction
A Word of Thanks
Genesis Chapter One, In the Beginning, God Created...
Creation by the Spoken Word
Spiritual Core Concepts: The Breath-of-Life
Spiritual Core Concepts: The Sons of Adam and the Daughter's of Eve Inhaled Drugs and they Became Living-Addicts
Spiritual Core Concepts: What is the Body, the Soul, and the Spirit of Man?
Spiritual Core Concepts: Our Purpose in Life Is to Work
Fellowship
Covenant Relationships: The First Marriage
Spiritual Core Concepts: Sabbath Rest
Spiritual Core Concepts: Imprinting
Spiritual Core Concepts: The Rhythm of the Creation
Spiritual Core Concepts: You Shall Surely Die
Spiritual Core Concepts: Did God Say...?"
The Occult I
The Occult II
The Tree of the Knowledge of Good and Evil
Spiritual Core Concepts: Fig Leaf Façade
Spiritual Core Concepts: If at First You Don't Succeed
Where Are You?
The Moment of Truth
Addiction Character Traits: The Blame Game
The Devil's Demise
Eve and Pain in Childbirth
And to Adam He Said...
Because of You
Covenant Relationships: Death Can't Can Wait
Covenant Relationships: The Adamic Covenant
The First Confession
Covenant Relationships: Leather Clothes
Paradise Lost
Genesis Four
Sibling Rivalry and Favoritism

The Way of Cain: No Regard
Covenant Relationships: Righteous Abel
The Way of Cain: Anger Management
The Way of Cain: Murder
The Way of Cain: The Fugitive
The Way of Cain: The Mark of Stigmatization and the Generational Curse
Apart from the Covenant We Cannot Really Know God
The Way of Cain: Anger Management II
Prayer
Wickedness on Earth and Righteous Noah
Noah Got Drunk
Spiritual Core Concepts: Give Me Your Blessing or Let Me Die
Sexual Abuse
The Serenity Prayer
Jesus Said, "You Must Be Born of the Spirit"
Spiritual Practices: Breathing and Relaxation
Step 1
Step 2
Step 3
Step 4
Step 5
Step 6
Step 7
Step 8
Step 9
Step 10
Step 11
Step 12
Addicted to Excess
Spiritual Practices: Incense
Spiritual Practices: Lifting Up Hands in Holy Worship
The Wisdom of Solomon
More Futility
Toxic to The Body and The Soul
The Drugs are a Façade That We Wear
Vanity Proof
The Occult III
Spiritual Core Concepts: Take a Hit
Spiritual Core Concepts: I Did Not Know Who I Had Become
Anxiety and Easy Does It
Drug Slaves
Spiritual Core Concepts: Addiction is a Second Fall
Spiritual Core Concepts: Sorcery is Recreational Drug Use

Drugs Strong Grip
Addiction Character Traits: Blaming
Addiction Character Traits: Grandiosity
Cigarettes and Marijuana Are Gateway Drugs
Case Study: Five Teens at a Sleepover
Spiritual Core Concepts: The Toxic Ritual of Using Drugs
Addiction Character Traits: Low Self-Esteem
The Beginnings of Faith
The Anointed One
Dig Down a Little Deeper in the Well
Drawing Near to God
Radical Change
Our Advocate
Meal-Time Prayers
Prayers
The Foggy Veil
Sharing in Our Lord's Suffering
Writing, Journaling, and Poetry
I Know In Whom I Have Believed
Things Just Happen
But seek first the kingdom of God
The Word of God: Law and Gospel
Restoring Our Minds
What Voice Will We Listen To?
We Are Temples of the Holy Spirit
Spiritual Practices: Yoked with the Lord Meditation
We Tried to Carry This Message to Addicts
The Spiritual Dimension
Our Thought Life
It is a Fearful Thing to Fall into the Hands of the Living God
The Dry Drunk
Spiritual Practices: A Sabbath Rest and Hibernating
Addiction Character Traits: Two Extremes - Impulsiveness and Procrastination
Spiritual Core Concepts: Born-of-the-Spirit
Spiritual Core Concepts: Jesus' Breath
Thomas Said, "My Lord and My God!"
A Renewed Relationship with God
The Word of God Guides Us
Our Purpose and Our Future
All Plans Are Soft Until…
Spiritual Practices: Our Safe Place
The Spiritual Life

Safe People
Resentments and Remembrance
Easy Does It
An Intervention
The Ten Commandments
How Firm a Foundation, Ye Saints of the Lord
Fellowship
We're in a Marathon Not a Sprint
What Must I Know as a Christian
Surrender
Spiritual Fathers and Mothers
Making Amends
Offering Forgiveness
Introspection
Spiritual Character Traits, The Fruit of the Spirit: Love
Spiritual Character Traits, The Fruit of the Spirit: Joy
Spiritual Character Traits, The Fruit of the Spirit: Peace
Spiritual Character Traits, The Fruit of the Spirit: Patience
Spiritual Character Traits, The fruit of the Spirit is: Kindness
Comfort
The Revealed Truth
Peel an Onion, There's Lots of Layers
The Theology of the Cross
The Reconciliation of All Things
Jesus and Zacchaeus
Our Personal Relationship with the Lord and The Aaronic Blessing
If It Had Not Been for the Lord
You Hurt the Ones You Love the Most
Case Study: Workaholic on Meth
Christian Spirituality: A New Way of Life
The Prayer of Saint Francis
Relapse Prevention and Restoration
Recovery Maintenance: Continue in What You Have Learned
Scripture Given for Our Benefit
Spiritual Practices: Singing Psalms, Hymns and Spiritual Songs
The Abundant Life
Meditation
The Glory of the Lord
The Heart of Man
God's Voice Guides Us Still
Spiritual Character from Trial by Fire
Sick-Love Verses Love-Sick
Cleansing from Character Defects

A Dumb Bird
It Is the Holy Spirit Who Sanctifies Us
And I Will Show You A Still More Excellent Way
With God's Help We Can Stay Clean
Healthy Boundaries: Samson and Delilah
Spiritual Practices: Ash Wednesday and Lent
Hitting Bottom
Our First Priority
Spiritual Practices: Breathing Exercise 4 by 4
From Glory to Glory Transformation
The Group Process I
Fellowship
The Reformation of Faith
One Life and One Master
Restoration
Maturity: Growing Up
Spiritual Practices: Meditation and the Breath-of-Life
Spiritual Practices: Our Prayer Life
By the Grace of God Alone
The Love of God Wins our Hearts Over
Progress Not Perfection I
More Than Meets the Eye
Progress Not Perfection II
Laugher is Good Medicine
Jesus Was Tempted
We Shall Also Bear the Image of The Man of Heaven
Becoming What We Hate
The Love of Christ Controls Us
Forensic Righteousness
Higher Power Verses God through Jesus Christ our Savior and Lord
Pity Parties Don't Happen Anymore, Right?
Healthy Boundaries
Trials: Testing and Temptation
The Lord's Prayer / The Our Father
The Temptation of Christ
One Day at a Time
This Too Shall Pass
Judgement and the Word Game
Strength in Weakness
The Whole Armor of God
Spiritual Signs and Wonders
Dope Made Us Stupid
The Occult IV

Smoke and Fire
Case Study: Through many Tribulations
Celebrate
Miserable, Desperate and Hopeless
Anselm of Canterbury: Religion Is Faith Seeking Understanding
Living in Remembrance
Free Will
Spirituality
Loving God Entirely
The Sabbath Rest
Grace and the Gift of Faith
Winning by Losing
Spiritual Practices: The Home Altar and Daily Devotions
The Group Process II
What Are Your Red Flags?
Our Purpose in Life
Uncover, Discover, and Recover
Ah,… Ah,… Ah Choo
Our Purpose in Redemption
The Transforming Power of the Word of God
Parallels
The Oral Tradition of the Word of God
Morning Prayer
Evening Prayer
Troubling Things Will Happen
Peer Pressure
We Are the Temple of the Holy Spirit
Slaves of God
Life Got You Down?
Transcendence
We Are Never Alone
Come, Thou Fount of Every Blessing
Spiritual Practices: Breathing and Meditation
We Can Decide Not to Use Anymore, but It Takes God to Get Us to Quit
The Lament Rather than a Pity-Party
Covenant Relationships: Codependency and Interdependency
Unconditional Positive Regard
Seeking the Lord
Spiritual Practices: Breathing and Envisioning
Being of Two Minds
The Blind Leading the Blind
Healthy Boundaries: Bridges, Fences and Gates
Maturity: From Childhood to Adulthood

God's Amazing Grace
Spirituality
Natures: Our Old and New Natures
Natures: Old and New
Sorcery: Recreational Drug Use
What to Do with Anger
Our Lying Nostalgic Memories
Maintenance Work
Natures: Our Old-Nature is Hostile Toward God
Covenant Relationships: Near and Dear to the Heart of God
The Mystery of our Faith
Following in the Example
Natures: Our Old Adamic Nature on Drugs
Natures: We are Simultaneously Sinners and Saints
The Way of Cain: Toxic Relationships
The God of Our Own Understanding
Natures: Our New Hearts
Participating in the Continuing Work of God
Saved to the Uttermost
Discipleship and Life Skills
Call for the Elders
The Spiritual Time of Day
Accountability
God Supports Marriage
Spiritual Core Concepts: The Anatomy and Physiology of Circulation
The Golden Rule
Reviving the Soul
Why We Cannot Recover on Our Own
Addiction Character Traits: Denial
The Christ Hymn
Case Study: A Generational Curse
Just Today Please
Eyes Forward
Turning Our Lives Over to God
Eureka
The Ups and Downs of Life
Healthy Boundaries: Abraham
Stewards of the Mystery
The Mount of Transfiguration
Alcohol is a Drug
The Flip Flop
Overcoming the World
I'm Not the Problem, They Are

Peel an Onion
I'm First
Guilt Not Shame
The Structured Life of Discipline
Owning Our Own Feelings
Our Calling in Life
Spiritual Practices: Mediation
Spiritual Practices: The Incense Ritual
The Complete Rebirth and Renewal of our Minds
Confessing Saving Faith
Think or Don't Think About the Future
The Routines We Thrive On
The Spirit's Help
Going Our Own Way
Guilt and Shame
Hot Potato
Generational Curses
Healthy Communication: Speaking the Truth in Love
We Have Today
Pox Christi
The Original Steps and The Oxford Group
The Logos of God
Our Purpose in Redemption
Saint Augustine
I Know the Lord
Prayer Over Anxiety
Natures: The Covenant of Our Baptism
Doing Whatever it Takes to Be Clean
Covenant Relationships: The Covenant of Our Baptisms
Covenant Relationships: Baptism and Putting on Christ
But Put on the Lord Jesus Christ
Mighty Because of the Lord
Spiritual Character Traits: Poor in Spirit
Spiritual Character Traits: Mourning
Spiritual Character Traits: Righteousness
Natures: Old-Self * New-Self
Spiritual Character Traits: Transcending Peace
Spiritual Practices: Worshipping with Holy Hands
Spiritual Promises
The Occult V
Where Are Your Accusers?
Healthy Boundaries: Bad Company
Spiritual Intimacy with God

Healthy Boundaries: Codependency
Switching Seats on the HMS Titanic
What About Hate?
Covenant Relationships: Married to Our Addiction
Spirituality: Detachment
Clean Mouths
Supernatural Help
Wellness: Being Good Stewards of Our Bodies
The Prodigal Son
It Is A Fearful Thing to Fall into The Hands of The Living God
God Does Not Give Us More Than We Can Handle
Maintenance in Recovery
Crisis: An Opportunity for Change
Alcohol and the Bible
That's a Big IF
Anxiety and Living One Day At a Time
John Wesley's Covenant Prayer
The Seeds of Recovery
Spirituality: Transcendence
We Are More Than Conquerors
Relapse and Recovery
Bringing the Message to Those Who Need It the Most
Maturity: Our Teenage Years
Step 1
Step 2
Step 3
Step 4
Step 5
Step 6
Step 7
Step 8
Step 9
Step 10
Step 11
Step 12
The Doxology
Appendix 1 The 12-steps of Narcotics Anonymous- How It Works
Appendix 2 The 12-steps from Narcotics Anonymous with Bible references.

Dedication
In memory of my beloved daughter,

Laura Ann

Oh, that I had wings like a dove!
I would fly away and be at rest.
Psalm 55:6

My Bio

For myself, I am an addict in recovery for thirty-four years at the time this book was first published in 2022. Some of what I share is from my own life, some of it is from the lives of other people who I have known, some in recovery, some not. I hold an undergraduate degree in Health and Wellness Education, and master's degrees in psychology, and divinity. I am an ordained Lutheran Pastor.

Preface

**And [Jesus] said to them,
"Therefore every scribe who has been
trained for the kingdom of heaven is like
a master of a house, who brings out of his
treasure what is new and what is old."
Matthew 13:52**

So much has already been written on drug addiction and recovery. Beyond that, if it hasn't been written down on paper for others to read, it has certainly been said by countless speakers, at countless meetings and treatment centers around the globe. A lot of it is the same basic things, all being said in slightly new or different ways. None of that is bad, these things need to be said. The newcomer certainly needs to know them. Those of us who have been in recovery for a while need to be reminded of these essential facts.

When I set out to research and write this daily devotional I dedicated myself to not entirely reinventing the wheel by simply repeating what has already been shared so widely, but I wanted to present as new and insightful an approach to recovery as I could. I wanted most of all to present something that would substantially help us as addicts to both get into recovery and to maintain our recovery for the course of our natural lives. In this devotional book I have worked to uncovered and bring to light many new Biblical insights into the spirituality of addiction and recovery.

Pastor Blaine MacNeil

Introduction

**But, as it is written,
"What no eye has seen, nor ear heard,
nor the heart of man imagined, what God has prepared for those who love him"— these things God has revealed to us through the Spirit. For the Spirit searches everything, even the depths of God. For who knows a person's thoughts except the spirit of that person, which is in him? So also no one comprehends the thoughts of God except the Spirit of God. Now we have received not the spirit of the world, but the Spirit who is from God, that we might understand the things freely given us by God. And we impart this in words not taught by human wisdom but taught by the Spirit, interpreting spiritual truths to those who are spiritual.
1 Corinthians 2:9-13**

This is a daily devotional for all of us who suffer with addiction. Unlike most devotionals these pages have no dates on them. It is necessary for everyone to start at the beginning because the sequence of the information as it is presented is needed to understand the pages that will follow.

I have written these pages in first person plural. The plural references are not rhetorical, they are inclusive of us all, I am an addict in recovery too. I want everyone reading this to always know that we are together in our recovery united by the fellowship of Christ's Church on earth through the Holy Spirit. With only rare instance have I used references *to you, them and their*, in order to avoid the appearance of separating myself out from among us as an addict in recovery. These pages are for all of us, myself included. I have written in the past tense about our drug use even though some of us may be still struggling to overcome active drug use.

The basic theme of this book is simple. In the beginning God formed Adam out of the dust of the earth. God breathed into his nostrils the breath-of-life and Adam became a living-soul. Then the sons and daughters of Adam inhaled the smoke of marijuana, coke, or meth and were fundamentally changed and we became *living-addicts*. Just as the birth of Adam took place when God put the breath-of-life into his lungs, when we inhaled the toxic drug laced smoke into our lungs, we were *re-birthed* in a parallel process that fundamentally changed us and we became living-addicts.

Adam was made in God's image and likeness, and as a result he resembled his Maker. God gave him a purpose, it was to join with him in caring for the Garden of Eden that he had planted. Adam and Eve chose to rebel and not participate with God in their lives. As a result they were booted out of the garden. As addicts we chose to go our own way too. We became addicts in the re-birthing experience we had with drugs. The drugs were like a new god in our lives. They were a demigod that ruled over us, they were both impersonal and yet demanding of our complete devotion whether we were willing or not. Our behavior changed, we fell away from fulfilling our God given purpose in our lives. We took up behaviors that were centered on using and acquiring more drugs. Our image and likeness was marred, we resembled our new demigod, we were addicts.

When we were ready to quit we came to realize that we could not do it on our own. We had to turn to God for that. Just as the breath-of-life from God had come into us at the beginning our lives, drugs re-birthed us into a horrible life of addiction. Now in order to begin our recovery we needed another birth to overcome our addiction. We all know that Jesus said we must be born-again. Do we all know that in that conversation he also referred to it as being born-of-the-Spirit? We needed this new spiritual birth in our lives to counter the toxic effects of the drugs we took into our bodies. Biblically and spiritually, this is what makes our recoveries possible.

Rather than write out my work in a chapter book that would have passed on information and provided an education as its goal I choose to present it in daily devotional. Spread throughout this book are the spiritual insights and practices that have I have used in my own life. These have enhanced my recovery greatly. They are practical and they explain why we are the way we are as addicts.

This is a day-by-day book on Christian Spirituality for the addict. It offers the hope that by practicing our faith with devotion we can remain clean and free of drugs. It offers no guarantees. This is not a self-help book, a treatment book, or a manual of any kind, and it should not be used as such. If you need professional help from a qualified licensed professional for yourself make an appointment with one and do not expect that this book is a substitute for one.

The earliest stories of human history hold a special place in our lives no matter how many centuries have gone by. These accounts tell us about our basic nature and about things that don't change over time. They are perfectly accurate in their telling of traits that have been and always will be basic to all of us. Case in point, Adam blamed Eve after the fall. Eve blamed the serpent, and today we still blame others for our own problems. As addicts the ill effects of the fall seem to have worked their woe in us twofold, which is to say they are frequently worse in our lives than in those who are not afflicted with addiction.

There is hope. There is really only one hope. Hope is found in the redeeming power of the life, suffering, death, and resurrection of Jesus Christ who is our Lord. He alone is our Savior from sin and for those among us who also suffer from addiction to drugs, he is twice our Savior. First he is our Savior from sin, and two, he is our Savior from addiction.

In the beginning of this devotional I have shared about the creation before the fall of Adam and Eve into sin. This is about how God made the heavens and the earth, and his original design for life before sin entered the world. By understanding these things we gain some insight into how we are to live our lives today. Following this I describe the fall of Adam and Eve into sin and the dramatic changes that followed. The book describes early human history and shows the progression of corruption, depravity, godlessness, and sin in the world. Then the book progresses and I share more about drug life and then Christian life in recovery.

A Word of Thanks

I have to give thanks to a few friends and special people who have helped in preparing this book for publication. By their encouragement and support I was able to bring this effort to completion. Thanks to Grant, Steve, Kyle, Chaplain Peter, and most of all to my wife Melanie.

Genesis Chapter One

In the Beginning, God Created...

... the heavens and the earth. ² The earth was without form and void, and darkness was over the face of the deep. And the Spirit of God was hovering over the face of the waters. ³ And God said, "Let there be light," and there was light. ⁴ And God saw that the light was good. And God separated the light from the darkness. ⁵ God called the light Day, and the darkness he called Night. And there was evening and there was morning, the first day. ⁶ And God said, "Let there be an expanse in the midst of the waters, and let it separate the waters from the waters." ⁷ And God made the expanse and separated the waters that were under the expanse from the waters that were above the expanse. And it was so. ⁸ And God called the expanse Heaven. And there was evening and there was morning, the second day. ⁹ And God said, "Let the waters under the heavens be gathered together into one place, and let the dry land appear." And it was so. ¹⁰ God called the dry land Earth, and the waters that were gathered together he called Seas. And God saw that it was good. ¹¹ And God said, "Let the earth sprout vegetation, plants yielding seed, and fruit trees bearing fruit in which is their seed, each according to its kind, on the earth." And it was so. ¹² The earth brought forth vegetation, plants yielding seed according to their own kinds, and trees bearing fruit in which is their seed, each according to its kind. And God saw that it was good. ¹³ And there was evening and there was morning, the third day. ¹⁴ And God said, "Let there be lights in the expanse of the heavens to separate the day from the night. And let them be for signs and for seasons, and for days and years, ¹⁵ and let them be lights in the expanse of the heavens to give light upon the earth." And it was so. ¹⁶ And God made the two great lights—the greater light to rule the day and the lesser light to rule the night—and the stars. ¹⁷ And God set them in the expanse of the heavens to give light on the earth, ¹⁸ to rule over the day and over the night, and to separate the light from the darkness. And God saw that it was good. ¹⁹ And there was evening and there was morning, the fourth day. ²⁰ And God said, "Let the waters swarm with swarms of living creatures, and let birds fly above the earth across the expanse of the heavens." ²¹ So God created the great sea creatures and every living creature that moves, with which the waters swarm, according to their kinds, and every winged bird according to its kind. And God saw that it was good. ²² And God blessed them, saying, "Be fruitful and multiply and fill the waters in the seas, and let birds multiply on the earth." ²³ And there was evening and there was morning, the fifth day.

²⁴ And God said, "Let the earth bring forth living creatures according to their kinds—livestock and creeping things and beasts of the earth according to their kinds." And it was so. ²⁵ And God made the beasts of the earth according to their kinds and the livestock according to their kinds, and everything that creeps on the ground according to its kind. And God saw that it was good. ²⁶ Then God said, "Let us make man in our image, after our likeness. And let them have dominion over the fish of the sea and over the birds of the heavens and over the livestock and over all the earth and over every creeping thing that creeps on the earth."

> ²⁷ So God created man in his own image,
> in the image of God he created him;
> male and female he created them.

²⁸ And God blessed them. And God said to them, "Be fruitful and multiply and fill the earth and subdue it, and have dominion over the fish of the sea and over the birds of the heavens and over every living thing that moves on the earth." ²⁹ And God said, "Behold, I have given you every plant yielding seed that is on the face of all the earth, and every tree with seed in its fruit. You shall have them for food. ³⁰ And to every beast of the earth and to every bird of the heavens and to everything that creeps on the earth, everything that has the breath of life, I have given every green plant for food." And it was so. ³¹ And God saw everything that he had made, and behold, it was very good. And there was evening and there was morning, the sixth day.

Creation by the Spoken Word

It is a great wonder to go out at night and view the stars that light up the sky. They are vast in their numbers and the great distances that they cover is unimaginable. All this was created by God in an instant, and isn't it amazing that he simply did it by the power of his spoken Word?

In the beginning God created order out of nothing. This means that in creating everything he also set things in their proper place and gave them a purpose. Out of the light that he spoke into existence out of nothing he created the expanse of stars in the heavens, the sun that would rule by day and the lesser light of the night, which is the moon, that would rule by night. With the creation of light he also made radio waves which make microwave ovens work and television and cell phones possible. Other things he created out of existing things, such as the animals and the birds which he created out of the already existent earth.[1] God created Adam out of the dust of the earth[2]. Eve's creation is also unique, completely unique. She was created not by the spoken word of God's voice, not out of the dust of the earth as was Adam. Eve was created out of an existing being. She was created out of her husband's rib.[3]

Everything God created he declared that it was good. That is a point that needs to be reemphasized. Everything he created was good. Some folks have mistakenly said perfect, but that is not the case. Along that same line, God made nothing that is inherently evil or sinful. How could he have or why would he have? Rather, things that he has made good can be misused, abused, and used in evil ways. That is a point to be remembered.

Although God gave names to everything, when Adam came along this task was given to him to name things. Adam was tasked with carrying on with the work that God started but wanted him to share in. When Eve came along, she too was included in this work of God's as well.

Heavenly Father, by your power you have made us for your glory. Empower us to live for you and to fulfill the purpose you brought us into this world for. Through Christ our Lord. Amen

---

[1] Genesis 2:18
[2] Genesis 2:7
[3] Genesis 2:21-22

Spiritual Core Concepts: The Breath-of-Life

**And the Lord God formed man of the dust of the ground, and breathed into his nostrils the breath of life; and man became a living soul.
Genesis 2:7 KJV**

    God spoke with his breath to bring about all of creation, but when he created Adam, it was more personal. His body was uniquely shaped by the hands of God. Of all the creatures on the face of the earth this is the only time that happened. It was with his own breath that God breathed life into Adam's nostrils. Adam was created in this intimate way and he was made in God's image and likeness. This tells us that there is a very personal connection between us, as the descendants of Adam and Eve, and God. We are God's children.

    Adam's first breath was not taken on his own. Life came as a gift from his Maker. Who knows what Adam's lifeless body first looked like? It might have looked like a corpse. Or maybe it was wrinkled from dehydration. It had no oxygen in it, perhaps it was blue or gray in color. As God gave Adam his first breath his lungs filled, his heart began to beat, and oxygen flowed to every cell in his body. It was a tremendous rush of vitality as God's *life-giving-spirit* flowed and pulsated in him from head to toe. Adam's life began with a face-to-face experience with his Holy Father. As God's breath flowed into the body of Adam he became a *living-soul* with a life that was almost all his own.

    Heavenly Father, thank you for your life-giving-spirit that is inside of us. Thank you for our lives. May we live in such a way that we always bring honor to your holy name. Through Christ our Lord we pray. Amen

Spiritual Core Concepts: The Sons of Adam and the daughters of Eve Inhaled Drugs and they Became Living-Addicts

And the Lord God formed man of the dust of the ground, and breathed into his nostrils the breath-of-life; and man became a living soul.
Genesis 2:7 KJV

It does not matter if the drugs are smoked, swallowed, snorted, or injected. Not only do they intermix with our body's chemistry, they also intermix with our souls. This is a spiritual process that runs parallel to the birthing experience when Adam was first simply a pile of dust in the loose shape of a man. Recall that it was when God breathed into him the breath-of-life and the result was that he became a living-soul. In our lives drugs had entered our bodies. In doing this they intermixed with who we were as a person at the bedrock of our souls. As a result, we were fundamentally changed, rather than simply being living-souls, we were rebirthed as living-addicts.

Adam and Eve had been given a purpose in life, to care for a garden that God planted. Even after the fall they were to continue on in God's purpose for their lives as farmers. When we, the sons and daughters of Adam and Eve, used drugs our lives took on new purposes. No longer were we interested in being participants in caring on in useful ways in the world that God created. "We used to live and lived to use."[4] Drugs increased the ill effects of the fall many times over in our lives. It was like putting our sinful nature on steroids and they magnified the worst in us. In recovery God breathed on us and put his Holy Spirit to work in us. God is working to sanctify us and is returning our lives to serving him and living according to his will.

Heavenly Father, reverse the effects of our drug use and restore us to the purposes you have made us for. May we live to fulfill your will in our lives again and may we bring glory to your name. Aid and guide us in our recovery and strengthen us for the journey. In Christ's name. Amen

---

[4] White Booklet Narcotics Anonymous, Narcotics Anonymous World Services, 2000.

Spiritual Core Concepts:
What is the Body, the Soul, and the Spirit of Man?

And the LORD God formed man of the dust of the ground, and breathed into his nostrils the breath of life; and man became a living soul.
Genesis 2:7 KJV

As the Genesis story tells us, we are living beings, or souls. In our totality, we are made up of a physical body, a soul, and a spirit. As life came to Adam by the breath-of-life from God, so also it comes to us and remains in us for the length of our days. This breath-of-life, or life-giving-spirit is not the same thing as the Holy Spirit. When death comes to us this life-giving-spirit returns to God.

The Human Body and the Dust of the Ground

The human body is self-evident. It is physical, therefore it can be seen and touched. The great sophistication of our many organs and systems tell us that we are made by God. As it was with Adam, we all require that God's breath-of-life, or spirit, be in us for our physical life to exist and continue. At death the body returns to the earth from which is was made, and the life of our soul is released from the body and enters heaven, and God's life-giving-spirit returns to him.

Regarding the body at the time of death, some well-intentioned but ill-informed persons have referred to it as "only" or "just" a shell. On the surface that may sound true, but it falls far short of the truth about our bodies. Our bodies are not a shell and they should not be referred to in such demeaning terms. We are all made in God's image and likeness, which includes our outward physical appearance. The body of course needs to be treated with all dignity and respect. It has been for us as Christians the temple of the Holy Spirit. It will be raised from the dead and transformed from a perishable and natural body into a spiritual and imperishable body.[5] Some of the details of these things remain a mystery to us, though we do understand them in part during our earthly journey. God willing we will understand this mystery fully when we go to heaven.

The Living-Soul

Our soul is somewhat of an intangible part of us, but while we live it is housed inside of our physical body. It was not preexistent prior to our

---

[5] 1 Corinthians 15:42-44

conception as is the life-giving-spirit we have from God. The soul is created at the time when the mother's egg is fertilized by the father's sperm. At that point the life-giving-spirit of God is given to the newly formed child. As it was with Adam, as the physical body receives the spirit of God, the soul of the person, yet to be born, is created, and given life. Our souls are created by the merging or blending of our physical body with God's living-giving-spirit.

In the Old Testament the Hebrew word for soul is *nephesh,* and the Greek New Testament word for soul is *psyche*. Behind their meanings, soul, is the idea of a gentle, throaty puff of air as it is exhaled.

It is housed in our physical bodies, with special concentrations found in the brain, the chest, heart, blood, lungs, and our abdomens. Our soul's expressions are seen most clearly in the functioning of our brain which houses the mind with which we think. Also credited to the soul are our emotions. These are thought to be located in our brain, heart, and abdomen.

There has been considerable debate over the centuries about whether the soul is immortal or mortal. The Bible does not describe our souls as either an immortal soul, or as a mortal soul. Theologians and Biblical scholars are divided over this, but they agree that the soul is raised in the resurrection of the dead and therefore it becomes eternal.

The Human Spirit and the Breath-of-life

The spirit we have is from God and because it is intangible it is a little hard to understand. This life-giving-spirit is not the same as the Holy Spirit. It is ours on a temporary basis, while we live it is ours, but God can take it from us at any time. When we die, it returns to God. Our physical life is dependent on it.[6] Clearly it is housed inside our physical bodies and while it permeates our entire being, it is very possible that it is centered or more concentrated in our chests, where the lungs and the heart are located.

In the Scriptures of the Old Testament the Hebrew word for spirit is *ruach,* and the Greek Scriptures of the New Testament the word for spirit is *pneuma*, which literally means air. In both the Hebrew and the Greek it can also mean a strong gust of air, as in a powerful blowing wind.

Heavenly Father, by your hands we were fearfully and wonderfully made. You hold our lives in the palms of your hands and you have made us for your glory. May we honor you in our physical bodies, praise you with our spirits, and always love you with all of our hearts, souls, minds, and strength. Through Christ our Lord we pray. Amen

---

[6] Job 33:4

Spiritual Core Concepts:
Our Purpose in Life Is to Work

The Lord God took the man and put him in the Garden of Eden to work it and keep it.
Genesis 2:15

From the beginning of time there are several things that God has made us for. On the sixth day of creation Adam and Eve were told to be fruitful and multiply.[7] Adam was also given the job of giving names to all the animals that God had created.[8] It is interesting to note here that up until this point God was the only person who had given names to anything. Now Adam is included in this work. Adam and Eve were also given careers, it was their responsibility as gardeners to care for the Garden of Eden that God had planted. The couple needed to do those things that would make it flourish by helping the plants and trees to grow such as: pruning, tilling the soil, harvesting the food, and saving seeds for the next planting. It is notable that the assignment of work came before and not after the fall. Work was to be a blessing in both of their lives and to give them a purpose which was to include them in maintaining what God had created.

Sometimes in the church we divide between secular and sacred occupations. The pastor and deacon have sacred vocations, the farmer and the welder have secular occupations. The truth be told, all occupations are given to us from God and should be seen as such. Though the work of a pastor is particularly important, have you ever considered what would happen if the farmer didn't do his job? We would starve. Therefore, it is best to see all our occupational callings as coming from God and as spiritual callings as well.

Heavenly Father, thank you for including us in the work that you have begun. Bless us and gift us with the skills we need on the job. This we ask through Christ our Lord. Amen

---

[7] Genesis 1:28
[8] Genesis 2:19

Fellowship

Then the LORD **God said, "It is not good that the man should be alone; I will make him a helper fit for him." Now out of the ground the L**ORD **God had formed every beast of the field and every bird of the heavens and brought them to the man to see what he would call them. And whatever the man called every living creature, that was its name. The man gave names to all livestock and to the birds of the heavens and to every beast of the field. But for Adam there was not found a helper fit for him. So the L**ORD **God caused a deep sleep to fall upon the man, and while he slept took one of his ribs and closed up its place with flesh. And the rib that the L**ORD **God had taken from the man he made into a woman and brought her to the man.**
Genesis 2:18-22

Adam needed a companion who could help him. God searched all the living creatures and reviewed their relationships to Adam. None of the animals could have been as good of companions as what God had in mind, which was to create Eve. So, God put him into a deep sleep and he took a rib from his side and created his mate, Eve. She was fashioned to be like him as a human, but different so that she was a female rather than a male.

From the beginning of human life God's design was to have the two genders, male and female. To assume that there are more than these, or that they can be changed is to play God, which is the continuation of original sin. Our task in life is for us to live as God has made us, a male or a female. As males we may not have bodies like Apollo or as females we may not look like a Venus, that doesn't matter, and it is no reason to abandon our God given gender. God has loved us as we are, male or female, and so should we love ourselves as we have been made by the hand of God.

Heavenly Father, thank you for our lives. Bless and care for us so that we can live according to your design. May we always honor you with our physical bodies as well. This we ask through Christ our Lord and Savior. Amen

Covenant Relationships: The First Marriage

So the LORD **God caused a deep sleep to fall upon the man, and while he slept took one of his ribs and closed up its place with flesh. And the rib that the L**ORD **God had taken from the man he made into a woman and brought her to the man. Then the man said,**

"This at last is bone of my bones and flesh of my flesh;
she shall be called Woman,
because she was taken out of Man."

Therefore a man shall leave his father and his mother and hold fast to his wife, and they shall become one flesh. And the man and his wife were both naked and were not ashamed.
Genesis 2:21-25

So, God saw that it was not good for Adam to be alone. Beyond that, he needed a helpmate to assist him in his God given purpose, which was to care for the Garden. For this God had to make a new being, Eve, who became his wife. She was like him in most regards, except she was a female and Adam was a male. Adam saw her and testified himself that she alone was his mate, being like him on the surface all the way down to the bones. You might say Adam and Eve had it all. Their marriage might not have been a match made in heaven, but it was one made in the paradise of the Garden of Eden.

So, Adam and Eve began their lives together. They lived in the best of places, the Garden of Eden, under the best of conditions, it was before the fall. They had God's blessing to be fruitful and multiply. They had God's instructions to have dominion over the earth, which meant that they were stewards of what God had made and they were the caretakers of it. Life was delightfully good for them.

Heavenly Father, bless the covenant of marriage that exists for many of us. For those among us who long for marriage prepare us to be healthy partners and bring us together for this purpose. This we pray in the name of your son, Jesus Christ. Amen

Covenant Relationships: Be Fruitful and Multiply

**God blessed them and God said to them,
"Be fruitful, multiply, fill the earth, and subdue it.
Rule the fish of the sea, the birds of the sky,
and every creature that crawls on the earth."
Genesis 1:28**

At the time when God first made Adam and then Eve, he endowed them with the responsibility of having dominion over the fish, birds, insects, and all living things on the face of the earth. Shortly after that be gave them a blessing to go along with their newly acquired responsibilities. He gave them a spiritual blessing and said that they should have productive lives, have children and be the stewards over all the living creatures on the earth.

This special blessing that he gave to our first parents is one that we have by all rights inherited. This passage gives to us God's blessing in life and it is still in effect today. By this directive God has also given us stewardship over the earth and all that it contains.

In our addictions we abandoned the spirituality of our God given callings. We neglected ourselves and all that was entrusted to us. We did not care the for earth, or the lives that we had been given. We gave up our aspirations and goals, even our hopes and dreams. Our homes were unkept, our contributions to society as employees or employers suffered. Our social skills went by the wayside and we offended countless people.

In recovery our lives began to return to what they should have been had we not lost our way and ourselves to drugs. This was made possible because God continues to uphold his blessings in our lives and to empower us to that end as we live in faithfulness to him. As our loving Father, he has always wanted what is best for us.

Dearest God, from heaven you came in the life of your son to the earth and lived among us. Continue to abide with us always and bless us so that we can fulfill your will in all that we do. Care for us in our recoveries and sustain us by the power of your might. Empower us to live clean and free of drug use, so that we may bring glory to your name. This we pray through Christ Jesus our Lord and Savior. Amen

Spiritual Core Concepts: Sabbath Rest

Thus the heavens and the earth were finished, and all the host of them. And on the seventh day God finished his work that he had done and he rested on the seventh day from all his work that he had done. So God blessed the seventh day and made it holy, because on it God rested from all his work that he had done in creation.
Genesis 2:1-3

There is a pattern, a certain rhythm and cadence to life and to all of creation. It was set in motion by God and continues to this day. It began as God spoke all things in creation into existence. The days of the week have a two-beat pattern, as the scriptures say over and over again in Genesis the first chapter, "And there was evening and there was morning..."[9] There was evening and morning, a time of darkness and resting followed by a period of light and work. It began on the first day of creation and it continues to this very day. On the seventh day, the scriptures say God completed his work and then he rested. This was a Saturday and because it was made special by the completion of creation God made it a holy day. This means that Sunday through Friday were considered common days, but Saturday was set aside for the purpose of being dedicated to God.

Now added to the rhythm and cadence of life is added this pattern. Working for six days and resting on the seventh. While we don't typically observe a formal sabbath day of rest on Saturday or on Sunday, the Lord's day, it is a good spiritual practice to take time to rest during the week and focus on our recovery and offer prayers and devotions to God.

Heavenly Father, by your grace we began our recovery journeys, through your grace may we continue day by day, living one day at a time and abiding in the freedom from drugs that you have provided for us. Through Christ our Lord we ask this. Amen

---

[9] Genesis 1:5, 8, 13, 19, 23, 31

Spiritual Core Concepts: Imprinting

**So God created man in his own image,
in the image of God he created him;
male and female he created them.
Genesis 1:27**

Is it safe to assume that everyone knows about a goose and how it bonds to its mother? How when the gooseling cracks open its egg and breaks free of it, the first living thing it sees becomes its mother, in its mind anyway. God forbid that it might see a chicken or a dog in the barn where it has been kept. Once the bond is made there is no way to break it. This is called imprinting. This is brought up because something remarkably similar happens to us in life. When Adam was formed God breathed into him his own breath, the breath-of-life, Adam then became a living-soul. The first man knew who his Maker was, it was imprinting from God himself. Adam knew he was made in his heavenly Father's image and likeness, it was undeniable. The breath-of-life, the life-giving-spirit of God was in him, and it informed him of these things.

It is not just these traits, of being made in God's image and likeness, that are passed on to us. It is not so uncommon to have members of the same family that look alike from one generation to the next. We resemble our parents, grandparents and sometimes we even look like our ancestors further back for many generations. Often times naturally occurring behaviors are seen in successive generations of the same family. A grandpa might be known for laboring away at a job and his mouth will be open and he has his tongue hanging out. Then the son and the grandson are noted to being doing the exact same thing. They are commonly unaware of it happening until someone else in the family points it out to them that they all do this.

Heavenly Father, you have made us in your image and likeness. May we as your children live in accord with your will and design for us in this life. Sustain us in our recoveries, help us to share the message of salvation and of recovery from addiction to drugs with those who need to hear them the most. This we ask through Christ our Lord. Amen

Spiritual Core Concepts: The Rhythm of the Creation

And God said, "Let there be lights in the expanse of the heavens to separate the day from the night. And let them be for signs and for seasons, and for days and years, and let them be lights in the expanse of the heavens to give light upon the earth." And it was so. And God made the two great lights the greater light to rule the day and the lesser light to rule the night and the stars. And God set them in the expanse of the heavens to give light on the earth, to rule over the day and over the night, and to separate the light from the darkness. And God saw that it was good. And there was evening and there was morning, the fourth day.
Genesis 1:14-19

From the beginning of measurable time, which began at the moment God said, "Let there be light," the pulse and rhythm of creation was set into motion. Time as we understand it had begun. For us we have the calendar year, which is set by the time it takes the earth to circle the sun. The year is divided by the four seasons of spring, summer, autumn, and winter. The seasons are defined by the type of weather that prevails in them. Then there are the phases of the moon, originally there were thirteen lunar months which goes from full moon to full moon. Now we have twelve calendar months. Next in the pattern of God's rhythm is the seven-day week, with six days for work and the last day of the week having been originally set aside for a day of rest. Finally, in the end is the measure of the day, which according to the Bible begins at sundown, "And there was evening and morning, the first day."[10]

All of these patterns are given to us as markers to guide us in how we live out our lives. Day and night tell us that it is time to work or to rest. The seasons tell us to plant, to water and pull weeds, when to harvest and when to let the land rest. By living in accord with this rhythm that God has set in motion we align ourselves with his work. This is part of his purpose for us in this life.

Heavenly Father, aid and guide us as we seek to join in with you in the care and maintenance of your creation. Sustain us in our recoveries, through Christ our Lord we pray. Amen

---

[10] Genesis 1:5

Spiritual Core Concepts: You Shall Surely Die

**And the Lord God commanded the man, saying,
"You may surely eat of every tree of the garden,
but of the tree of the knowledge of good and
evil you shall not eat, for in the day that
you eat of it you shall surely die."
Genesis 2:16-17**

Adam and Eve lived in Paradise. It was the most beautiful, wonderful place on earth, God himself planted it. True, the couple had to work there, but the work wasn't that hard, and this was God's purpose for their lives. They were now included in God's work by providing for its maintenance. God visited them in the evenings, at twilight, when the sun would set and the vastness of the heavens were revealed. If they had need of anything that they could not provide for themselves all they needed to do was to ask God.

The Holy Scriptures as we know them had not been written down yet, but then there wasn't much to record at this point either. Adam and Eve had the Word of God direct from its source, the Lord God Almighty. Adam and Eve shared in direct fellowship with God. They both knew this one commandment from their personal relationship with God. This passage was simple, direct, and to the point. It left no room for doubt in anyone's mind. The short and simple truth of it was clear: that tree, that fruit, don't eat it, don't touch it. Why? Because it is deadly. That is right, you will die in the same day you eat it. No ifs, ands, or buts about it. Death will follow, this is sure, certain, and final.

Heavenly Father, guard and keep safe our lives. Empower us to live according to your will, strengthen us for our recovery journey. May we steer clear of the temptations we face in our lives and help us to always embrace the way of recovery so that we may live for your glory. This we ask through Christ our Lord. Amen

Spiritual Core Concepts: Did God Say...?"

Now the serpent was more crafty than any other beast of the field that the Lord God had made. He said to the woman, "Did God actually say, 'You shall not eat of any tree in the garden'?" And the woman said to the serpent, "We may eat of the fruit of the trees in the garden, but God said, 'You shall not eat of the fruit of the tree that is in the midst of the garden, neither shall you touch it, lest you die.'" But the serpent said to the woman, "You will not surely die. For God knows that when you eat of it your eyes will be opened, and you will be like God, knowing good and evil." So when the woman saw that the tree was good for food, and that it was a delight to the eyes, and that the tree was to be desired to make one wise, she took of its fruit and ate, and she also gave some to her husband who was with her, and he ate.
Genesis 3:1-6

Not eating the fruit was easy enough to do for a long time, apparently. Then came the day. Adam and Eve were together when this crafty, snaky looking fellow showed up. He was not the devil, though he acted like one. He was in fact acting in the agency of the devil, which is to say that he was acting on the behalf of the devil.

Here's the break down on what happened. The serpent asked Eve a question rather than making a statement. He questioned the authenticity of the Word of God. Eve responded correctly, quoting the Word of God. The serpent lied, saying they will not die. This is a direct lie by the way, it contradicts God's Word. The serpent lied again telling her that there were benefits she and Adam could have by eating the forbidden, deadly fruit. These lies are half-truths. The serpent had corrupted the truth and twisted it for his own purposes because half-truths are also lies.

What isn't apparent to us is this, by eating the fruit of the tree of the knowledge of good and evil, Adam and Eve believed that they would come into knowledge that would empower them to be able to control good and evil in their lives. What else we need to know in order to understand this text is that the Hebrew root words for good and evil are the same root words for pleasure and pain, *Tov* and *Rah.* By having this imagined control over good and evil, Adam and Eve believed they could choose to have what good and pleasurable things they wanted in life and choose not to have whatever evil or painful things might otherwise come their way. The trouble for them was that it did not work that way for them in the end. It was actually pretty bad how things turned out, it made things worse for them. The serpent lied to them saying, "You will be like God, knowing good and evil." The problem with this was that it was another lie. They wouldn't be like God, they won't be able to know and control good and evil the way God does.

As the couple fell into this sin they wanted to be able to bypass God and control good and evil for themselves. God's plan for them was that they should have trusted him and had faith in him for all that would have come their way in life. They were to give thanks for the good things and rely on him in the painful parts of life. The lie they came to believe in was that they could gain control of good and evil for themselves. This is the nature of original sin, trying to do for ourselves what only God can do for us.

Eve came to believe that the lie was true and she further reasoned that the tree could make her wise, so that she could control pain and pleasure. So, she ate it. She gave it to her husband too. Their eyes were opened to new knowledge alright, but it was not what they hoped for. It was a nightmare.

Heavenly Father, keep us from presumptuous sins and safeguard us from attacks of the evil one and his agents. By your might empower us to live in recovery, free and clean from drugs. Help us especially to trust you in all the comes our way in life, in the good times and in the difficult times as well. This we pray through the name of our Lord and Savior, your son Jesus Christ. Amen

The Occult I

Now the serpent was more crafty than any other beast of the field that the Lord God had made. He said to the woman, "Did God actually say, 'You shall not eat of any tree in the garden'?" And the woman said to the serpent, "We may eat of the fruit of the trees in the garden, but God said, 'You shall not eat of the fruit of the tree that is in the midst of the garden, neither shall you touch it, lest you die.'" But the serpent said to the woman, "You will not surely die. For God knows that when you eat of it your eyes will be opened, and you will be like God, knowing good and evil." So when the woman saw that the tree was good for food, and that it was a delight to the eyes, and that the tree was to be desired to make one wise, she took of its fruit and ate, and she also gave some to her husband who was with her, and he ate. Then the eyes of both were opened, and they knew that they were naked. And they sewed fig leaves together and made themselves loincloths.
Genesis 3:1-7

    This snaky fellow in the garden was not the devil himself. He was working on the behalf of the devil though. He presented himself as though he had special knowledge that was withheld from them by God. He says things that are lies which are imbedded with half-truths at best. He even goes so far as to say that God knows that these things are true, that your eyes will be opened and you will know good and evil. Moreover, he says they will be like God by doing this thing.

    All this is the beginning of the occult, a word that means hidden or secret, and by implication means hidden or secret knowledge. The occult includes a wide variety of superstitious or religious beliefs and practices. They all are categorically contrary to our Christian faith. Unfortunately, some Christians have been lured into checking them out or have even been involved in them. Just like Adam and Eve's involvement was to their ruin, it can lead to the ruin of a Christian's life as well. We are well advised to avoid the occult in all of its forms.

    Heavenly Father, deliver us from evil and protect us from all harm. Shield us from all attacks of the evil one and bring us into the glorious Kingdom of your son, Christ our Lord. Amen

The Occult II

**But the serpent said to the woman,
"You will not surely die.
For God knows that when you
eat of it your eyes will be opened,
and you will be like God,
knowing good and evil."
Genesis 3:4-5**

Adam and Eve were made in God's image and likeness, and that should have been enough. Still, they fell to the temptation to be "like God." In the presence of the serpent Eve's thinking for herself was shutting down and Adam said nothing. Eve was lured in by a false offer to become something she already was. She and Adam were already like God, they were made in his image and likeness. This offer to know good and evil was not something the serpent could really offer them, but Eve didn't know that. She should have already known that she and her husband were supposed to trust God for the good and evil things that might come their way in life. Perhaps she was thinking like some teenagers do who don't believe they could die or even get hurt in life and therefore undertake dangerous risks.

This offer of special knowledge that was supposed to come their way is much like what the occult attempts to offer people. The occult attempts to offer people hidden knowledge that will empower them to act with the power of a demigod. The problem is that it does not deliver on that promise. What it does is lead people astray, giving them false notions of what they can perform. They falsely imagine they will have superhuman abilities with magical thinking and believe they can do the impossible. When that doesn't happen in reality they slip into a world of fantasy and make believe. Add to that the use of drugs, which is quite common among occultists, and they enter into the world of the unreal. Fantasy becomes reality for them, and reality is lost. That combination of things in any lifestyle makes a person vulnerable to addiction and mental illness.

Father in heaven, you are our God and we have allegiance to you alone. We entrust our lives to your care and credit you with the success of our recoveries. In you we have security and you are the firm foundation that we build our lives upon. Through Christ our Lord we pray. Amen

The Tree of the Knowledge of Good and Evil

**And the Lord God commanded the man, saying,
"You may surely eat of every tree of the garden,
but of the tree of the knowledge of good
and evil you shall not eat,
for in the day that you eat
of it you shall surely die."
Genesis 2:16-17**

People have wondered, was this a real tree or was it a metaphor for something else? This tree, the tree of the fruit of the knowledge of good and evil, is an actual tree. And yes, its fruit is deadly. Up until this point in their lives the couple had been trusting God over those issues that could cause pain or that brought them pleasure. That was God's plan for them, that he would bring them times of pleasure in their lives and that he would support them through the times of pain in their lives.

If their plan had worked, to have control over good and evil, or pleasure and pain in their lives, they would of course chosen only the good and pleasurable things for their lives. Equally true, they would have chosen to not experience any of the evil or painful things that would come to them in their lives. They would no longer have needed to live in a trusting and faith-based relationship with God. They would have been able to do for themselves what only God could do for them up to that point.

Needless to say, they did not think their plans through very well, because nothing turned out the way they had thought it would. Their sin was trying to do for themselves what they were supposed to trust God for. Now, in their fallen state their lives were about to become much more difficult for them. In turn, in the face of the increased difficulties in life, they would need to rely on God all the more, not less.

Heavenly Father, in our addiction we tried to control life by bringing ourselves only pleasure by using drugs and eliminating the pain. We turned our backs on the challenges of life trying only to have good things to enjoy. We joined our first parents in original sin when we tried to live our lives that way. Forgive us and renew us in faith so that we may trust you in all things no matter what the course of our lives brings us. This we ask through Christ Jesus our Lord and Savior. Amen

Spiritual Core Concepts: Fig Leaf Façade

**Then the eyes of both were opened,
and they knew that they were naked.
And they sewed fig leaves together
and made themselves loincloths.
Genesis 3:7**

After their fall into sin Adam and Eve immediately came to see themselves differently. They saw that they were both naked and it was embarrassing to them. It was like that almost universal dream that some of us have, that we are naked in public, and there is nothing we can do about it. Only in the case of Adam and Eve, it was not a dream, it was painfully real.

This situation left them restless to say the least. Their solution to the problem was instinctual and entirely wrong, but how would they have known that? The ill effects of the fall were already apparent in their lives. They were supposed to go to the Lord for help in their painful situation. Instead they followed their own understanding. Unfortunately for them, what they did made matters worse. To overcome this monumental problem they used something from their own resources. They went to the trees they kept to solve their problem of nakedness. The leaves of the fig tree are large, leathery, and durable. They sewed these together and wore them as garments. These worked well and brought them relief for their nakedness at least temporarily.

This all worked fairly well until that evening. That was when God came around and the thin veneer of the leaves no longer shielded them from their sense of nakedness. The idea of coming face-to-face with God left them feeling completely inadequate. So, what did they do? They raced as fast as they could and crouched down low behind the trees that they had harvested the leaves from. If their thin garments helped them, perhaps the great girth of the tree's trunk would suffice to hide their nakedness before God, right? Wrong.

God, we did not want to trust you for our needs and the difficulties we faced. We tried to fix our situations quick and easily by getting high. Our actions only made our lives increasingly worse. Forgive us our sins. Lead us forward into our recoveries and strengthen us for the journey. This we ask through the one who died and rose for us, Christ Jesus our Lord. Amen

Spiritual Core Concepts: If at First You Don't Succeed
TRY, TRY AGAIN

**And they heard the sound of the LORD God
walking in the garden in the cool of the day,
and the man and his wife hid themselves
from the presence of the LORD God
among the trees of the garden.
Genesis 3:8**

Adam and Eve had eaten the fruit hoping to be empowered to control the painful things that would come their way in life. As if coming into the knowledge that they were naked wasn't bad enough, now God was coming near and it was time to have a panic attack. Their problems didn't go away, they were multiplied. They thought they had power over nakedness, and before each other that was true, but not before God. Before him they were powerless.

When God came around that evening, things changed. Adam and Eve were again aware of their nakedness, to their great surprise. So, they hid themselves from him among the trees of the garden. It could be that they were hiding behind the very fig trees they got their leaves from. What they had done here is this, the fig leaves were only thick enough to cover their nakedness to each other, but not before God. They hoped that the large trunks of the trees might be thick enough to hide them from God. Needless to say, their plans did not work the way they had hoped.

What also needs to be said is that these covering for their nakedness, leaves and trees, was their attempt to cover or hide their sins. Their use of the leaves and even the trees were works of self-righteousness because this was from their work, that they did for themselves. They could not atone for their sins, only God could and their attempts to make amends for their sins in their own way only made the problem worse.

Dearest God, help us to not hide ourselves or what we have done in life from you. Guide us in our confessions of sin and aid us in making amends for those we have hurt and offended. Lead us in your ways and empower us to live fully in recovery. This we pray in Jesus' name. Amen

It Was the Best of Times, It Was the Worst of Times

**And they heard the sound of the Lord God
walking in the garden in the cool of the day
and the man and his wife hid themselves
from the presence of the Lord God
among the trees of the garden.
Genesis 3:8**

Eden was paradise. It was a place of great beauty and it yielded very abundant crops. What more could a person want? Adam needed a helpmate. Not a problem, God provided the most perfect wife for him. They had employment and the work wasn't too difficult to do. They were horticulturists in the world's foremost private garden. In the cool of the evening their Maker came down from Heaven and visited them.

This reference, "in the cool of the day" has a special meaning to it. As the sun sets the temperature drops and there is a gentle breeze, literally a spirit, that flows in to offset the pressure differences that come from the cooling of the air. For Adam and Eve, it was a time when they could find relief from their labors and the heat. It was also a time to relax and prepare for sleep.

At that hour the sky's blue dome fades away and the stars of the night sky appear. This is a very spiritual time of the day. With the appearance of the heavens comes the revelation of the greatness of God. It was at this spiritual time that God would visit with Adam and Eve. The couple should have anticipated his coming and been anxious to turn to God for the help they needed. That seems simple enough. However, in their fallen state what might have seemed so simple had become complex. There is a blindness that comes from sin which overtook them and instead of doing to the right things, the wrong thing to do seemed right and that is what they did.

God, help us to learn from our ancestor's mistakes and allow us to avoid repeating them. Let us come to you daily in prayer, worship, and meditation so that we may be renewed in faith and receive wisdom from you. By your grace lead and guide us in our recovery journey and aid us in living clean and free from drugs. Through Christ our Lord we pray. Amen

Where Are You?

**But the L<small>ORD</small> God called to the man and said to him,
"Where are you?"
Genesis 3:8-9**

God made his presence known as he called out to Adam. He did this in a very pastoral and gentle way. To be certain, God knew everything that had transpired. God didn't go directly to them, instead he let them hide. God didn't say to them, "I know exactly where you are and I saw what you have done." Saying that would have put the couple into a highly defensive stance, much more than they already were. God went along with their plan and asked, "Where are you?" This question was not just about their location. God was also asking them about their state of affairs.

What soon follows is what is sometimes referred to as a *come to Jesus meeting*. It was a time for the man and the woman to come clean about what had happened and to accept their consequences. This was a highly charged situation. Adam and Eve needed to take a look at where they were and what had become of their lives. They had never before felt naked, or had to wear clothing. They never before had to hide from God. In the past God would visit them at this spiritual hour and it was always a favorable time. The tide of things had changed and the uncertainty of the hour was extremely frightening to them. They already knew that they would be facing capital punishment for what they had done in eating the forbidden fruit.

Dearest God, like our earliest ancestors we have hidden from you. We were also lost and without hope in finding our way back to you. We are grateful that you came to us in the life of your son, our dear Lord Jesus Christ. You have redeemed us from our sins and delivered us from our addictions. Lead us as we follow you in our lives that we may do your will, and in our recoveries that we may live free and clean to the glory of your name. This we ask through Christ our Lord. Amen

The Moment of Truth

**And he said,
"I heard the sound of you in the garden,
and I was afraid, because I was naked,
and I hid myself."
Genesis 3:10**

Adam's response was quite simple and honest. He and Eve were living out that terrible nightmare about being naked again, only this time it was infinitely worse. It was real. It was an absolute horror in their minds. That was because the thin leaves did not help them this time, and neither did the thick girth of the trees. Their senses were acutely sharp at that time and at the first sound that God was nearing them for a visit they bolted in a panic attack and hid behind the trees of the garden.

After God called to him Adam was honest about his situation. He was living in fear he said. He was afraid of God because he was naked. We have to ask why wasn't he fearful about having eaten the fruit though? In his sinful and fallen state he could see that he and Eve were naked, but he could not see the real cause of their problems. He had disobeyed God, eaten the forbidden fruit, and fell in sin. Ironically, he could see they were naked, but he could not see the root of that problem. So it would be for all of mankind, we are blind to many of our problems and we need God to guide us to the truth.

God, of course, showed his concern about why Adam knew that he is naked. Note that Adam did not boast that he had gained power through the knowledge of good and evil as the two had expected they would get. He said nothing about being more like God, as the serpent said they would be. They had no such power. They had not become more like God. It was just the opposite. They were less god like, their innocence was gone, and they were now rebellious sinners.

Heavenly Father, when we had gone astray you came to us in the life of your son and redeemed us from our sins. Through him you joined us in our pain and suffering when he died on the cross for our sins. As you provided for Adam and Eve in their time of need, provide for us every day of our lives so that we may have the strength we need to live for your glory, clean and free of drug use. Through Christ our Lord. Amen

Addiction Character Traits: The Blame Game

**He said, "Who told you that you were naked?
Have you eaten of the tree of which
I commanded you not to eat?"
The man said, "The woman whom
you gave to be with me, she gave me
fruit of the tree, and I ate."
Then the Lord God said to the woman,
"What is this that you have done?"
The woman said,
"The serpent deceived me, and I ate."
Genesis 3:11-13**

In his answer to God Adam threw his wife under the bus and blamed her for his eating the forbidden fruit before he admitted to his own involvement. Adam was there the whole time while Eve was being tempted by the serpent. He said nothing as his wife sparred with the most crafty and deceitful wild beast that ever lived. Then in his round about admission of sin he blamed her, and then he blamed God because he gave her to him. He avoided a direct admission to his own inaction in this as well.

God asked Eve what happened, and she also passed the blame. Was she copying her husband's example or was this now her nature too? Probably both. In essence, the woman said, "It was that snaky looking fellow over there. He is the responsible one."

A confession of sin is what was needed; blaming each other was what they did. Their natural reaction was everything it should not have been. It was nothing close to what they needed to do. Their inclination was of no help, rather it was a great hindrance, making matters far worse for them both. Taking personal responsibility for their actions was something they would have to learn to do.

Dear God, help us to learn not to blame other people, not to blame circumstances or anything else. Help us to learn to take personal responsibility for all of our actions. Guide us in working to correct the wrongs we have worked in our lives. Thank you most of all for the forgiveness we needed for our sin through the suffering and death of your son our Lord, who lives and reigns with you and the Holy Spirit, one God now and forever. Amen

The Devil's Demise

**The LORD God said to the serpent,
"Because you have done this,
cursed are you above all livestock
and above all beasts of the field;
on your belly you shall go,
and dust you shall eat all the days of your life.
I will put enmity between you and the woman,
and between your offspring and her offspring;
he shall bruise your head,
and you shall bruise his heel."
Genesis 3:14-15**

So, the serpent got what he had coming, and it wasn't pretty. God did not ask him why he did it or any questions for that matter. The snaky beast was working on behalf of the father of all lies, the devil. God's judgement was immediate and harsh. He was cursed by God. In humility he would now have to crawl on his belly and be something of a bottom dweller, eating dust all the days of his life. What followed this is the most interesting part.

God put hostility between the serpent and the woman, and her descendants and the descendants of the serpent. What this means is that from among the woman's descendants will come the Savior. Jesus will bruise the head of the serpent and the serpent will bruise Jesus' heel. What this is understood to mean is that that Lord's suffering and death on the cross for our sins was like a mere heel bruise compared to the damage the devil suffered and will still suffer.

Father, save us from the time of trial and protect us against all the attacks of the evil one. Guard our souls and cover us with the blood of Jesus so that no evil may come upon us. We look to you in humility for all that we need, for our daily bread and all the provisions we need for our lives. Strengthen us by your Holy Spirit, may we bring you glory, through Christ our Lord. Amen

Eve and Pain in Childbirth

To the woman he said,
"I will surely multiply your pain in childbearing;
in pain you shall bring forth children.
Your desire shall be contrary to your husband,
but he shall rule over you."
Genesis 3:16

Pain in any circumstance has a certain grip on the person experiencing it. It has a way of bringing us to our knees if it is severe enough. When it is that bad all we can think about is the pain and wanting relief, now. Eating the forbidden fruit was supposed to allow the couple to control pain in their lives. Here, for Eve, who tangled with the devilish creature, the problem of pain has not been reduced but rather it has been greatly increased. Adam and Eve had not had a child yet, but that would come soon enough. The pain of childbirth before the fall would have been rather minor. Now, because of her sin, it would be greatly multiplied.

Eve also found another painful experience would exist for her. She was going to find that her interests in life were not going to be entirely compatible with her husband's, hence they would clash. She would not be getting her way in those family spats. Adam was given the upper hand by God in the case of their family and now he will be ruling over her.

They had been blessed by God who said to them, "Be fruitful and multiply and fill the earth." This was God's will for them both before and now after the fall.

God, lead and guide us in discerning your will for our lives. Help us to fulfill your purpose for our lives, especially when it gets difficult for us. If times are good and pleasant or difficult and painful may we trust you in all that comes our way. Strengthen us in our recovery and help us to mature in you as we grow and go through the steps. This we pray in Jesus' holy name. Amen

And to Adam He Said…

**"Because you have listened to the voice of your wife
and have eaten of the tree of which I commanded you,
'You shall not eat of it,'
Genesis 3:17**

Adam also suffered under what was to be. He listened to the voice of his wife. That in itself was not the problem though. It is what wasn't said there, which was that he listened to the voice of his wife and didn't think for himself. Further, what we need to understand about this verse is how their culture in that ancient day differs from our own. In Adam and Eve's culture if you listened to someone, it meant that you: heard their voice with your ears, listened with your mind to what they were saying, and automatically did what they were asking of you. In our American culture it is different. We might only hear their voice but pay them no further attention. We might go the next step and let what they said register in our head. We might even react to them in one of several ways: we might not say anything, we might disagree with them, we might agree with them, we might do contrary to what they have asked, and lastly we might do what they have asked.

Adam shouldn't have listened to her and ate the fruit. Instead he should have merely heard her voice and not done as she did because he was thinking for himself. In listening to Eve's voice he allowed God's voice and commandment to be drown out.

In the end, it is not a bad thing to hear the voice of your spouse. Someone told a joke about that once: A husband heard his wife yelling at him, "Are you listening to me?" His response to her was simply this, "Why do you always start our conversations by asking me that question?" Enough said.

Heavenly Father, may we always listen first to you and live out your will for our lives. Help us to ignore the demands that this world puts on us when they are contrary to your will and Word. Be close to us in our recovery from addiction and lead us so that we will serve you and you alone with our lives. Through Christ Jesus our Lord we ask this. Amen

Because of You

And to Adam he said, ...
"cursed is the ground because of you;
in pain you shall eat of it all the days of your life;
thorns and thistles it shall bring forth for you;
and you shall eat the plants of the field.
By the sweat of your face you shall eat bread,"
Genesis 3:17-19

It is hard to say between these two, Adam and Eve, who would suffer more in the days and years that were still ahead of them. In the man's case God drives home the point that Adam was disobedient to the commandment not to eat the fruit. That is in sharp contrast to Eve who ate first because she was deceived. As a result of his sin God pronounced what the consequences were for him. Rather than be a gardener eating the fruits of Eden he was to be a laboring farmer who would painfully try to grow food in the ground that is cursed. He will grow wheat for the bread he will eat, but there was a problem. Along with the wheat, weeds with thrones and thistles would also grow in his crop. The ground was going to be hard and he must break it up in a labor intense effort.

Sweat dripping from a dirty face in the scorching heat can be an extremely uncomfortable experience. It was so difficult and hot for Adam that as he quenched his powerful thirst the water immediately ran out his pores as his body tried to cool itself. What Adam had to look forward to in life was not very pleasant. He had to do this sweaty and painful work all his life. Even as he ate his meals he would be made miserable by the heat and sweat that followed.

What is unseen and unspoken here is interesting. Adam and Eve were thinking they could be less dependent on God by eating the fruit. Here they are going to have to be even more reliant on God for the help they both needed in the difficulties they have brought on themselves. For Eve in painful childbirth and for Adam in farming and producing food.

Dearest God, aid us in our difficulties so that by your strength we may fulfill your will in our lives and live clean and free of drugs in our recoveries. In Christ's name. Amen

Covenant Relationships: Death ~~Can't~~ Can Wait

And the LORD **God commanded the man,
saying, … in the day that you eat of it
you shall surely die."
Genesis 2:16-17**

It had been a bad day for these two to say the least, but the day was not over. Remember that the matter of their deaths was referred to. That death would happen on the day they sinned. They did not die though, neither spiritually, metaphorically, nor physically. Yet, God said they would die. So, what happened to fulfill God's Word which cannot fall void?

Some have said that Adam and Eve died metaphorically on that day. Others have said they died spiritually. Still others have said that their relationship with God was dead and they were cut off from him. But there is another possibility that is more likely than all these.

God is the Almighty and therefore for his Word is absolute. If he says you will die, then it is true you will die. There is no negotiating, no explaining it away and there is certainly no getting around it. They ate the fruit, therefore death had to come to them. Can you hear yourself saying, "But they didn't die on that day!" Adam went on to live 930 years before he died. True he and Eve didn't die that day, but someone did die. It was a substitutionary death that happened. An animal died that day for the first man and his wife.

Their relationship with God did not end on that day either. To the contrary, there relationship continued on as evidenced by God showing up that day. After the fall God spent a large amount of time with them, doing some highly significant things with them and establishing a covenant with them called the *Adamic Covenant*.

Heavenly Father, you sent your son to die in our stead and by it you have given us forgiveness for our sins. Thank you for the sacrifices you made and help us to live with servant's hearts as we continue to live under your care. Empower us in making forward progress in our recoveries from addiction. This we pray through Christ our Lord. Amen

Covenant Relationships: The Adamic Covenant
The First Confession

On that day when the couple sinned God called to his side a lamb, which despite the fall, was without fault, spot, wrinkle, or blemish. It came willingly and tenderly as it stood by his side, and nuzzled against God's thigh. Then God called the couple to his side and had Adam place his hand on the lamb's head. God lead him saying, "Confess your sins and the sins of your wife by saying that you ate the forbidden fruit of the tree of the knowledge of good and evil." Adam and Eve nervously looked at each other, guilt was on their faces. They wondered for a moment if they could trust the Lord and then Adam said these simple words, "We have eaten what was prohibited, we ate the fruit of the tree of the knowledge of good and evil. We broke your commandment and in doing so we have sinned against you." The Lord nodded, smiled, and encouraged him to say more. Adam and Eve knew there was more to their sin than just that alone. Eve shared, "I spoke with the serpent, I should have simply told him to leave us alone. I thought what he was saying was true, even though it went against what you had said, my Lord. I doubted your Word and believed in his lies." Adam then shared, "I was there, but I said and did nothing. I failed my wife and helpmate as her husband. I did not protect her from the evil one. I did not stop her from eating the fruit and I freely ate it too. I disobeyed you and for that I know this day we must die."

As Adam said those final five words his heart and Eve's heart as well, sank low and dread set in. They could not have been more sorrowful for their actions. Tears streamed down their faces as they looked to each other in love, knowing that they would not be able to be with each other ever again. The pain of their trespass against the Lord, their failure to each other was overwhelming and no words could express their deepest regret.

To the surprise of the man and his wife the Lord looked at them both and said, "Because you have confessed your trespasses before me your sins are forgiven you. By the laying of your hand on this lamb, your sins have passed from you and your wife to it. The guilt and punishment for your trespasses have been transferred from your family to the lamb and it will die in your place as a holy sacrifice."

Adam and Eve were not sure of what all was now unfolding. There thoughts raced and their emotions flipped about rapidly. They felt the greatest sense of relief for their sins, for that their hearts sored to new heights. However in fear they looked on as the Lord drew out a knife and in one swift movement of his hand he sliced through the neck of the lamb. So quickly was it done that the lamb suffered nothing as it fell to the ground, lifeless and still. They felt absolutely horrified at its death and still more horrorstruck because it was for their sins that the innocent lamb had died. They were grateful to the Lord and to the lamb that this had been done for them and there was a reverent awe that settled on their hearts in the end.

Then God instructed them that they needed to confess their sins to him in prayer on a daily basis. Further, he told them how they needed to atone for their sins annually. They needed to sacrifice an animal, a lamb, a goat, or a bull, yearly just as he did for them. The head of the household needed to place his hand on the animal and confess the sins of the family, which allowed for the transfer of their sins from them to the animal. Then the animal was to be put to death by the slicing of its neck in one swift movement of a knife. Finally, they needed to include their children in this ritual and instruct them to carry this practice on in every generation until one day the Messiah would come.

Lord, you sent your son Jesus, the Lamb of God, to die for us. We are grateful for the salvation he won for us on the cross and by his resurrection we find daily strength to live as your people. Help us to be faithful to you all the days of our lives and live in recovery from our addiction to drugs. This we pray in his name, Jesus Christ our Lord. Amen

Covenant Relationships: Leather Clothes

And the Lord God made for Adam and for his wife garments of skins and clothed them.
Genesis 3:21

Who doesn't love a leather jacket or coat? Granted they are a bit expensive, but they do last a long time and they look really nice on us. If you are into motorcycles a leather jacket and pants are almost required. Many of the motorcycle leathers have body armor added to them to protect the rider in the case of a fall or an accident.

Now if God gave Adam and Eve garments of skin, meaning leather, then the question needs to be asked where did the garments of skin come from? And the answer is that they came from lamb that had been sacrificed by God because of their sins.

There is something especially important that is portrayed in the choice of clothing that Adam and Eve made for themselves and in the leather clothes the God gave them. Imagine for yourself that God is looking at them and what does he see? In the case of the fig leaves he sees that they sinned because they wanted to be too much like him. He sees that they tried to right their sin by wearing clothes they made for themselves from the garden that they were keepers of. These are all signs of their self-righteousness because they were trying to fix in their own way what they could not fix for themselves. Only God could fix it.

God took away their fig-leaf clothes and in exchange he gave them the leather ones he had made. Now, as God looked upon them, he saw the blood sacrifice that was made for the forgiveness of their sins. He saw that the requirements of his Law, death for sin, was met. God saw Adam and Eve as righteous because of the covenant he made with them.

Heavenly Father, thank you for the blood of the eternal covenant whereby we have the forgiveness of our sins. May we walk in righteousness before you all the days of our lives. Bless us in our recoveries and aid us that we may not sin against you by having a relapse. Help us to progress and recover the lives you have designed for us. This we ask through Christ our Lord and Savior. Amen

Paradise Lost

Then the LORD **God said, "Behold, the man has become like one of us in knowing good and evil. Now, lest he reach out his hand and take also of the tree of life and eat, and live forever—" therefore the L**ORD **God sent him out from the garden of Eden to work the ground from which he was taken.**
Genesis 3:22-23

We don't know why Adam and Eve never ate from the Tree of Life to become immortals when they had the chance. When they ate from the forbidden fruit and they knew death would come, that would have seemed like reason enough to do it. That would have saved them from the awful fate of death, or so it seemed. However, in their fallen state their bodies were now susceptible to illness, injury and disease. If they ate of the tree of life they would have lived eternally in their fallen bodies. That would mean that as they aged and their organs wore out, they would never find relief through a natural death. When they developed heart failure, dementia or cancer, the diseases would continue to ravage their bodies with no end to it for all of eternity. It would have been truly unthinkable that God would have allowed them to have access to the tree of life given the horrid outcome that would have forever forced them to live in eternity in those dreadful states.

We thought we had found a little piece of paradise for ourselves when we were high. We loved how it made us feel and wanted it more and more. Before long we needed to use more of the drugs to get the same high. Over time we were not able to get so high on them anymore. Then, when we weren't high we felt awful, and it was getting worse. We used more and more of the drugs to ward off the lows that we felt. We also found that we were enjoying the high of drugs less and less. We were trapped in addiction and being sucked in deeper every day. We were frightened, but our solution to that was to get high which only made things worse. The paradise we had made for ourselves by getting high was now turning into a living hell for us.

Gracious God in heaven, thank you for rescuing us out of our addictions and bringing us to salvation through the redeeming death of your son Jesus Christ, in whose name we pray. Amen

Genesis Four

Now Adam knew Eve his wife, and she conceived ...

... and bore Cain, saying, "I have gotten a man with the help of the LORD." ² And again, she bore his brother Abel. Now Abel was a keeper of sheep, and Cain a worker of the ground. ³ In the course of time Cain brought to the LORD an offering of the fruit of the ground, ⁴ and Abel also brought of the firstborn of his flock and of their fat portions. And the LORD had regard for Abel and his offering, ⁵ but for Cain and his offering he had no regard. So Cain was very angry, and his face fell. ⁶ The LORD said to Cain, "Why are you angry, and why has your face fallen? ⁷ If you do well, will you not be accepted? And if you do not do well, sin is crouching at the door. Its desire is contrary to you, but you must rule over it." ⁸ Cain spoke to Abel his brother. And when they were in the field, Cain rose up against his brother Abel and killed him. ⁹ Then the LORD said to Cain, "Where is Abel your brother?" He said, "I do not know; am I my brother's keeper?" ¹⁰ And the LORD said, "What have you done? The voice of your brother's blood is crying to me from the ground. ¹¹ And now you are cursed from the ground, which has opened its mouth to receive your brother's blood from your hand. ¹² When you work the ground, it shall no longer yield to you its strength. You shall be a fugitive and a wanderer on the earth." ¹³ Cain said to the LORD, "My punishment is greater than I can bear. ¹⁴ Behold, you have driven me today away from the ground, and from your face I shall be hidden. I shall be a fugitive and a wanderer on the earth, and whoever finds me will kill me." ¹⁵ Then the LORD said to him, "Not so! If anyone kills Cain, vengeance shall be taken on him sevenfold." And the LORD put a mark on Cain, lest any who found him should attack him. ¹⁶ Then Cain went away from the presence of the LORD and settled in the land of Nod, east of Eden.

Sibling Rivalry and Favoritism

**Now Adam knew Eve his wife,
and she conceived and bore Cain, saying,
"I have gotten a man with the help of the LORD."
And again, she bore his brother Abel.
Now Abel was a keeper of sheep,
and Cain a worker of the ground.
Genesis 4:1-2**

What this Scripture passage doesn't tell us is more revealing than what it does tell us. Of course Adam was the father of Cain. Still Eve gives credit to God for his help with his birth who is immediately referred to as a man rather than as an infant or as a child. In this ancient culture typically when a child was born it was seen as having the potential to become a man, or a woman in adult life. To attain to that stature they needed to take on a trade, have a career and contribute to society. To show how much Cain was held in high esteem, he was immediately granted the status of manhood even though his accomplishments to date amounted to absolutely nothing. Clearly he had a highly favored status as he went into the family business of farming.

When Abel the second born son came along, he was referred to as merely the brother of Cain, not as Eve's son or Adam's son. Because of that, Abel lived in the shadow of his older brother and he didn't go into the family business. He was a keeper of sheep. What must be known about this career path is that it was despised by everyone else. Sheepherders smell like sheep and their manure. They had to live in the pasture lands and keep moving their sheep frequently to new fields and to water. Because of that they could not keep up close social relationships with others and they didn't have the best social skills for lack of interaction with others on a regular basis.

Family dysfunction is quite common among us. Frequently we used drugs to give us a sense of being valued because we did not receive that from our roles in our families of origin. At other times we used because we had a sense of entitlement, meaning we felt like we deserved the right to get high to feel especially good about ourselves.

Dearest God, you loved us from the day of our conception. You love us still even though we have been rebellious and were using drugs. Thank you for our redemption and for bringing us into recovery, through Christ Jesus our Lord and Savior. Amen

The Way of Cain: No Regard

**In the course of time Cain brought to the
Lord an offering of the fruit of the ground,
but for Cain and his offering he had no regard.
So Cain was very angry, and his face fell.
Genesis 4:3, 5**

Beginning with the fourth day of creation God set into place a revolving cycle; of night and day, of lunar months, and the four seasons that make up a calendar year. This cycle has generationally repeated itself ever since the beginning of earth's first days. On the day of the fall God added to the calendar an annual event for the atonement of sin. It began on that day when God showed Adam and Eve how to receive forgiveness for their sins when he made the first animal sacrifice. This practice was continued by our first parents and with the birth of their children, they too were included in the rite and were taught how to do it for themselves when they became adults. Cain and Abel knew they were expected to continue this practice and also pass it on to their children to observe until the Messiah would come.

One year at the appointed time for the atonement rite Cain sacrificed, but it was not an animal sacrifice. He brought produce from the ground and in return he received God's disapproval. There was a time of year to offer this kind sacrifice, it is a thanks offering for a bountiful harvest. This was not that time of year. Cain found out soon enough what the consequences were for his improper offering to God and his mistaken beliefs associated with it. Cain had avoided bartering with his brother for the lamb that was needed for the sacrifice. Instead he made his own self-styled offering, but no blood was spilled into the ground, instead it was the sweat of his brow that fell to the ground as he harvested his produce. From this he made an ill-fated attempt to atone for his sins. By offering produce he did not have to experience humility in the confession of his sins or experience transference of his sins from his life to the life of an innocent lamb as he laid his hand on its head. Cain sidestepped the pain of seeing the lamb become his substitute and having to put his knife to its throat as it died in his stead. He chose to excuse himself from experiencing its death for the forgiveness of his sins.

God could have never been satisfied with Cain's sacrifice of his crops for the forgiveness of sin no matter how large it was, no matter how sincere Cain thought he was, or with whatever he may have had in mind. In the final measure of any sacrifice for the forgiveness of sin is not determined by Cain or by any single person or group of people. Here is why, Cain's sin, and for that matter all sin, is an offense to God.

Therefore, God is the only one who can appropriately determine what penalties and punishments for forgiveness had to happen for righteousness to be restored.

For us in recovery we need to know from this that we must follow God's prescribed ways. Our ways will lead us astray and cause us to act in ways that are contrary to his will. Adam and Eve tried to deal with their sin problem and their fig leaf garments did not work. Cain tried to appease God with fruit and vegetables and that didn't work. They needed to sacrifice a lamb. For us, God sent his son to be our lamb, and to die for our sins and redeem us.

Heavenly Father, thank you for delivering us from sin and bondage, and from addiction to drugs. As your son rose victoriously from the death and the grave, so also bring us into his victory over sin and drugs in our lives. In his name we pray. Amen

Covenant Relationships: Righteous Abel

**And Abel for his part brought of the
firstlings of his flock, their fat portions.
And the LORD had regard for Abel and his offering.
Genesis 4:4**

Abel and the sacrifice he made was approved by God because it followed in the pattern he had already established from the day of the fall. What followed was simple, Abel followed God's requirements and Cain did not. If sacrificing was so hard a thing for Cain to bring himself to do then he needed to consider Abel. It wasn't easy for him either, he was supposed to keep the sheep and protect them from harm. If the sacrifice went against Cain's nature, then it was more so for Abel. Even so, Abel followed the religious practice of sacrificing a lamb just as his parents had taught him, just as they had been taught by God.

What this is telling us is that Abel confessed that he was a sinner, that is why he sacrificed the lamb. As a result of having confessed his sins and sacrificed an innocent lamb for them, his sins were removed from him and placed on the lamb who died in his place. In essence the lamb became sinful and suffered death as its punishment. The lamb's innocence was passed to Abel in the process. As a result of this God saw Abel as though he was righteous, and he was given God's approval for having made things right in this way.

In addiction our sins were many. The lifestyle of addiction multiplied our sins and they wore heavily on us. We felt shame, guilt, hopelessness, and helplessness. Our misery was without measure. Our own solution was to get high again. That not only continued the cycle but it also enflamed it and made that pattern in our behavior more deeply entrenched. In recovery we did what God had planned for our deliverance since before the foundation of the world was laid. We turned to him through the life of his son Jesus Christ. We called on his name and prayed for salvation from our sins and deliverance from our addiction. God saved us from both.

Heavenly Father, thank you for providing us salvation from our sins and our addiction. By the redeeming death and resurrection of your son we have life again. In Jesus name. Amen

The Way of Cain: Anger Management

**But for Cain and his offering he had no regard.
So Cain was very angry, and his face fell.
The Lord said to Cain, "Why are you angry,
and why has your face fallen?
If you do well, will you not be accepted?
And if you do not do well,
sin is crouching at the door.
Its desire is contrary to you,
but you must rule over it."
Genesis 4:5-7**

Cain took being rejected by God extremely hard, as he should have. He was angry and that emotional energy it generated was like high octane fuel. That kind of fuel was intended to empower Cain to overcome his resistance to making a blood sacrifice for his sin. However, Cain took this powerful energy and focused it on himself. His face fell which is describing him as being depressed. God's intensions for him was to not stay stuck there with his anger but to do the right thing. His will for Cain was for him to make the sacrifice and then find acceptance. In an exceedingly kind and pastoral way God also issued him guidance and a warning. God said that if he didn't make the sacrifice then sin would have its way with him and he would fall prey to a grave sin. God told him that he needed to master his anger and direct it in the right course of action.

As is common to most of us when our back is pushed against the wall, we tend to do one of two things. One is to rise to the occasion and react in noble ways. The other is to sink to our lowest and act in some of the worst ways, and Cain's back was against the wall. Some call it survival behavior because that is all we can think of doing, just surviving. It is shortsighted and can be extremely dangerous for us. In addiction we were stuck and held captive by our insatiable cravings to get high. We were on a wild ride that never ended and we could not just jump off of it and take our chances on where we might land. We needed help to quit. In recovery we were freed from our using and cleansed of our sins. God in his mercy delivered us and through his son's life and death he provided the sacrifice for the forgiveness of our sins.

Gracious God, thank you for sending your son to rescue us from our sins and our addictions. By his sacrifice we are clean, free, and living according to your will. In Jesus name we pray. Amen

The Way of Cain: Murder

**Cain spoke to Abel his brother.
And when they were in the field,
Cain rose up against his
brother Abel and killed him.
Then the LORD said to Cain,
"Where is Abel your brother?"
He said, "I do not know; am I my brother's keeper?"
And the LORD said, "What have you done?
The voice of your brother's blood
is crying to me from the ground.
Genesis 4:8-10**

Cain did not take mastery over his anger and the energy it provided. He did not use it as the motivation he needed to make the right decision and take the right action. Instead of bartering for a lamb from his brother the shepherd, he killed the shepherd who kept the sheep. Anger is not inherently a bad emotion, what we do with it can be either for good or bad, or even evil as it was in this case. Cain first turned his anger inward and was depressed, then he expressed it outwardly against his brother. His brother had received the approval from God that he sought. However, Cain was unwilling to do what his brother had done to receive it. He wasn't willing to admit to and confess his sins. He did not receive the forgiveness that he needed. His failure to confess his sins before God and make the sacrifice lead him to commit the sin of murder. He turned his back on the prescribed method of forgiveness and it led him into a very dark place.

In the blindness that comes with his sin filled mind Cain was unaware that God knew all about what had happened. As it was with Cain's parents on the day of the fall when God came to them pastorally, hoping to ease the way for them to confess to him, God also came to Cain in a pastoral way. God brought up the matter of his brother in a way that was hoped would aid him in his confession of sin. His response was to lie and make the sarcastic remark, "am I my brother's keeper?" Sarcasm is born out of anger and it is a very unhealthy expression. Soon Cain would suffer a tragic but fitting outcome for his punishment.

In our addictions the drugs we used controlled our emotions. They controlled our physical sensations. They controlled our minds and thoughts. The smoke that we inhaled choked off our souls and the life-giving-spirit of God in us. We were in trouble and in turn many of us got into more serious trouble by our actions and our words. We did not have mastery over our lives, instead we were overtaken by a cruel and harsh taskmaster that was impersonal and cared nothing for what was best for our lives. The drugs fueled our addictions, and our addictions craved the drugs. We had neither the ability to catch our breath in this out of control lifestyle, nor to retake what was once ours, our own lives.

In desperation we responded to God's offer of salvation. We were in no place in our lives to assume we could eventually get over our addiction. Many of us saw our own deaths coming if we had continued on using. God rescued us and delivered us into freedom from drugs. He breathed into us new life through his Holy Spirit and we were clean and ready to live our lives in accordance with his will. Daily we learned to turn to him for the temptations that would come trying to lure us back into that dark way of living. We walked in the light of his Word and in fellowship with the church who shared with us in lives of faith.

Heavenly Father, by your mighty and omnipotent right hand you have delivered us from the desperate life of an addict and given us new life. When we had no hope you came to us and worked miracle after miracle. Shed your light before our paths that we may continue evermore in the lives you have restored to us. May we remember to always give you the glory for all that you have done and are doing for us, through Christ our Lord. Amen

The Way of Cain: The Fugitive

[The Lord said,]
"And now you are cursed from the ground,
which has opened its mouth to receive
your brother's blood from your hand.
When you work the ground,
it shall no longer yield to you its strength.
You shall be a fugitive and a wanderer on the earth."
Then Cain went away from the presence of the
Lord and settled in the land of Nod, east of Eden."
Genesis 4:11-12

The Mosaic Law of an eye for an eye, and a tooth for a tooth was not yet enacted. Cain's life had been spared him. However, his life as he knew it was now over. When his parents fell in sin God pronounced to them that the ground was cursed because of their sin. Now because of his murderous sin Cain was cursed from the ground. He had inherited the family business and was raised to be a farmer. He was intimately attached to the ground and the seasons of planting, growing, and harvesting. It was his life. Now he was sentenced to be uprooted from the ground and he could never be a farmer again. Even if he wanted to disobey God and continue working the fields they would no longer grow enough food for him to live on. He was forced into the life of a vagrant without a home. If he wanted to eat, he would have to travel great distances in order to find enough food to survive. He had despised his brother who wandered the fields as he brought his flocks to green pastures. Now Cain would be the one who was wandering infertile fields for the reason that he had murdered his brother.

This reference to being a fugitive also meant that he had refused to participate in the Adamic Covenant and make the yearly animal sacrifice that God required of all people. Because of Cain's refusal to take part in the covenant, God reluctantly set up an armistice for him to live under. This was something of a truce because the two parties had reached a stalemate. For Cain, he was not going to be able to live in peace but would be haunted for the rest of his life with the guilt of being a murderer. Also take note that there is a play on words in the text that is lost in translation. It says that he settled in the land of Nod. The land of Nod means the land of restlessness and this is where he wandered.

In addiction we had refused to live as God asked. We were deceived and drawn in by a lying impersonal demigod, drugs. They enslaved us and took everything from us. We were restless and wandered in many ways. Our minds were filled with confusion and our thoughts were twisted. We tried to avoid thinking about what our lives had become and used drugs to help us avoid worrying about our present state and what we were heading towards. Our restlessness existed on many levels and there was no solution for it.

The day came when God came to us and offered to have us join with him in a covenant relationship. He had already made the blood sacrifice for us when he offered up his only begotten son in death on the cross for our sins, which were many. All had been prepared and we were welcomed to have fellowship with him. God promised us deliverance, cleansing and a new life. We received his offer and have been walking in that covenant relationship with him ever since.

God, we had gone far astray and were lost in our sin and addiction. Our needs were great and then you came to us. You have delivered us from destruction and death, and have brought us into covenant relationships with you through the blood of your son. We give you our heartfelt thanks and praise your holy name for all that you have done and are doing. This we offer to you through your son who suffered, died, and rose again to redeem us. Amen

The Way of Cain:
The Mark of Stigmatization and the Generational Curse

**Cain said to the Lord, "My punishment is greater than I can bear.
Behold, you have driven me today away from the ground,
and from your face I shall be hidden.
I shall be a fugitive and a wanderer on the earth,
and whoever finds me will kill me."
Then the Lord said to him,
"Not so! If anyone kills Cain,
vengeance shall be taken on him sevenfold."
And the LORD put a mark on Cain,
lest any who found him should attack him.
Genesis 4:13-16**

Cain had committed capital murder. It was a serious crime. Who would feel safe around him, or even trust him for anything ever again? If he killed once, what was to prevent him from doing so again? His worry was that he was at great risk and would be put to death by someone for the crime he had committed. As an amendment to the armistice God agreed to do what he could to safeguard his life for him, and a mark was put on him. What exactly the mark was, no one knows. This was a form of branding or a stigma that he had to wear because of the seriousness of the situation and it was his for life.

In contrast to that, whenever one person saw another, they were reminded that all people were made in God's image and likeness. For this reason respect and dignity was due them. Cain had not respected God, he had not respected his own brother, he murdered him. In Cain's case the stigma that he wore was well deserved. There was an opportunity for him to be redeemed from his murderous sin, that was to return to the covenant by sacrificing a lamb for his sins as prescribed by God. But he refused to his dying day to do it.

Many of us in addiction were stigmatized long before we were called addicts by others or by ourselves. The whole world is dysfunctional, and don't we know it. We grew up in that world. Many of us were stigmatized at an early age. It could have come from our families, from childhood friends, from school, work or any number of places or people. In a family setting one child might have been labeled as a smart kid or maybe a good child. In turn the other child in the family was called, or at least it was implied, that he was stupid or the bad one. As a result of these stigmas the family created an environment that supported the labels given to the two children. The good kid could do no wrong and so he got away with everything. The bad child could do nothing good and even got blamed for things he did not do. Everything he did, good or bad, was automatically identified as bad. This child didn't want to contradict his family's unwritten rules and show anyone that they were wrong about him, so he lived down to the stigmatization that he was labeled with.

Unfortunately, this kind of a family setting in a child's developmental years has far reaching effects on them in their adult lives and in their core beliefs about themselves. Just to make things still worse, this sets up a pattern for the next generation to follow in. That in turn perpetuates it until someone steps up, breaks dysfunctional family rules, and stops it.

For us in recovery we might have been raised in a family with this dynamic going on. If we were subject to stigmatization we need to advocate for ourselves and not accept the dysfunctional roles that we were forced into. We may need to seek out some counseling from a competent Christian counselor or a pastor to help us in our recovery.

Heavenly Father, forgive us all our sins for the sake of your son Jesus Christ our Lord. Teach us your ways and sustain us in righteousness. Empower us to live up to our full potentials, help us to break free from the stigmas that we were wrongly labeled with. This we pray in Jesus' name. Amen

Apart from the Covenant We Cannot Really Know God

**Cain said to the LORD,
"My punishment is greater than I can bear.
Behold, you have driven me
today away from the ground,
and from your face I shall be hidden.
Genesis 4:13-14**

Cain had all that he needed. His parents had done the annual sacrifice with him since the day he was born. He knew how to do it for himself and most likely had for years before that one year when he decided not to. God came to him in a truly kind and pastoral way to guide and encourage him into doing the right thing. What possessed him to not do it? Why in the world would he kill his own brother over it? He was sinful and just as Adam and Eve blamed each other for their sin, he blamed his brother for his problems. Only he took blaming to a new level by murdering his brother over it.

Because Cain would not participate in the Adamic covenant God established the armistice with him. In great spiritual pain he cried out that his punishment was unbearable. He came to realize that outside of the covenant he would not have access to God in the same way as he had before. He said God's face would now be hidden to him. This reference to God's face is their culture's way of saying he would not be having a personal relationship with God anymore. This means for all people, of all time, that outside of God's covenant they cannot know God in such a personal way anymore.

As addicts we know what it is like to feel like we are cut off from God. We know that we cannot repair the separation that our sin and addiction had caused. Half measures, bargaining and all the plans that we dreamt up were worthless. It was only through the blood of Jesus Christ that he shed on the cross for us that we could have access to God.

Dear Heavenly Father, you gave your only begotten son over in death to redeem us from all of our sins and our addiction. By the power of your Holy Spirit you raised him to life again. So also by the power of your Holy Spirit raise us up to new life in him and keep us free and clean from drug use. This we ask through Christ our Lord. Amen

The Way of Cain: Anger Management II

Lamech said to his wives:
"Adah and Zillah,
hear my voice; you wives of Lamech,
listen to what I say:
I have killed a man for wounding me,
a young man for striking me.
If Cain's revenge is sevenfold,
then Lamech's is seventy-sevenfold."
Genesis 4:23-24

With the onset of a growing population who are all fallen in sin, things have gone from bad to worse and will only continue to grow still worse. Lamech was from the seventh generation out from Adam and Eve. It needs to be known that seven in the Bible is a number that tells of completion, such as in the passing of seven days that completes one week. In Lamech's case, he is born as member of that generation, and is a descendant of murderous Cain. His example reveals that in the fullness of this time period, evil in the lives of many people has grown to a grievously severe level since the fall. Now in the fullness of that generational curse Lamech in his out of control rage has murdered not once but twice. Apparently, he did not learn the first time. He was wounded and that most likely was from a fight he got himself into. In the second incidence he was not wounded, though he was hit by someone, again from another fight he got himself into.

This is a generational curse that had surfaced, and it will continue until the end of time on earth. As we all know anger issues plague mankind. Lamech knows his guilt and fears revenge, which he believes would rightly be seventy-seven times worse than what Cain suffered with. It is highly likely that all of Cain's descendants were told about his punishment and the armistice, but were not instructed by their parents about practicing the Adamic Covenant and the forgiveness of their sins by sacrificing a lamb.

Heavenly Father, lead us away from the temptations that come from unrestrained anger. Show us better ways to express our feelings and to live with others in peace. Most of all nurture us in your love and sustain our recoveries so that we may live for your glory and that of your son's, in whose name we pray, Christ our Lord. Amen

Prayer

At that time people began to
call upon the name of the Lord.
Genesis 4:26

For reasons that can only be guessed at people had forsaken the Lord for perhaps up to seven generations. They had not been calling on his name in prayer and worship. Along with that they had ceased to make their annual sacrifices for their sins as was established with the Adamic Covenant. By default, when they did not participate in the covenant, they fell into living in the armistice that God had established with mankind because of Cain's unrepentant heart.

In the fall God pronounced to Adam and Eve the things that had changed because of their sin. These two things, the increased pain in childbirth, and the great difficulties in growing food to eat were now going to be commonplace. The people learned through Cain that they had the options of living under the armistice or the covenant were they to turn back to God. With the ill-effects of the fall continuing to roll out the earth was continually yielding leaner crops. Difficulties like that have a way of humbling us and bringing us to our knees in prayer with the intension that they cause us to cry out to God for help. Perhaps this is one reason why the people began to call on the name of the Lord again.

In active addiction we faced increasing difficulties because our disease is progressive. The troubles that came our way were not by chance, our using lifestyle brought them directly to us. The difficulties were there to warn us that we needed to get into recovery. When we realized we couldn't simply stop on our own we were being told by our circumstances that we needed help from outside of ourselves. In spite of the signs that we had a problem and needed help we continued to use and our troubles continued to multiply. The difficulties were warning signs meant to turn us back to the Lord. Because of our addiction we were instead motivated to continue our drug use. Typically it is a crisis that finally tells us we have had enough and then we got help.

Heavenly Father, thank you for the warning signs you put before us when we were using. Lead us in our recoveries to follow your ways and live to do your will. In Jesus' name. Amen

Wickedness on Earth and Righteous Noah

When the Lord saw that human wickedness was widespread on the earth and that every inclination of the human mind was nothing but evil all the time, the Lord regretted that he had made man on the earth, and he was deeply grieved. Then the Lord said, "I will wipe mankind, whom I created, off the face of the earth, together with the animals, creatures that crawl, and birds of the sky for I regret that I made them." Noah, however, found favor with the Lord.
Genesis 6:5-8

In only seven generations of lives from the fall, from the life of Cain to the life of Lamech, the Bible records the wickedness of men growing and going from bad to worse. The next time the wickedness of the earth is mentioned is in the days of Noah. Life had declined in a downward spiral to the point that the human heart was now focused on evil all of the time.

The Genesis text doesn't give us the details of what their sins were. Other readings in the Bible give us a good idea of what they most likely were because they are common to all of society due to the fall:

Covetousness	Envy	Murder
Strife	Homosexuality	Maliciousness
Gossip	Slander	Haters of God
Sorcery/drug use	Inventors of evil	Faithlessness
Sexual immorality	Theft	Jealousy
Idolatry	Adultery	Drunkenness
Lying	Fits of Anger[11]	

Heavenly Father, truly strengthen us in our repentance from sin and lead us in the way that is everlasting. Refresh us in our weariness, strengthen us in weakness and may this day be a blessing to us. This we pray in Jesus' name. Amen

---

[11] Romans 1:24-32, 1 Corinthians 6:9-10, Galatians 5:19-21, Ephesians 4:19, Colossians 3:51.

Noah Got Drunk

Noah began to be a man of the soil, and he planted a vineyard. He drank of the wine and became drunk and lay uncovered in his tent. And Ham, the father of Canaan, saw the nakedness of his father and told his two brothers outside. Then Shem and Japheth took a garment, laid it on both their shoulders, and walked backward and covered the nakedness of their father. Their faces were turned backward, and they did not see their father's nakedness. When Noah awoke from his wine and knew what his youngest son had done to him, he said, "Cursed be Canaan; a servant of servants shall he be to his brothers." He also said, "Blessed be the LORD, the God of Shem; and let Canaan be his servant. May God enlarge Japheth, and let him dwell in the tents of Shem, and let Canaan be his servant."
After the flood Noah lived 350 years.
All the days of Noah were 950 years, and he died.
Genesis 9:20-28

    The full corrupting effects of the fall were still continuing to roll out in human culture. This was seen with the rise of anger in Cain and then amplified in Lamech. Things were continuing to worsen, even after the flood that had just cleansed the earth.

    Noah had found favor with the Lord, that is why he and his family were spared from the deadly flood. After they were able to leave the ark he grew grapes in a vineyard he planted. Grapes were not new to him, but something about them apparently was. The fullness of the earth gave him a harvest of fruit, and the decay of the fallen creation made their juice decay. It appears that grape juice had now been corrupted resulting in the formation of alcohol. The concern for Noah was not just about his drinking it, it is about his drinking and subsequent intoxication. Then he laid naked where others could see his indiscretion. Clearly, as a result of the fermentation Noah was also corrupted by it.

    Nakedness is viewed differently in many cultures. There is a very conservative group of people on an island off the coast of Europe whose people bath with their clothes on, and only change their clothes in the dark. In other parts of the world where is it extremely hot and humid some of the men and women go around scantily dressed. The universally accepted practice is to always have our personal parts covered in public. That was first learned on the day of the fall.

    Noah had no excuse for his nakedness. He was drunk and he should not have been. He was in his tent, but he was naked, and his family still had access to him. He was irresponsible and acted badly. If his behavior then were assessed by a drug and alcohol counselor he would highly likely have been diagnosed with alcoholism. This would have been especially true if he did this more than once. Being drunk is one thing, and it is never a good thing, but his nakedness in this case was immoral and a sin.

His son Ham was not without excuse either. Apparently, he was indiscreet about how he dealt with the issue of his father's nakedness. He had options, before going into his father's tent he could have called out to him. If he did not answer, then he should have left whatever his concern was until the morning. Call Ham stupid, but he could have kept the matter of his father's nakedness to himself and said nothing. It seems that he recklessly opened his mouth and told his brothers. Shem and Japheth together knew just what to do for this crisis and they did it discreetly. In light of their father's boundary issue, they created a healthy boundary. Shem and Japheth handled the crisis very well. They took a blanket and walked in backwards so their eyes saw nothing as they covered him up.

For us in recovery we can follow in Japheth and Shem's example. This can be done by working discreetly to care for others in their difficulties, and making the help they need available to them. We need to practice Saint Peter's instructions knowing that "love covers a multitude of sins."[12]

Heavenly Father, thank you for bringing us into recovery and helping us to make amends with those we harmed. Help us to grow and mature, to be of help to other addicts in need, and to reflect by our own lives how your grace is restoring us to sanity, in Jesus' holy name. Amen

---

[12] 1 Peter 4:8

Spiritual Core Concepts: Give Me Your Blessing or Let Me Die

The same night he arose and took his two wives, his two female servants, and his eleven children, and crossed the ford of the Jabbok. He took them and sent them across the stream, and everything else that he had. And Jacob was left alone. And a man wrestled with him until the breaking of the day. When the man saw that he did not prevail against Jacob, he touched his hip socket, and Jacob's hip was put out of joint as he wrestled with him. Then he said, "Let me go, for the day has broken." But Jacob said, "I will not let you go unless you bless me." And he said to him, "What is your name?" And he said, "Jacob." Then he said, "Your name shall no longer be called Jacob, but Israel, for you have striven with God and with men, and have prevailed." Then Jacob asked him, "Please tell me your name." But he said, "Why is it that you ask my name?" And there he blessed him. So Jacob called the name of the place Peniel, saying, "For I have seen God face to face, and yet my life has been delivered." The sun rose upon him as he passed Penuel, limping because of his hip.

Genesis 32:22-31

A little background on this story is necessary. Jacob was born a twin along with his brother, Esau. They were not identical. As a matter of fact, it appears from the details of their birth that Esau was probably only eight months gestational age, and Jacob was a full nine months gestational age. The reason this is suspected is that Esau came out reddish and furry.[13] That happens to unborn infants at about the eight month of the pregnancy after which the hair falls off and their skin takes on a normal color tone. Jacob was most likely conceived first and then a month later Esau was conceived. At birth Esau would have been smaller than Jacob making it easier for him to have fit through the birth canal first. On the other hand, Jacob was a gestational month older, which made him larger and less likely to be the one opening the birth canal. Also, we need to know that there is commonly some time that passes between twin births, typically it is twenty minutes to more than an hour or even two hours. Esau was born first but Jacob immediately reached out and grabbed his heel. It is as if he knew he was the oldest. It was like he was saying by his actions that he was the oldest and believed he should have been first to come out of the womb.

As the twin's father, Isaac, approached the end of his days he prepared to bestow a blessing on his children to pass on his good will and

---

[13] Genesis 25:25

earthly goods to them. Esau as the first born would receive the vast majority of it, if not all of it. Isaac was also blind. Jacob's mother Rebekah knew that her husband was planning on giving his final blessing to Esau. So she conspired to have her other son, Jacob, deceive her husband so he could get the blessing meant for the first born. Her plan worked too and Jacob received the blessing meant for the firstborn. When Esau learned what happened he became homicidal and sought to kill Jacob and the younger brother had to flee for his life. He lived in exile until many years later when he returned home.

During those years of exile Jacob was subject to a schemer named Laban, who became his father-in-law. Jacob got an unrelenting dose of himself as a schemer for many years from this man. Yet, because of the blessing that he was given from his father the Lord looked out for him and he prospered in all that he did. He became an exceedingly wealthy man while he lived in exile. He longed to return to his home and finally did, but it was not without great risk. Not only could he and his large family have faced death from Esau, there was another deadly problem that Jacob needed to face as well. This is where this Bible text picks up.

In the dark of the night God showed up at the side of the river where Jacob was standing alone. The two wrestled through the entire length of the night and neither of them seemed to be able to conquer the other. The night was now passing and the day would be breaking with the dawn. This presented a profoundly serious problem. If anyone sees God's face, then he sees them and if he sees them he sees their sin. Then he will have to do something about their sin, he will have to make them account for their sin and that means they must die because of them.[14] The darkness that hid God's face from Jacob and protected him from death was giving way to daylight.

God asked Jacob to let him go to spare his life for him but Jacob refused to let go even if it meant losing his very life. He was willing to die unless he received this one special blessing from God. Think about it, he already had received his father's blessing. He had a lot to live for, he was incredibly wealthy. Yet Jacob was bound and determined to get this one blessing or die trying.

Remember that in Jacob's scheming he became guilty of identity theft? His name Jacob is not a complementary one. Literally it means a *heel*, as in someone who walks on you, which is very offensive. It also means a *deceiver*. He certainly has lived up to his name by living down to some very lowly behavior. He was a scoundrel and a despised man. He was hated by his brother, and he hated that he had acted unethically and what he had become because of it.

---

[14] Exodus 33:20, Romans 6:23

Jacob was unwilling to continue on in life as he had been, a man of despicable character. He wanted the kind of transforming change that only God could bring about. He wanted it so bad that he would get it or die in the trying rather than continue on as he was.

At this point God asked him his name, which seemed a little strange. After all, God knows all things, why did he ask him this question? The answer was simple. God was asking for a confession of his sins. Jacob gave him his name and in so doing he admitted that he was truly a heel, a deceiver, a scoundrel, and a sinner. With that confession God gave him the blessing he asked for. Jacob's life was transformed and he was redeemed from his sinfulness. As a sign of this a new name was given to him, *Israel*, meaning someone who walks with God. No longer would he be someone who was a heel and treated others with disrespect.

In our addiction we became rogues. We were unethical and immoral in our behavior. Our behavior was reprehensible and we did things that we now deeply regret. In our recovery we turned to God and turned our lives over to his care so that we could be transformed just as Jacob was.

Heavenly Father, because of our addictions we became heels. We used others and treated them badly. We put ourselves first and lived to use drugs. We have looked to you for freedom from our addictions, and you were faithful to deliver us. Now we look to you daily for the transformation we need, to take away our character defects and replace them with godly qualities just as you did for Jacob. Mercifully sanctify us and reform us into the image of your son, Christ Jesus our Lord in whose name we pray. Amen

Sexual Abuse

**Now Dinah the daughter of Leah,
whom she had borne to Jacob,
went out to see the women of the land.
And when Shechem the son of Hamor the Hivite,
the prince of the land, saw her,
he seized her and lay with her and humiliated her.
Genesis 34:1-2**

    Sexual abuse is an ancient sin and crime, and tragically it continues on to this day. The legal system has not done enough to protect us from it, especially with repeat offenders. As a society we have not done enough to prevent it. Among all of us as addicts it seems that the rate of sexual abuse runs especially high. Some reports put the rate of sexual abuse victims among alcoholics as high as 70 to 90 percent for women. For men it is put at 50-70 percent, and it is believed that the actual rate is higher because of underreporting. Regardless of what the actual frequency may be, the truth is that this tragedy occurs with great frequency among our numbers.

    Whether the rape alone was the sole contributing factor to the development of addiction in a person's life or not, it is always a highly significant factor. Just as the use of drugs altars our souls and creates the life of an addict in us, so also our sexual experiences have a creative effect on us. Sex is a gift to us from God and it is given for two basic purposes in the context of marriage. First it is creative, for making children. Secondly, it is recreational. It is meant to refresh and fulfill the husband and wife in their physical love for each other. Sex re-creates us, as the Scriptures have said, "Therefore a man shall leave his father and his mother and hold fast to his wife, and they shall become one flesh."[15] In the case of a rape, because of the fundamental creative nature of sex, it also changes the person being abused and re-creates them. This is especially true if this is the first time they have had sex, voluntarily or involuntarily. This experience is formative and re-creative. Its impact goes deeply down to the most foundational level of our souls and our self-identity. Do not forget that in the sexual experience we have the potential to be pro-creating because God has empowered us in this way. Because the pro-creative power of God is being abused, its impact is severe. It has the potential to create in its victim the false belief that they are not worthy of respect and can simply be abused sexually by almost anyone or abuse anyone as they were.

---

[15] Genesis 2:24

The mere pages of this book are not near enough to help any sexual abuse survivor heal. Therefore, in this area it is highly recommended that anyone who has been sexually abused seek professional counseling from a competent licensed Christian therapist who has experience in this area.

Dearest God, help us to find healing in our most difficult and deepest wounds. Bring healing to those among us who have been treated so badly through rape and sexual trauma. Help to make our world a safer place for all to live. Aid and guide us in our recoveries so that we may live to make your will happen in our lives. In Jesus' name. Amen

The Serenity Prayer

God, give us grace to accept with serenity
the things that cannot be changed,
Courage to change the things
which should be changed,
and the Wisdom to distinguish
the one from the other.
Living one day at a time,
Enjoying one moment at a time,
Accepting hardship as a pathway to peace,
Taking, as Jesus did,
This sinful world as it is,
Not as I would have it,
Trusting that You will make all things right,
If I surrender to Your will,
So that I may be reasonably happy in this life,
And supremely happy with You forever in the next.
Amen

Reinhold Niebuhr
1892-1971

Jesus Said, "You Must Be Born of the Spirit"

**Jesus answered,
"Truly, truly, I say to you,
unless one is born of water and the Spirit,
he cannot enter the kingdom of God.
That which is born of the flesh is flesh,
and that which is born of the spirit is spirit.
Do not marvel that I said to you,
'You must be born again.'
The wind blows where it wishes,
and you hear its sound,
but you do not know where it
comes from or where it goes.
So it is with everyone
who is born of the Spirit."
John 3:5-8**

Back in the seventies being born-again, or born-of-the-Spirit, became very vogue. It was a time of great renewal in the faith by many. Some Christians wondered if they were born-again, others were told they weren't. The truth be told we all must be born-again, or born-of-the-Spirit. As John wrote down in Greek what Jesus said about it, he used the emphatic tense, meaning you *must absolutely* be born-again. This is true we must be. We know that some Christian traditions really emphasize that they are born-again Christians more than others.

We need to understand a few things on the matter of being born-of-the-Spirit as Christians and it needs to be put into perspective. Know this, most of the books and letters of the New Testament do not mention this topic at all. Out of the four Gospel accounts written about Jesus' life, Matthew, Mark, and Luke, three out of the four make no mention of it whatsoever. Paul mentions it, as does Peter, James, and John. But to keep it in perspective Jesus said we MUST be born-of-the-Spirit, it is that important. Just as those three Gospel authors made no mention of it many Christians don't know that they are born-again even though they are. Regardless, anyone who is a Christian, who believes in our Lord for their salvation, is of necessity a born-of-the-Spirit Christian, if they know it or not.

Being born-of-the-Spirit happens at the time of our conversions. The famous late evangelist Billy Graham could recall a specific time, date, and place when he was born-of-the-Spirit. It was when he first believed in the testimony of Jesus Christ and received the Lord as his personal Savior in prayer. This was his conversion. His wife, Ruth Graham, grew up in a

Christian home in China where her parents were missionaries. She remembers from her earliest years always believing in Jesus as her personal Savior and Lord. She cannot recall a specific time, date, or place in her life when she had a conversion experience, but her faith was as genuine as could be nonetheless. Of course, they are both born-of-the-Spirit. Their routes of salvation may have varied on the outside but they were both born-again, born-of-the-Spirit Christians.

We need to know that it is perfectly fine to simply *realize* that we are a person who has received Jesus' testimony and now believe in him. This is what makes us a Christian, and yes it makes us born-again, born-of-the-Spirit Christians. We also believe that we have times in our lives when we go through periods of spiritual renewal in our faith. In these events we are not being born-of-the-Spirit a second or third time. Instead these awesome experiences remind us that we go from faith to faith as we mature over the length of our lifetimes.

Being born-of-the-Spirit is a critical message in this book. As has been said, when the first man was created, God personally formed him out of the dust of the earth, shaping and designing him to be made in God's image and likeness. Then God breathed into his nostrils the breath-of-life and Adam became a living-soul. In addiction we, the sons and daughters of Adam and Eve, inhaled the smoke of marijuana, meth or some other drug and we all became living-addicts. It is as if the drugs we abused gave us the equivalent of a second-birth and we were no longer the same. In our recreated lives as addicts we acted out in the image and likeness of the toxic drugs that we had taken into our lungs.

In order to recover from that life of addiction another birth was necessary to replace the poisonous lives that the smoke of the drugs created in us. We all need to be, must be born-of-the-Spirit of God, which is what makes recovery possible.

Heavenly Father, your son died to give us second birth. By his blood shed on the cross you have cleansed us of our sins and freed us from addiction. By your Spirit living in us strengthen us in our faith and in our recoveries as well. This we ask in the name of our risen Lord Jesus Christ. Amen

Spiritual Practices: Breathing and Relaxation

Their Redeemer is strong; the LORD of hosts is his name.
He will surely plead their cause, that he may give rest to the earth.
Jeremiah 50:34

Many of us in addiction and recovery have suffered great abuse. As a result, we frequently have our guards up, sometimes they are constantly up. We can be hypervigilant, tense, and ready to react to the mere appearance of an attack of any kind on us. It is a conditioned posture that we have learned to be in so that we don't suffer any further. The problem with this is that we live with nearly constant tension in our muscles. Also, our minds are anxious and watchful too. This makes us very weary and causes chronically tired muscles. Because of this our minds don't get the rest they need, and we are at times driven to near exhaustion by it. Our muscle tension from bracing in hypervigilance leaves us tired too.

For us as Christians there is a Sabbath rest that we can enter into that will counter the effects of this kind of tension. We need to know that the word *Sabbath* is best defined in this way: it literally means that we take in a deep breath, then exhale and sigh, as we shrug our shoulders and relax. To use our breath to relax is very spiritual because it is the breath of God that gave us life. Breathing in combination with both tensing and then relaxing our muscles is a highly effective way to reduce the tension and stress we have in our bodies and minds.

In this exercise we can either recline or lay down. Begin by taking a deep breath in and hold it for a moment and focus on what it is like to hold your breath in. No doubt it is a little uncomfortable. Release your breath and with it let go of some of the muscle tension you are holding that makes you uncomfortable. Continue to breathe and as you do work to slow your breathing, taking long slow breaths in your nose and exhaling through your mouth. After several cycles of this breathing pattern, tense and flex your neck muscles as hard as you can. If you are reclining in a chair or laying down push your head down hard against the furniture that you are resting on. Hold this for a moment and then relax those tense muscles as you exhale. Continue taking long, slow breaths in and out. Focus on relaxing your neck muscles. As you exhale focus hard on relaxing deeply.

After a few cycles of more slow and rhythmic breathing tense up your shoulders as hard as you can, just as you did with your neck. Hold this for a moment and then relax those tense muscles. Continue taking long, slow breaths in and out. Focus on relaxing your neck muscles. As you exhale focus hard on relaxing deeply.

Continue to follow this pattern as you perform it again with your forehead, arms and hands, abdomen, buttock, legs and feet. Repeat the exercise with any part of your body that seemed resistant to relaxing the first time through.

As an aid to doing this exercise consider what other supportive measures to relaxing that you can do. Suggestions for this include soft music, incense, turning the lights down low and meditating on a Scripture verse related to relaxing or resting in the Lord.

When you are done take time to simply remain in this relaxed state of rest. Enjoy the time and reassure yourself that you can trust in the Lord to care for you in all situations. Tell yourself that you can relax throughout all of your day and that you don't need to wear your stress on your body or be hypervigilant in your mind.

Dear loving Heavenly Father, you rested on the seventh day from all of your work, and blessed and made that day holy. You have invited us to share in observing your sabbath rest. We give you thanks that you care so much for us in this way. Bless us now and bring us into your rest, that we may cease our striving and live our lives in confidence of your care and protection. Through you son's name, Christ our Lord we pray. Amen

Step 1. We Admitted We Were Powerless Over Our Addiction

For when I am weak, then I am strong.
2 Corinthians 12:10

There is a certain spiritual mystery that exists for us in recovery. This is what it is, when we openly admit to our addiction, in front of others, it helps us recover. If we simply admit it to ourselves, in our thoughts, it is of really no redeeming value in aiding our recovery. If we go so far as to admit that we are addicts to ourselves out loud, it is also of little redeeming value. Part of the problem is that our addiction loves to keep itself a secret. It lies to us and gets us to deny to ourselves that we are addicted. When we know that we are addicted but don't really like to think about it, the addiction can continue to keep us under its control. Addiction works best when it can keep our dirty little secret from ourselves and others. That gives it great power over us. When we admit to ourselves and others that we are addicted, its tight grip on us begins to loosen.

But there is more to this spiritual mystery of being weak to become strong. When we go to a meeting and say to the group, "Hi, my name is _____, and I am an addict," it strengthens us in our recovery. The benefits of admitting to our weaknesses continues. At the meeting when it is our turn to share we can open up about just about anything. We can admit to all kinds of our failings and fallings. We can share with great confidence because what is shared will be received by caring and compassionate souls that we trust and who have our best interests at heart. At the meeting we find out that they have struggled too. The result of this openness is that we find we are not alone, we are heard in a nonjudgmental way, we are accepted, and we find hope and strength.

One word of caution is needed here. Just because we experience the great benefit of being strengthened in our recovery is no reason to get overconfident about it. We must not come to the false conclusion that we can now control our use and return to using on a limited basis.

Heavenly Father, help us in our weaknesses to rely solely on you for the strength we need to be in recovery. Aid us in our failings, lift us up when we stumble and lead us today so that we may live out your perfect will in our lives. This we ask through Christ our Lord. Amen

**Step 2. We came to believe that a Power
greater than ourselves could restore us to sanity.**

**For it is God who works in you,
both to will and to work for his good pleasure.
Philippians 2:13**

In our addiction we certainly could not return to sanity on our own. We were hooked on drugs. We could not shake their grip on our lives. Neither could we begin to work on fixing the problems they caused, let alone our problems that lead us to using them in the first place. It was vicious what they had done to us. We were boxed in from all sides and without a hope in ourselves. We imagined what our lives might have been like if we could turned back time. That way we could have avoided the problems we were now having. That was as close as we could get ourselves to quitting, but it was of course only imagined and not the real help that we needed.

Early in recovery we had gotten to that point where we knew and admitted that we were powerless over our drug usage. We had now arrived at this new place, believing that God was our only hope. We had tried what we could to quit, it was all to no avail. Our attempts to quit were worthless and waisted our time as our personal problems went from bad to worse, and then on to severe or even direr. We knew desperation, and now we were willing to humble ourselves and turn to God for the help that we needed and only he could offer.

Simply put, faith in God is putting our trust in God. This wasn't easy to do. It meant turning to him and trusting that he could do what we could not. We knew the impossibility of quitting, it couldn't be done up until now. No one else had been able to help us either. Why would the invisible God be any different we wondered? We were made in his image and likeness, so were the others who tried to help us quit. If we couldn't do it, how was he any different we wondered? Nevertheless, we were at the end of our ropes and had run out of other options. We put our trust in him and moved forward from there.

God, we put our trust in you and we renew our trust in you. You are who you say you are and we are grateful to you for all the help you have been. Strengthen us in faith and empower us for the journey so that we may continue on in faithfulness through Christ Jesus our Lord. Amen

Step 3. We made a decision to turn our will and our lives over to the care of God as we understood Him.

But as for me and my house, we will serve the Lord.
Joshua 24:15

There comes a time in our lives when we need to do something different because what we had been doing did not work out the way we hoped. We tried to quit, it didn't work. We tried harder to quit, our addiction got worse. It had a strangle hold on us that only got tighter the harder we tried. Though it may not have seemed logical, we needed to quit trying to quit. Now if that was all we did our addiction would progress as diseases do and it would have continued to overtake us. What broke the cycle was that we quit trying to quit, and we turned to God for his aid. We turned our lives over to the care of God. We simply let him take over the control of our lives, and why not? We had no control over our own lives any more anyway, drugs were in control.

Now, turning over our wills and lives to God's care is what we did, but there was a little more to it than just that. God is all powerful, and we don't exactly act on him because we are weak and he is the Almighty. Rather, God works on us and we are the passive recipients of his will. His will is of course to be the Master of our lives and he wants to be intimately involved with us. In turning to God for help, we surrendered to him and we stay surrendered to him for the entire length of our lives. If we tried to add to what God was doing to bring us into recovery, or believe for some reason that we could now go it alone we were almost guaranteed that we would relapse. The way to avoid that relapse is to always return to this step and do it again, surrendering to his will for our lives and trusting in him for his care over our lives.

Heavenly Father, forgive us our sins and lead us in the way that is everlasting. We yield to you in surrender, trusting in you and yielding to your will for our lives. Keep us this day and everyday living clean and free of drugs and sustain our recoveries as you always have. Through Christ our Lord. Amen

**Step 4. We Made a Searching and
Fearless Moral Inventory of Ourselves**

**Search me, O God, and know my heart!
Try me and know my thoughts!
And see if there be any grievous way in me,
and lead me in the way everlasting!
Psalm 139:23-24**

Step four is a very bold step forward in our lives of recovery. It requires that we take a serious and honest look at ourselves and what we have done as well as what our values have been. It can be a nerve-racking thing to look into our own eyes in the mirror for fear of what we might see. In our addictions we became experts at denying the truth to ourselves; in recovery we worked to become experts at self-examination.

This step can be so difficult that there is a need to approach it slowly and return to it several times before we get to the deepest parts of our lives. Maybe the first time we came to it we only began to think about what it meant for us. Then, the second time we came to it we coughed up a few of our more mild offenses in life. It was stressful, but it also held the promise of relief for us and we considered the direction it would take us, which was to step five. There we would be making amends with those we had mistreated. Hard as it might be to humble ourselves and confess our sins to them and ask for their forgiveness, in the end it is very healing for them and for us.

Then each time after that, we dug a little deeper. We found that it would not kill us to do this, and that we could find some relief for the guilt of our past. We found that we were helping those we had hurt in the past and saw them heal from our confession to them. Soon enough we got the hang of it and we were able to see spontaneously when we needed to amend our ways and ask for their forgiveness right away.

Heavenly Father, you showed the ultimate sacrifice when you sent your son to die for our sins. Help us to live in his example and grant us humility so that we can truly examine our past and make amends for all the offenses we have brought to others by our addictions. In Jesus name we pray. Amen

Step 5. We admitted to God, to ourselves, and to another human being the exact nature of our wrongs.

**And no creature is hidden from his sight, but all are naked and exposed to the eyes of him to whom we must give account.
Hebrews 4:13**

The confession of our sins to God is both a very intimidating thing as well as an act that will bring us great relief. Going before our Maker and admitting to our sins with particular emphasis on those sins related to our drug use will help us. We have this promise before we begin, that our heavenly Father will forgive us our sins for the sake of his son who died on the cross for our forgiveness. We can in humility have a certain confidence, not that we can justify our sins, but that the blood of Christ shed on the cross for us will cleanse us from all our sins. The relief this will bring is vital for us in breaking the cycle of shame and continued drug use. Rather than falling back into that unhealthy practice, we are able to deal with our guilt in a healthy way. We came to believe that God could and would restore sanity to our lives. Step five is a giant step that takes us in that direction. That is because this has been God's plan for us ever since the day of fall of Adam and Eve when he sacrificed a lamb for the forgiveness of their sins. By trusting in Jesus, the Lamb of God, and his death for our sins, we are living out the will of God in our lives.

The second part of step five is for us to take our confession to another person and share it with them. There are many persons who we can choose from for this. This includes a sponsor, a pastor, or someone in our local 12-step group who is gifted in this area. Some people have also gone to a nun in their area who is practiced in hearing confessions and offering spiritual care. This step is valuable because when we do it we are taking ownership for our actions. This along with the other steps is part of a healing process that will lift the heavy weight of our addiction from our shoulders and cover us with God's grace instead.

Loving Father, care for us as we move from shame and addiction, to forgiveness and recovery. We long for your presence in our lives and love you deeply. In Jesus' name. Amen

**Step 6. We were entirely ready to have
God remove all these defects of character.**

**Now the Lord is the Spirit,
and where the Spirit of the Lord is,
there is freedom. And we all,
with unveiled face, beholding the glory of the Lord,
are being transformed into the same
image from one degree of glory to another.
For this comes from the Lord who is the Spirit.
2 Corinthians 3:17-18**

We have heard that we cannot change others, we can only change ourselves. The first part of this certainly seems true but we need to be challenged about the validity of the second half of that statement. There are somethings about ourselves that we cannot change, being addicts is one of these. Once an addict, always an addict, this is true of us for life. There are more things that we cannot change as well. For these problems, these defects in our character, we need God's help, we need him to make the changes in us.

Our forebearers Adam and Eve were created in a state of innocence and in God's image and likeness. They fell in sin and we ourselves were born in original sin. We are what we are and because we are the problem as sinners, we cannot be part of the solution, we cannot contribute to our own salvation from sin or in the changing of our own character defects. In recovery we have to step back and confess our problems and in humility give ourselves over to the will of God. In this state of surrender we can see ourselves transformed by the hand of God. This miracle of change is not our own, and we can take no credit for it. It comes from the Lord, therefore it is spiritual, it is God acting on us for Christ's sake.

Heavenly Father, you sent your only begotten son to teach us and make us his disciples. He gave his life for our redemption from sin and addiction, and in him we die to ourselves, to sin and to addiction. Because he was raised from the dead we share in his resurrected life. We pray that by the power of your Holy Spirit you will transform our lives, allow us to die to ourselves daily and rise to newness of life in him. In Jesus name we pray. Amen

Step 7. We humbly asked Him to remove our shortcomings.

**If we confess our sins, he is faithful and just to forgive us
our sins and to cleanse us from all unrighteousness.
1 John 1:9**

It is not just our addiction that we had no control over. Along with that we also had no control over our shortcomings. That is not to say that we could not manage some of our behaviors and exercise some level of self-restraint. We could manage some of our behavior, but there were some that were part of the addiction and we had no control over them. The list included lying, cheating, manipulation, denial, selfishness, being close-minded and unwillingness. Our addictions tainted virtually every area of our lives, that is their nature. Our lives were centered around our selfishness, around getting high, getting more drugs, and getting high again. All of our behaviors were subjected to that brutal cycle. We may have quit using, but our shortcoming behavior continued on until we were changed by God.

We know how hopeless we had been to quit using and to quit our drug related behaviors. We needed to get to a place where we despised how we conducted ourselves in those ways. We needed to also cry out to God for help because we could not simply make them go away. Early on our minds were closed and our eyes were blinded to them. As we progressed in our recoveries, our eyes started to open and our minds started to recognize what we had been like. That was a frightening experience. We were naturally inclined to be in denial about it, to lie to ourselves and not believe that it was true about us. We needed God's help, not in part, but in whole.

God works on us through his Word and so we need to read our Bibles and be a part of a Bible Study group. God works on us through 12-step meetings, so we must go to them. Counseling may be in order as well as treatment.

Dearest God in heaven, holy is your name. Work on the bedrock of our souls and redeem us from our shortcomings. May the conduct of our lives reflect the glory of the salvation your son won for us on the cross of Calvary, for we pray in Jesus' name. Amen

8. We made a list of all persons we had harmed, and became willing to make amends to them all.

So if you are offering your gift at the altar and there remember that your brother has something against you, leave your gift there before the altar and go. First be reconciled to your brother, and then come and offer your gift.
Matthew 5:23-24

While the idea of doing this can be somewhat frightening, as it applies to our recovery it is also essential and incredibly valuable. Trying to skip it or putting it off can also delay our recovery's progress and weaken our sustainability too. We need to become accountable for our actions, specifically for the harm we caused others because of our addictions. In doing this step we are learning the very lessons that we have skipped in the past, but still need very badly to learn. The very act of going through step eight and then nine, provides us with the very experiences we need to learn so that we don't continue to offend and harm others by our addictive character traits. Experience in this will show us that we do need to be very thorough in making our list of those we harmed and what we did that was harmful.

The spirituality of this goes all the way back to the Garden of Eden after the fall. Adam and Eve were instructed by God to make a confession of their sins. That is what we are doing. To not do this is to follow in the way of Cain who refused to admit to his sins and make the sacrifice.

It is in this step, and we do just one step at a time least we be overwhelmed, all we need to do is make a list and become willing to make amends. No need to go beyond that. By doing this we are opening our own eyes to the extent of our addiction and looking at how far it has taken control of our lives by the harm we brought to others.

Great God in heaven, by your grace we have been forgiven by you. Help us to progress in recovery by completing this one task. Bring our hearts to full repentance over the sins from our former way of living. Lead us in your paths for the sake of Jesus Christ your son our Lord. Amen

Step 9. We made direct amends to such people wherever possible, except when to do so would injure them or others.

I will arise and go to my father, and I will say to him, "Father, I have sinned against heaven and before you. I am no longer worthy to be called your son. Treat me as one of your hired servants."
Luke 15:18-19

In getting clean from drug use we need to come clean over our sins to both God and others. When we can, we should do this in person. When distance is a problem a phone call will work equally well. It has even been done over social media platforms. The others we did harm to will heal much better if we apologize and ask for their forgiveness. We can if we want to, but it is not required, to tell them that we are now in recovery from drug addiction. There is one caution though. Bringing up the harm we did from the past could reopen old wounds, that we need to safeguard against. When it is something we are uncertain about, if it would cause further injury to them or others, then it should be discussed with someone like our sponsor or our confessor from step 5.

We need to be prepared for whatever reactions might come our way. Some may not admit to remembering the harm we are bringing up. They may remember it entirely different then us. Remember, we were on drugs and they probably weren't. It might be best to give them the benefit of a doubt when memories differ. Some may not appreciate our effort and will take offense at us. Others were truly hurt by our actions and will still be in pain over it. We need to show them our sincerity and that we are making a heartfelt effort to right the wrongs that we had brought. In the case where money was taken or their property was damaged we need to do what we can to restore to them the full value of their losses. By God's grace all will go well and we will be able to make full amends for all that we did when we brought harm to them.

Heavenly Father, we are truly and humbly repentant of our former sins against others and wish to bring them healing. Empower us, we pray, to this end. Through Christ our Lord. Amen

Step 10. We continued to take personal inventory and when we were wrong promptly admitted it.

**Search me, O God, and know my heart!
Try me and know my thoughts!
And see if there be any grievous way in me,
and lead me in the way everlasting!
Psalm 139:23-24**

With step ten we are into the first of the maintenance steps of the recovery program. This is where we add to our new recovery oriented lifestyles what is intended to be a continuous and lifelong revolving cycle of practices. As our lives roll on, we have old memories that surface, we need to work on them as we did in steps four, five, eight and nine. We want to be thorough, and we want to go deep. In recovery we don't want to leave unfinished business behind because it will become a stumbling block for us and of that there can be no doubt. We desire to bring healing to those we have harmed, we want to live shame and guilt free.

Along with all this hopefully we came to find out that it is okay to not be, try to appear to be or believe that we are uncapable of making mistakes in life. We are not perfect, but we are making progress in our lives. When we were wrong we used to gloss over it in one way or another. Now we can admit to it right away and not let it fester in us. By admitting to it right away, it does not become an issue between us and the others in our lives. We can find immediate relief by simply saying something like, "I goofed, I was wrong, I made a mistake, forgive me." Our friends will be relieved, we will be relieved, and all will be the better because of it.

Heavenly Father, by your grace we have come this far and by your grace we will continue, day-by-day, and step-by-step, to live as your people. Empower us to live for you and inspire us in the difficult things so that by your strength we can fulfill your will in our lives. This we ask through the one who died and rose again, Jesus Christ our Lord and Savior. Amen

Step 11. We sought through prayer and meditation to improve our conscious contact with God as we understood Him, praying only for knowledge of His will for us and the power to carry that out.

**Jesus said to him, "I am the way, and the truth, and the life.
No one comes to the Father except through me.
If you had known me, you would have known my Father also.
From now on you do know him and have seen him."
John 14:6-7**

Because of Jesus we are able to have a relationship with God. The Lord, the son of God, is our mediator to the Father. By his blood we are forgiven and made to be participators in the covenant that the Father established when Jesus died on the cross for our sins. This is also why we pray in his name when we call on him. Additionally, though Jesus is seated at the right hand of the Father, the Holy Spirit was sent to us in his name and lives in us always. God has extended to us a relationship with him, and because of this we are connected to God. This way we can look to God and seek to know his will for our lives. Because the Holy Spirit lives in us on a permanent basis, thanks to Jesus, we can be empowered to carry out God's will for our lives.

We need to also be reading God's Word on a daily basis. His Word speaks to us and helps us to know his will for our lives. When God speaks to our hearts it will always be consistent with his Holy Word in the Bible. God also confirms his will to us by the witness of the Holy Spirit speaking to our hearts. Sometimes his will comes to us from multiple sources. We might hear from a Christian friend, a pastor, or a friend in our 12-step group confirmation about what we believe we are hearing from God and about what we need to be doing to fulfill his will in our lives. As we carry out this step on a continual basis we need to remind ourselves that it is a maintenance step that builds on step three and us turning our will and lives over to God.

Dearest God, we are your servants and we seek to know and do your will with our lives. Help us to continue in the work you began in the days of creation and to know our place in this world. This we ask through Christ Jesus, who is Lord and Savior to us all. Amen

Step 12. Having had a spiritual awakening as a result of these steps, we tried to carry this message to addicts, and to practice these principles in all our affairs.

**Come and hear, all you who fear God,
and I will tell what he has done for my soul.
Psalm 66:16**

Step twelve has three points to it and the first part is about how our recovery is a spiritual awakening. For some it is, or leads us to, a conversion and becoming a Christian. For those among us who were already Christians but fallen away, it is a special time of spiritual renewal, growth and coming into what our inheritance as children of God includes.

Our newfound freedom in Christ is wonderful and we have a reason for sharing what God has done for us. As our recovery continues we will have opportunities to share what our experiences have been. For those we know who are still using we can say just a word to plant the first seed. Or, have a heart to heart with them and share the message of recovery.

Finally, we work the program by working all 12-steps in a continuous cycle. *Easy does it*, we don't want to feel overwhelmed by it, that is why we take it one step at a time, one day at a time. As we do these things they begin to take on a natural feel to them, then in time it becomes part of our routine thinking and living. In a while we don't even give it a second thought until we look back and see that we automatically and naturally worked the steps.

Gracious heavenly Father, you have delivered us out of the kingdom darkness and into the glorious Kingdom of light in your son. Abide closely with us in our journey as we make progress in our lifelong journey of living clean and free of drug use. Through your son's name we ask, Jesus Christ our Lord and Savior. Amen

Addicted to Excess

**And whatever my eyes desired I did not keep from them.
I kept my heart from no pleasure,
for my heart found pleasure in all my toil,
and this was my reward for all my toil.
Then I considered all that my hands had done
and the toil I had expended in doing it,
and behold, all was vanity and a striving after wind,
and there was nothing to be gained under the sun.
Ecclesiastes 2:10-11**

    King Solomon was an extraordinarily rich man, perhaps one of the richest in all of history. His wisdom continues to be renown, and to this day it is believed that he was the wisest man that ever lived. He shares in this passage from his personal experience about what he came to believe in his mind and heart. His great wealth, power and influence afforded him every imaginable luxury. He took full advantage of his lifestyle and gave himself every pleasure available to a man in his day. This included the satisfaction earned from hard work and completing many exhausting accomplishments like his extensive building projects and civic improvements. The trouble with all the excesses of life that he enjoyed, in his own words, was that that it was all for vanity.

    Vanity is not a word that continues to be in common use today. It comes from the Hebrew word, *hebel*. This is a picture word, if you can image it visually, it means having something in your hands and then in an instant, poof it is gone like dust in the wind. Note too that in his final comment here he seems to be expressing a bit of pessimism.

    The only answer for us, to prevent such letdowns, is to put our hope for personal fulfillment in the Lord daily. We must follow after Christ, daily living in his will, and living out our God given potential, this is how we will experience the abundant life that Jesus has promised us.

    God, by your graciousness to us we have been restored to sanity and our lives are clean and free of drugs again. By your bounty our lives are being restored to us fully and abundantly. Aid and guide us in our journeys so that we may abide in you and walk in your ways to the glory of your name. This we ask through Jesus Christ our Lord and Savior. Amen

Spiritual Practices: Incense

O Lord, I call upon you; hasten to me!
Give ear to my voice when I call to you!
Let my prayer be counted as incense before you,
and the lifting up of my hands as the evening sacrifice!
Psalm 141:1-2

As part of our daily devotion to the Lord consider burning some incense during this time that has been set aside for prayer, meditation, Bible reading and worship. Scripturally, there is a strong basis for doing this. The priests in the temple burned incense to the Lord on a daily basis. The Bible refers to incense as being symbolic of our prayers and praises rising up to God. As they are joined with the incense they become a pleasant aroma rising up to God's nostrils.

Consider using frankincense, it has a very sweet and encompassing aroma. It has a stimulating effect on our nasal septum and brings our senses into sharper focus. In general, the effects of incense has its most powerful effects on us right away and then it slowly diminishes. Once it has been started take a slow and deep breath in your nose, hold it for a few seconds, and then slowly exhale out your mouth. Incense can have an emotionally calming and physically relaxing effect on us while at the same time stimulating our senses, bringing a new height to our mental and spiritual concentration. You can cup your hand and draw its smoke into your nostrils to increase its aromatic effects on you.

When we were using the smell of the drug's smoke filled the room and our eyes were sometimes mesmerized by it. That is part of a toxic spirituality that deceived and lead us astray. Now, in recovery we can truly find our spiritual experiences enhanced by the righteous use of incense and its smoke.

Heavenly Father, we offer heart felt prayers and worship as we come before you today. We worship and adore you, we glorify you, we love and adore you. Hear our prayers this day that we offer for the needs of our lives and addicts everywhere. Though Christ our Lord we ask this. Amen

Spiritual Practices: Lifting Up Hands in Holy Worship

O Lord, I call upon you; hasten to me!
Give ear to my voice when I call to you!
Let my prayer be counted as incense before you,
and the lifting up of my hands as the evening sacrifice!
Psalm 141:1-2

Worshipping God is important, in fact it is vital. This not only includes Sunday worship in church, but it should include day to day worship as well. Worshipping him invites his presence into our lives and keeps us closer to him throughout the day. Showing our devotion to God daily aligns our lives, thoughts, feelings, and everything we are so that we are centered in him.

Things that we can do in worship includes offering thanks to him. We thank God for the things he has done for us. To that should be added worshipful praise, and we praise him because he is worthy of our praise. We should also read from the scriptures as part of our daily devotion to our Maker. This can be a time for us to be reminded that we are addicts and without him in our lives we would relapse. We can reaffirm that we have turned our wills and our lives over to him. It is also helpful for us to look to God for his aid in removing our character defects, and to be reminded that we cannot escape them without him transforming our lives. In this time of devotion we should be seeking to know and have his will affirmed to us so that we can live it out daily.

While it may not be part of our faith tradition for many of us, lifting up our hands as an act of surrender to him is very appropriate. It is a physical act that demonstrates us turning our lives and will over to him. As a practical exercise in worship it aids us as addicts to live out this especially important part of our recovery. Surrendering in this way empowers us to live out his will and not our own.

Heavenly Father, we surrender our lives to you, to do your will. We die to self daily as we pick up our crosses to follow our Savior, Christ the Lord. Strengthen us in our recovery, help us to grow daily. Let us know your will and empower us to live it out fully in our lives. This we pray in Jesus' name, for he lives and reigns with you and the Holy Spirit, both now and forever. Amen

Covenant Relationships: The Nazarite

**And the L<small>ORD</small> spoke to Moses, saying,
"Speak to the people of Israel and say to them,
when either a man or a woman makes a special vow,
the vow of a Nazirite, to separate himself to the L<small>ORD</small>,
he shall separate himself from wine and strong drink.
He shall drink no vinegar made from
wine or strong drink and shall not drink any
juice of grapes or eat grapes, fresh or dried.
All the days of his separation he shall eat
nothing that is produced by the grapevine,
not even the seeds or the skins.
Numbers 6:1-4**

Prophets had their callings that separated them apart so they could serve God. The Levites were dedicated to supporting the Temple. The descendants of Aaron were the priests who ministered in the temple, but anyone could become a Nazarite. Anyone, including women, who wanted to dedicate their life to the service of God could undertake this vow and devote their life to the Lord. In many ways the Nazarites were revered and viewed as more holy than the priests.

The purpose of becoming a Nazarite, which means *consecrated one*, was to be devoted to God and to serve him. The vow could be for a time limited period or for the entire length of a person's life if they so choose. Among the many people who undertook this vow are included: Samson, Samuel the prophet, as well as his mother Hannah, and John the Baptist. In recovery we devote ourselves, as did the Nazarites, to a more formal and structured spirituality before God, knowing that our continued success is dependent upon our daily devotion to him.

There aren't any modern-day Nazarites. However, as Christians in recovery we have similarities in our lifestyles. Just as we need to abstain from all drugs, including alcohol, so also the Nazarite was forbidden to drink anything fermented in any way. They were not even allowed to have grapes, grape juice or even raisins for fear that they might have unknowingly fermented.

Gracious God, you have called us to follow your son and live as his disciples. Sustain us in our recoveries, transform us from our former lifestyles and lead us this day in all that we do. May our lives bring glory to your name, this we pray through Christ our Lord. Amen

The Wisdom of Solomon

**The words of the Preacher,
the son of David, king in Jerusalem.
Vanity of vanities, says the Preacher,
vanity of vanities! All is vanity.
What does man gain by all the toil
at which he toils under the sun?
Ecclesiastes 1:1-3**

At the time when Solomon became king, he said a very solemn prayer. He asked God for wisdom to rule his people with. God granted him this request. In turn one of the things that he did was to set out and study life in its entirety. He is also credited with writing three books in the Bible.[16] In his book Ecclesiastes he writes about many of his observations and conclusions about life.

Ecclesiastes offers a very somber and sobering look at the world because so many, though not all, of his conclusions are pessimistic. Among his many recorded observations he wrote that, "Our eyes are not going to be satisfied with seeing, neither are our ears going to be satisfied with hearing.[17] He also said about the same thing about wealth. Though a fabulously rich man himself, he said that we are not going to be satisfied with earthly riches.[18] He went on to say that we labor hard for the food that we eat, but our appetite is never satisfied.[19] To all of this he regularity reminded his readers that life, "is vanity, and a striving after wind."[20]

Solomon worked extremely hard and provided great civic improvements in his nation. He became very rich and found pleasures in all that he did, but then he came to hate life.[21] He said our end in life is the same as our beginnings, we came naked into the world and we will leave the same way, meaning that we cannot take anything with us when we leave.[22] He said a person who lives a godly and righteous life may sadly die young, but a man who lives out an evil life sometimes lives a long time.[23] Sometimes the righteous person receives nothing but tragedy in his life, and a wicked person may prosper.[24] He said that even though you

---

[16] Proverbs, Song of Solomon, and Ecclesiastes
[17] Ecclesiastes 1:8
[18] Ecclesiastes 4:8, 5:10
[19] Ecclesiastes 6:7
[20] Ecclesiastes 1:14
[21] Ecclesiastes 2:1-11, 17
[22] Ecclesiastes 5:15
[23] Ecclesiastes 7:15
[24] Ecclesiastes 8:14

might be the fastest in a race you very well may not win. The strongest person in a fight doesn't necessarily have the winning edge. The smartest person has no guarantee of becoming rich. In all these situations, the odds of success can be unfavorable to those best qualified.[25]

Solomon believed that because of the great difficulties we face we need to enjoy life as best we can, relishing in the fruit of our labor, and eating our meals with cheerful and glad hearts.[26] He believed these are all gifts that God gives to us.[27] For those who are married we are to enjoy our lives together with our spouses.[28] He believes that whatever we end up doing for our careers we need to do it wholeheartedly and with all our might.[29] Solomon wisely concluded that apart from God life does not hold much enjoyment for us.[30] He made a very promising statement that tells us that if we set out to achieve a goal and apply ourselves, we have a very good chance at succeeding.[31]

His conclusion is a very fitting one that strongly supports the Narcotics Anonymous (NA)[32] eleventh step: We sought through prayer and meditation to improve our conscious contact with God as we understood Him, praying only for knowledge of His will for us and the power to carry that out.[33] Solomon's wisdom for us as addicts in recovery is very practical. It sheds an honest light on the realities of the world that we live in. By adapting his views we can be better adjusted to living with the ups and downs that come our way. At the end of the Book of Ecclesiastes, Solomon's conclusion in all the things he writes about is simple and most wise:

The end of the matter; all has been heard.
Fear God and keep his commandments,
for this is the whole duty of man.
Ecclesiastes 12:13

God, grant to us wisdom to live each day one day at a time. Help us to see your hand at work in the world. By your grace may we accept the

---

[25] Ecclesiastes 9:11
[26] Ecclesiastes 8:15
[27] Ecclesiastes 3:13
[28] Ecclesiastes 9:9
[29] Ecclesiastes 9:10
[30] Ecclesiastes 2:25
[31] Ecclesiastes 11:1
[32] Who, What, Why and How, The White Booklet, 2000, Narcotics Anonymous World Service, Inc.
[33] Who, What, How and Why, White Booklet, Narcotics Anonymous World Services, Inc., 2000.

world as it is, and strengthen us for service in it. Lend to us your peace so that we may rest secure that in all things no matter what comes our way. May we be reminded that we are in your care by day and by night. This we pray in the precious name of your son, Christ Jesus our Lord and Savior. Amen

More Futility

**For the creation was subjected to futility,
not willingly, but because of him who subjected it,
in hope that the creation itself will be set free
from its bondage to corruption and obtain the
freedom of the glory of the children of God.
For we know that the whole creation has been
groaning together in the pains of childbirth until now.
Romans 8:20-22**

So, the question begs to be asked, "Why was creation subjected to futility?" This brings up the Genesis fall story. Adam and Eve wanted to have the knowledge of good and evil. That way they could be like God, knowing and controlling good and evil for themselves. If that was possible then they would no longer need to trust in God for the good and evil, or the pleasant and painful things that would come their way in life. That leads to the simple answer that is needed to understand this problem of creation being subjected to futility. We all need to trust God, in all things and for all things. If creation was not subjected to futility, then whatever a person set out to do would most likely happen for them and without much difficulty at all. Everyone would be glad to take credit for their own success rather than give credit to God. This would lead to conceit, self-righteousness, and continued hostility toward God. Given the fallen nature of all things in creation everything has been made harder to accomplish. This leads us to humility so that we are brought to faith and devotion to God, and so that we will live in dependency of him.

In addiction our spirituality was hijacked by the drugs. We were made by God to be dependent on him. Drugs took advantage of that and made themselves the focus of this dependency. In recovery our dependency was recaptured and returned to the Lord, where it rightly belongs. For this reason we live a devoted life, active in our Christian faith, ever mindful of the need we have to maintain our focus on the Lord our God who made us for his glory alone.

Heavenly Father, all thanks, praise, and glory are yours. By your omnipotent right hand you have saved us from addiction and brought us in the Kingdom of your son, Jesus Christ. Grant to us all that we need to live this day according to your bounty in heaven. In Jesus name. Amen

Toxic to The Body and The Soul

And the LORD **God commanded the man, saying,
"You may surely eat of every tree of the garden,
but of the tree of the knowledge of good and evil you shall not eat,
for in the day that you eat of it you shall surely die."
Genesis 2:16-17**

The argument for using drugs because they are part of nature has been coming up forever. The trouble with using the, *"they are all natural"* argument is that it really doesn't work. Implied with the claim to being natural is that therefore they must be okay. In the case of marijuana, it is a weed by definition. In the fall one of the serious outcomes of Adam and Eve's sin was that weeds would grow in abundance and that would be a problem not some kind of blessing. The truth is that there are many things natural to this world that are absolutely deadly, beginning with the fruit of the tree of the knowledge of good and evil. After that, there is cyanide, ricin, and botulism to name only a few of the world's naturally occurring deadly substances. Looking at the problem in another way we need to know that before the fall we know that God had created all things and he pronounce them to be good. We know that after the fall creation was changed and it fell from grace.

The addict in us worked just like the serpent in the garden when we were tempted. We heard our own thoughts tell us this will take all our cares away. In a short while we will be feeling no pain, it will be great, we will love it. That is not far removed from what the serpent implied. The outcome for us in using drugs is as bad as it was for them when they ate the forbidden fruit.

In recovery we came to see through the lies we made up and believed in. We came to know the truth about our sinful nature and we turned to God in repentance calling on him to save us from our sins and our addiction. Our desperation forced us to pray with great sincerity and because we called out to him in faith, he heard our prayer and delivered us from our bondage.

God, now in recovery we walk day by day with you, calling on your name and trusting that you are fully able to keep us. Guard us from the evil one and shield us from relapse. Lead us into a deeper relationship with you, for the sake of your son Jesus Christ we pray. Amen

The Drugs are a Façade That We Wear

**And they sewed fig leaves together and made themselves loincloths.
Genesis 3:7**

Prior to the fall Adam and Eve lived together in innocence. They were naked and that was not a problem for them. In their sin after the fall their nakedness was unbearable to them. They quickly made clothes for themselves out of the hardy leaves of a fig tree. This created a solution for the needs of their relationship. However, when God showed up they were feeling frightfully inadequate again in his presence. For that they hid behind the thickness of the tree trucks from where they got the leaves. The reason they got themselves into this situation was that they aspired to be something that they were not and could not become, they wanted to be too much like God.

For us in our active using days we got high for, among other reasons, to feel better. That surge and its rush made us feel like we were conquering the world around us. On drugs we were as wise as we wanted to imagine ourselves to be. We felt great about ourselves and what a relief it was compared to how much our inner self image was hurting. In truth we were depressed, lacked confidence, and shamed ourselves often. We thought getting high would remedy all that. What the drugs did for us was only temporary. It was an illusion of greatness that was followed by some of the worst lows that were beyond our imaginations. The façade that we had put on when we got high lead to the nightmare of addiction from which there was no apparent escape.

In recovery we surrendered to God. That also meant that we let our façade fall by the wayside and we admitted to God and others the depth of how far we fell. Hard as that was to do it also brought to us a great sense of relief. We found acceptance for who we were and for where we were. From there our journey into recovery began. We found comfort knowing that God loved us and redeemed us. We learned how to trust him in all that came our way in life.

God, thank you for saving us from ourselves and from our addiction to drugs. Praise you for your greatness, your mercy, and your love. Thank you for turning our lives around and restoring them to us. This we pray in the name of your only begotten son, Christ Jesus our Lord. Amen

Vanity Proof

**And whatever my eyes desired I did not keep from them.
I kept my heart from no pleasure, for my heart found pleasure in all my toil, and this was my reward for all my toil. Then I considered all that my hands had done and the toil I had expended in doing it, and behold, all was vanity and a striving after wind, and there was nothing to be gained under the sun.
Ecclesiastes 2:10-11**

In our literature we have a statement, "one is too many and a thousand is never enough."[34] This simply tells us that if we returned to using drugs, even if we intended to do it just one time, it is dangerous. We would lose all the ground gained in our recovery and we would go back to being a full blown active addict again. Using once more often than not leads to continual use. We are never satisfied with using just one time, let alone satisfied with a thousand, ten thousand or even a million times.

It was King Solomon in his infinite wisdom who described this phenomena best. He said that "the eye is not satisfied with seeing, nor the ear filled with hearing." [35] And again, "He who loves money will not be satisfied with money, nor he who loves wealth with his income."[36] For as bad as that sounds, our being unsatisfied is not limited to just these areas. Solomon went on to say that our "souls are not satisfied with life's good things"[37] And, just to add to our misery, he tells us that though we sweat and labor for the food on our tables, our appetites are not satisfied either.[38]

Our natural man objects to these claims though. The very purpose of the eye is to see, the purpose of the ear is to hear. God commanded Adam and Eve to be fruitful. Why then is the eye not satisfied with fulfilling the very purpose it was created for? Why isn't the ear satisfied with fulfilling its purpose in life? Why is the acquisition of personal property not fulfilling? Why is laboring for food and then eating it not enough to satisfy our appetites? For as bad as all this sounds, this is not the end of this terrible news. It continued to grow worse.

J.P. Getty was the world's first billionaire. While there are many people who can boast of such great wealth today, in Getty's day it was quite a phenomenon. He made his great wealth in the oil industry. In those

---

[34] Who, What, Why and How, The White Booklet, 2000, Narcotics Anonymous World Service, Inc.
[35] Ecclesiastes 1:8
[36] Ecclesiastes 5:8
[37] Ecclesiastes 6:3
[38] Ecclesiastes 6:7

days someone said to him something like, "Now hold on here. You have acquired a lot of wealth. How much is going to be enough for you.?" To which he replied, "Just a little bit more." With a mindset like that it is easy to see how he was driven without an end in sight to his accumulation of wealth. With that for a motivating force his goal for more money was never met, nor could it ever be met, and consequently he was never satisfied. Solomon in his wisdom knew this too, he had accumulated untold riches as well. This is why he was speaking from experience when he said, "He who loves money will not be satisfied with money, nor he who loves wealth with his income; this also is vanity.[39]

Brace yourself, the end this is not yet, it is about to get still worse again. Now that issue of Solomon calling something *vanity* is significant for us. It is a word rarely heard now a days. In the Scriptures it has a specific meaning. It is a picture word that is best described this way. Image you have something like a stack of money in your hands. There are twenties and fifties and hundreds wrapped in a paper ring. You have worked, no, labored with sweat to accumulate it. You are proud of it and proud of how you earned it too. Then suddenly your large stack of bills crumbles and disintegrates into a small pile of paper dust that blows away right before your very eyes. There was nothing you could have done to prevent it and there is no way to recover it from whence it has gone. That is vanity, it is irony at its worst. And isn't this the mirror image of what many of us have seen in our lives because of our addictions? We had a job, spouse, children, car, house, and savings. But in our addictions we had ruined our careers, destroyed our marriages, alienated our children, and lost everything of value. We lost it all because we gave ourselves over to our addictions without reservation. Before long we realized that we could not stop on our own. We were reduced to the lives of slaves who cooperated with our addiction because we had no other choice. We saw that before long our addiction would get us arrested and we would have to face prison time. Worse, we saw that it would lead us to using enough drugs to kill us.

We desired to stop and made that commitment, but we were unable to carry it out. We turned to the Savior and believed that he alone could bring us into recovery. Prayerfully we turned our lives and our wills over to his care. Jesus became our Lord and his strength was greater than the power of our addiction. He freed us and brought us into recovery. In our devotion to him we are held by his love for us.

Savior, Lord, Redeemer, we love you so dearly. By your resurrection power you have restored us to life and freed us from

---

[39] Ecclesiastes 5:10

addiction. By your grace strengthen us for our earthly journey, reveal your will to us and lead us in discipleship all the days of our lives. Amen

The Occult III

**Manasseh was twelve years old when he began to reign,
and he reigned fifty-five years in Jerusalem.
And he did what was evil in the sight of the Lord,
according to the abominations of the nations
whom the Lord drove out before the people of Israel.
For he rebuilt the high places that his father Hezekiah
had broken down, and he erected altars to the Baals,
and made Asheroth, and worshiped all the host of heaven
and served them. And he built altars in the house of the Lord,
of which the Lord had said, "In Jerusalem shall my name be
forever." And he built altars for all the host of heaven in the
two courts of the house of the Lord. And he burned his sons
as an offering in the Valley of the Son of Hinnom,
and used fortune-telling and omens and sorcery,
and dealt with mediums and with necromancers.
He did much evil in the sight of the Lord,
provoking him to anger.
2 Chronicles 33:1-6**

There were times in the life of God's chosen people when they fell away from faith, and they fell far away from following as his faithful people. The occult and so-called new age are nothing new. Their names have changed according to contemporary times, but they have been around for nearly as long as people have. Other so-called gods are not gods at all, and in some cases, they may be a fallen angel who is now a demon in disguise. All of their rituals and rites, practices, and beliefs, whatever they do, is evil. Make no doubt about it, they are sinful. Beyond that they are terribly dangerous for anyone to be involved in.

If the occult is dangerous, and it is, then the occult and drugs in combination are absolutely deadly. You might say in combination there isn't much worse that you could get involved in. *Sorcery* is the Bible's word for drug use. We need to know that the mind on drugs is very vulnerable to spiritual attacks from the devil and all of his evil spirits.

There is one hope for all of us who crossed that threshold into involvement with the occult. We have a Savior, our Lord and Savior Jesus Christ. He breaks the bonds and chains that have held us in the devil's power. By his grace we can live free and be restored to our right minds. If any of us have been involved in the occult in any way, even in the smallest way, seek out spiritual care from your pastor so that your needs for spiritual freedom from the occult are assured.

Lord Jesus Christ, the demons are subject to your name and you had complete control over them. Cleanse our hearts and bodies, our minds and thoughts, our souls, and spirits from their influence. Keep us safe from all evil and guard us day and night. Cleanse our homes and everywhere we go so that by your grace, we may serve you with our whole hearts. Lead us in our recoveries and make us strong in the power of your might. Amen

Spiritual Core Concepts: Take a Hit

And the LORD **God formed man of the dust of the ground,
and breathed into his nostrils the breath of life;
and man became a living soul.
Genesis 2:7**

Recovery came to us thanks to God and his immeasurable love for us. We understand that God made Adam. His dusty, lifeless body received God's life-giving-spirit and his lungs were filled. This got things going, Adam's chest rose, then his heart started to beat, and his blood moved through the arteries and carried oxygen to all parts of his body. His muscles and organs came to life. Then Adam opened his eyes and saw his Maker.

Addiction became a problem when the sons and daughters of Adam and Eve inhaled drugs into their lungs. Parallel to the birthing process that gave life to Adam is the pathway to addiction. God's breath went into Adam's nostrils and he became a living-soul, and his sons and daughters inhaled the smoke of drugs and they became living-addicts. First, we were made in God's image and likeness, but because of our drug use we were recreated into people dependent on drugs. Just as the breath-of-life from God gave life, so also this smoke brought fundamental changes to who we were. With the use of drugs, a new allegiance was formed. No longer could we be devoted to God. Our personal allegiance was transferred to the demigod of drugs that then ruled over us.

The life-giving blood that God's son shed for us redeemed us not only from sin but also from addiction. Though he died for our sins, the grave could not hold him. By the limitless power of the Holy Spirit he was raised to life. It is by that resurrection power that we are freed from the bonds of addiction and brought into recovery. Thanks be to God!

Most holy God, we give you thanks this day because you have shown us your power by raising your son from death to life. So also bring life to our mortal bodies that we may live for you in all that we do and say. May we be empowered by you to live free and clean, may we know and do your will, may we be wholly devoted to you through Christ Jesus our Lord. Amen

Spiritual Core Concepts: I Did Not Know Who I Had Become

For I do not understand my own actions. For I do not do what I want, but I do the very thing I hate. Now if I do what I do not want, I agree with the law, that it is good. So now it is no longer I who do it, but sin that dwells within me. For I know that nothing good dwells in me, that is, in my flesh. For I have the desire to do what is right, but not the ability to carry it out. For I do not do the good I want, but the evil I do not want is what I keep on doing. Now if I do what I do not want, it is no longer I who do it, but sin that dwells within me.
Romans 7:14-20

Many of us in recovery have found that the person we were prior to using was hugely different from the person we had become. Drugs of abuse have a personality that is all their own and just as the smoke permeates our souls, so also its personality dominated in our lives. Adam and Eve were, as are we all, made in the image of God and we resembled him. Our drug use and addiction changed us into someone else and it was not a better person that we became. It was our worst version of ourselves and more. We were in survival mode, trying to satisfy a drug demon who could not be satisfied, ever.

Because of the drug use we began to change and, in the addiction, those changes went extremely far and became semi-permanent. In recovery we found that we had become a new person in Christ and were more like who we were originally in life. We found that because of faith in Christ we were in fact a new creation. We came to see our character flaws and by God's transforming grace we were being changed miraculously by his power. We had hated our drug addicted lives but we came to love our new lives and all that God was bringing us into. We developed a hunger and a thirst for more of what God was holding for us and our future.

Heavenly Father, thank you for our new lives that are fresh and exciting. Thank you for all that you have done and are continuing to do in us and for us. Bring us by your grace forward into progress in our recoveries day by day, one day at a time. This we ask in Jesus' name. Amen

Anxiety and Easy Does It

**Strengthen the weak hands, and make firm the feeble knees.
Say to those who have an anxious heart,
"Be strong; fear not! Behold, your God will come with vengeance,
with the recompense of God. He will come and save you."
Isaiah 35:3-4**

In addiction we sometimes did a thing called self-medicating. This means that we were trying to treat a problem of ours, like anxiety, with street drugs, illegally obtained prescription medications or abusing over the counter drugs. Anxiety is common among everyone, among addicts though it hits some of us pretty hard. Sometimes it is the result of just living, sometimes it is from trauma of one kind or another, and sometimes it is the result of our drug abuse. If we have self-medicated for our anxiety, we may have inadvertently created an ever-growing downward cycle of anxiety, drug abuse, worse anxiety, and increased drug abuse.

We need to know that *anxiety* is a word that literally means we aren't getting any oxygen to breath, like being choked off. That of course will cause all of us some serious anxiety, because if we are being choked, we will pass out and die from it. We want quick relief from anxiety because it is so alarming to us, as though our very survival is at stake. Our addiction may have worsened our anxiety, and our anxiety may have made our addiction worse.

In recovery we quit using and our anxiety may have actually worsened in the short run. That may have made for some exceedingly difficult days for us as we went through withdrawal. We may have or should have sought help from a medical doctor who is familiar with treating addiction. We may have needed to be treated with properly prescribed medications during our initial withdrawal period, or for an ongoing time if the doctor believed we needed the help for chronic anxiety.

Heavenly Father, you have given us all good things, medical doctors, and medications for our illnesses. Thank you for all that you provide, through Christ our Lord. Amen

Drug Slaves

**They promise them freedom,
but they themselves are slaves of corruption.
For whatever overcomes a person, to that he is enslaved.
2 Peter 2:19**

Firsts are things we remember. Most of us remember the first time we rode our bicycle without help, or the first time we drove a car. They were exciting events for us. The thrill of riding a bike, the independence of driving a car all told us that we had attained something new and exciting in our lives. They were milestones and we were changed a little by them. In the same way using drugs had a specific changing effect on us. Many of us used thousands of times and most of those experiences were not very memorable to us. Yet, the first time we used we all remember. There was the thrill of the rush that hit us, the feeling of relief from our daily burdens, the sense of release from our normal self. We can visualize the room we were in and recall who was with us.

God created Adam by breathing life into his nostrils. When the sons of Adam, or the daughters of Eve, inhaled the drugs smoke it had a similar creative effect on us. The drugs re-created us into its own image, an addict dependent on using them over and over again. Our lives were reorganized around it, it became our god, we lived for it and gave ourselves over to it in an act of surrender to its power.

God took us where we were and gave us new spiritual birth. In our conversions we were joined with Jesus on the cross and died with him to our sins. Because we shared with him in his death, we will also share with him in his resurrection.[40] So it is with our recoveries, by daily dying with him on the cross we are freed from our addiction.

Heavenly Father, by the suffering, death, and resurrection of your son you have freed us from addiction. May we be empowered by you to live as he lived, this we pray in Jesus name. Amen

---

[40] Romans 6:5

Spiritual Core Concepts: Addiction is a Second Fall

He who digs a pit will fall into it.
Ecclesiastes 10:8

Genesis doesn't actually use the word *fall* for what happened when Adam and Eve sinned. Nevertheless, it is commonly and rightly referred to as the fall anyway. So, you might say that becoming addicts is something of a second fall for us. Addiction is something that makes our sinful nature all the more tenacious, inflexible, and resistant to doing God's will.

Just prior to the flood the Scriptures said that men's hearts had grown wicked and their thoughts were continually evil.[41] The flood came about one thousand years after the days of creation. That means that it took quite a while for the progression of evil to become so widespread and prevalent. There is one thing, more than anything else, that will speed up the decay of any society. That is the use of drugs. Drugs work like steroids to speed up the process of societies moral and ethical decay.

For us and for everyone that is faced with addiction in their lives there is one answer. We must turn to God in repentance from the choices that we made to use drugs. The pathway to recovery is almost identical to the path to salvation. It is by Jesus' sacrificial death for us that we are saved and it is by his death that we are freed from addiction. It is by his blood that we are washed clean of our sins and cleansed from our addiction. It is because he rose victoriously from death and came out of the grave alive that we can live, forgiven, and also clean and free.

Heavenly Father, we see your great love for us through the sacrifice you made when you gave your son in death for our forgiveness and our freedom. We see your greatness in his resurrection and thank you that by it we too share in his victory. In his name, Jesus, we pray. Amen

---

[41] Genesis 6:5

Spiritual Core Concepts: Sorcery is Recreational Drug Use

Now the works of the flesh are evident: sexual immorality, impurity, sensuality, idolatry, sorcery, enmity, strife, jealousy, fits of anger, rivalries, dissensions, divisions, envy, drunkenness, orgies, and things like these. I warn you, as I warned you before, that those who do such things will not inherit the kingdom of God.
Galatians 5:19-21

Popular culture has made the word sorcery seem like it is not so much of a problem. With the story of King Arthur and Merlin they make it mythical, with Disney and the Sorcerer's Apprentice they make it into a magical children's bedtime story, anything but what it is. Sorcery in the Bible is recreational drug use, and in some cases it was used as a hypnotic drug to lure and manipulate others.

In the Old Testament the ancient Hebrew word for sorcery that was used is *kesheph*. In the Greek of the New Testament the word *pharmacopeia* is used. It is translated as sorcery and sometimes as witchcraft, meaning magical arts. It is frequently associated with occult practices and pagan religious rites such as child sacrifice and the worship of idols.

The practice of sorcery drug use reared its ugly head in many places in the Bible. One of the more outstanding references is found in 2 Chronicles 33. There the Scriptures talk about the righteous King Hezekiah who had torn down altars that had been put up to the idol Baal and put an end to the worship of false gods. His son Manasseh became king after him and he returned to the evil ways that his father had rid the nation of. He rebuilt all of the altars to Baal that his father had destroyed and he lead the people astray in worshipping false gods. He went so far as to put some of those pagan altars in the holy temple along with an idol god that he had made. Among the worst of his evil practices was that he sacrificed his sons and burned them as an offering to the false god Baal. He practiced occult arts such as fortune tellers and mediums and relied on their predictions, practiced sorcery drug use, and dealt with witches practicing dark arts.

As Christians we need to be wise about the ways of this world, especially when they are contrary to our faith. All occult practices, no matter what they are called such as new age, are evil and we should have nothing to do with them. Drugs are sometimes used in connection to occult practices too. This is also evil. Even simply following our horoscope is a spiritual problem and we shouldn't be doing that either. The use of drugs combined with any and all occult practices compounds their evil grip on our lives. They most certainly opened us up to spiritual evil in our lives.

In recovery we were freed from addiction and restored by God to our right minds. Spiritually we were delivered from the kingdom of darkness where the devil rules. We were brought into the Kingdom of light, into the Kingdom of God's son, Jesus Christ our Lord. We are his subjects and God is not willing to share us with another. We must avoid being involved in anything that would weaken our relationship to our Savior. Our allegiance is to him who gave his all for us and our response is to give our all to him in return.

Thank you God for bringing us into freedom from spiritual evil, thank you for freeing us from addiction to drugs. Guard and protect us from all evil and the devil. Lead us in your ways and nurture us in your everlasting love that you bear for us through Christ Jesus our Lord, who lives and reigns with you and the Holy Spirit. Amen

Drugs Strong Grip

**Formerly, when you did not know God,
you were enslaved to those that by nature are not gods.
Galatians 4:8**

Spiritually there are reasons why drugs have terrible power of addiction over us. This can be seen in several ways:

- With marijuana use we inhaled and held it in the lungs for a long time to get a fuller effect. Even when we wanted to exhale or cough, we resisted and forced it to be held in our lungs for a greater buzz. This holding action overcame our bodies natural resistance to the drug. By holding it in we were training ourselves to forgo our most basic need to breathe and placed the drug ahead of our need for oxygen. When we resisted our bodies natural response of coughing it out and wanting to exhale we rewired ourselves so that we would do drugs even if it meant we were jeopardizing our health and our lives.
- When we inhaled the smoke of any drug that was lit up in a joint or pipe, we were yielding ourselves to a toxic air. Our hemoglobin normally carries oxygen to our cells, but it likes smoke more than it does oxygen. That means that it chemically bonds to the smoke very readily, and it bonds to the smoke even though oxygen is available to it. More than that, hemoglobin holds on to the smoke a lot longer than it does oxygen, up to about 200 times longer than it holds onto oxygen. This is a direct mirror image of how the addiction so tenaciously holds our souls in its evil grip and resists recovery.
- We all know how we can breathe in an excited pattern to stimulate our nervous system or breathe slowly and meditatively to tap into our nervous system to bring about a relaxation response. Slowing our breathing in this way can slow our heartbeat and relax tense muscles. These practices are very spiritual by nature. Smoking or snorting drugs also taps into our nervous system through our breathing pattern. This is a toxic and poisonous spiritual practice.
- When the drugs were injected directly into our blood stream they had a terrible and evil grip on our souls. First, as addicts doing this we wanted the fastest, most immediate high and the greatest rush we could get. That meant we had to mainline it into our bloodstream. This need for the highest level of immediate gratification is a contributing factor to the strength of this addiction. We need to know that the Bible says that the life of flesh

is in our blood.[42] Blood is used in establishing God's covenant with us, though the blood of lambs in the Old Testament and Jesus' blood in the New Testament. By injecting the drugs into our bloodstream we were in essence creating a covenant like relationship with the drug. This left us honor bound to submitting to its demands in our lives.

When our Lord died, he breathed his last and said, *"It is finished."*[43] This meant that our salvation had been secured, the sacrifice was complete and our sins were all forgiven. It also meant that all that was necessary for our deliverance from addiction was complete as well. In recovery we can live and find security in those three words, "it is finished." We have been given our freedom, we have been made clean and our Lord did it all for us.

Heavenly Father, you knew from before the foundations of the world were laid that you would need to send your son to redeem us from our sins by his death. By his death you have also released us from bondage to addiction and delivered us from drugs. You have made us your sons and daughters, and inheritors of the Kingdom of your son. Lead and guide us in our new lives and fill us with the knowledge of your will and give to us the power to live it out in our lives. This we ask in Jesus' name. Amen

---

[42] Leviticus 17:10
[43] John 19:30

Addiction Character Traits: Blaming

He said, "Who told you that you were naked?
Have you eaten of the tree of which I commanded you not to eat?"
The man said, "The woman whom you gave to be with me,
she gave me fruit of the tree, and I ate."
Then the Lord God said to the woman,
"What is this that you have done?"
The woman said,
"The serpent deceived me, and I ate."
Genesis 3:11-13

Blaming is a human trait that began in the garden. Because of addiction the traits of our fallen nature are greatly multiplied in us. The reasons for it include fear of punishment, not wanting to look bad in front of others, not wanting to lose face, and not wanting to admit to imperfection.

From this initial pattern we can see something about how it works. Though God came to the couple in a very pastoral way they hid themselves. Adam blamed her. He also blamed God because God gave her to him. Eve did no better, she blamed the serpent. She said he deceived her, which was true, but it was only part of the truth. She admitted that she ate the fruit, but she totally avoided taking personal responsibility for her actions, and did not admit to her real reasons for eating it. She wanted to be like God. She did not confess that she wanted to eliminate God from her life and exchange her will for his. What they should have done was to come completely clean and admit what they did and why they did it. This revealed what human behavior had become.

We need to know in our recoveries that the drugs we used exaggerated this trait and others like it to a greater extreme in our lives. We need to learn to recognize when we want to blame others to avoid taking personal responsibility for our actions and then take responsibility for ourselves. Though addiction had amplified our worst traits in us, in recovery by God's grace we can reflect his glory and show Christ-like traits in all that we do.

Heavenly Father, by your Holy Spirit living in us you are transforming our lives and working sanctification in us. Lead us in your ways, to your glory through Christ our Lord. Amen

Addiction Character Traits: Grandiosity

**For by the grace given to me I say to everyone
among you not to think of himself
more highly than he ought to think,
but to think with sober judgment,
each according to the measure
of faith that God has assigned.
Romans 12:3**

The drugs have a way of twisting our thinking with great irony. In addiction many of us were at our worst. Our personal hygiene was horrid, we might have been homeless, broke, unemployed, down and out on our luck, and without a friend. Yet, when we got high those troubles no longer bothered us, in fact in our minds they no longer existed. We felt great and believed that we were on top of the world. We thought of ourselves as geniuses, captains of industry, possessors of magical powers and models of high fashion. If the drugs we used were not so impersonal, they might have been having a great laugh over us and our state of affairs.

In psychological terms we were suffering with an inferiority complex. We knew that we were in a bad way and we felt awful about our condition. To compensate for this we went on to have a drug induced superiority complex. At heart we were living at our worst and full of self-loathing. So what we did, rather than get the help we needed for our addiction, was to continue using drugs so that we could counter our sense of self-loathing. The drugs masked our true state and by giving us a quick high, they also gave us what seemed like a quick fix to all of our problems.

In recovery the fog that our minds had been immersed in started to clear. We were able to slowly admit to ourselves and others how low our lifestyles had fallen. We returned to work and began earning our own way again. We came into new friends who supported us in our recovery because they were where we had been and were now in recovery too. God began to give us a healthy sense of who we were and in humility we grew in him.

Heavenly Father, forgive us for the vanity of our minds. We accept that we are but mortal and our frames are of flesh and bone. It is you who has redeemed us from our sin and delivered us from addiction. You alone are worthy of praise and glory, through Christ our Lord we pray. Amen

Cigarettes and Marijuana Are Gateway Drugs

**They promise them freedom,
but they themselves are slaves of corruption.
For whatever overcomes a person, to that he is enslaved.
For if, after they have escaped the defilements of the world
through the knowledge of our Lord and Savior Jesus Christ,
they are again entangled in them and overcome,
the last state has become worse for them than the first.
2 Peter 2:19-21**

Having come into recovery there is a specific temptation that will come our way. That is the false idea that marijuana and tobacco are okay to use because they are not as bad as meth, or heroin, or the other drugs of abuse. We need to dispel that lie from our thinking. Researchers have found that for many people the addiction to cigarettes is in some cases even more powerful than addiction to heroin. Marijuana is a mood altering, mind twisting, thought distorting drug that is addictive. Use of either of these two drugs can easily lead to addiction to them. For us in recovery, if we use them we have returned to active addiction again and are in a relapse. Worse, their use can lead to a return to using other more dangerous and deadly drugs too.

In recovery we are indebted to the One who delivered us from the domain of darkness and brought us into freedom through Christ our Lord. We were set free in order to live for God and not for ourselves. God as our Maker never intended for us to use recreational drugs under any circumstances. The freedom of a Christian is one that loves God in return because he first loved us and sent his son to die for our freedom from sin, death, the grave, the devil, and drugs. We were set free so that we would not need to use drugs anymore.

Heavenly Father, as your children we praise you and give glory to your Name. You have set us free from sin and addiction. In our freedom we worship and adore you. You have empowered us by your indwelling Holy Spirit so that we can do your will with our lives. Help us to always abide in you and your son Jesus Christ, in whose name we pray. Amen

Case Study: Five Teens at a Sleepover

**Behold, the wicked man conceives evil
and is pregnant with mischief and gives birth to lies.
He makes a pit, digging it out, and falls into the hole that he has made.
Psalm 7:14-15**

Derick and a few other friends were sleeping over at Jim's that Friday night. They had set up a tent in his backyard and made plans to get high after his parents had gone to sleep. Then they were going to go out and run around in the neighborhood.

It was only about midnight when they ventured out. They wandered around without much purpose. They stopped under a streetlight and in their boredom they wondered what could they do. One teen said, "We probably shouldn't be standing out here in the open under the light, someone will see us." The others agreed, but in their state of mind no one did anything about it like move to a more concealed area. Soon enough a car turned the corner and drove right by them. One said, "What if it is the cops?" The others agreed, "What if it is the cops?" However no one moved. With that for a suggestion they all hallucinated seeing a police car. It was a real car, only they all saw it as a police car. They saw the red lights on the top, the police logo on the side of the vehicle and two officers inside. Still, in their altered state they did not run, they did not hide, they did nothing.

To their amazement the car drove right past them and into a garage. Then out came Milford, the local drunk. He stumbled out of his car, out of the garage and onto his driveway. He wiggled with some effort to stand up straight and then he strained his eyes as he looked at the teens. He wondered what they were up to but did and said nothing before he stumbled into his house.

This experience of hallucinating about the police gave the teens a sense of immunity against being caught. So to cure their boredom they thought of something dangerous to do. At the corner of the block there were apple trees. They went there and picked up rotten apples that had fallen to the ground. They went to the next block were there was a street with occasional cars passing by. The teens hid behind some bushes and then when the next car came by they pelted it with the rotten apples. They hoped it would get the driver to chase them, but no, he kept going.

That did not discourage the teens one bit. They decided to go over to the Steven's house and throw apples at their back door. The Steven's were an older couple who kept to themselves. They stood under a street light that was in the back ally way. They all took their turns throwing apples and hitting the back door to the house. Soon enough a light in the house went on. That only encouraged them to continue. Then a flood light came on and the back door opened. At that point the teens all ran back to their tent. Once they settled in and the excitement subsided, they were left with drug enhanced anxiety as they worried that they would be caught, but none of their trouble making caught up with them.

When we got high we did things we normally would never have done. Drugs had a way of lowering our inhibitions and emboldening us to act unwisely. Before long in addiction, even though we weren't high, we were doing things we normally never would have when we were straight. In recovery that all changed. We were devoted to our relationship with God and concerned with how our actions would support or hinder that. We loved being free and clean and we made choices that would keep us that way.
Dearest God, you have loved us as no other could and we are grateful for our redemption from sin and the freedom you have given us from addiction. Reveal yourself to us more and more and let us baste in your love that supports us by day and by night, through Christ our Lord. Amen

Spiritual Core Concepts: The Toxic Ritual of Using Drugs

**But I say, walk by the Spirit,
and you will not gratify the desires of the flesh.
For the desires of the flesh are against
the Spirit, and the desires of the Spirit
are against the flesh, for these are opposed
to each other, to keep you from doing
the things you want to do. But if you are
led by the Spirit, you are not under the law.
Now the works of the flesh are evident:
... sorcery ... I warn you, as I warned you before,
that those who do such things will
not inherit the kingdom of God.
Galatians 5:16-21**

It is simply a coincidence that the word spiritual has for a pseudo root word, *ritual* in it. Even still it is a good place to start. Spirituality frequently involves rituals, or religious ceremonies, in which things are done in a certain way, with certain tools, at a certain time, by certain people. Rituals are specific routines that happen with some formality to them. Take for example the Methodist Church. They started out as a Bible study group that had a certain *method* for how they approached the Bible in their studies. That is how they were given the name *Methodists*.

In drug use there are also rituals, albeit toxic rituals. For example in marijuana use, it was almost always kept in a specific type of bag that was rolled up in a certain way. When a joint was rolled, it was done the same way every time. The way it was lit was done in virtually the same way by everyone. Again, if the joint was being passed around there was a customary tradition to do it in a certain way. All this made it a ritual. And, because it had a mood altering effect on us, because as smoke it was similar to a spirit, it was a pseudo-spiritual toxic ritual that we once shared in.

In recovery we replaced our old using rituals with new and healthy ones. Our time of daily devotion with prayer and Bible reading was one of them. We attended worship at church and went to NA meetings, both of which contained several group rituals.

Heavenly Father, we look to you this day for all that we need and want. Most of all we give you thanks that by the blood of the covenant you have redeemed our lives from sin and addiction. Reveal your will to us and lead us as we seek to fulfill it in our daily lives. This we ask through the One who died for us, Jesus Christ our Lord and Savior in whose name we pray. Amen

Addiction Character Traits: Low Self-Esteem

**So I find it to be a law that when I want to do right,
evil lies close at hand. For I delight in the law of God,
in my inner being, but I see in my members another law
waging war against the law of my mind and making me
captive to the law of sin that dwells in my members.
Wretched man that I am! Who will deliver
me from this body of death?
Romans 7:21-24**

Drugs and addiction have a way of magnifying in us our worst traits. In the case of our low self-esteem, it goes back to the Garden of Eden. Satan used the serpent to pry away at a weak point in Adam and Eve's life. While they were already like God, having been made in his image and likeness, he offered a way to them so they could be more like God by acquiring the knowledge of good and evil. We know the story well. As a result the two realized they were naked, which was also a sign of low self-esteem in their lives.

In our lives we used drugs to mask our feelings of inferiority. We used drugs to give us a boost and make us feel better about ourselves. When the drugs wore off, we found that our low self-esteem had slipped even lower. Then began that nightmarish cycle of trying to lift-up our tumbling self-esteem by using the very thing that made it fall lower in the first place.

In recovery that downward spiral was stopped. We no longer based our self-esteem on the same things as before. Our hearts were lightened because we came into the knowledge that we were loved by God no matter what. We took heart knowing that for Christ's sake our sins had been forgiven us. We felt loved and valued because while we were still sinners Jesus died for us. Our self-esteem was raised, not because of what we did or didn't do, but because of what God had done for us in Christ.

Heavenly Father, thank you for your everlasting love that you love us with. Thank you for sending your son to rescue us when we went astray. You have made us your children and inheritors of your Kingdom. We love you, though Christ our Lord we pray. Amen

The Beginnings of Faith

**Yet you are he who took me from the womb;
you made me trust you at my mother's breasts.
On you was I cast from my birth, and from
my mother's womb you have been my God.
Psalm 22:9-10**

Adam was in direct fellowship with God from his conception. He had no doubts about God's existence, he knew from the moment he came to life that God made him and was his Father. Eve too was created by God's hand and Adam's rib. Not so with the rest of us who were created with the help of God and our parents. Nonetheless, God has designed this process of natural birth so that we come to know him through our relationship with our mother.

Contrary to the evolutionists, we know that we did not come into existence spontaneously. Life begets life, that is the way it has always been and that is the way it will always be. Without life existing in the first place life cannot come into existence. You might say that is a law of science. From being nurtured at our mother's breast, being feed from a bottle with formula or simply being held, we knew that there was *someone* greater than ourselves. God has designed this process of child rearing so that we come to know him through our relationship with our mother and other care givers. By their loving embrace we knew that someone greater than ourselves existed, namely God our Father and Creator.

In addiction we tried to have our needs met by using. Instead the drugs only made our needs greater and they grew to the point that no one but God could help us. In recovery we are cared for by God who delivered us from using and brought us into freedom. Like hungry infants we longed to be nurtured by him by being fed from his Word and filled with his Holy Spirit.

Loving God, you took us from our desperation and held us in your arms as a mother cares for her child. By your strong grip in our lives you keep us safe from harm and lead us so that we may do your will in our lives. Thank you for your salvation, through Christ Jesus we pray. Amen

The Anointed One

And the scroll of the prophet Isaiah was handed to [Jesus]. Unrolling it, he found the place where it is written: "The Spirit of the Lord is on me, because he has anointed me to proclaim good news to the poor. He has sent me to proclaim freedom for the prisoners and recovery of sight for the blind, to set the oppressed free, to proclaim the year of the Lord's favor." Then he rolled up the scroll, gave it back to the attendant and sat down. The eyes of everyone in the synagogue were fastened on him. He began by saying to them, "Today this scripture is fulfilled in your hearing."[44]
Luke 4:17-21

As our Lord began his public ministry he read this text in the synagogue during worship. Following his baptism God his Father sent the Holy Spirit to him and anointed him for the work of the ministry. Jesus declared here what he was equipped for. As addicts we know that he is gifted to aid us in our recovery. We are the ones who more than most were held captive by our addiction and made blind by its grip. We were deeply oppressed by its weight and needed to be liberated.

During his three years of ministry our Lord performed miracles and healed the sick. He walked on water and fed thousands. He died for our sins and was raised from the dead.

We know how terrible drug addiction is. We couldn't stop on our own. This left us without hope and feeling like we didn't have a future. We had every reason for deepest despair. When we had lost all hope in ourselves then we became ready to surrender to God and to his son. Then we were ready to step out of the way and let our lives be yielded to God. Then our time of using could stop and we began our recovery. All this was made possible because God sent his son.

Father, you sent your son knowing that he would be put to death. By his resurrection we have hope, just as the grave could not hold him, neither can addiction hold us. In his name. Amen

---

[44] Jesus is quoting Isaiah 61:1-2

Dig Down a Little Deeper in the Well

A woman from Samaria came to draw water. Jesus said to her, "Give me a drink." (For his disciples had gone away into the city to buy food.) The Samaritan woman said to him, "How is it that you, a Jew, ask for a drink from me, a woman of Samaria?" (For Jews have no dealings with Samaritans.) Jesus answered her, "If you knew the gift of God, and who it is that is saying to you, 'Give me a drink,' you would have asked him, and he would have given you living water." The woman said to him, "Sir, you have nothing to draw water with, and the well is deep. Where do you get that living water? Are you greater than our father Jacob? He gave us the well and drank from it himself, as did his sons and his livestock." Jesus said to her, "Everyone who drinks of this water will be thirsty again, but whoever drinks of the water that I will give him will never be thirsty again. The water that I will give him will become in him a spring of water welling up to eternal life." The woman said to him, "Sir, give me this water, so that I will not be thirsty or have to come here to draw water."
John 4:7-15

The story of Jacob's life is amazing. Though his life we see the heights and depths that can come our way in leading a spiritual life. He had a vision of angels rising up to highest heaven and descending to the earth.[45] We saw him wrestle with God all night long where he could have lost his life.[46] Here this unnamed woman refers to Jacob's well, saying that he gave her people this well. We don't have the details about the well, we don't know if he dug it, or merely took possession of it for his family and their descendants.

In this context of Jacob's well is where we as addicts in recovery benefit. Wells are deep and whoever wants to drink its water from it must drop their bucket down to its very depths. So it is in our recovery that we must dig deeply into our past and deal with our stuff. We have a saying, peel an onion there are lots of layers. For us as Christians in recovery, we need to dig a little deeper into the well of our lives and bring up the problems of the past and work through them so that we can heal from them. Left alone they become triggers for a relapse because they can sabotage our recoveries. Some of the events of our past are of such a tragic

---

[45] Genesis 28:10-17
[46] Genesis 32:24-32

and damaging nature that we may need to see a professionally licensed Christian therapist to help us work through them. If this is true of us, then seeing a counselor should not be long delayed.

The woman in the story asked Jesus, "Are you greater than our father Jacob?" The truth is, yes he is greater than our patriarch in the faith, Jacob. For our difficulties with our past we have the Lord who is there to aid us in all of our needs. We can take confidence that our Lord is with us and will always be with us as we work through our difficulties from our past, of our present and he will be there as we move forward into our futures.

Lord Jesus Christ, you offered living water to the woman at the well. Give us also this living water so that our souls may be refreshed, and we may continue our life's journeys in confidence of your continuous support. Bring healing to us for all the things from our past that cause us pain, give us courage to make amends with those who we have offended. By your suffering you have joined with us in our suffering. By your atoning death you have freely given us the forgiveness of our sins. Because of your resurrection from death and the grave, you have given to us the victory that we could never attain to. To you belongs all thanks and praise, glory and honor, power and might. Amen

Drawing Near to God

Make a joyful noise to the LORD**, all the earth!**
Serve the LORD **with gladness!**
Come into his presence with singing!
Know that the LORD**, he is God!**
It is he who made us, and we are his;
we are his people,
and the sheep of his pasture.
Enter his gates with thanksgiving,
and his courts with praise!
Give thanks to him; bless his name!
For the LORD **is good;**
his steadfast love endures forever,
and his faithfulness to all generations.
Psalm 100

In our daily devotional time this psalm serves as a guide to entering into God's presence through singing, even if we don't believe we are particularly good at singing. In doing this we grow in our relationship with God and we come to know him better. We come to know we are his personally. The psalm guides us to give thanks to God, which is something we do for what he has done for us. By giving thanks we come closer to him, which is like entering into the gates of the fence that surrounds his front yard. Entering into his courts is like coming closer to God by going in the front door of his house. We praise God in worship because he is worthy and this comes next. By praising him we come even closer to him by entering his courts, which is a reference to the inner court of his holy Temple. By doing this the revelation of who he is and what he is like continues to unfold. We come to have confidence in his never-ending love and faithfulness to us.

In addiction we were short-sighted. We knew what drugs would and wouldn't do for us. Even though they did not continue to meet our needs we used them anyway. We hoped for a better high and that our problems would go away. Instead our problems grew and we sank to new lows. In our growing relationship with God we came to trust him more. We found out that we could rely on him because he is faithful to us.

Father in heaven, by your love you have cared for us in our greatest needs. Help us to know you more personally day by day. Reveal yourself to us through your Word, in our worship and throughout our day in the circumstances of our lives. This we ask in Jesus's precious name. Amen

Radical Change

The Passover of the Jews was at hand, and Jesus went up to Jerusalem. In the temple he found those who were selling oxen and sheep and pigeons, and the money-changers sitting there. And making a whip of cords, he drove them all out of the temple, with the sheep and oxen. And he poured out the coins of the money-changers and overturned their tables. And he told those who sold the pigeons, "Take these things away; do not make my Father's house a house of trade."
John 2:13-16

While the problem in the temple was not drug use, this example shows that when there were terrible problems, then radical action was needed to solve them. And we need to remember our bodies are the temple of the Holy Spirit.[47] In our lives, especially when we first got clean, we needed to have some radical changes made in our lives. Many of us had close friends or relatives who used with us, sold drugs to us, or supported our addictions. For the extreme problem of drug addiction, safeguards and boundaries were needed to protect us as addicts in recovery.

In recovery necessary actions we needed to take may have included cutting out from our lives everyone who might have compromised our full recovery. It may have been necessary to change jobs, or move out of where we were living. We may have needed to block phone calls and reject text messages from certain people. If we owned our home it may have been necessary to have others move out or even have them removed if they do not want to stop using and get into recovery along with us. We cannot minimize the dangers of addiction, or the risk of relapse if we accommodate others who wish to continue using. In their active use, they do not fully understand the dangers and sometimes fragile state that some of us can be in.

Dearest God in heaven, we daily surrender to you and your loving care for our lives. May we abide in you and you in us. Let the love of your son richly fill our lives and let it be our motivation to live for you, free and clean of drugs. In Jesus Christ's name we pray this. Amen

---

[47] 1 Corinthians 6:19

Our Advocate

If we say we have no sin, we deceive ourselves, and the truth is not in us. If we confess our sins, he is faithful and just to forgive us our sins and to cleanse us from all unrighteousness. If we say we have not sinned, we make him a liar, and his word is not in us. My little children, I am writing these things to you so that you may not sin. But if anyone does sin, we have an advocate with the Father, Jesus Christ the righteous. He is the propitiation for our sins, and not for ours only but also for the sins of the whole world.
1 John 1:8-2:2

    Many of us grew up in a church where we practiced the corporate confession of sin and received God's forgiveness. This letter from John the Apostle was written as a sermon to be read to the members of the church during worship. John is very pastoral in how he shares about sin in our lives and what we need to do about it. He says, "if anyone does sin…" Of course we sin, we are sinners by nature. Yet, he says "if" as a gentle and pastoral way of approaching the subject which is wonderful, because we all feel guilty enough about our failings. Of course we sin and when, not if, we do we don't have to get all riled up about it, we don't have to get defensive, deny it, hide it, or react in any negative way. Why? As John says we have an advocate who is Christ the Lord.

    This term that John uses, translated as *advocate* is a fantastic word for us. In the Greek Bible it is the word *paraclete*. It means someone who is close at hand, who is at our side and is there to aid us in our difficulties. It can also be translated *attorney*, as in Attorney at Law.

    When we sin we know we are guilty. As addicts we tend to take our failures in several ways. We may take it extremely hard when we fail, too hard in fact. We also commonly try to put up a good front and on the surface make light of it. Yet deep inside we are in turmoil over it. Worst of all, in both cases we shame ourselves. All this can be a terrible trigger leading us to fall back into our old ways of behaving. It can even be a trigger to use again. Sometimes we have gotten so hardened by sin working in our lives that we are callous to the truth about our problems.

    Thankfully as believers we have an advocate, the Lord, who will help us. Through Jesus' blood we can go straight to our loving Heavenly Father and confess our sins and receive all the forgiveness we need. We have other options too. We can talk to a pastor, priest or minister and get their wise counsel and hear them tell us that our sins are forgiven. If we have a sponsor, a spiritual director, a deacon, a close friend, or a mentor we can call and talk to them. We can go to a recovery meeting or to church and get help there too of course. Most of all we need to feel the relief of forgiveness from our sins and feel the never failing, ever enduring love that God has for us.

In addiction we were hostile toward God, in recovery some of that may have carried over. We do not need to nurture that attitude. God loves us and wants the best for us. We do not have to harbor our sins and delay going to God to confess them and receive his forgiveness. Delaying doesn't make them go away or make them any less sinful. If we are struggling with habitual sins, the sooner we get help from a counselor or a pastor the better. We do not have to stay stuck in our problems and remember recovery is all about progress not perfection.

Gracious and forgiving Father, we are but flesh and our frames are only bones. If it was not for your help we would be turned again to dust. Strengthen us for the journey of recovery. Aid us in knowing and fulfilling your will in our lives. Lead and guide us today, help us to grow in our personal relationship with you, through Christ Jesus our Lord, our Savior, our All. Amen

Meal-Time Prayers

**And they devoted themselves to the
apostles' teaching and the fellowship,
to the breaking of bread and the prayers.
Acts 2:42**

It is always nice when someone brings some treats to eat at the recovery meeting. Coffee is almost always available. Sometimes there is a gathering or a potluck for Thanksgiving and Christmas too. It is always a good thing. Providing food along with the fellowship warms the atmosphere and generates a deeper bond. For those of us who bring food, it says that we care about the others and want to be a part of the nurturing that happens there. For those who drink the coffee and eat the food, they feel cared for and are appreciative of the gift we have blessed them with.

As Christians in recovery there is an ancient tradition of gathering and breaking bread together, which is the Bible's way of saying that they shared in a meal together. When the situation is right and safe consider inviting one or more recovery friends to your home for a meal if you have the gift of hospitality. This is a time for deeper bonding with each other, and for building trust and friendship.

According to the Book of Acts, the Christians also shared in prayers together. A meal-time prayer for the food is a must to begin with. In the ancient tradition of the Jews, their meal-time prayer was actually a blessing they said to the Lord for giving them the food. Over the centuries this tradition changed to us giving thanks to God for the food and asking him to bless us. In our meal-time devotion both can be done. Add to that prayers for the needs of the day, for people in distress of any kind: illness, surgery, active addiction and whatever is needful. By living out these practices our lives and our recoveries will be strengthened and enriched in ways that will warm our hearts and homes.

Heavenly Father thank you for Christian fellowship. By the unity granted to us by your Holy Spirit make our times together sweet and nurturing. Build us up as the body of Christ and use us to do your will. This we ask in Jesus' holy and precious name. Amen

Prayers

**Seven times a day I praise you for your righteous rules.
Great peace have those who love your law;
nothing can make them stumble.
Psalm 119:164-165**

In some Christian traditions long prayers are practiced, in others short prays are practiced. Biblically speaking in the Old Testament there are references to praying seven times a day which is probably based on this psalm and when they should teach and learn the Word of God:

> You shall teach them diligently to your children,
> and shall talk of them when you sit in your house,
> and when you walk by the way,
> and when you lie down,
> and when you rise.[48]

What this means is that when we sit for meals, breakfast, lunch, and supper is three times for prayers. When we walk by the way is when we are going to work and when we are walking home from work, which is two times for prayer. Finally, when we go to bed and when we wake up that is two times for prayer, for a total of seven times daily.

There are also several references to praying three times a day.[49] Those times are loosely defined as evening, morning and at noon. In the New Testament there is an exhortation to "pray without ceasing.[50] In the historical church there are eight traditional prayer times:

> *Matins* are nighttime prayers.
> *Lauds* are early morning prayers while it is still dark.
> *Prime* at the first hour of daylight or 6 am.
> *Terce* at the third hour which is our time 9 am.
> *Sext* at the sixth hour which is our 12 noon.
> *Nones* is at the ninth hour which is our 3 pm.
> *Vespers* is sunset in the evening.
> *Compline* which is the end of the day or bedtime.

---

[48] Deuteronomy 6:7
[49] Psalm 55:17, Daniel 6:10
[50] 1 Thessalonians 5:17

Prayer is one of the most spiritual things we do. It is a time to meet with God and he is personally there for each one of us every time we call on him. The things we can consider praying for includes:

Family, relatives, friends, government, the president and his staff, congress, governors, mayors, fire fighters, schools, teachers and staff, police, emergency workers, paramedics, nurses, doctors, healthcare workers, churches, pastors, church staff, safety, travelers, work/career, peace, military service men and women, evangelism, recovery 12-step groups, ourselves, home and house, neighbors, the economy, prayers of gratitude and thankfulness, wisdom, the power to carry out God's will in our lives, protection from all harm, and peace of mind.

Father in heaven, make us strong in prayer and give us the hearts of spiritual warriors. Teach us how to petition you for the needs of the world, the church, and our own lives. Let us enjoy the warmth of your presence and grow in our love for you. This we ask in Jesus' name. Amen

The Foggy Veil

Even if our gospel is veiled, it is veiled to those who are perishing. In their case the god of this world has blinded the minds of the unbelievers, to keep them from seeing the light of the gospel of the glory of Christ, who is the image of God.
2 Corinthians 4:3-4

A healthy fog like veil occurs in our lives after a critical incident happens. Our minds commonly create a mental fog to protect us. For example, after the death of a close friend or a relative a fog surrounds us for about a year. It is our minds way of trying to shield and protect us from the harsh reality of having lost someone in death. This fogs helps us to slowly take in and get used to the trauma over a longer period of time. It helps us to function in that difficult year of adjustment to living without them.

In our addiction there was a veil like fog that existed besides the smoke coming off the joint or pipe. The high itself fogged our minds, our thoughts and more. The high also veiled up and blurred our emotions so that we were no longer connected to them very well. The high worked to hide the problems we needed to face and work through. The drug induced foggy veil was a mental cloud of confusion, an emotional blunting, and it was spiritually blinding. As Paul said to the church in Corinth, the god of this world, who is the devil, blinds people to keep them from believing in the saving message of the Gospel.

In recovery our minds returned to normal and by God's gracious intervention in our lives we were granted our sanity. Our eyes were opened and we could see how blinded we once were. Now in recovery we were given spiritual insight into what we had once been in bondage to.

Lord God Almighty, deliver us from our blindness. Open our eyes so that we can see the world as you see it. Give us clarity in our thoughts and clear our minds so that your truth may guide us all of our days. Help us in our lives to be in touch with our emotions, and help us to heal on every level, that we might live to serve you all of our days, in Jesus' holy name. Amen

Sharing in Our Lord's Suffering

**Surely he has borne our griefs and carried our sorrows;
yet we esteemed him stricken, smitten by God, and afflicted.
But he was pierced for our transgressions; he was crushed for our
iniquities; upon him was the chastisement that brought us peace,
and with his wounds we are healed.
Isaiah 53:4-5**

There is a reciprocal sharing that happens in our lives of faith between us and our Savior. Jesus came and suffered terribly and then died for our sins. There was a reason for his suffering too, he did it on our behalf, meaning that he suffered for us. His suffering was our suffering that he took upon himself. Someone once said misery loves company, but in our case the one who took our suffering upon himself did it because he loves us. He was whipped in a dreadful way, and beaten to pulp by professional soldiers. Many of the victims of this kind of torture died from it before they could be executed. Our Lord in his innocence took the punishment that we deserved upon himself. Not only that, but the suffering we have known as victims of abuse, no matter what it was, he has also joined with us in that suffering and shared in it intimately with us.

In God's divine way he wants us to embrace our Lord's suffering and death in our lives. By doing this we find that we can be healed from our own suffering in this life. Our Lord rose from the dead and brought a message of peace to the disciples on Easter. So also God brings us peace to our lives when we journey with Jesus to the cross of his suffering and death. It is then that we can enjoy the benefits of his resurrection.

Father, by your son's passion you joined with us in our earthly suffering. Give us the courage to journey with our Lord in his passion too, that we may share with him there and enjoy the healing that he knew in his resurrection as well. This we ask in his name. Amen

**That I may know him and the power of his resurrection,
and may share his sufferings, becoming like him in his death,
that by any means possible I may attain
the resurrection from the dead.
Philippians 3:10-11**

Writing, Journaling, and Poetry

**And [Jesus] said to them,
"Therefore every scribe who has been trained
for the kingdom of heaven is like a master of a house,
who brings out of his treasure what is new and what is old."
Matthew 13:52**

Because of drug use we were cut off from ourselves and had become strangers to who we were. Alienation was not only common, it was the rule. We may have been using in order to escape from dreadful memories of untold kinds of abuse and neglect. In our recovery we not only stopped using, we also began to regain what our lives were supposed to have been like. Because of drug use we had blackouts and lost memories of what we had done, and what might have been done to us. As is true of traumatic memories and how the brain first stores them, we may not have put words to the memories we have stored deep inside of us.

Writing can be a great healing remedy for us. We might not be ready to say out loud what happened to us either to ourselves or to another person. Writing it down can be a safe way to say something without much risk. Journaling, letter writing, poetry or any form of writing can be very revealing and healing to us. Seeing in our minds the visual memories and putting them to words is immensely helpful in dealing with trauma and other frightful events. Should any of the writing cause excessive distress, or if it is about serious abuses that we or others suffered, seeing a competent, licensed Christian therapist is a good idea.

Lord Jesus, you suffered untold and unimaginable torture at the time of your death. You were able to forgive those who mistreated you. You were able to heal from all that you suffered. Help us who still suffer from trauma and abuse to heal. Help us to be restored to healthy minds and to have peace in our hearts from all that we have had to endure. Amen

I Know In Whom I Have Believed[51]

Paul then stood up in the meeting of the Areopagus and said: "People of Athens! I see that in every way you are very religious. For as I walked around and looked carefully at your objects of worship, I even found an altar with this inscription: TO AN UNKNOWN GOD. So you are ignorant of the very thing you worship— and this is what I am going to proclaim to you.
Acts 17:22-23

The NA program refers to our Higher Power, which is a very generic reference to God. This is done so that even an atheist can work the program. NA does refer to God, "For our group purpose there is but one ultimate authority—a loving God as He may express Himself in our group conscience."[52] For us as Christians we might squirm a little at the notion of God being referred to as merely our Higher Power. For us, we know in whom we have believed, it is the Lord our God who has sent his son Jesus Christ to be our Savior. NA and like groups have, with good cause in mind, worked to keep the program open to all and exclusive to no one in the hopes of helping everyone and rightly so.

In our own minds and hearts we need to always keep in the forefront of our thoughts and beliefs that God has revealed himself to us best in the life of his son Jesus. We have a personal relationship with him by faith and through him we have a personal relationship with the Father. We can and do call on his name in prayer, praise, and worship. His name is powerful to the tearing down of the devil's strongholds and for deliverance from active addiction. By his shed blood on the cross he has established his covenant with us forever and we are eternally his children.

Heavenly Father, thank you for revealing yourself to us and bringing us into a covenanted relationship with you through the blood of your son. Help us to grow in this relationship you have made with us and nurture us with your love. Through Christ Jesus our Lord. Amen

---

[51] 2 Timothy 1:12
[52] Who, What, How and Why, White Booklet, Narcotics Anonymous World Services, Inc., 2000

Things Just Happen

**As he went along, he saw a man blind from birth.
His disciples asked him,**
"**Rabbi, who sinned, this man or his parents, that he was born blind?**"
"**Neither this man nor his parents sinned," said Jesus, "but this happened so that the works of God might be displayed in him. As long as it is day, we must do the works of him who sent me. Night is coming, when no one can work. While I am in the world, I am the light of the world." After saying this, he spit on the ground, made some mud with the saliva, and put it on the man's eyes. "Go," he told him, "wash in the Pool of Siloam" (this word means "Sent").
So the man went and washed, and came home seeing.**
John 9:1-7

As addicts we were addicted to chaos. We frequently went from crisis to crisis. Sometimes we recognized when we were at fault, sometimes we didn't. If we did see the connection between our actions and the consequences we commonly would not admit to our part in it anyway. As addicts we were good at blaming others for our situation. Drugs blinded us to what was incredibly obvious to everyone else. It is also true that sometimes due to no reason other than chance in the wind things happened to us. Life can be random. Random things happen in life to everyone and we need to recognize that too. When that happens no one needs to be blamed or held accountable.

In our recoveries we need to take on the views and values that Jesus portrayed in this situation with the man born blind. When we are in the midst of troubles, if we caused the troubles or not, let's work to show our faith in God. We need to take responsibility for our actions when we contributed to the problem. Our role is to trust God to carry us through the mess, and to bring glory to his Name in the end by our faith in him in all situations and circumstances.

Heavenly Father, guard us by the presence of your Holy Spirit that no evil befalls us. When we are challenged in life, help us to abide in faith and trust you in all things. Let us, by our lives, bring glory to your name, so that others will know that you love and care for all your children, in Christ's name we pray. Amen

Jesus said,
"But seek first the kingdom of God and his righteousness,
and all these things will be added to you.
Matthew 6:33

Recovery is dependent on being in a relationship with God and our following the program. The program consists of the 12-steps and going to meetings among other things. Prior to Dr. Bob and Bill W. with the 12-steps there was the Oxford Group, and before that was the Temperance Society. These last two groups found that recovery, a sustained recovery, was possible by more or less simply doing those things that a Christian should be doing anyway. As Christians who are addicts our recovery works when we are dedicated and consistent, intentional, and structured in living an active and focused Christian life. This includes these things:

Already true of our lives of faith we should believe these things:
- We should believe that we are sinners by nature, we are in bondage to sin and cannot free ourselves.
- That God is our Father and Jesus Christ is his only son, we are their subjects.
- Jesus is the only way of salvation, that he suffered and died for our sins, and was raised on the third day by the power of the Holy Spirit.
- We should be trusting that God will care for all of our needs.
- We should also be seeking in our lives to fulfill his will and purpose in our lives.

We should be regularly practicing these things:
- Leading a daily life of faith and repentance, confessing, and receiving forgiveness for our sins.
- Directly asking for forgiveness from anyone that we have sinned against.
- Sharing in fellowship with believers several times a week.
- Daily prayers and prayers several times a day.
- Daily Bible reading and study.
- Sharing our faith with others, especially those in need.
- Worshipping in church and confessing our sins.
- As addicts we need to share about our recovery with addicts not in recovery.

For anyone with specific or deeply rooted issues or sins in their lives a more intensive Christian walk is needed. For example, if someone has been found guilty of embezzling money we would not want them working around cash funds. Rather, we would want to steer them clear of situations where they would be needlessly tempted. We would want to create a supportive and nurturing environment where they could grow in self-restraint and good character. Likewise, for ourselves as addicts we want to live this active and devout life so we can be nurtured in healthy lifestyles and be steered clear of both direct temptations and the triggers that could lead to a relapse.

Seeking God's Kingdom is a matter of letting him have full dominion over our lives. Seeking his righteousness is a matter of several things. Repentance and confession of our own unworthiness is a good beginning. Then living by faith, as the Scriptures have said, *the righteous shall live by faith*.[53] In and of ourselves we are unrighteous and anything we do that might seem to be righteous, well the Bible says our righteousness is like a filthy garment that we wear.[54] We need to allow the Holy Spirit to do its work in us and sanctify us to bring about God's righteousness in us. We need to seek to know and do his will in our lives.

Father, by the life of your son you redeemed us from sin and freed us from addiction. Now we pray that you will aid us as we journey ever forward and seek to make progress in our growing faith. We yield our lives up to you so that the work of your Holy Spirit may continue in our lives unhindered. Sanctify us, reveal your will to us and empower us to serve you this day, and every day, one day at a time. In Jesus' name, our Lord and Savior we pray. Amen

---

[53] Romans 1:17
[54] Isaiah 64:6

The Word of God: Law and Gospel

**For all have sinned and fall short of the glory of God,
and are justified by his grace as a gift,
through the redemption that is in Christ Jesus.
Romans 3:23-24**

The Great Reformer Martin Luther taught that the Word of God comes to us in one of two forms: Law and Gospel. Without this basic understanding of the Scriptures there is a lot of confusion that can arise when studying it.

The Law is found in those parts of the Bible that condemns us in our sins. The Law tells us in no uncertain terms that we are sinners, that we have offended our Maker and for that reason, because the offense is so great, that we deserve to spend an eternity suffering in hell. The Law removes from us any vain hope that we might have that somehow we can contribute to our own salvation by doing good works to merit forgiveness, we can't. It also causes us to look for help from outside of ourselves.

The Gospel, on the other, is found in those parts of the Bible that tell us that while we are sinners deserving of punishment, God loves us. God has done something about our sinful state and calls on us to repent and believe in his son Jesus Christ. The Gospel tells us that Jesus came to the earth from heaven and took our punishment upon himself and died for us on the cross to fulfill God's righteous demands. The Gospel tells us that Jesus rose victoriously from the grave and ascended into heaven where he is now, sitting at God the Father's right-hand side. When we confess faith in him, by God's free and gracious gift alone we are saved from our sins, forgiven them, and made to be a child of God.

Never should the two of these be shared separately. The Law alone will cause a person to despair and feel condemned with no relief by salvation. The Gospel alone will cause a person to take for granted that we have been redeemed at great cost, by the death of Jesus on the cross. Together the Law prepares the heart to receive the message of salvation, and the Gospel assures us of our salvation by faith alone, by grace alone.

In the same way, as addicts, we need a Savior. Just as the way the Law works on us concerning our sins, so also in the beginning of our recovery we despair of ourselves as we come into the truth that we have a problem. In that early stage we realize that just as we cannot contribute to our own salvation, neither can we quit using on our own. We might try to regulate our use, thinking that we can cut down, using less each time and by using less frequently. Typically these efforts are short lived and frequently result in a net increase in our using rather than a decrease.

When we become honest we admit that we cannot quit and we turn outside of ourselves for help.

In recovery we receive the message of hope, that given the right kind of help we can quit. This is similar to how the Gospel's message of salvation works on us. Having been properly prepared by realizing that we cannot quit on our own we gladly cling solely to the hope that we can recover from our addictions by turning to God and working the program. As Christians in recovery we know that our higher power is not just an impersonal, indirect reference to our Maker. As people of faith we know that God, Our Father and his only son, Jesus Christ our Lord are the two people that make our recovery possible.

The program says, *we came to believe that a power greater than ourselves could restore us to sanity.*[55] As Christians who are addicts we have come to know that the drugs have power over us. We also believe that God is not only more powerful than ourselves, but he is also more powerful than the drugs dominance over us. By believing in our Lord and Savior we are delivered from active addiction. By living an active and devout Christian life we maintain our recovery from drug addiction.

God, thank you for the gift of your Word. Without the truth we would be lost and without hope. By your living Word we have been shown how to live and who to believe in. By your Word we know who our Savior is. Nurture us by your Word daily and may its message permeate in us richly. This we ask through the name of the one who rose victoriously, Christ the Lord. Amen

---

[55] Step 12. Who, What, How and Why, White Booklet, Narcotics Anonymous World Services, Inc., 2000.

Restoring Our Minds

But it is the spirit in a person, the breath from the Almighty, that gives anyone understanding.
Job 32:8

You may ask, "How important is this matter of breath and breathing?" And what does it have to do with spirituality? It is vitally important. It was Job who said, "The Spirit of God has made me, and the breath of the Almighty gives me life."[56] Just as the spirit of God in us gives us life in our mortal bodies, so also it gives us the ability to understand. Some of the greatest thinkers in history such as Sir Isaac Newton gave credit to God for the discoveries they came to understand.

In contrast to the way the life-giving-spirit of God works in us, drugs do just the opposite. The toxic smoke that we inhaled was readily absorbed by our hemoglobin which normally carries oxygen to our cells. This process prevented oxygen from reaching our brains and limited our ability to think. Further, the drugs themselves twisted our thoughts, blunted our rational minds, and caused us to think in crazy ways. Drugs also shut down our ability to think for ourselves. They captured our interests and got us to focus on getting high and finding more drugs to get high with.

When we got clean our thinking slowly began to work again, but sometimes it remained very twisted for months, even years. Attending meetings and learning how our addiction had affected us was especially important in supporting us in living in recovery. We needed to hear from others what they had also suffered with and how their thinking was affected. It was necessary for us to hear from others about their old ways on drugs and how now in recovery they had changed for the better. This interaction stimulated our brains to work again for us.

Lord, restore to us again our mental health and give us clarity in our thinking. Heal our minds and our hearts so that we will have nothing keeping us from serving you fully. Send your Holy Spirit to us so that our lives will be renewed in you. Through Christ our Lord we ask. Amen

---

[56] Job 33:4

What Voice Will We Listen To?

**And your ears shall hear a word behind you, saying,
"This is the way, walk in it,"
when you turn to the right or
when you turn to the left.
Isaiah 30:19-21**

On the day of the fall Adam listened to and obeyed the voice of his wife as they both ate the forbidden fruit. God spoke to him about this very thing, and pointed out to him that he would suffer the consequences of listening to the voice of his wife rather than listening to God's voice which had told him not to eat the fruit that was forbidden.

In addiction we did not listen to and act in accordance with the warnings we had heard about drug use. We ignored the things we were taught in school about the dangers. We didn't listen to and act in accordance with what others warned us about. We even silenced our own thoughts that reminded us not to do it. Consequently, we went on to develop the medical diagnosis of being chemically dependent.

Our actions are a carryover from the day of the fall when Adam silenced the voice of God and listened exclusively to the voice of his wife. In the context of using, we listened to the voice of friends, strangers, or relatives and what they told us about drugs and what they would do for us. They encouraged us to use and we believed in their lies. As a result some of us were put into a temporary psychotic state and we heard voices in our heads telling us dangerous and dark things.

When we turned to the Lord for salvation and began our recovery we began to put to silence the voices that had been lying to us. When we cut off contact from former friends and relative that used we silenced their voices and stopped them from influencing us. Our minds could rest and be restored by the Lord as we listened to his voice as we read the Holy Bible and waited on the Holy Spirit who spoke the truth to our hearts with loving words.

Heavenly Father, forgive us for not listening to the warnings that you sent to us through others. Restore us to sound minds and bodies so that we may serve you in righteousness all of our days. For you are worthy of all praise and glory, honor, and power. In Jesus name. Amen

We Are Temples of the Holy Spirit

**Or do you not know that your body is a temple of the
Holy Spirit within you, whom you have from God?
You are not your own, for you were bought with a price.
So glorify God in your body.
1 Corinthians 6:19-20**

Life first came to Adam when God breathed into his nostrils the breath-of-life. This breath-of-life is from God, it is a life-giving-spirit from him but it is not the same as the Holy Spirit. This word for his life-giving-spirit could also be translated as a powerful wind. When this powerful life-giving-spirit came into Adam's body he became a living-soul. The word soul could also be translated here as a gentle puff of air. Addiction came to us when we inhaled the toxic smoke of our drug of choice. That toxic smoke intermingled with our soul and in turn our lives were altered by it and simply put, we became living-addicts.

Spiritual birth came to us and we were given the Holy Spirit who resides in us right now. We are the temple of the Holy Spirit. When as a Christian we take into our bodies the smoke of meth or marijuana, snort coke or something else we are deeply grieving the Holy Spirit living in us. We have personally experienced, or we know because of what others have told us, that using again as a Christian puts us into a very miserable state. Within us we spiritually feel the grief that God is experiencing from us using drugs.

Paul, who wrote this text, reminds us that we are not our own, we were purchased with the price of Jesus' life and his shed blood on the cross. Our lives are not our own, they are owed to God. We need to be faithful to the one who has redeemed us.

Heavenly Father, forgive us when we stray and lead us back to the way that is eternal. Help us to throw aside all the things that hinder us in our devotion to you. This we ask though Christ our Lord. Amen

Spiritual Practices: Yoked with the Lord Meditation

**Jesus said,
"Come to me, all who labor and are heavy laden,
and I will give you rest.
Take my yoke upon you, and learn from me,
for I am gentle and lowly in heart,
and you will find rest for your souls.
For my yoke is easy, and my burden is light."
Matthew 11:28-30**

Many of us struggle with muscle tension and carry our stress around in our shoulders. For us we have this verse from the Lord himself. The yoke that is referred to in this verse is a halter that gets strapped around a team of oxen's shoulders so that they can pull a plow to till a field. Not uncommonly the two oxen are not equally matched. One animal might be smaller than the other, one might be stronger and able to bear more of the load than the other. The yoke was custom made for them as a pair. That way it fit perfectly across both their shoulders and the load was evenly distributed so that the stronger ox carried the greater load according to its abilities. So, what the Lord is saying to us in this metaphor is that he teams up with us and carries the greater part of the load. By joining with him in our daily lives he helps to make our burdens lighter and easier for us.

In practical terms there is a spiritual application for this verse. Take this time to use it to relax by and take a short breather. Lay down and close your eyes. Meditate on this verse, if not by reciting it word for word at least by focusing on its image and its meaning in your mind. Then slow your breathing down. Breathe in through your nose to the count of four and then relax and let your breath freely flow out of your mouth to the count of five. Gently force a little extra of the residual air out of your lungs before repeating the cycle. Continue to meditate on the words and the image of the pair of oxen yoked and working together. Add to this the thought of Jesus working with you and you with him. Continue to focus on this and then roll your shoulders forward as you breathe in and then roll them backwards as you relax and exhale. After doing this a few times stop and focus on relaxing every muscle in your shoulders and neck. Focus on relaxing your upper arms too. Roll your neck from side to side, and round and round. If you are having trouble feeling your muscles release their tension try flexing them tightly for about three to five seconds and then relaxing them. Practice this for anywhere from five to fifteen minutes for the best results.

Heavenly Father, make real to us the understanding that we are equally yoked with our Lord. Let us know that we are never alone, but that you, our Lord Jesus Christ, and the Holy Spirit are with us in all that we do and everywhere that we go. This we pray in Jesus' name. Amen

For freedom Christ has set us free; stand firm therefore, and do not submit again to a yoke of slavery.
Galatians 5:1

We Tried to Carry This Message to Addicts[57]

**The LORD is near to the brokenhearted
and saves the crushed in spirit.
Psalm 34:18**

Addicts needing recovery are more likely to get help when they are in a crisis. It makes sense too if everything seems to be going well then why change? In our twelfth step we commit to carrying our message to other addicts. You might say that we become evangelists for the program. It is sufficient to let them know in a subtle way that we are a Christian and that God has made our recovery possible. Their need for help is the most important thing while they're in crisis.

Some addicts will enter into recovery by going to inpatient or outpatient treatment. Others will go to 30 meetings in 30 days. Some will need to get into a detox center or possibly a hospital to ensure a safe withdrawal period. That is especially true when they have been using high levels of any drug. It is a good idea to invite them to your meeting. Let them know what the format is and that they don't have to say anything. Assure them that it is entirely anonymous and explain to them what that exactly means. We will want to share about our self and our recovery in general.

Keep in mind that at their core, they are a very tender and wounded person. Remember to use inclusive language, meaning we, us and our for example. Never appear to be pointing a finger of accusation at them. They know they have a problem so don't drive that point home. Assure them of the success countless numbers of people have found in admitting to their powerlessness over their addiction, and that turning their will and lives over to God's care brought them into recovery. If they are ready to take action or not, at the very least, plant the seeds in them so that when they are ready, they will know where to turn and how to get help.

Dearest God, there are souls trapped in the rot and horror of addiction who need your merciful deliverance. Help us to help them. Help them turn to you and bring them into recovery. Restore to them the life you have prepared for them, through Christ our Lord we pray. Amen

---

[57] Who, What, How and Why, White Booklet, Narcotics Anonymous World Services, Inc., 2000

The Spiritual Dimension

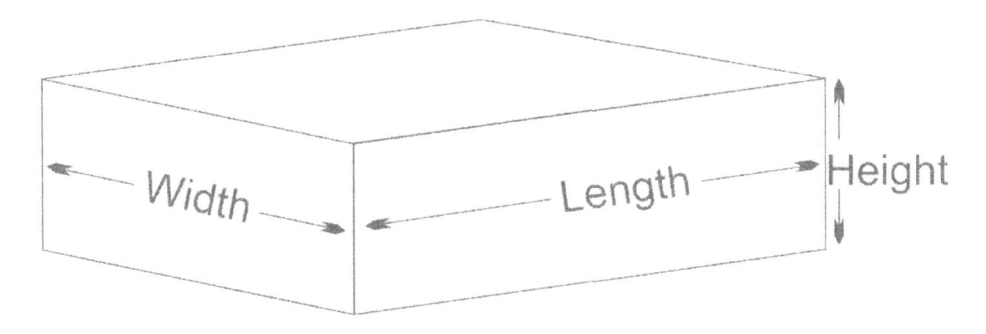

> **I pray that you may have the power to comprehend,
> with all the saints, what is the breadth and length
> and height and depth, and to know the
> love of Christ that surpasses knowledge,
> so that you may be filled with all the fullness of God.
> Ephesians 3:18-19 NRSV**

It was Solomon who in his wisdom said that the eye is not satisfied with seeing, the ear with hearing and the lover of wealth with gain.[58] In fact, life can be very unfulfilling when lived apart from a relationship with God. So then begs the question how does a relationship with God make things any better? And the answer is this: God made us for his glory, so then our fulfillment is found in fulfilling his will for our lives.

Here in what Paul writes to the church in Ephesus is a great mystery that is in part revealed to us. The apostle wants us to experientially understand God's love, and Christ's love for us. This is fulfilling for us. The spiritual mystery of it is seen in how he describes God's love, saying that it has four measurements. The length of it makes it one dimensional, add to that width which makes it two dimensional. To this he adds height which makes it three dimensional, which is where we live, in a three-dimensional world. To these three dimensions he adds yet another measurement, depth. This makes God's love in Christ for us four dimensional, which is the spiritual dimension. It is in this spiritual dimension that we find a supernatural fulfillment in our lives.

Heavenly Father, we long to know and do your will in our lives. Reveal to us what you would have us do and lead us in your ways. Through Christ our Lord we pray. Amen

---

[58] Ecclesiastes 1:8

Our Thought Life

**Finally, brothers, whatever is true, whatever is honorable, whatever is just, whatever is pure, whatever is lovely, whatever is commendable, if there is any excellence, if there is anything worthy of praise, think about these things. What you have learned and received and heard and seen in me— practice these things, and the God of peace will be with you.
Philippians 4:8-9**

Back in our using days our minds became an unhealthy and unholy playground for whatever whims caught our interests. Our minds wondered recklessly, were diverted by popular culture, and rode the wild ride of insanity from the drug's power over us. Our ability to deny the realities of life grew by leaps and bounds. Spurred on by the intoxicating power of the drugs we lied to ourselves about the state of our lives. We lied saying; that it wasn't as bad as all that, that we were not using as much as we were, that drug use was so common that we were just doing what most other people were doing, that we could handle it and that we deserved a break and drugs provided that for us. The lies grew with our ever-increasing drug use. We rehearsed them often in our own thoughts.

In the days leading up to our recovery we grew more and more exhausted by our lifestyles. We finally were able to get into recovery. One of the challenges we faced was to get our thinking to change. No longer did we want to think about using, we did not want to think about simply living however we pleased. We wanted to have clarity in our thoughts. We wanted to have clean thoughts because we were tired of our old ways. So, we undertook to actively decide what thoughts we would and would not entertain. Because our thought life was crucial to our recovery we also read the Bible and began to meditate on the Holy Scriptures.

Heavenly Father, you came into our lives and delivered us from drug addiction. Continue to fill our lives with thoughts of your love for us, with remembrances of all that you have done for us, of your love and the redemption of our souls from sin. Fill us evermore with pure and righteous thoughts so that in all the recesses of our minds you will always be honored. In Jesus' name. Amen

It is a Fearful Thing to Fall into the Hands of the Living God
Hebrew 10:31

As addicts it is obvious that we cannot quit on our own. That is just one of the distinguishing characteristics of being an addict. The drugs had more power over us than our own self-control, discipline, and wimpy will-power. Therefore, we needed to enlist the help of someone who was not only more powerful than ourselves, but also more powerful than the drugs and their power over us. This is God's place in our lives, he is the Almighty God.

The problem is that many, maybe even most of us, were afraid of turning to him for help. We had sinned, we screwed up, we were in a terrible place in our lives and we knew it. And isn't this exactly what Adam and Eve did when they sinned? Rather than turning to God they hid from him. Turning to the one person who could help us was what we needed to do, but like our first parents we did just the opposite of what we should have. There is another problem too, as the Bible verse says, "It is a fearful thing to fall into the hands of the living God. Why is that so? The Scriptures say that we cannot see God's face and live.[59] Why is that? Because if we see him, he sees us. If he sees us, he needs to do something about our sin, which is to call us to account for our sins, with our lives, meaning our death is required.[60]

Now all that paints a very gloomy and doom filled future, or so it would seem. The story of our redemption doesn't end there, not at all. The Bible also says this:

**Therefore, since we have been justified by faith,
we have peace with God through our Lord Jesus Christ.
Romans 5:1**

God, thank you from coming to us in the life of your son and making peace with us. Help us to live in the covenant of his blood and by it fulfilling your purpose for our lives. In Christ's name we pray. Amen

---

[59] Exodus 33:20
[60] Romans 6:23

The Dry Drunk

Some addicts stop using but go no further in their recovery work. That is admirable. In the alcoholic recovery community they are called a dry drunk. In the drug addict community we have no similar name, but maybe we should. The dry drunk is the person who has quit using but nothing else has changed. They still behave in all the same dysfunctional ways as before, lying, cheating, manipulating, using people, and on and on. Perhaps there are a rare, an exceedingly rare, few individuals who clean up their behavior with little to no outside help such as counseling and meetings. That doesn't work for the vast majority of us. Recovery truly needs to be more than just not using. It especially means that we work on our character flaws, and typically we have a lot of them.

Recovery also means to recapture what our life should have been like had it not been for the devastation that drug use brought us. This includes things like an education, a career that we may have dreamt of having in our younger years, a spouse, children, home, car and all the rest. Jesus said he came to bring us abundant life.[61] Also, very importantly we need to understand that our life and what it will be is in God's hands as the Scriptures have said,

For you have died, and your life is hidden with Christ in God.
When Christ who is your life appears,
then you also will appear with him in glory.
Colossians 3:3-4

Heavenly Father, our lives fell into ruin with our drug addiction. Now in recovery we humbly pray that you will sanctify us by the indwelling of your Holy Spirit and remove our character defects. Bring us to a better way of living and relating to others. We pray that what our lives should have been like will be granted to us once again by your gracious and loving hand. Forgive us our sins and lead us in the way that is everlasting, though Christ Jesus our Lord and Savior. Amen

---

[61] John 10:10

Spiritual Practices: A Sabbath Rest and Hibernating

There were times when our Lord withdrew from public life because he needed to be alone for a while. Before he chose his twelve disciples he went up to a mountain to spend the night in prayer.[62] When his cousin John the Baptist was murdered he also sought to be alone.[63] Equally true, in our recovery we have times when we need to be alone. The demands in our lives can pull on our souls from every direction. This can distort us, pull us off track and jeopardize our recovery.

Sometimes we need to calm our minds and souls because they have had too much stimulation coming at them, too much noise, lights, phone calls, emails, people wanting our attention, and on and on. We need to clear out our short-term memories that have too much clutter in them. Sometimes we need to be alone so we can hear our own thoughts, recall our memories, get in touch with ourselves again.

Things that we can do that will help with making it a spiritual time include checking in with our sponsor, and letting our closest friends know we are taking some needed time for rest and relaxation. We can take a few days off from work if we need to and have some downtime. This time should be spiritual too, this should be seen as a Sabbath rest for us. We might need a little, meaning in moderation, comfort food, quiet time, time to nap and get caught up on our sleep, or just vegetate in front of the TV to watch a good movie or two. We can burn some incense, pray, worship by singing spiritual songs and hymns, read our Bibles, meditate on God's Word, read a Christian book, watch a Christian movie, ask our pastor to serve us communion, or go on a prayer walk. Things to do include not receiving phone calls, let them roll into voice mail, stay off the internet, no Facebook or email, only Christian TV shows or, maybe no TV at all.

Heavenly Father, help us to enter into your rest and turn our focus toward you. Let us be refreshed in our weariness, strengthened in our weakness, and filled with your Holy Spirit. This we pray in your son's holy name, Jesus Christ our Savior and Lord. Amen.

---

[62] Luke 6:12-16
[63] Matthew 14:1-13

Addiction Character Traits: Two Extremes – Impulsiveness and Procrastination

So I find it to be a law that when I want to do right, evil lies close at hand.
Romans 7:21

Do not grow weary in doing good.
2 Thessalonians 3:13

If you can believe it, and oddly enough, as addicts we can suffer from two opposites in life: procrastination and impulsiveness. How can that be you may ask? Shouldn't it be maybe one but not the other? No, it isn't that way. Some of it is how our brains are wired, some of it is how we have lived our lives as addicts and who really knows what else?

Our impulsiveness relates to original sin and to the tree of the knowledge of good and evil. In the Hebrew language of the Genesis three text, the words *tov* and *rah* are used. Tov is good, rah is evil. These two words are also the root words for pleasure and pain. In plain language, it is in every person's nature to seek out pleasure and avoid anything that is uncomfortable or painful. Simple enough, right? The problem is that Adam and Eve choose to sin and eat of this fruit even though they had been warned it would be to their own demise and death. This is impulsiveness, it is part of our nature. We must learn to master it by living the spiritual life of a Christian disciple and in the program of recovery.

Now, procrastination, which is on the other end of the spectrum, is also something we do as addicts. Here again we want to avoid the painful and difficult things in life, but who doesn't? Our problem is that we want to avoid them by not doing anything to resolve the problem.

God, grant unto us that in our recovery we might learn from you how to manage our impulsive natures. Help us also to live in accordance with your will so that we may act, work, and accomplish all that is needful in our lives rather than practice procrastination, through Christ Jesus our Lord we pray. Amen

Spiritual Core Concepts: Born-of-the-Spirit

**Jesus answered,
"Truly, truly, I say to you, unless one is born of water and the Spirit,
he cannot enter the kingdom of God. That which is born of
the flesh is flesh, and that which is born of the spirit is spirit.
Do not marvel that I said to you, 'You must be born again.'
The wind blows where it wishes, and you hear its sound,
but you do not know where it comes from or where it goes.
So it is with everyone who is born of the Spirit."
John 3:1-7**

Matthew, Mark, and Luke all wrote accounts of the life of Jesus of Nazareth. Not a one of them said anything about spiritual birth. Long after they wrote, and late in his own life, John wrote his account of Jesus' life. He included many of the things the others left out. High on the list of importance is that Jesus said we must be *born-of-the-Spirit*. This is commonly referred to as being born-again, and less commonly referred to as being born-from-above. For us as addicts being *born-of-the-Spirit* is an essential truth that we must embrace for our recovery.

Jesus spoke of being born-of-the-Spirit using immensely powerful words. He insisted strongly, demanding adamantly, that we must be born-of-the-Spirit. John wrote in Greek using their imperative case, meaning that it is an absolute requirement for us a Christians, no exceptions are possible, we must be born-of-the-Spirit.

Adam became a living-soul when God breathed into his nostrils the breath-of-life. We, the descents of Adam, became living-addicts when we inhaled the poisonous and toxic smoke of our drugs. Now, when we are born-of-the-Spirit we not only become Christians who are born of God, we are also delivered from being active addicts. In this act where God gives us spiritual birth we are made to be in recovery by him as well.

Heavenly Father, thank you that you did not abandon us in our addictions but you provided spiritual birth for us. This we pray through Christ our Lord. Amen

Spiritual Core Concepts: Jesus' Breath

**On the evening of that day, the first day of the week,
the doors being locked where the disciples were for fear of the Jews,
Jesus came and stood among them and said to them,
"Peace be with you." When he had said this,
he showed them his hands and his side.
Then the disciples were glad when they
saw the Lord. Jesus said to them again,
"Peace be with you. As the Father has sent me,
even so I am sending you." And when he had said this,
he breathed on them and said to them, "Receive the Holy Spirit.
John 20:19-22**

When does being born-of-the-Spirit happen? And how does it happen? For the apostles it was on Easter. Jesus miraculously appeared among them. He offered them this special greeting of peace. This greeting is one that has great depth of meaning. It means not just peace as we understand it, but also good health and prosperity, good relations with your family, friends, and neighbors. Most of all in this circumstance it means peace with God because by Jesus' death for our sins and his resurrection we have been reconciled to God.

Jesus also did something that we don't do in our culture. He breathed on them. In that middle eastern culture, back in that day, they shared their breath with each other in their conversations. As one person talked the other person inhaled some of their breath. So important was this that if you didn't do it they would be offended. As Jesus greeted each of them he would have hugged them and said, "Peace." As he breathed out, they breathed in according to their custom. By his breath he gave each one of them the gift of spiritual birth and they received the indwelling of the Holy Spirit. Now by this the disciples were born-of-the-Spirit.[64]

Heavenly Father, you sent your son Jesus to bring us spiritual birth through his death and resurrection. Grant that through our Lord's death we may die to self, sin, and our addictions, and rise with him to newness of life through spiritual birth. This we pray in his name. Amen

---

[64] John 3:1-21

Thomas Said, "My Lord and My God!"

Now Thomas, one of the twelve, called the Twin,
was not with them when Jesus came.
So the other disciples told him,
"We have seen the Lord."
But he said to them,
"Unless I see in his hands the mark of the nails,
and place my finger into the mark of the nails, a
nd place my hand into his side, I will never believe."
Eight days later, his disciples were inside again,
and Thomas was with them.
Although the doors were locked,
Jesus came and stood among them and said,
"Peace be with you." Then he said to Thomas,
"Put your finger here,
and see my hands; and put out your hand,
and place it in my side.
Do not disbelieve, but believe."
Thomas answered him,
"My Lord and my God!"
Jesus said to him,
"Have you believed because you have seen me?
Blessed are those who have not seen and yet have believed."
John 20:24-29

    When the scriptures were first being written down paper was an expensive commodity. It was commonly in short supply. The scribes frequently wrote from one edge of the paper all the way to the other edge to ensure the maximum use of their limited resources. Writing styles from that period also reveal that they sometimes wrote with economy, meaning that they used a minimum of words to convey their message. So, that should make you wonder why, with paper being in short supply, why would they take up the space to write down that Thomas is a twin? And why would it need to be written down three times, isn't once enough?[65]

    The answer is found in John twenty. Thomas, as a twin, had a built-in affinity with his twin sibling, whose name we never knew. Thomas shared qualities with this sibling that are common among twins, for being able to almost share thoughts, feelings, and conversations almost mystically as do most twins. They frequently seem to be able to know what the other is thinking or feeling. They share in some remarkable

---

[65] John 11:16, 20:24, 21:2

qualities. One may start a sentence, the other finishes it. As adults they may live in separate residences but dress identically on the same day. They may have been separated at birth, grown up apart but gone into the same career and both married similar looking women with the very same names. All that to say that Thomas was already inclined toward having this special affinity of kinship with his twin and now he shares something at the same level spiritually with the resurrected Lord.

Every time you have heard someone talking about this text you probably heard about, "Doubting Thomas." The text doesn't say that Thomas doubted anything. He said he would not believe unless he also saw Jesus' hands and side. There is a difference. Thomas was an apostle like the other ten. If he was to be a witness to the resurrection, he too needed to be an eyewitness, so that he had the same experience to match the authority of his office as an apostle. That said, take another look at the reading from John twenty and consider deeply what it is describing.

Imagine for yourself what Thomas felt as his hand examined Jesus chest wound. He might have shied away from placing his hand inside the wound. Perhaps Jesus gently guided his hand. As Thomas' hand entered the wound, he first felt the warmth of his Savior's body. Then he would have felt the rise and fall of Jesus' chest and he felt the movement of air as he breathed in and out. Finally, as his hand went deeper, he felt the beating of the Lord's heart. What an awesome experience! Thomas' response was to fall to his knees and confess his faith, "My Lord and my God."

For as awesome as Thomas' experience was there is more that can be said about it. In Jesus lives the fullness of God.[66] We know that we must go through Jesus to see the Father and have a relationship with him.[67] Thomas was able then to touch the very heart of God in this experience.

Father in heaven, through Christ our Lord we come to you. We pray that you will give us the same intimacy with you that Thomas shared with your son. Challenge us to grow in our faith and lean on you more fully every day. In Jesus' name we pray this. Amen

---

[66] Colossians 1:18
[67] John 14:6,9-10

A Renewed Relationship with God

**Then you will call upon me and come and pray to me,
and I will hear you. You will seek me and find me,
when you seek me with all your heart.
I will be found by you, declares the LORD,
Jeremiah 29:12-13**

Our drug use alienated us from ourselves, others, and most importantly from God. The more we used, the further we pushed ourselves away from God. The more we used the closer we got to the demigod of our drug of choice. When we were ready to return to the Lord, we needed to know that he had already been long awaiting for us to turn again to him. This time it was not a quick prayer that we rattled off with no intention of returning to being faithful to him. Our sincerity was real, we were being genuine. We were desperate to recover and get clean. We had decided not to use any more, but it would take God and his strength to get us into recovery and to get us to stop using.

As Christians we need to know that when we invoke God's name, the Lord, by calling on him, he will hear our cry and listen to our prayer. He is able to judge our thoughts and the intents of our hearts to see if we are sincere or merely paying him lip service again. He has promised to answer us and be there for us. Even before we ask, he has already promised to forgive us our sins. Like any relationship, it takes time to get to know the other person. God promises that he will be there for us and that he we reveal himself to us more and more.

Dearest heavenly Father, we give you thanks for the love that you have lavishly shown to us. You were very patient with us while we lived in rebellion and used drugs. Thank you for being there for us when we turned away from our sins and called upon your holy name. Care for us as your children and lead us in our recovery journey so that we may live in faithfulness to you. This we ask in the name of your precious son, Jesus Christ our Savior and Lord. Amen

The Word of God Guides Us

**Your word is a lamp for my feet,
a light on my path.
Psalm 119:105**

There was an ancient practice that is still in use today regarding lighting our way in the dark of the night. Back then, and to this day, we have city streetlights that light up our roads and sidewalks. We supplement them when we drive our cars and we put our headlights on. If we are on a bicycle we can add a bright headlight to it. If we are walking we can also use a flashlight. Psalm 119's reference to a light for the path is like a streetlight that floods the general area with light. The psalm's reference to a lamp for our feet is like the headlights on our cars, bicycles, or a flashlight in our hands. The light to our paths is like a streetlight that lights the general way and gives us a long distance view to where we are going. The lamp to our feet gives us immediate and specific guidance to the things we might encounter such as a pothole or a bump in the road.

In active drug use we did not consider our future very well. We avoided thoughts that we might be arrested for drug use or dealing. We did not look at how we were jeopardizing our health or risking our financial security. We had become blind to the way we were living and offending others by our addictive character traits.

In recovery our eyes were opened again to what our life had become and more importantly, to what our lives could be. We relied on the experience of others who had been in recovery to help guide us in our new journey. As Christians we opened our Bibles and began again to live according to God's will for our lives. His Word became our guiding light both by day and by night.

Gracious God, thank you for coming to our rescue when we lived in bondage to drugs. Thank you for restoring our lives to fullness again. Lead us in all that we do and keep us in your care by day and by night. Help us to grow and become mature Christians and use us to bring you the glory that is due your name, through Christ our Lord. Amen

Our Purpose and Our Future

**For I know the plans I have for you, declares the Lord,
plans for welfare and not for evil, to give you a future and a hope.
Jeremiah 29:11**

Drug use has a way of shutting down our thinking and with it our thoughts about the future went by the wayside too. The exception to this was that we were only thinking about when we could get high again and where our next score would be coming from. This was a dangerous state of mind to be in. It caused many of us to act impulsively, dangerously, and even criminally.

Sometimes our motive for getting high again was because we had nothing else to look forward to in our lives. We had lost hope and no longer believed that we would be able to accomplish anything worthwhile in life. With that lost hope we had nothing to look forward to other than misery and more dashed dreams about what we wanted for ourselves in life. It was a downward spiral that didn't like to release its captives.

God had different plans for us, as addicts he had made a future for us that was good. First, he wanted to redeem us from our sins and active drug addiction. For some of us we might have been miraculously delivered from using. For others it meant going into treatment, out-patient, in-patient short-term or even long-term. We all needed help to work through the issues that led us to using in the first place. We needed God's help to recover from drug related character flaws and other terrible traits that we had come into. That you might say was our first priority in recovery.

God wants to rebuild, or build for the first time, a healthy and productive lifestyle for us to have. God wants us to hold down a job, maybe volunteer in a worthwhile organization, enjoy a home, family, having friends and having us pursuing some of our dreams. This was the life he had planned for us but drugs and addiction ruined it. In recovery, not only do we stop using, but we also get back the life that God meant for us to have.

God, just as you raised up from the dead your son also grant unto us the restoration of the lives you first had in store for us. This we pray in his name, Jesus Christ our Lord. Amen

All Plans Are Soft Until...

**Come now, you who say,
"Today or tomorrow we will go into such and such a town
and spend a year there and trade and make a profit"—
yet you do not know what tomorrow will bring.
What is your life?
For you are a mist that appears for
a little time and then vanishes.
Instead you ought to say,
"If the Lord wills,
we will live and do this or that."
James 4:13-15**

Someone once said, "If you want to hear God laugh, just make plans." For us in recovery we need to keep the temporary nature of this world in the forefront of our minds. Planning is good, but the future is uncertain. This passage from James, the brother of Jesus, guides us about how to think about our plans for the days ahead. His advice is that we always keep in mind that all plans are soft until confirmed according to God's will.

In recovery we do need to plan out our days, weeks, and months. Asking questions about how we will spend our time is wise and even necessary. Asking ourselves: how many meetings do we need to get to this week? That date is an anniversary of something difficult from my past, should we spend it with friends, go to a meeting or hibernate? We are on vacation then, should we find a meeting or two in that city to go to before we travel? We are newly clean, and we used to always get ripped by binging on Friday night and all day Saturday, what should we do instead? Planning how to spend our time helps us stay clean.

All this planning needs to be kept in perspective. Frequent or sudden changes in a rigidly managed lifestyle can be a trigger for us to use. Equally true too, much flexibility in a loosely structured lifestyle can also lead to relapse. Finding the balance is necessary. The question to ask is this, what do we need to do to keep from having a relapse and then planning around that.

Heavenly Father, help us to plan our days so that we may make the most of them. Guard our time so that it may be given to you for fulfilling your will in our lives. Through Christ Jesus our Lord we pray. Amen

Spiritual Practices: Our Safe Place

**You are a hiding place for me; you preserve me from trouble;
You surround me with shouts of deliverance.** *Selah*[68]
Psalm 32:7

There are times when we need to withdraw from everything that is going on in our lives and take a spiritual retreat. The reasons can be many, and as long as they are for good reasons who cares? Sometimes we feel overwhelmed; emotionally, mentally, physically, or spiritually. Our safe place offers us rest and security away from the demands of our active lives.

In our using in the past we retreated by getting high. Using drugs offered us anesthesia to numb our sense of shame and give us temporary relief from the memories and thoughts we wish we didn't have. It was a dangerous way of coping with life that ultimately put the problems we were running from back in front of us. When we did face our problems again they had multiplied which led us to into a repeating cycle of using and neglecting our responsibilities.

For us as Christians our safe place and times for retreats need to include the Lord rather than drugs. We can seclude in our homes, our bedrooms, or take a trip and rent a room. We should definitely include prayers, Christian music, relaxation exercises, maybe some incense or aroma therapy, art work like drawing, and reading from God's Word. Remember, even though we may be feeling very overwhelmed, these few things that we take the effort to include will be worth the extra effort. This is a time to still our minds and thoughts, rest our bodies, quiet our emotions, seek the Lord and find solace and comfort in him.

Heavenly Father, we long for your presence in our lives. You are our desire and our love for you grows daily. May we abide in you and grow in our relationships with you constantly. May we find all that we need in this life by your grace working in us. Bring us into your rest and refresh us in our weariness. This we ask through Christ our Lord. Amen

---

[68] Selah means to take a thoughtful pause and consider what you have just read before going on.

The Spiritual Life

**With my whole heart I seek you;
let me not wander from your commandments!
I have stored up your word in my heart,
that I might not sin against you.
Blessed are you, O LORD;
teach me your statutes!
Psalm 119:10-12**

    The spiritual life that we are inherently called to live began before the days of creation. God's plan for us in his creation was for us to be in a relationship with him first and foremost, then in relationships with others, and then in relationship with his creation. If we don't follow this model for our lives we can expect problems to come up in our lives related to it. This will continue until the spiritual balance is restored and God comes first in our lives again.

    God's Word was given to us to be a blessing in our lives. At one time or another we resented his Word because it was contrary to what we wanted to do with our lives or believe in our hearts and minds. The truth is that his Word is there for us so that we can, by following it, avoid countless problems in our lives. His Word also brings blessings to our lives. When others see that we are people with good moral standards, are people of integrity, who respect others and are true to our own word, they will trust us. Trust is basic to every relationship and from it healthy relationships in all areas of our lives can grow and flourish. Drugs worked to destroy what God wanted for us. In recovery we work to be restored and to grow into all that God has planned for us.

    Heavenly Father, you love us, each and every one of us in a special way. Thank you for your love that brings us into your blessings for this life. Be with us evermore and allow us to draw nearer to you through Christ our Lord in whose name we pray. Amen

Safe People

**Behold, a king will reign in righteousness,
and princes will rule in justice.
Each will be like a hiding place from the wind,
a shelter from the storm,
like streams of water in a dry place,
like the shade of a great rock in a weary land.
Isaiah 32:1-2**

When we were active in our addictions we hung out with some shady characters. As the saying goes, there is no honor among thieves. It is sad to say, but neither is there safety among addicts. As addicts we used people and loved to get high. We were not honest, we were liars, and sometimes we were thieves, and worse. One dealer sold his clients over a thousand dollars in rocks. That same week his clients ran out of money and could not afford groceries. So, the dealer spent sixty-five dollars at the store and got them some food. They thought he was a good person for helping them out in this way. The truth was extremely far from it, but in the twisted value system of addicts they saw it as a good thing. In recovery we need to disassociate from dealers and addicts alike. The scriptures says, "Do not be deceived: Bad company ruins good morals."[69]

In addiction we are vulnerable to being used and abused. In recovery we need to be on guard against falling into any of those situations in our recovery. The good news here is that there are safe people in this world who we can trust. These can include a mentor, a sponsor, a pastor, and other members in the recovery community. If you have a hunch that someone is not safe, go with your instincts, avoid them. Find friends and associates you like, and God willing, they will be good people. If not, dump them. If red flags come up keep them at a safe distance. A safe person will respect your boundaries. They will ask permission and accept it if you say "no". Surround yourself with these people, let them know you appreciate their friendship and why you do.

Dearest God, bring safe people into our lives so that we will have healthy relationships with others. Continue to work on us, make us safe people to be around as well. Keep us secure in our recoveries and help us to grow daily in you. This we pray through Christ Jesus our Lord. Amen

---

[69] 1 Corinthians 15:33

Resentments and Remembrance

**Put on then, as God's chosen ones, holy and beloved,
compassionate hearts, kindness, humility, meekness,
and patience, bearing with one another and,
if one has a complaint against another,
forgiving each other;
as the Lord has forgiven you,
so you also must forgive.
Colossians 3:12-13**

Hard as it might be to forgive others, and for some of us who were treated in absolutely criminal ways it can be extremely hard to do. Even still, we still need to work to forgive those who offended us and work through our woundedness. Unforgiveness is the place where resentments live and flourish in our lives. Resentments are giant landmines in addiction and recovery. When we come across them they can do much damage to our spiritual walk with the Lord and send us back into active addiction.

We need to know that the word *resent* simply means to *re-sense*, or to feel in that way all over again. The problem with this is that every time we recall our resentments, we relive those negative experiences again. In reliving them we rekindle the emotions we had with the event, and it keeps those horrible experiences alive and active in us. This leads to living in constant stress over them and acting with vigilance in all our interactions. Because of unforgiveness our view of life becomes biased by the skewing of our perceptions with prejudice.

Our recovery is made unstable by us holding onto events from our past with resentment. Their recollection can trigger a pity-party in us or give us a flimsy excuse for using again. There is a better way to live and deal with these difficult problems that we are holding onto as resentments. In order to get through this we need to deal with them in a healthy way, find healing from God and grow from the experience, rather than letting them sidetrack us over and over again.

For many of our past experiences we may need to enter into counseling with a professionally licensed Christian counselor. Drug and alcohol counselors are specifically trained to work with our kinds of problems. They can be extremely helpful because they understand how the disease works in our lives.

Among our many reservations as addicts we worry that if we heal from our past and forgive the offender we will make ourselves vulnerable to reinjury. Healing should bring us to a place where we can recall those memories by our own choosing and not have them intrusively coming up. Remembering them should not be nearly as painful as it was, while at the same time we are able to maintain healthy boundaries that provide a reasonable degree of safety for us. Moreover, we are able to live a life that is not constantly on high alert for new offenses of that kind.

Hard as it may be to imagine, in forgiving our offenders we need to consider Jesus' example of forgiving others. At his execution he forgave the ones who were nailing him to the cross. In his resurrection he bore no resentments towards his disciples, all of whom abandoned him in the garden at the time of his arrest. He has lead the way for us to forgive others and will abide with us closely as we intentionally journey towards healing in our spiritual walk.

Lord Jesus Christ, you readily forgave those who mistreated you. Help us to forgive those who have mistreated us. Bring healing to our wounded lives, restore our lives fully to us. Help us to find strength and security in you we pray. Amen

Easy Does It

Now as they went on their way, Jesus entered a village. And a woman named Martha welcomed him into her house. And she had a sister called Mary, who sat at the Lord's feet and listened to his teaching. But Martha was distracted with much serving. And she went up to him and said, "Lord, do you not care that my sister has left me to serve alone? Tell her then to help me." But the Lord answered her, "Martha, Martha, you are anxious and troubled about many things, but one thing is necessary. Mary has chosen the good portion, which will not be taken away from her."
Luke 10:38-42

Aren't we like one of these two at some time in our lives? Martha was a perfectionist who set her standards too high. She wanted to be an ideal hostess by providing an abundance of hospitality. In their culture hospitality was a necessity. Even still, Mary was listening at Jesus' feet. Martha went to her honored guest and assumed he would agree with her. Jesus responded with a term of endearment saying her name twice, "Martha, Martha." Our Lord let her know that she was troubling herself too much. Being the perfect hostess was not necessary. For as important as hospitality was in their culture the most important thing there was seen in what Mary was doing.

For us in recovery from our addictions we can learn from this story. When we set our standards too high, we also see that soon enough we cannot live up to them. Our reaction could be to see ourselves as some sort of failure. If being that good is not something we can do, then we might be tempted to say to ourselves, "What else matters? What a letdown, I need a pick me up, I'm going to get high." What we need to do for our recovery is to have and maintain an attitude of *easy does it*. We don't need to be uptight or perfectionistic in this fallen world. We need to be simply fine with letting good enough be just that, good enough.

Heavenly Father, guide us in all that we set out to do. Help us to be realistic in the expectations we put on ourselves and on others. May we be ready to accept things even though they may not be as good as we had hoped for. This we ask through Christ our Lord. Amen

An Intervention

My brothers, if anyone among you wanders from the truth and someone brings him back, let him know that whoever brings back a sinner from his wandering will save his soul from death and will cover a multitude of sins.
James 5:19-20

Perhaps we began our journey in recovery because a caring person had a love filled heart to heart talk with us, or a group of family and friends met with us. There may come a time when we will need to initiate such actions or we are asked to be part of an intervention. This is part of the fellowship we share in both as an addict in recovery and as a Christian.

Unless there is a mature Christian who is very experienced at interventions among those involved it is best to ask for help from a licensed professional in the field of drug and alcohol treatment. Those selected for the task need to be people who can objectively and with love in their hearts share in a nonjudgmental way how the person's drug use has adversely affected them. Anyone who might fall short of that could by their bias sabotage the intervention.

The group will need to meet in advance of the intervention, perhaps several times to prepare and to have the time to research the things they will need to know. There needs to be a prearranged appointment for the person to be professionally evaluated for a diagnosis of chemical dependency. Also, it is best to have been in contact with at least one treatment center that can meet the specific needs of the addict.

In a preparatory meeting appoint one person to be in charge of communicating to the all the members things like times and places where the group will meet. One member of the group should be able to give clear instructions to everyone about things like the nature of the disease. This includes the highly developed sense of denial regarding the disease that is universal among addicts. Everyone needs to know that drug use alters the way the brain functions and that their thinking is twisted because of it. All members should share their experiences with regards to the addict's behavior and drug use. Shedding light on the secrecy that has existed will help for the intervention to have the desired effects.

Everyone should make notes or write out a manuscript of what they want to share. Sharing about specific times and incidences is necessary. Share how the addicts behavior negatively impacted your life in very specific terms. Use "I" statement, such as "I feared for my life when you drove me home under the influence. Your driving was extremely dangerous as you ran stop signs and red lights." It works best to rehearse what you will say with the others and get their help on revisions.

The location for the meeting should be a familiar one where the addict will be comfortable. The meeting should not take longer than an hour to an hour and a half at the longest. The addict may react adversely to the meeting and become verbally abusive. Be prepared to respond without taking the insults personally. They may even react severely and if they make physical threats or act out violently call 911 immediately.

The addict at some time may ask you what you want them to do. It is best though if they decide for themselves to get into treatment rather than go because you asked them to. Even if they do not accept your challenge to go into treatment for themselves, you will have planted the seeds that will hopefully take root before too long.

Heavenly Father, through Christ our Lord we come before your throne to pray and intercede for those addicts still using drugs, for those who we personally know and for those unknown to us but personally known to you. We ask that you intervein in their lives. Save them from their suffering and the bondage of addiction. Deliver them from the clutches of the devil's power and deliver them into the glorious Kingdom of your son, Christ our Lord. In your love reach out and by your Holy Spirit speak to their hearts, calling on them to seek the help they need. Bring Christians in recovery into their lives who will share with them how you freed them from their drug use. Provide places of treatment for all in need, provide sober houses, 12-step meetings, and sponsors to aid them in their journey toward recovery. This we pray with all earnestness and fervency, through Christ our Lord. Amen

The Ten Commandments
From Martin Luther's Small Catechism

I am the Lord your God.

The First Commandment Thou shalt have no other gods.
What does this mean?
Answer: We should fear, love, and trust in God above all things.

The Second Commandment. Thou shalt not take the name of the Lord, thy God, in vain.
What does this mean?
Answer: We should fear and love God that we may not curse, swear, use witchcraft, lie, or deceive by His name, but call upon it in every trouble, pray, praise, and give thanks.

The Third Commandment.
Thou shalt sanctify the holy-day.
What does this mean?
Answer: We should fear and love God that we may not despise preaching and His Word, but hold it sacred, and gladly hear and learn it.

The Fourth Commandment.
Thou shalt honor thy father and thy mother that it may be well with thee and thou mayest live long upon the earth.
What does this mean?
Answer: We should fear and love God that we may not despise nor anger our parents and masters, but give them honor, serve, obey, and hold them in love and esteem.

The Fifth Commandment.
Thou shalt not kill.
What does this mean?

Answer: We should fear and love God that we may not hurt nor harm our neighbor in his body, but help and befriend him in every bodily need.

The Sixth Commandment.
Thou shalt not commit adultery.
What does this mean?
Answer: We should fear and love God that we may lead a chaste and decent life in words and deeds, and each love and honor his spouse.

The Seventh Commandment.
Thou shalt not steal.
What does this mean?
Answer: We should fear and love God that we may not take our neighbor's money or property, nor get them by false ware or dealing, but help him to improve and protect his property and business.

The Eighth Commandment.
Thou shalt not bear false witness against thy neighbor.
What does this mean?
Answer: We should fear and love God that we may not deceitfully belie, betray, slander, or defame our neighbor, but defend him, speak well of him, and put the best construction on everything.

The Ninth Commandment.
Thou shalt not covet thy neighbor's house.
What does this mean?
Answer: We should fear and love God that we may not craftily seek to get our neighbor's inheritance or house, and obtain it by a show of right, etc., but help and be of service to him in keeping it.

The Tenth Commandment.
Thou shalt not covet thy neighbor's wife, nor his man-servant, nor his maid-servant, nor his cattle, nor anything that is his.
What does this mean?
Answer: We should fear and love God that we may not estrange, force, or entice away our neighbor's wife, servants, or cattle, but urge them to stay and do their duty.

What Does God Say of All These Commandments?
Answer: He says thus: I the Lord, thy God, am a jealous God, visiting the iniquity of the fathers upon the children unto the third and fourth generation of them that hate Me, and showing mercy unto thousands of them that love Me and keep My commandments.
What does this mean?
Answer: God threatens to punish all that transgress these commandments. Therefore we should dread His wrath and not act contrary to these commandments. But He promises grace and every blessing to all that keep these commandments. Therefore we should also love and trust in Him, and gladly do according to His commandments.[70]

---

[70] https://en.wikisource.org/wiki/Luther%27s_Small_Catechism

Dearest Heavenly Father, by your Word to us we know that we are sinners deserving only eternal punishment. We have failed to be faithful to you. We have sinned and sinned grievously against you and against others. We turn to you seeking to be strengthened in our repentance and given grace for the forgiveness of our sins for your son's sake. Strengthen us for our journey and empower us to live faithfully to you and all your commandments. This we most humbly pray in the name of your beloved son, Christ Jesus our Lord and Savior. Amen

**Let the word of Christ dwell in you richly, teaching and admonishing one another in all wisdom, singing psalms and hymns and spiritual songs, with thankfulness in your hearts to God.
Colossians 3:16**

There are certain spiritual songs and hymns that are of particular value to us in recovery. Their words and phrases seem especially meaningful to us and all that we must endure as addicts in recovery. Take time to find the tune on a CD or the internet and sing it aloud.

How Firm a Foundation, Ye Saints of the Lord

How firm a foundation, ye saints of the Lord, is laid for your faith in His excellent word! What more can He say than to you He hath said, to you who for refuge to Jesus have fled?

Fear not, I am with thee, O be not dismayed, for I am thy God, and will still give thee aid; I'll strengthen thee, help thee, and cause thee to stand, upheld by My righteous, omnipotent hand.

When through the deep waters I call thee to go, the rivers of sorrow shall not overflow; For I will be with thee, thy troubles to bless, and sanctify to thee thy deepest distress.

When through fiery trials thy pathway shall lie, my grace, all sufficient, shall be thy supply; The flame shall not hurt thee; I only design thy dross to consume, and thy gold to refine.

E'en down to old age all My people shall prove my sovereign, eternal, unchangeable love; And then, when grey hairs shall their temples adorn, like lambs they shall still in My bosom be borne.

The soul that on Jesus hath leaned for repose, I will not, I will not desert to his foes; That soul, though all hell should endeavor to shake, I'll never, no, never, no, never forsake!

Published 1787 by John Rippon

Heavenly Father, bless our recovery with this hymn. Help their words and the meaning they hold to ring in our hearts throughout the day. In Jesus name. Amen

Fellowship

A Song of Ascents. Of David.
Behold, how good and pleasant it is when brothers dwell in unity!
It is like the precious oil on the head, running down on the beard,
on the beard of Aaron, running down on the collar of his robes!
It is like the dew of Hermon, which falls on the mountains of Zion!
For there the LORD has commanded the blessing, life forevermore.
Psalm 133

In our addictions we shared getting high with others. It was an unhealthy relationship for that reason alone. God delivered us from that and brought us into the fellowship of the church. Gathering for fellowship is meant to be a blessing. In the days of the early church Christians met together and shared in the breaking of bread, meaning they ate meals and spent time together.[71]

There is a difference between having friends and having Christian friends. We call our interactions with Christian friends, *fellowship*. This comes from the Greek language of the New Testament. It is the word *koinonia*, which means having things in common. Christian friendship has a certain special quality, which is the addition of the Holy Spirit that dwells in us all. Even Jesus referred to himself as being intimately involved with us together saying, "For where two or three are gathered in my name, there am I among them."[72] This is not to say that we will never have issues with other Christians. Hopefully this does means that when those problems arise they are simpler, fewer, and farther in between, and easily resolved. We also hope that because of our common faith that we will be able to live peacefully with each other in spite of our differences.

Heavenly Father, you delivered us out of darkness and brought us into the fellowship of your people. Bless us all as we live and share our lives with each other. In Jesus' name. Amen

---

[71] Acts 2:42, 48
[72] Matthew 18:20

We're in a Marathon Not a Sprint

**Do you not know that in a race all the runners run,
but only one receives the prize?
So run that you may obtain it.
Every athlete exercises self-control in all things.
They do it to receive a perishable wreath, but we an imperishable.
So I do not run aimlessly; I do not box as one beating the air.
But I discipline my body and keep it under control,
lest after preaching to others I myself should be disqualified.
1 Corinthians 9:24-27**

An elderly woman was being treated for emphysema brought on by decades of tobacco abuse. Her physical conditioning had slipped to the point that she was too weak to walk. She was slowly getting stronger with physical therapy. Finally she was able to go outside for a short walk. The therapists encouraged her and when she had gone a short distance without assistance she was allowed to sit down and rest. They praised her for her achievement and she felt great about it. Then she told them how much she would enjoy having a cigarette now that she was outside.

Too often as addicts in recovery we feel great about having some clean time and we reward ourselves with getting high. As a result we fall back into active using. We can easily get cocky and falsely believe that we can control our use this time. We want to reward ourselves for clean time and rightly so. The problem is that sometimes we don't think far enough ahead about what would be a proper reward. A reward for good behavior does not include behaving badly.

In recovery we need to always keep in the forefront of our thoughts that we are addicts in recovery and we are in it for the long-haul. We need to remind ourselves that when we live *one day at a time*, each day we reset the clock back to day one, because we do best living just one day at a time.

Heavenly Father, help us to be ever mindful of our recovery and guide us to do nothing to jeopardize it. Let us live as disciples of your son Jesus and empower us to follow his teachings. May we grow daily, each day, one day at a time. This we ask in his name, Christ our Lord. Amen

What Must I Know as a Christian

But in your hearts honor Christ the Lord as holy, always being prepared to make a defense to anyone who asks you for a reason for the hope that is in you; yet do it with gentleness and respect.
1 Peter 3:15

In the dark ages and into the days of the renaissance most Christians had no idea what the basic beliefs of our faith were. This was a spiritually dangerous state to be in. These problems continue to this day despite the availability of Bibles and Christian books for us to read. As people of faith and in recovery we need to know the basic most elements of our faith. To that we need to add those things that are specific to us as addicts in recovery. It was Martin Luther who wrote out the following explanations of the Apostles Creed so that everyone in his day could have this foundation for their faith to rest secure on.

The First Article: Of Creation

I believe in God the Father Almighty, Maker of heaven and earth.

> What does this mean?
> Answer: I believe that God has made me and all creatures; that He has given me my body and soul, eyes, ears, and all my members, my reason, and all my senses, and still takes care of them, he also gives me clothing and shoes, food and drink, house and home, wife and children, land, animals and all that I have; He richly and daily provides me with all that I need to support this body and life, protects me from all danger, and guards me and defends me from all evil; and all this he does out of fatherly, divine goodness and mercy, without any merit or worthiness in me; for all this it is my duty to thank, praise, serve and obey him.

The Second Article: Of Redemption

And in Jesus Christ, His only Son, our Lord; who was conceived by the Holy Ghost, born of the Virgin Mary; suffered under Pontius Pilate, was crucified, dead, and buried; He descended into hell; the third day He rose again from the dead; He ascended into heaven, and sitteth on the right hand of God the Father Almighty; from thence He shall come to judge the quick and the dead.

What does this mean?
Answer: I believe that Jesus Christ, true God, begotten of the Father from eternity, and also true man, born of the Virgin Mary, is my Lord, who has redeemed me, a lost and condemned creature, purchased and won me from all sins, from death, and from the power of the devil, not with gold or silver, but with His holy, precious blood and with His innocent suffering and death, in order that I may be [wholly] His own, and live under Him in His kingdom, and serve Him in everlasting righteousness, innocence, and blessedness, even as He is risen from the dead, lives and reigns to all eternity. This is most certainly true.

The Third Article: Of Sanctification

I believe in the Holy Ghost; one holy Christian Church, the communion of saints; the forgiveness of sins; the resurrection of the body; and the life everlasting. Amen.

What does this mean?
Answer: I believe that I cannot by my own reason or strength believe in Jesus Christ, my Lord, or come to Him; but the Holy Ghost has called me by the Gospel, enlightened me with His gifts, sanctified and kept me in the true faith; even as He calls, gathers, enlightens, and sanctifies the whole Christian Church on earth, and keeps it with Jesus Christ in the one true faith; in which Christian Church He forgives daily and richly all sins to me and all believers, and at the last day will raise up me and all the dead, and will give to me and to all believers in Christ everlasting life. This is most certainly true.[73]

Heavenly Father, grant to us knowledge of our faith that we might know and be secure in those things essential to our spirituality. Give us wisdom to see your design in all of life so that we may know your will and live it out in our lives day by day. Most of all empower us by your Holy Spirit so that we may live according to your Word as disciples of our Master, in whose name we pray, Jesus Christ. Amen

---

[73] https://en.wikisource.org/wiki/Luther%27s_Small_Catechism

Surrender

**Jesus said to Simon Peter,
"Simon, son of John, do you love me more than these?"
He said to him, "Yes, Lord; you know that I love you.
John 21:15**

Following his resurrection Jesus appeared multiple times to his disciples. During that time Peter had returned to his former career as a commercial fisherman. In this instance Jesus was with Peter and his fishing companions were nearby. Jesus challenged his loyalty by asking Peter if he loved his Lord more than anyone else. Peter became irritated with Jesus' questioning, but he also failed to say that he loved the Lord more than everyone else in his life. Peter's answer was merely affirming that he loved Jesus but not that he loved him more than everyone else.

In our using days we loved our drugs. In our addiction we loved drugs a lot, and while we may have hated what they were doing to our lives, we were solely devoted to them. We loved the high they gave us and even when the high was no longer all that great, we still remained devoted.

Now we are Christians in recovery and for us to be successful at it, we cannot be like Peter was during that time in his life. We need to love our Lord more than everyone else, as well as more than everything else. This love needs to be so consuming that there is no room left for even occasional drug use. We need to love our Lord so that all that we do, and think, and believe in life revolves around our love relationship with him.

Yes, Lord Jesus, we love you more than all these. We love you more than all that this world can offer to us, or tempt us with. We love you more than using, we love you because you first loved us and gave yourself fully for us. Amen

Spiritual Fathers and Mothers

**I do not write these things to make you ashamed,
but to admonish you as my beloved children.
For though you have countless guides in Christ,
you do not have many fathers.
For I became your father in Christ Jesus through
the gospel. I urge you, then, be imitators of me.
1 Corinthians 4:14-16**

In life as we grow and become adults our own families become less influential in our lives. We move out and we see them less often. New people come into our lives and take the place of our siblings and parents and they become the regular figures in our lives who are there for us day by day. In recovery and in our spiritual walk, it is a good idea to have a relationship with a mature figure who has an established walk with the Lord that can be a spiritual father or mother to us.

In recovery, in Christ, we have many individuals who are spiritually significant to us. Among them should be included our pastor or priest, and our sponsor or mentor. These people are something of a spiritual father, or mother to us. They may take us under their wings and help us in our lives. Their role is especially vital to us in maintaining our recovery and aiding us in a growth-oriented lifestyle. Our pastor is there for us spiritually, has been called by God into public ministry and has been recognized in the church where they serve. Our sponsor or mentor is someone who has been stable in their own recovery from addiction for several years at a minimum, say three to five to be on the safe-side. Anything less than that could put us at risk. Unless what we are going through is a major crisis, the pastor may not appreciate being called in the middle of the night, so speak to them about that first. Your sponsor is a person who should be okay with middle of the night calls if you are struggling, especially if you are at risk of a relapse.

Lord Jesus, you are with us always. Give us mature leaders who can guide us in our lives. May their experience be beneficial to us. Help us to bond with our spiritual fathers and mothers, and our sponsors so that we can be strengthened in our recoveries. Amen

Making Amends

**[Jesus said,] So if you are offering your gift at the altar and there remember that your brother has something against you,
leave your gift there before the altar and go.
First be reconciled to your brother,
and then come and offer your gift.
Matthew 5:23-24**

Asking for forgiveness can be difficult to begin with. For us as addicts it can feel like a near death experience until we become accustomed to it. There are reasons for that. As addicts we have at our core very tender and sensitive hearts. There may be many layers of false fronts that we put up to cover over it, but it is universal, we are tender at the core. It is hard for us to admit that we are not perfect, that we errored, made a mistake, or were wrong. To do that opens us up to vulnerability and we fear being further wounded. We fear rejection, we fear that they will not forgive us, we fear they will exploit our admission to imperfection. We are in such a wounded state that we fear any further injury that we might open ourselves up to because it will only further overwhelm us. In recovery we are empowered by God to do the right things and making amends is one of them.

In making amends we try to restore not only the relationship but also to repay the other for their losses. Whether it be money, property, social standing, or something else, we try to right the wrong that we brought to them. If we cannot repay them in kind at the time we can still make the effort and pledge to them that we will do what we can to right the wrong regardless of whether they forgive us or not.

Forgiving God, you sent your son to earth to die for the forgiveness of our sins. May his example be our guide and motivation to seek forgiveness from all those who we have hurt and offended. Give us courage to thoroughly do this task in life and give us grace to overcome our reluctance. This we ask through our precious Lord and Savior's name, Jesus Christ. Amen

Offering Forgiveness

And forgive us our debts, as we also have forgiven our debtors.
Matthew 6:12

When someone comes to us seeking our forgiveness this can be a hard thing to give to them. As addicts we may have liked to be vindictive, to bear grudges and even allowed our emotions to get stirred up over any offense. We may call our reaction righteous indignation, meaning that we have a right to it and can act on it with impunity. Admitting that someone was able to hurt us can also be hard to admit to. Our exterior image that we portray to others, as someone who is secure because we have our act together, could be compromised. Offering forgiveness may show that we are not emotionally untouchable, and we might have suffered. We may be tempted to make light of it and say it was nothing when it really was something hurtful.

At the very least, the person coming to us is acting in humility and we need to recognize that. They are hoping to receive our forgiveness. They are hoping to bring healing to our wounds, to restore us and help us by their actions.

Scripturally, we know that our sins have been forgiven, and that they were great offenses to God. He forgave us and at great cost. That is a strong argument for us not to withhold our forgiveness to others. Even still, as addicts while we know that it makes all the sense in the world, we are not always ready or willing to forgive others.

Some offenses against us may be profoundly serious. Someone may have committed crimes against us. We may not be ready to offer them forgiveness in these serious situation. We may need time and with its passing to seek professional counseling for more serious injuries we have received. In some cases, forgiveness may only come late in life after many years of being in recovery. Sometimes we need to hear and be reassured that we can forgive someone of the greatest offense without letting ourselves become vulnerable to them again. Even if they do not come to us and ask to be forgiven, we can forgive them.

Dearest God, help us to forgive others as you have forgiven us. In Jesus' name. Amen

Introspection

But be doers of the word, and not hearers only, deceiving yourselves. For if anyone is a hearer of the word and not a doer, he is like a man who looks intently at his natural face in a mirror. For he looks at himself and goes away and at once forgets what he was like.
James 1:22-24

In active addiction we lost touch with ourselves. The drugs had that power over us. They overrode our own emotions and twisted our thoughts. They replaced our feelings with other powerful sensations and confused reality in our minds. This was especially true when our reasons for using was to numb our feelings and trying to create an amnesia to block intrusive memories of images, thoughts, and feelings that we desperately wanted to forget but could not escape.

Frequently in addiction we were cut off from family and friends because of our behavior. We may have wondered whatever did we do to offend them? As addicts we had acted terribly towards them and in our sickness we were blinded to our own behavior and did not see what we had done. Further, while we were the one offending others, we took on the role of being the victim, and treated others as if they were the offenders. This terrible role reversal we played out was part of our illness of addiction.

As we heal in recovery there are opportunities to correct many of these problems. As James wrote, we should not be like the person who looks at himself in a mirror but forgets what he has been like. We should look introspectively at ourselves and then take corrective actions. These are the actions of steps four through nine in the NA program. These are the actions that will lead to us to reconnecting with our own emotions and actions, and bring healing where we have offended others in our time of using.

Heavenly Father, bring healing to our lives for the damage our drug use brought. Turn our hearts so that we can see ourselves in true light and by your grace help us to change for the better. Help us to bring healing to those we offended. Through Christ our Lord we ask. Amen

Spiritual Character Traits

But the fruit of the Spirit is love, joy, peace, patience, kindness, goodness, faithfulness, gentleness, self-control; against such things there is no law.
Galatians 5:22-23

Spiritual Character Traits
The Fruit of the Spirit: Love

This love that is at the beginning of the list is a unique love. It is the New Testament Greek word *agape*. This is the most special love that God has for us. It is the highest form of love that there is. The way that we see this love lived out in God's relationship with us is in the life of his son. Even though we had offended God by our sinful living, he found a way to forgive us by letting his beloved son's life be sacrificed for our redemption. Even though we sinned, and sinned grievously, our heavenly Father bore no ill-will against us, but worked for our best good out of his benevolent agape love for us.

God pours out this love of his upon us in great abundance, so much so that it overflows from our hearts. What love we can generate is conditional on our meager resources and further limited by our ability to show it to others. The love of God in our lives is one that goes beyond our finite ability to generate love. It also goes beyond our ability to reach out to others and share it with them. It is God's special love, working through us and reaching out to others.

Heavenly Father, thank you for your special love that you bear for us. Thank you that in your love you found a way to redeem us from our sins. Thank you that you share your love with us in such abundance that it overflows from our hearts and makes its way to others as well. Though Christ our Lord we pray. Amen

Spiritual Character Traits
The Fruit of the Spirit: Joy

We don't hear or use this word joy that often. Perhaps it is poorly understood. We like to use the word happy, which is loosely related. Happy is from the word *happenstance*. It means that if our circumstances in life are favorable, then we feel good about it, or we are happy. The problem with being happy is that the good feeling goes away when our circumstances are not favorable. Joy, as a fruit of the Spirit of God, is not that way. Joy is not dependent on our circumstances at all. We can have joy in our hearts when our lives are in ruin. That is because the source of our joy is God, not this world and the circumstances we find ourselves in. Joy itself can be described as having gladness in our hearts, and being delighted regardless of our circumstances.

In our drug using days we relied on drugs to control our moods. That was dangerous because they fouled up our brain chemistry. We had very little tolerance for feeling down, or feeling anxious. The drugs brought us up emotionally when our circumstances were bad. We were not motivated to resolve our problems in life, instead we got a quick fix and we were falsely made to feel better. We had neither joy or happiness, all we had were problems and addiction.

In recovery our brain's chemistry slowly returned to normal again. We learned that we could tolerate life's difficulties without getting high anymore. As we lived with an active faith we found joy in our relationship with God and relied on his help through prayer. He gave us joy in our relationship through the forgiveness that was ours because of the death of his son for our sins. We found joy in our hearts because we knew without a doubt that God loves us, will care for us, and will carry us through all of life's trials. We found that this joy was there in the good times, and in the bad times, and in those times we found the comfort we needed to weather the storms of life.

Dearest God, you have sent joy into our hearts and filled us with your love. You have made us to love our lives again. Sustain us in our recoveries, uplift us in your strength, and fill us ever more with joy in all of life's circumstances. May the love we have for you overflow in our hearts and may glory be given to your most holy and precious name, through Christ our Lord. Amen

Spiritual Character Traits
The Fruit of the Spirit: Peace

    For the Christian in the first few centuries there was not much peace, instead there was persecution. Nevertheless, there was a certain peace that ruled and reigned in their lives. It was a stout peace that was resilient. It defied being wore down by both a constant barrage of harassment and by the assault of massively unsettling events in life. It was not that those first century Christians were untouched by their difficulties or callous to them, they were deeply moved in every way. For them and for us in any kind of similar situation, as Christians we are upheld by the Lord God Almighty.

    Jesus said he would not leave us as abandoned orphans, but that he would send us the Holy Spirit to be near to us and to help us in all of our needs.[74] There are events in life that are traumatic, that are overwhelming, and that will bring us to our knees. We live in a fallen world and we are subjected to the greatest of difficulties at times. It is when we put our trust in God and pray to him that he carries us through. Because of this we can have peace not just in the absence of trials and temptations, but in the midst of the greatest of difficulties. We cannot generate this kind of peace ourselves, we have no such resources and no such strength. God alone can bring us this kind of peace.

    And what is this peace? It is a calm and gentle assurance because we have the inward calming presence of God's Holy Spirit living inside. We have this peace because God shares in our suffering through the suffering of his son. We know that he will never leave us or forsake us.

    Heavenly Father, thank you for your love for us. Thank you for the gift of your peace in our lives. We pray that you will help us to abide in this special peace daily and help us to share your peace with others. This we ask in the name of the one who died and rose, Christ Jesus our Lord. Amen

---

[74] John 14:16-18

Spiritual Character Traits
The Fruit of the Spirit: Patience

In our lives, prior to drug use, many of us suffered with impulsive behaviors. In some of us it was related to Attention Deficit Disorder/Attention Deficit, Hyperactivity Disorder (ADD/ADHD). We acted first, and thought second, if we thought about it at all. This got us into trouble in school, and on and off the job. This behavior of impulsiveness put us at risk for taking dangerous actions, such as using drugs without forethought. Worse, because of impulsiveness, we never learned from the consequences of our actions.

In leading the spiritual life, the conditions existed so that we could change by the grace of God. We were focused on pleasing God rather than ourselves. We were newly able to be sensitive to our actions and how we affected others. We prayed for God's help in how we led our lives and God answered our prayers and wonderful changes followed.

Patience, sometimes called long-suffering, can be a natural quality that we have, or it can come to us from God as well. It can be exceedingly difficult for us to wait for something, especially if we are in some kind of pain, such as physical or emotional pain. Pain has a way of controlling us so that we urgently seek immediate relief, it is a survival instinct. When we are in pain, we don't think about the future, our thoughts are focused on the here and now, and getting relief.

Living in Christ we know that he was long-suffering in his passion, as he was whipped and tortured, and then when he suffered death on the cross. As Christians we are called to share in his suffering and death. Because of this, God gives us the grace to endure the difficulties that come our way with patience. In our limited resources for living we could not endure as he did. As we live for him and rely fully on him, we learn that his grace is sufficient for us in all things.

Jesus, dear Savior, you endured the pain of crucifixion for the joy set before you. Through your suffering and death we are forgiven our sins. Help us in our times of suffering, help us in our impatience, to rely not on ourselves but on you and your strength. Amen

Spiritual Character Traits
But the fruit of the Spirit is: Kindness

Fred Rogers from the Mr. Roger's Neighborhood television series said, "There are three ways to ultimate success:

The first way is to be kind.
The second way is to be kind.
The third way is to be kind."

Mr. Rogers was also a Methodist minister. Right he was about the importance of kindness. His show ran for thirty-three years and it was filled with examples of his kindness towards others. His calming and always relaxed voice gently invited everyone to share in his kind and neighborly ways.

Many of us in addictions have been abused, some of us were severely abused. Life was unkind to us, people were unkind to us, and in our addictions we were unkind to ourselves and to others as well. We didn't care about others unless it was so that we could get drugs and get high on them.

In our recovery we are encouraged to humbly ask God to remove our defects of character. That is because just as we cannot quit using without his help, neither can we stop acting like addicts in all those ways without his help again.

The kindness that is a spiritual character trait is one that comes from God. It is able to overcome the harsh realities that we have faced and can keep on being kind a thousand times over. The Holy Spirit is the one that empowers us to have this unlimited kindness in our hearts. It is by God's unlimited grace that we can show it to others who are treating us with the utmost disrespect.

God of all kindness and grace, by your mercy you befriended us and brought us into a better lifestyle. Help us to live in you and may your kindness overflow in our lives to others so that they may see your good works in us and give you glory. Through Christ our Lord. Amen

Comfort

Comfort, comfort my people, says your God.
Speak tenderly to Jerusalem,
and cry to her that her warfare is ended,
that her iniquity is pardoned.
Isaiah 40:1-2

Who knows what percentage of us used drugs to kill the pain of traumatic memories? Who among us knew that we used drugs to mask the fear of God because of our sins? Most, perhaps all of us as addicts used because of distress of one kind or another in our lives. Pain and suffering, sorrow and even torment were among our daily experiences. Who wouldn't want to get relief from that? Life does not always turn out right and there are many injustices that go on without resolution. For some of us, we had a low threshold for these difficulties. For some of us we had a high threshold for suffering and so we did little about it until it pushed us off into the deep end of things and we cracked.

The pursuit of comfort is very much a prime motive in all of our lives. It goes way back to the first century of time when Adam and Eve were in the Garden of Eden. They wanted to have the power that comes from knowing good and evil. They believed that with this knowledge they could control the good things that would then come their way. We all know it did not work out that way.

Comfort can come our way in life without the use of drugs. From this text from the Prophet Isaiah, comfort was being promised because the coming of the Savior Christ our Lord was being foretold. The greatest comfort we can have is in knowing that our sins have been forgiven us by God through his son's redeeming death on the cross. Comfort can come to us because we have the promise of our Savior, that he is with us, and will never leave us or forsake us.[75]

Loving God, you alone are our comfort and security. May we always look to you for these needs and rest peacefully in your gracious care for our lives. Through Jesus Christ our Lord. Amen

---

[75] Hebrews 13:5

The Revealed Truth

**The secret things belong to the Lord our God,
but the things that are revealed belong
to us and to our children forever,
that we may do all the words of this law.
Deuteronomy 29:29**

There are spiritual things in life that are a mystery to us and always will be, at least until we get to heaven where we hope they will be revealed. Other things are spiritual mysteries to us now, but over the course of our lifetimes they will be made known to us. Spiritual mysteries are always exciting to us. Some of them we know and understand in part, but the greater part of it is veiled to our minds. In the case of some of these mysteries we have wondered and searched the Scriptures to understand it. We have waited on the Lord, asked others about their understanding, and over time the fullness of the mystery was revealed to us and how exciting that was.

Some secularists have told us that we need to study every religion there is to find the truth. That is this world's way of it. As people of faith we believe that God has revealed the truth to us, in the Word, which is the Holy Scriptures of the Bible. We accept their revelation as true, not because we have studied all the religions of the world and came to a logical conclusion about it. We accept them by faith because of the witness of God's Spirit speaking to our spirit about the truth of his Word.[76]

God has revealed himself to us through the words of the prophets and apostles as recorded in the Bible. However, the most complete revelation of God our Father comes to us in the very life of his only begotten son, Jesus Christ our Lord, who gave himself for the forgiveness of our sins.

Thank you God for revealing yourself to us in the life of your son Jesus of Nazareth. Thank you for bringing us into a covenant relationship with you. May we be faithful to you to live as true disciples of Christ, to love you first in our lives and bring glory to you. In Jesus name. Amen

---

[76] Romans 8:16

Peel an Onion, There's Lots of Layers

**The heart is deceitful above all things, and desperately sick;
who can understand it?
"I the Lord search the heart and test the mind,
to give every man according to his ways,
according to the fruit of his deeds."
Jeremiah 17:9-10**

There is this saying, *peel an onion, there's lots of layers*. In our case as addicts in recovery it might be more accurate to talk about peeling back the layers of our hearts. When we do this we need to be ready to see the worst of ourselves, and given our addiction, it can get pretty bad. According to the Prophet Jeremiah, the state our hearts, all of them, is not good. We have this moral and spiritual sickness and the only cure is in the hands of our God.

In recovery we learned about ourselves in addiction. We learned about our highly developed trait of denial. We worked hard to dismantle it too. We learned how to think introspectively and to self-examine our thoughts and emotions. We worked to unravel the tangled mess of our past. We dealt with memories of things we had not cared about due to the callousness of our hearts. In recovery we came to terms with things about our lives and our past that were difficult to make amends for. We had lied, stole, and cheated others. We had been abusive to others in multiple ways. As time passed, we were able to admit to ourselves what terrible things we had committed. As more time passed we were able to admit to others the nature of the wrongs we had committed. When we could we made things right between ourselves and those we had hurt.

In our relationship with God we came to find that just as he accepted and forgave us we could be confident that he would always love us. This gave us the assurance that no matter what we had done we could face up to it, admit to it and allow him to change our flawed character traits.

Gracious God in heaven, thank you for the hope we have in you. By the example of your beloved son we are encouraged daily and want to be more and more like him in all our affairs. By your Holy Spirit work changes in us so that we may live according to your Holy Word in all that we do and say, through Christ our Lord. Amen

The Theology of the Cross

That I may know him and the power of his resurrection, and may share his sufferings, becoming like him in his death.
Philippians 3:10

There is no resurrection without Jesus' crucifixion, and without his suffering there is no death. The Apostle Paul asked to share in his suffering and death so that he could come to know the power of his resurrection. In examining our Lord's suffering and death we are reminded that he suffered in our place. The same is true about his death, he died for us and in our place. His passion and our suffering are intricately tied together and we need to be intricately tied to his death.

This is the basis for our theology, which is our understanding of who God and his son are. It is called *the theology of the cross*. We understand that God suffered for us and with us in the life of Jesus. In our recovery we learned that we cannot long avoid the difficulties of life. The past for many of us holds great trauma. We would rather not revisit it, but we learned that we cannot get around it as we move forward in life. We must somehow find the courage to go through it, again, deal with it, relive it, and hopefully heal from it this time. To leave the wounds of the past still open and festering can leave us wide open for a relapse into our former way of living as addicts.

In faith we come to mystically share in the suffering of our Lord. We come to find his presence in our lives as we look to him in our suffering. We know that because of him we do not suffer alone, but find that God is intimately there with us.

In his resurrection we are reminded that when he appeared to his disciples he showed them his wounded hands and side. We are reminded that Thomas was invited to examine the wounds and place his hand into his wounded side. Somehow, in the mystery of Jesus' appearance in the upper room, they realized that his wounds were no longer painful to him and that he held no ill feelings towards them for abandoning him in the garden. By believing in this about our Lord we find that we too can come to a place with him where our wounds are also healed.

Father, from heaven your endured our Lords' suffering and death. Help us to also endure with him and to be joined with him in his suffering and death, so that we may know the power of his resurrection in our lives. Though his name, Jesus Christ we pray. Amen

The Reconciliation of All Things

**In him all the fullness of God was pleased to dwell,
and through him to reconcile to himself all things,
whether on earth or in heaven, making peace by the blood of his cross.
Colossians 1:19-20**

Reconciliation is especially important for us as Christians. God, in the life, suffering and death of Jesus has reconciled us to himself. All of our sins, large and small, were of great offense to him. Along with the reconciliation of our sins God made it possible for us to be reconciled to others who we have offended in life because of our abusing drugs. Equally true, God has made it possible for reconciliation to come to us for all those who have offended us in life.

This is particularly important for us in recovery. Reconciliation is there, and not just for our sins, but for all things. What that means is that for things that we deeply regret, such as if there was a terrible accident that we were involved in, there is reconciliation. Imagine, for example, that two young men were riding on an ATV and one fell off. It was an accident and there was nothing irresponsible being done. The accident caused him to have a concussion and brain damage. The friend said he felt worse about this accident than the worst of his sins. He found hope and relief for his guilt in this verse that told him God has reconciled all things, not just our sins but all things that we regret, by the blood of the cross.

In our addiction we may have caused a great deal of offense to countless people. In blackouts, in our obtuse and callousness we ticked off people everywhere. We fell into a deep sense of denial in order to escape our unhealthy sense of shame and lived inside a hardened shell for protection from criticism. In recovery we found a new hope in the light of the Gospel, that God had done all to make us whole again.

Heavenly Father, you are the healer of all ills and you alone can restore us to wholeness again. We pray for those we have offended by our actions and by our inaction, bring your healing to them as well. This we pray through Christ our Lord. Amen

Jesus and Zacchaeus

He entered Jericho and was passing through. And behold, there was a man named Zacchaeus. He was a chief tax collector and was rich. And he was seeking to see who Jesus was, but on account of the crowd he could not, because he was small in stature. So he ran on ahead and climbed up into a sycamore tree to see him, for he was about to pass that way. And when Jesus came to the place, he looked up and said to him, "Zacchaeus, hurry and come down, for I must stay at your house today." So he hurried and came down and received him joyfully. And when they saw it, they all grumbled, "He has gone in to be the guest of a man who is a sinner." And Zacchaeus stood and said to the Lord, "Behold, Lord, the half of my goods I give to the poor. And if I have defrauded anyone of anything, I restore it fourfold." And Jesus said to him, "Today salvation has come to this house, since he also is a son of Abraham. For the Son of Man came to seek and to save the lost."
Luke 19:1-10

Zacchaeus had big problems in his life. He was a tax collector for the occupying Roman Empire. He collected taxes from his own people and gave it to the foreigners ruling over his country. For this reason he was hated and despised by all of his own people. Perhaps his short height had motivated him to try and achieve great things. Unfortunately, he betrayed his nation by collaborating with a foreign power. No doubt he lost friends because of this. The money he had accumulated by his career was a great sum. On the day Jesus came to town he had to climb a tree to see him because he was short and the crowd that had gathered was large. Our Lord broke with all social protocol and called on him to be his host as he stayed in that town. Everybody baulked at the Lord because this man was a sinner that stood out in their minds from among them, and they were right too, he was pretty bad. As the Lord befriended him, he made a pledge to restore the money that he had defrauded others.

For us in our drug use, at times we felt like worse sinners than the rest. We sought to self-justify by pointing fingers at others and saying they were the bad ones because they were the dealers, or they were thieves and robbers, or they were self-righteous. This did not relieve our sense of guilt or shame though.

When we came to the Lord in repentance, our prayer may not have been the best. We may have even compared ourselves to others in the hopes of lessoning the heavy weight of our guilt. Regardless of our shortcomings, the Lord heard the prayer of our desperation and answered us according to his mercy and grace.

Isn't it amazing how great we feel when the weight of our guilt and shame has rolled away because God has forgiven and accepted us? By grace he saved us and we did nothing to deserve his goodness towards us. What a relief it was to us, beyond what words could describe, right? Zacchaeus was so relieved that he restored with interest the money he over charged people. What might we still need to do to make proper amends to others for our offences? Because God has forgiven us so great a debt, we find we want to make amends and bring healing to others.

Heavenly Father, thank you for sending Jesus your son to die for the forgiveness of our sins. Thank you for saving us from our sins and freeing us from our drug use. Help us to bring the message of your forgiveness through Jesus Christ to others, especially to those who suffer as we have with drug addiction. We thank and praise you, worship and adore you, for you have done great things and holy is your name, through Christ Jesus our Lord we pray. Amen

Our Personal Relationship with the Lord

A man who had just heard the message of the gospel responded by saying, "How can anyone believe in a man who died two thousand years ago?" To which the response was, "He rose from the dead, he is alive right now, and he is seated at the right hand of God the Father." It must seem strange to some who aren't believers that as Christians we believe Jesus of Nazareth is alive and well. It must also seem strange to them that we claim to be able to pray to him, that we believe he hears us and answers us. Yet isn't that the basis of a relationship with someone? This is in a large part what we are talking about when we say we have a personal relationship with God. In a relationship of any kind we spend time with them, talk with them, listen to them, and we think about them when we are apart. However, nowhere in the Bible does it say in those exact words, that we have a personal relationship with God or Jesus. Even still, we need to know that though our relationship with Jesus is not referred to as a personal relationship in the Scriptures, it is shown as a personal relationship with him in all ways.

We need to know that the ancient culture of the Bible uses its own language to describe the personal relationship that we have with Jesus and with the Father through him. It is found in these words:

The LORD bless you and keep you;
the LORD make his face to shine upon you and be gracious to you;
the LORD lift up his countenance upon you and give you peace.
"So shall they put my name upon the people of Israel,
and I will bless them."
Numbers 6:24-27

The Bible's way of saying we have a personal relationship with God is found in these words: to have the Lord's *face shine on us* and to have *the Lord life up his countenance upon us* is to be face to face with him in a close, personal, and even intimate relationship.

Thank you Father for loving and caring for us in such a wonderful way. Through your son we have this relationship with you and we praise your name eternally. In Christ's name. Amen

The Aaronic Blessing

The L<small>ORD</small> spoke to Moses, saying,
"Speak to Aaron and his sons, saying,
Thus you shall bless the people of Israel:
you shall say to them,

The L<small>ORD</small> bless you and keep you;
the L<small>ORD</small> make his face to shine upon you and be gracious to you;
the L<small>ORD</small> lift up his countenance upon you and give you peace.

"So shall they put my name upon the people of Israel,
and I will bless them."
Numbers 6:22-27

In more formal worship settings this blessing is given to the people at the conclusion of the worship service. It was given by God to Moses who was instructed to give it to his brother Aaron so that he could say it over the people as a blessing to them. Its references to the Lord's face and countenance are the Bible's way of saying that God has a personal relationship with us.

This blessing in particular has an incredibly special effect on all who receive it. It marks us with the name of the Lord! Many of us in addiction were labeled and stigmatized in life. We were sometimes treated as troublemakers and outcasts. That kind of treatment contributed to our suffering and low self-image. Even admitting, truthfully, that we are addicts can be extremely hard for us to do, though it is ultimately good for us in recovery.

This blessing is for us and it is powerful to take away all the stigmas, the name calling, and labeling that we received. This blessing puts the name of the Lord on us, and we are marked with it forever. This lets us and the world know that we have a personal relationship with God through our Lord Jesus Christ.

Dear God, thank you for coming to us in the life of your son and establishing your covenant relationship with us by his blood shed on the cross for us. We are blessed and give you our praise for all that you have done to redeem us fully from our sins and addictions. In his name. Amen

If It Had Not Been for the Lord

If it had not been the LORD **who was on our side,**
let Israel now say if it had not been the LORD **who was on our side**
when people rose up against us, then they would have swallowed us
up alive, when their anger was kindled against us; then the flood
would have swept us away, the torrent would have gone over us;
then over us would have gone the raging waters. Blessed be the LORD**,**
who has not given us as prey to their teeth!
We have escaped like a bird from the snare of the fowlers;
the snare is broken, and we have escaped!
Our help is in the name of the LORD**, who made heaven and earth.**
Psalm 124

Of the things from our past that we need to remember, and remember often, is the sense of desperation that we suffered within our addictions. We were without a hope. Many of us were in prison, but its walls were not enough to keep the drugs away from us. We had made countless promises to others and ourselves that we were done, that this was the last time we would use, and a lot of good that did us too. We didn't want to admit that we had no control over our addiction. We were living in the lie and were thoroughly deceived by our own selves and our addiction.

Finally, the day came and we got the help we needed. We entered into treatment, or we went to 30 meetings in 30 days. Maybe, for some of us we were miraculously delivered from our addiction by the Lord. We were clean, we had a week, thirty days, six months clean, all one day at a time. One of the most powerful motivators we had in those early days was the recent memory of our absolute desperation to get off drugs and get clean. We should never, ever loose tract of that memory and the intense feelings that go with it. It will help us continue the journey.

Heavenly Father, by your omnipotent right hand you delivered us from the dominion of the devil and from our addictions. You have saved our lives so that we may live for your glory and we praise you. Ever keep us close to you, through Christ our Lord. Amen

You Hurt the Ones You Love the Most

**The heart of the wise is in the house of mourning,
but the heart of fools is in the house of mirth.
It is better for a man to hear the rebuke of the wise
than to hear the song of fools.
Ecclesiastes 7:4-5**

In our addiction we would take this statement, *"you hurt the ones you love the most,"* and use it as permission to treat others badly. We were self-centered, egotistical and didn't care about the feelings and rights of others. We thought only about ourselves and what we wanted. We were out of control. We used others and justified ourselves erroneously believing we had a right to do whatever we wanted.

In recovery we use this statement, "you hurt the ones you love the most," as a confession in the fourth and fifth steps, and we worked to make amends to those we offended. Often times in tears we admitted to our faults and what we did wrong to others. We asked for their forgiveness and prayed for their healing. Because we were dealing with our past abusive behavior we came face to face with ourselves and who we had become on drugs. It was hard, but to recover we had to do this for the ones we hurt and for ourselves. We looked to God in desperation so that he would deliver us from drug use, and in humility we asked him to remove these character defects from us. We did not want to behave that way ever again. Many of those we made amends to forgave us and in their healing we found that we were healed too. In gratefulness we relished in our recovery and rejoiced in our healing.

Loving God in heaven, thank you for giving us the gift of being transformed by your will. Thank you for your help in making right the wrongs of our past. Bring healing to those we have offended. Lead us in the way that is everlasting, for you alone are God and you alone we will worship with praises and shouts of thanksgiving. Through Christ our Lord. Amen

Case Study: Workaholic on Meth

**For this reason I bow my knees before the Father,
from whom every family in heaven and on earth is named,
that according to the riches of his glory he may grant you to be
strengthened with power through his Spirit in your inner being.
Ephesians 3:14-16**

Westley was a man who came from a working-class family. Everyone was in the union. Even some of his great grandparents had fought hand and foot to form the union decades before. For all the men in the family their career choice was decided for them from before they were even born. Work was in their every waking thought and in their blood. For generations unending they had this extraordinarily strong work ethic that was lived out and passed on to every up and coming generation. To those very few family members who choose to go to college or into other fields of endeavor, well they were treated as second class family members at best.

Westley, was having trouble fitting into the family mold. He had been thinking about the possibility of going to college and studying for a different career. He mentioned the idea at the dinner table and the noisy group went dead silent. That was such a shock to him that he shut down, his thoughts froze, and he didn't know what to do. He felt rejected. After that meal his family hardly spoke to him and when they did it was in a shaming and critical way. He gave up all his hopes of going to college or of exercising his right to choose his own path in life. He grew depressed. A week after he graduated from high school his father woke him up early one morning. He told Westley that his summer break was over, and he took him down to the union hall. He was signed up as an apprentice. While most of his family members started at ninety percent of journeyman wages when they became apprentices, he was start at the bottom of the pay scale. Nothing was said to him about it, but he knew why that was done to him. It was because he said he wanted to go to college.

He begrudgingly continued on this track for his life for a few years. He eventually became a journeyman, but it took him longer than most people. That was due in part to his lack of enthusiasm and partly because his co-workers were family members who progressed him through his training at a slower than usual pace because they resented what he said that one night.

On the job his family criticized him often and unnecessarily to keep him in his place. He was getting tired of not measuring up. Then he learned about coke and crack. The drugs made him feel good and that was something that was sadly lacking in his life. He didn't actually like all of their affects very much because he felt like it was harder for him to function on them. That was contrary to the family work ethic that he was trying to live up to. Then he tried meth. He purchased enough to get high several times, but when he started smoking it, he could not stop. He smoked it until it was all used up. He didn't really like the high that meth offered him, and it tasted awful. It was the other things that it did for him that he liked best. Soon he found out that he could use it to stay awake for days at a time. He also learned that he could use it to improve his performance at work. Then he volunteered for extra hours of overtime whenever they became available. He also asked for extra hours if they weren't offered. However, that was not enough to keep him busy when he was high. So, he went on to get additional non-union jobs which allowed him to work second and third shifts at a factory for up to a week at a time. He worked and worked, sometimes over 100 hours a week. He worked until he had ridden out the high. He timed his use so that he could crash on a weekend when he would sleep those days through.

He loved to work. He loved the money, but it all went back into purchasing more meth. Before long, his lifestyle started to deteriorate. He lost his apartment. Then he went to live with some relatives. It was not long before they realized that Westley never slept for days at a time and that he would sleep nonstop every weekend. When they asked him about it, he mumbled a feeble excuse to them and soon moved out. After that he stayed with other relatives or friends but not long enough for them to catch on to his lifestyle.

His work performance did not suffer at first. He out preformed everyone else. But he became angry that they were not working as hard as he was. Their complaints about his work continued unchanged even though his work was excellent, and his productivity was outstanding.

Eventually, things changed for the worse. He was burning out physically and his mind was thinking crazy thoughts. Before long it all came to a head as his life was nearing complete ruin and he got busted for drugs. He had a large amount on him in his car, so much so that he was charged with intent to sell. The courts confiscated his car. What little he saved was used up by his lawyer. He was looking at five to twenty years in prison. That was when he went to treatment and got clean.

Drugs seemed to offer to Westley things that would not have normally happened in his life. By using he thought that he was accepted among his peers and that made him new friends. The drugs made him feel good about himself and he had been lacking that. They were his recreation and he felt entitled to have some relief from his mundane life. In Westley's mind he thought that they would bring him a sense of acceptance in his family. In the beginning it seemed to work but as his addiction grew worse they had a reverse effect on him and things went from bad to worse. He wanted the enhancements that drugs seemed to be offering and he lied to himself about the bad side effects. Things progressed until there was no longer much benefit to using. In his addiction he had reached the point where he was using just to feel less awful because they really didn't offer him much of a high anymore.

    At some point we got into recovery and quit using. At that point the progression of our disease was stopped. Because we applied ourselves to the program we were able to grow as we worked the steps and went to meetings. We prayed, worshipped, read our Bibles, and lived devoted lives. Because of our spiritual pursuits to become closer to God we grew more and more in our recoveries. By the grace God extended to us we were being blessed and the lives he intended for us to live were being restored to us.

    Heavenly Father, your love for us overwhelms us and we love you all the more. You have blessed us with recovery and extended your grace to us. Teach us more about yourself and help us to live in relationship with you, through Christ Jesus our Redeemer, Lord and Savior. Amen

Christian Spirituality: A New Way of Life

**Thus says the Lord:
"Stand by the roads, and look, and ask for the ancient paths,
where the good way is; and walk in it, and find rest for your souls."
Jeremiah 6:16**

    This world by and large, though created by God, does not function as a place that is still committed to his glory. It can be a very dysfunctional, impersonal, discouraging, and sinful place. There were times and places in history when it seemed like most of the people lived for the Lord. It was easy to be a Christian then because our faith was widely practiced and we were viewed with favor by the rest of the population. These were like golden years when conditions seemed ideal for living as a person of faith.

    As addicts we did not want to live in this world as it was, so we dropped out and sank deeper into addiction. In our using days we may have longed for a better lifestyle. We wanted to return to an older way of living that was the way life was meant to be lived by God who created everything. We may have nostalgically remembered idyllic times from our own past and longed to return to living in those days. We cannot turn back time and return to the past where life was more ideal for us. However, we can look to God for the guidance we need to live in this world as it is, and also have a special sense of peace and serenity in our lives.

    Loving and gracious Father in heaven, you have given us freedom from addiction and restored our lives to us. Help us to accept all that life brings our way and give us your peace in the midst of our trials, strength for our weaknesses and patience for our journeys. In the name of your beloved son, Jesus Christ our Savior and Lord. Amen

The Prayer of Saint Francis

Lord, make me an instrument of your peace
Where there is hatred, let me sow love
Where there is injury, pardon
Where there is doubt, faith
Where there is despair, hope
Where there is darkness, light
And where there is sadness, joy
O Divine Master, grant that I may
Not so much seek to be consoled as to console
To be understood, as to understand
To be loved, as to love
For it is in giving that we receive
And it's in pardoning that we are pardoned
And it's in dying that we are born to eternal life.
Amen

Relapse Prevention and Restoration

**Brothers, if anyone is caught in any transgression,
you who are spiritual should restore him in a spirit of gentleness.
Keep watch on yourself, lest you too be tempted.
Bear one another's burdens, and so fulfill the law of Christ.
Galatians 6:1-2**

A drug and alcohol counselor told her class that relapse is part of recovery. Upon hearing that the class squirmed a little in their chairs. She went on to explain that if any of them was to relapse into using again, they needed to have a plan for getting back into recovery again before it happens.

As addicts we need to watch ourselves for the warning signs. Knowing ourselves and what happens to us when we are reaching our maximum threshold for stress is key. Some people say that their red flags are the temptation to use again, to want to reach out to someone socially who uses, or go to a place where drugs are likely being used or sold. Other people say that negative emotional overload puts them at risk. Anniversaries of difficult life events or the occurrence of something like a death, a change in health status, or loss of a job can increase our risk of a relapse too. Other red flags include feeling pity for oneself, being over-confident, needlessly calling in "sick" to work, or not being responsible in other ways.

Knowing the things that are needful when the red flags of a relapse warning comes or when a relapse occurs is necessary. Have a sponsor and call them. Get to a meeting, get to as many meetings as you might need to. Call a clean and free friend and invite them over. Prevention is well worth the extra effort too. Eat healthy meals, at least two a day. Get your sleep, bathe, do the laundry. Manage your stress, check in with a therapist. Exercise, read, enjoy music, or see a movie.

Heavenly Father, it is by your grace that we are forgiven, and living clean and free. Protect us from temptations to return to our former way of living and sustain us in our recovery for we long to bring glory to you name by all that we say and do, in Jesus name. Amen

Recovery Maintenance: Continue in What You Have Learned

**But as for you, continue in what you
have learned and have firmly believed,
knowing from whom you learned it
and how from childhood you have been
acquainted with the sacred writings,
which are able to make you wise for
salvation through faith in Christ Jesus.
2 Timothy 3:14-15**

Will-power is not enough to get us to quit using. Oh, we might achieve some clean time for a little while on our own, but it will not last for long. There is also more to recovery than just having a short period of clean time. Recovery needs to go far beyond merely being clean. We need to deal with our fallen character defects. That requires a new and growth-oriented lifestyle.

Times change and we must change with it. That is not to say that we need to adopt any of the popular culture changes that come about. Rather, we need to grow and mature in our recovery to maintain ourselves from anything that causes our recovery to be jeopardized. That is where the devout life comes in. We must be quick to respond to anything that would put us at risk and cautious to adopt anything new that we are leery of.

In our love for the Savior who delivered us from our sins and our addictions we need to be steadfast and forward growing. This text that Paul wrote to Timothy focuses on the value of the Holy Scriptures. We are reminded by them of our need to be reading and studying our own Bibles on a daily basis. This spiritual practice refreshes our knowledge of his Word and brings us growth by bringing us into new and deeper revelations of the revealed truth from God.

Heavenly Father, by day and by night hold us in the palm of your hand and sustain us in our faith and in our recoveries. Our prayer is that we may lovingly honor you and your son in all that we do. Help us to grow over the course of our lifetimes, that we might more fully live out your will in our lives to your glory, through Jesus Christ our Lord we pray. Amen

Scripture is Given for Our Benefit

**All Scripture is breathed out by God and profitable for teaching, for reproof, for correction, and for training in righteousness, that the man of God may be complete, equipped for every good work.
2 Timothy 3:16-17**

Paul wrote to his young disciple Timothy and spoke to him as a father might wisely and lovingly encouraged his son. He directed him to continue in what he had already learned and believed, and to rely on the Scriptures that make one wise unto salvation. He explained four specific things that the Scripture are profitable for. First is teaching about what is right and true. Second is reproof, which is how to identify what is not right or untrue. Third is correction which is how to get right with the Lord. Lastly, the fourth benefit is training in righteousness which is how to stay right with the Lord.

In our daily walk we need to wisely maintain what is ours, namely our recovery. The Apostle Paul explained that the Scriptures will help us to do just that. None of us are infallible, we can and do error. With the Scriptures as our guide we need to know what they are telling us. Then we must compare our lives against what the Bible says our lives should be like. We need to make occasional corrective changes in our lives so that we do come into alignment with the Word of God.

These four things, teaching, reproof, correction, and righteousness, we need to make them part of a constant cycle in our lives. This is how the Word of God works his will in our lives so that we can grow day by day, year by year, and mature wisely in our spirituality. By this we will come to be skilled at walking with our Lord in growth oriented lives that are clean and free of drug use.

Heavenly Father, by your grace you have saved us so that we may live for your glory. In our daily lives help us to grow both closer to you and to mature into all that you have planned for us in this life. Through Jesus Christ our Lord and Savior we pray. Amen

Spiritual Practices: Singing Psalms, Hymns and Spiritual Songs

**And do not get drunk with wine, for that is debauchery,
but be filled with the Spirit, addressing one another in psalms
and hymns and spiritual songs, singing and making melody
to the Lord with your heart, giving thanks always and for everything
to God the Father in the name of our Lord Jesus Christ.
Ephesians 5:18-20**

We know that alcohol is also a drug and should not be viewed differently for any reason. As addicts we know about cross addiction and even though alcohol may not be our drug of choice, we are subject to addiction to all drugs, including alcohol. The Scriptures clearly condemns all recreational use of drugs, which are referred to under the term sorcery. Alcohol use in the Bible is referred to in both the context of it being bad for us, and as something some people can consume under certain conditions. Those conditions include are that we don't drink too much and get drunk. One thing is certain for us, as addicts we should not tempt ourselves and drink alcohol.

In our spiritual life we have alternatives to drinking which are strongly encouraged such as singing Christian songs of several types. The Psalms of the Bible are one of those types, other types include hymns and the last type is the spiritual songs. The Psalms of the Bible are written in various poetic forms. We know that many of them were meant to be sung, but there are no surviving musical tunes from those days. The word hymn is a Greek word, *hymnos*, meaning a song of praise. Both psalms and hymns are specifically songs of adoration and praise for God and have theological statements in them. Qualities of a song that makes it a hymn is that it is poetic and has a certain literary style to it. In all cases, the songs direct our thoughts to things that God has done, is doing, and has promised to do for us, and they are about his character. Hymns have a melody that is referred to as a hymn tune. Its melody is described as commonly being in 4-part harmony. The tune of the music and the words of hymns have a certain pairing quality that joins them together very closely.

We don't have a clear historical understanding of what Paul meant when he referred to spiritual songs. Perhaps they were something akin to the contemporary praise songs of the last century.

Our worship of God and the Lord is vital to our spiritual wellbeing. Because God has been so good to us in so many ways with things that only he could do, we respond to him with our highest expressions of love and adoration. That is why we sing.

Martin Luther reminded the church that when we sing, we pray twice. The importance of singing in worship because of what the Lord has done for us cannot be over stressed. We invite his Holy Spirit's presence to be among us in this way. This can have a very soothing and calming effect on us, especially when adversity strikes. Paul and Silas were on a missionary journey when they were arrested, beaten, and thrown in jail. There they were praying and singing hymns to the Lord. As a result many of the other prisoners were saved by their witness.[77]

For us in recovery we need to know that there is a relationship between using drugs and being filled with God's Holy Spirit. You can do one, but not the other. Being high or drunk is entirely antagonistic to being in fellowship with God. We were saved from our sins and active addiction so that we could serve God fully, not so that we could use on an occasional basis which would put us at risk for a full relapse.

Worshipping God, in our church services, in a small group or when alone can be a wonderful experience with God. It can be exhilarating and a time of elation. It is a good idea to include playing a song or two on a CD player in our daily devotions because it will bring us closer to the one we love, Jesus our Lord.

Father, you have called us to be your people and given us hearts to worship you. Empower our hearts and voices to sing your praises and tell of your glory. Receive our worship as we give glory to your name, through the one who died and rose for us, Christ Jesus our Lord we pray. Amen

---

[77] Acts 16:12-34

The Abundant Life

**Jesus said,
"The thief comes only to steal and kill and destroy.
I came that they may have life and have it abundantly."
John 10:10**

Jesus could just as easily have been talking about a drug dealer when he said, "the thief comes only to steal and kill and destroy." We know that is entirely true. Our occasional drug use cost us money, then it became an addiction and it started to take whatever it wanted. Our paychecks, the money in our wallets and even our bank accounts were taken by it. Our credit was also destroyed and it didn't stop there. Our debts continued to rise because we borrowed money from others even though we had no way of paying them back. We borrowed off the value of our cars and homes too. Even still, the path of its destruction was ever widening. Our careers suffered, we lost our jobs. We lost friends and alienated our families. We were miserable but none of this stopped the blood sucking addiction that would never be satisfied no matter how much it stole from us. We may have even overdosed, but then survived because someone got us to the hospital. That wasn't enough to get us to quit though.

It wasn't until we turned to God Almighty and surrendered to him that we found the supernatural help we needed to intervene in our lives. We were delivered from addiction and freed to live in a new way. Our lives as they should have been without drugs began to be restored to us by the Lord. Sometimes friendships were restored, sometimes our family members were able to be healed and they were restored to us. We were able to hold down a job again and our financial situation began to be turned around. We felt good about ourselves and the lives we were leading again thanks to Jesus Christ who came to bring us abundant life again.

Dearest Heavenly Father, through your sharing with us your son's victory over death and the grave, you have blessed us with abundant life. Because he rose again we too have found new lives free from active addiction with him. Though his name, Jesus Christ our Savior we pray. Amen

Meditation

**Let the words of my mouth and the
meditation of my heart be acceptable in your sight,
O LORD, my rock and my redeemer.
Psalm 19:14**

Studies have shown that our minds are continually occupied with thinking. Much of it is the repeating of the same thing over again and again. The Psalmist, David, was very conscious of the nature of his thought life, praying here that his thoughts would be favorable to God.

For us, we need to be mindful of what thoughts we allow and which ones we don't. Even though a thought comes that is not acceptable in God's eyes, we don't have to own it. We can say we reject it, we don't need to agree with it, and we won't act on it or feel condemned for it then.

An example of this might come to us while we are driving in our car. Someone may not let us change lanes, or they may cut us off. They may have unknowingly or intentionally done something offensive in this way. Our first reaction may not be a pleasant one. We might immediately think I will show him, I will... . Then we realize that those are not our values, we don't care to think or react that way. Even though our first thought was to do something foolish we can know that we would never actually act on it. Even if we might have in our using days done something inappropriate, that is not where we are now. We can reassure ourselves that we are a forgiving and understanding person who does not, and will not act, or speak unkindly to anyone for any reason, in our car or in any situation.

The thoughts that we want to occupy ourselves with are those that are consistent with living a Christian and godly life. We want to live, so much as is possible, at peace with all people. We don't want to give into our old sinful nature and allow negative thoughts to dominate our minds. Even though it may be a struggle at times, we have this prayer from the psalms to offer to God. We also have the Scriptures to meditate on and spiritual songs to sing in our heart or out loud.

Dearest God in heaven, we join with King David in his prayer, asking that our thought life be honoring to you in all ways. Sanctify our minds in your truth. In Jesus' name. Amen

The Glory of the Lord

**And we all, with unveiled face,
beholding the glory of the Lord,
are being transformed into the same
image from one degree of glory to another.
For this comes from the Lord who is the Spirit.
2 Corinthians 3:18**

We need to know this about the glory of the Lord. Glory can mean so many things. It could refer to Hollywood glamor or stardom, it could refer to fame, fortune or even a battle commander's success in the field of conquest. Our Lord's glory is all about his reputation. And this is God's reputation, that though as sinners we deserved to die for our sins, and suffer an eternity outside of his presence, he loves us and redeemed us. On the one hand, God's condemnation of sin is so absolute that there was no way around it. On the other hand, our God loves us and did not want us to suffer that terrible fate, but what could be done about it? That is what is called a problem worthy of God, because the solution was inconceivable to us and otherwise unsolvable by mankind. Yet, God found a way to meet the righteous demands of his absolute Law, which cannot be compromised, and he also redeemed us from our sins. God did the impossible for us!

The way our redemption works is that he sent his son to us, Jesus Christ, who was incarnated and became man. As such he could die, and therefore die for our sins. While no one person can die for another person's sins, Jesus having become a man who could die, and being God who can do all things, could then die for the sins of all mankind. This way the righteous demands of God's Law were satisfied and our sins were forgiven in full.

As the Scripture says we are transformed by God who did the impossible by redeeming us. We are close and personal in our relationship with God as we look with awe at his glory. We are being transformed in our relationship with him, becoming more like him, one day at a time.

Heavenly Father, we love you so much. We pray that by your Holy Spirit we may be transformed from our former way of living into saintly lives dedicated to living in the example of your son, Christ our Lord in whose name we pray. Amen

The Heart of Man

Again, the Lord said to [Moses], "Put your hand inside your cloak." And he put his hand inside his cloak, and when he took it out, behold, his hand was leprous like snow. Then God said, "Put your hand back inside your cloak." So he put his hand back inside his cloak, and when he took it out, behold, it was restored like the rest of his flesh.
Exodus 4:6-7

Ever wonder what is in our heart? Moses found out that as sinners it is nothing good. He put his hand inside his cloak next to his heart, and then saw that it was full of the awful sin disease of leprosy. The Bible says that if you had this skin disease that you were contagious and unclean. Because of it you were cut off from the mainstream of society. There were no cures. Your only hope was a miracle healing which were incredibly rare. Worse, and yes there is a worse to this problem for the leper, you were unclean before God. You could not go to the synagogue, you could not venture anywhere near the temple in Jerusalem. You could not worship God and you worried your prayers may not even be heard by him because of your very terrible sinful condition.

As addicts we suffered with terrible self-images. At our core our hearts were tender from being wounded. Drugs could make us feel better about ourselves. But that didn't last. Soon their seemingly positive influence diminished and before long we are using just to feel less terrible about ourselves and any good feelings were long gone.

In recovery we can find joy in knowing that while we were still sinners, Christ died for us.[78] God loves us with an everlasting love even though we were living in rebellion to his will. God will always love us with his everlasting love.

Thank you heavenly Father for your love that you have loved us with. You amaze us that even in our darkest sins your love was undiminished for us. This we pray in Jesus' name. Amen

---

[78] Romans 5:8

God's Voice Guides Us Still

**And your ears shall hear a word behind you, saying,
"This is the way, walk in it,"
when you turn to the right or
when you turn to the left.
Isaiah 30:21**

Anyone who has taken one of those psychological tests with the question in it about being able to hear from God has thought twice before answering that question. We worried that if we admitted that we believed God has spoken to us, they would think we were crazy. The right answer is that we believe God speaks silently to our hearts. If the person scoring the test has a problem with it they can always follow up with us and ask further questions to see that we are not crazy.

As Christians we have a personal relationship with God. God speaks to us through his Word, the Bible. God speaks to us through our pastor's sermons, through other Christians and sometimes he speaks directly to our hearts. He does this through his Holy Spirit who lives in us. Sometimes he speaks to us with what is called a witness of his Spirit. This might be a feeling of restlessness which may correlate with a *no* answer to the situation. Sometimes it is a feeling of peacefulness with a situation that may be a *yes* answer. Other times God may speak to us in the form of an answered prayer. It could also be that God reveals something to us, which might be what is called a word of knowledge.

For us in our recovery we should be reading our Bibles daily and finding strength in it. We need a good sense of what it says about how we should be living our lives, and then living that way. We also should have a growing ability to sense what God's Holy Spirit is saying to us. We need to know what to do when we are uncertain about what we are hearing. God will never speak to us in any way that contradicts what the Bible says. If we are confused we can turn to the Scriptures, to our pastor, a Christian sponsor, mentor or elder at our church.

Dear God, help us to hear you speaking to our hearts and to be faithful in how we respond. For this and for all your blessings we are grateful and praise you. Through Jesus' name. Amen

Spiritual Character from Trial by Fire

**Not only that, but we rejoice in our sufferings,
knowing that suffering produces endurance,
and endurance produces character, and character
produces hope, and hope does not put us to shame,
because God's love has been poured into our hearts
through the Holy Spirit who has been given to us.
Romans 5:3-5**

Have you ever wondered how iron is made and refined? If you merely put iron ore in a big metal pan and heat it up to extract the iron, the pan will melt down in the heat. Smelters devised a way to heat up the ore to refine metal without having their pan melt down in the process. They use a device called a crucible. This is a large metal pan with some special cooling channels in it that water is forced through. The water carries the heat away from the pan so it doesn't meltdown. However, the blazing intense heat reaches the iron ore inside the pan and it becomes molten liquid. In that molten state the impurities in it, called dross, float to the top where they are scraped away leaving just the refined iron metal behind.

In a remarkably similar way, life's challenging events can act to refine us. 12-step meetings and treatment also work like a crucible in our lives. If the circumstances are at a crisis level it can do several things to us. It can drive us to our knees and to God where we seek his mercy and intervention. It can also lead us into the temptation of relapse. If that is the case we might sink to our lowest levels of immoral and unethical behavior. Hopefully, that is not what we do.

Turning to God we find strength to do as this scripture instructs, we rejoice in our trials, not because of them. Hard as it might be, giving God thanks and praise, and rejoicing in him has an action like the cooling water of a crucible that prevents it from melting down. This sets in motion the progression: suffering producing endurance, producing good character, leading to hope.

God of all glory, we have set our hopes on you. By your grace we grow and mature day by day. Help us to rejoice in our trials and in them turn to you for the help we need. We praise you by day and by night as well as in the good and the bad, through Christ our Lord. Amen

Sick-Love Verses Love-Sick

It is actually reported that there is sexual immorality among you, and of a kind that is not tolerated even among pagans, for a man has his father's wife.
1 Corinthians 5:1

How horrible it is that such a wonderful gift from God has been abused so much and to such great extremes. In the first century there was a new church in the city of Corinth. It was an immature church and they suffered from many problems because of this. The worst one was likely this one, of sexual immorality. The Apostle Paul said that at least one of their members had gone beyond what godless pagans tolerate. Apparently it was a situation where a man had taken his stepmother for his lover. Because it doesn't say that the father had passed on, it is reasonable to assume that the father might still have been living.

In our day we have had our eyes opened and opened very widely. The internet has made pornography widely available to everyone including our children whose innocence it has stolen. Sex trafficking was hardly heard of a generation or two ago. Now it is in the news on a regular basis and it is shocking as well as tragic how widespread it is and who is involved in it at all levels of our society. Sex abuse is a leading cause of people turning to drug use and many go on to become addicts. Those participating in the sex trade at any level can develop a sex addiction just as easily as someone becoming addicted to drugs.

In recovery we need to abstain from all drugs that have an addictive nature to them. We also need to abstain from involvement in anything sexual outside of the bonds of marriage. God has reserved sex in this way so that it is a blessing for us and not a curse when we engage in it outside of marriage.

Heavenly Father, bless and sustain us in our marriage unions, bring those who long for marriage together and lead them to the altar. Help to keep us pure in our relationships with all people so that we honor you with our physical bodies, through Christ our Lord. Amen

Cleansing from Character Defects

**If we confess our sins, he is faithful and just to forgive us
our sins and to cleanse us from all unrighteousness.
1 John 1:9**

Our desperation to escape from our former lives of drug addiction has also motivated us to place our shortcomings behind us and be rid of them. For us, we understand that we cannot simply step out of our former lifestyles and walk away from them. We know that we will be dragging them with us. It takes a miracle from God in our lives so that we can by his grace alone have our faults and character defects removed. Thankfully, God is glad to do this and ready to do this for us. We do not become saintly overnight through, at least not in most cases. We have the program that we need to work and we take it one day at a time.

As addicts, when we were high, the drugs had a way of erasing and overwriting much of our developmental years training in manners. What was written on our souls because of the drugs was all about getting high, staying high and getting more and more drugs to do that with. We were selfish to say the least, untrustworthy, and ill-mannered. In recovery the damage done can be arrested and even reversed. The program re-parents us, correcting us when we are wrong and instructing us in how to conduct ourselves in life again. We know how difficult, if not impossible, these kind of changes are to come by. That is why in our weaknesses we turn to God for the impossible because with him it is not impossible any longer. God found the way to forgive us our sins against him. Along that same path comes the cleansing of our souls by the blood of Christ that empowers us to lead lives of good moral and upright behavior.

Dearest God in heaven, thank you for the shed blood of your son that washes us clean and rejuvenates our lives. Lead and guide us this day, that we might live for you and reflect your glory in all that we do. This we pray through Christ our Lord. Amen

A Dumb Bird

**And Jesus said to them, "You will all fall away, for it is written,
'I will strike the shepherd, and the sheep will be scattered.' ..."
Peter said to him, "Even though they all fall away, I will not."
And Jesus said to him, "Truly, I tell you, this very night, before
the rooster crows twice, you will deny me three times."
But he said emphatically, "If I must die with you,
I will not deny you." And they all said the same.
Mark 14:29-31**

**But he began to invoke a curse on himself and to swear,
"I do not know this man of whom you speak."
And immediately the rooster crowed a second time.
And Peter remembered how Jesus had said to him,
"Before the rooster crows twice, you will deny me three times."
And he broke down and wept.
Mark 14:71-72**

On the night of his betrayal Jesus said that all of his apostles would fall away. Impulsive Peter said something like, "No I won't!" It was a strong-willed person who made that assertion. As it turned out Peter did deny knowing Jesus, not once, not twice, but three times. He even had been warned by the roster who crowed during his second and third denials.

What is interesting here is that at this time of night rosters are asleep. This dumb bird woke up because he heard the arguing going on and had to be a part of the verbal parley. The bird had no idea of what the fight was about, it didn't matter to him, he wanted to win and get the last word in. Peter gave him no mind until the bird's second boast and got the last word in his argument.

In recovery we must remember that our will-power is never enough. Peter tried to do the right thing on his own and he failed. We need to give way and yield to God, surrendering to him even when it goes against our will. It is by God's grace that we recovered and by his daily grace to us that we stay in recovery.

Thank you Father this day for our recoveries that you have blessed us with. May we live faithfully for you by the power of your Holy Spirit living in us. In Jesus' name. Amen

It Is the Holy Spirit Who Sanctifies Us

Therefore, my beloved, as you have always obeyed, so now, not only as in my presence but much more in my absence, work out your own salvation with fear and trembling, for it is God who works in you, both to will and to work for his good pleasure.
Philippians 2:12-13

In addiction our lives fell and fell far. Many of us committed criminal acts, we lied, we cheated, stole, manipulated, destroyed our families, marriages, trashed our careers and alienated our friends. The boundaries we were taught about how to live and behave in our childhood were all crossed. The values we were given before our addictions were abandoned. The addiction lifestyle that we came into with our drug use was immoral and unethical.

In recovery we returned to a better way of living. It was not easy and we even stumbled at times. With the support meetings, with treatment and with one-on-one work with counselors we began to live a healthy lifestyle again. We found our old way of life was very resilient. Often times we found ourselves being deceived by the cunning nature of our old way of life. By working the program we made steady progress in recovering our lives as God meant them to be lived.

In the seventh step of NA we humbly ask God to remove our character defects. That is because drugs had taken over our lifestyle and we were powerless to do anything about it. We could not quit using on our own and equally true we could not change ourselves and rid ourselves of the terrible lifestyles we had come into.

God calls us to live peaceful and holy lives. It is only by the power of his Holy Spirit living in us and through us that we are able to do this. In our spiritual maturity we come to rely more and more on God's help for the lives we wanted to live.

Loving God refine our lives and remove our character defects by the sanctification of your Holy Spirit so that we may serve you in holiness in all that we do. Through Christ our Lord. Amen

And I Will Show You A Still More Excellent Way
1 Corinthians 12:31

If I speak in the tongues of men and of angels, but have not love, I am a noisy gong or a clanging cymbal. And if I have prophetic powers, and understand all mysteries and all knowledge, and if I have all faith, so as to remove mountains, but have not love, I am nothing. If I give away all I have, and if I deliver up my body to be burned, but have not love, I gain nothing. Love is patient and kind; love does not envy or boast; it is not arrogant or rude. It does not insist on its own way; it is not irritable or resentful; it does not rejoice at wrongdoing, but rejoices with the truth. Love bears all things, believes all things, hopes all things, endures all things. Love never ends. As for prophecies, they will pass away; as for tongues, they will cease; as for knowledge, it will pass away. For we know in part and we prophesy in part, but when the perfect comes, the partial will pass away. When I was a child, I spoke like a child, I thought like a child, I reasoned like a child. When I became a man, I gave up childish ways. For now we see in a mirror dimly, but then face to face. Now I know in part; then I shall know fully, even as I have been fully known.
So now faith, hope, and love abide, these three;
but the greatest of these is love.
1 Corinthians 13

Everyone knows about 1 Corinthians 13 don't they? This is frequently read at weddings and it has been called the love chapter of the Bible. The introduction for this chapter is actually in chapter 12 where Paul says, "But desire the greater gifts. And I will show you a still more excellent way." In Chapter 12 Paul was instructing the church in spiritual gifts, about harmonious relationships within the body of Christ, and its administration and leadership. For important as healthy leadership is, for as vital as the gifts of the Spirit are and for as necessary as harmony is, there is one thing that is greater than all, that being love.

God, reign in our hearts and pour out your love in our lives so that we may have such an abundance that we can show it to others and they may glorify you. In Christ's name. Amen

With God's Help We Can Stay Clean

**No temptation has overtaken you that is not common to man.
God is faithful, and he will not let you be tempted beyond your ability,
but with the temptation he will also provide the way of escape,
that you may be able to endure it.
1 Corinthians 10:13**

At every recovery meeting we attend there is universally one thing that gets us to stop and take notice. That is whenever anyone announces how much clean time they have. We all take that moment to clap in celebration of their achievement by the grace of God. Getting clean is never easy and we know that it is only by God's grace that it happened. With time and from applying ourselves to the program it does become easier for us to live clean and free. With working the program our desire to use diminishes. Our character deficits, lying, cheating, and using people comes to an end. Our social interest and our contributing to society as productive members rises.

We could not do any of this except by the grace of God in our lives. His gifts to us in the success of our recovery is not to be underestimated or understated. He is the one who empowers us to get clean and stay clean, day by day, one day at a time. As the Holy Scriptures promise to us, our Heavenly Father will not allow us to be tempted beyond our ability to successfully resist, again by his grace in us. This is a promise that we need to cling to, our lives may very well depend on it.

None of this is to say that it is easy to resist and overcome temptation, it isn't. As addicts we need to always take personal responsibility for ourselves and our actions. To do otherwise can only contribute to the dangers of a relapse. God provides for us sponsors, meetings, fellowship, counseling, books and literature, education, and treatment programs, sober houses, halfway houses and more, all supporting us in having a sustained recovery unto the end of our natural lives.

Heavenly Father, thank you for providing all that we need to live for you free and clean. Thank you for restoring our lives to us and refining us by the working of your Holy Spirit so that we may continue in the path of disciples, serving you with our whole hearts. In Jesus name. Amen

Healthy Boundaries: Samson and Delilah[79]

**And the woman bore a son and called his name Samson.
And the young man grew, and the Lord blessed him.
Judges 13:24**

The ancient nation of Israel lived out an alternating pattern of being faithful and following God, and then falling away and doing what was evil. Because they had been unfaithful to God they fell into the domination of the Philistines who were a very pagan and ungodly people. After about 40 years of living under their rule there was a man named Samson, who had been raised as a Nazarite, who rose up to lead Israel.

Samson came into a startling revelation about himself one day when he was attacked by a lion. Because of his covenant relationship with the Lord as a Nazarite the Holy Spirit fell on him and gave him superhuman strength. He not only fought the lion, he was able to tear the lion to pieces with his bare hands. Samson realized the gift that he had, and he used it to his advantage against the oppressive Philistines. Even though Samson was raised as a very devout man of God, he seemed to have at least one weakness that plagued his life. He had unhealthy boundaries, he was attracted to and gave himself to a Philistine woman. This great weakness in his life ultimately lead to his demise, and his death. At the end of his life a woman named Delilah, who he was in an unmarried and unhealthy relationship with, manipulated him into telling her the secret of his strength. His strength was dependent on his keeping his vows and not cutting his hair.

For us as Christians who are in recovery we need to practice conservative values. God has given us the gift of sex to be a blessing, but outside of a marriage between one man and one women it can quickly become a curse to us.

Heavenly Father, thank you for the grace you have extended to us. Bless us and make us healthy people who can be in healthy relationships with others. Make us wise to see unhealthy people and help us to provide them with examples of better ways to live. In Jesus name. Amen

---

[79] Judges 13-16

Spiritual Practices: Ash Wednesday and Lent

**By the sweat of your face you shall eat bread,
till you return to the ground, for out of it you were taken;
for you are dust, and to dust you shall return."
Genesis 3:19**

More than half of all Christians belong to denominations and traditions that observe Ash Wednesday and the Church Season of Lent. This is a church season for Christians to devote themselves to renewing their faith and preparing for Holy week and Easter. Lent begins on Ash Wednesday. It is forty days long and ends on the Saturday preceding Palm Sunday and the celebration of Jesus' Triumphal Entry into Jerusalem. Some churches have revival meetings in the summer season, others have them at random times throughout the year. Lent is also a time of returning to the Lord, to be renewed in our repentance, to rededicate ourselves to living the devout life. At the heart of the Season of Lent is a very spiritual foundation that can only strengthen our devotion to the Lord.

In preparation for this special service of Ash Wednesday palm leaves from the prior Palm Sunday are burned and their ashes are prepared for use. At Ash Wednesday worship the pastor or priest does a very spiritual thing. He takes these ashes and applies them to the forehead of all who present themselves. As he does this, he says the very words that God told Adam and Eve on the day of the fall.

Remember that you are dust and to dust you shall return.

This is a very mortifying and humbling act to be the recipient of. In a very real sense, it is us picking up our cross, dying to self and following after our Lord as he carried his cross to Golgotha on Good Friday. It is by dying to ourselves and surrendering our wills and lives over to God that we can live clean, free and in recovery.

Heavenly Father, help us to live humbly before you and remind us that we are of the dust. Strengthen us in our earthy journeys and sustain us in our recoveries. In Jesus's name. Amen

Hitting Bottom

The LORD **is near to the brokenhearted
and saves the crushed in spirit.
Psalm 34:18**

Maybe you have heard that we need to hit bottom as our wakeup call in order to get the help we need. While that might be true for some, it is not true for all of us. What is true for all of us is that we came to realize that we are powerless over our addiction, and that our lives had become unmanageable.[80]

When we as Christians become overwhelmed and crushed under by the weight of this heavy burden of addiction then we are ready to take the next step. You can call it repentance. What we need to do is turn away from our using and turn towards God who is able to save us from our addiction. This is where we come to believe that a Power greater than ourselves, namely God Almighty, could restore us to sanity.[81]

At this point we need to add actions to the realizations that we have come into. It is time to turn our will and lives over the care of God as we understand him[82], and as Christians we know and understand him best through the life of his son, Jesus Christ our Lord and Savior.

A heart made tender by a crisis is very pliable in the hands of our loving God. When the circumstances of our lives are a crushing weight over us it can quickly create the right atmosphere for changes. If our addiction has brought us to a crisis, or if it came into our lives for any other reason, God can use it to bring us closer to him.

God, you sustain us and carry us through all of our trials. Uphold us by your omnipotent right hand and empower us to live as disciples of our Lord, in whose name we pray. Amen

---

[80] Who, What, How and Why, White Booklet, Narcotics Anonymous World Services, Inc., 2000.

[81] Who, What, How and Why, White Booklet, Narcotics Anonymous World Services, Inc., 2000.

[82] Who, What, How and Why, White Booklet, Narcotics Anonymous World Services, Inc., 2000.

Our First Priority

**But seek first the kingdom of God and his righteousness,
and all these things will be added to you.
Matthew 6:33**

In addiction we knew what our priorities were. Getting high and getting more drugs to get high on. At first we carried out what seemed on the surface like a normal life, but then things began to show. We had secret friends that we bought from, other secret friends we used with. Our behavior suffered, we began to act erratically and our friendships suffered. As our addiction grew and money got tight we failed to pay our bills, we borrowed money from friends but were unable to pay them back. Our homes fell apart, our relationships with relatives and family went from bad to worse. We tried to maintain our jobs because that was providing money to get drugs with but this too suffered and we lost jobs, frequently. Our priorities were to maintain the addiction at all costs and in the end it cost us everything that was once important to us. Then we turned to get help and God turned our lives around.

Some of us in recovery will say that it is our number one priority to stay clean. However, it might be better to think of our priorities in another way. Our first priority should be to God, who is the One who made our recovery possible, and who is the One who sustains us day by day. By having our relationship with God our number one priority, then in most cases the other parts of our lives will fall into their proper places. Many of us have reported that with fulfilling God's will for our lives as our first priority that many of our other problems in life have gotten straightened out. That this was especially true in our relationships with others we were close to. That rather than focusing on straightening out the relationship problems as our number one priority, we focused on our relationship to God and the rest just fell into line.

Heavenly Father, you sent your son to seek and save the lost. We were lost but now are found, thanks to you and your son Jesus. Keep us ever in your sheepfold and close to our shepherd. May we never take our eyes off of you and your son, in whose name we pray. Amen

Spiritual Practices: Breathing Exercise 4 by 4

**I cried aloud to the Lord, and he
answered me from his holy hill. Selah
Psalm 3:4**

This breathing exercise has been called by a few names, both tactical breathing, and also combat breathing. It was developed to help de-escalate high-stress situations by activating our own relaxation response through a specific pattern of breathing. Simply put, when our emotions want to dominate our actions, this will return us back to being dominated by the thinking part of our brains.

When a stressful event happens in our lives and we are overrun with anxiety our bodies try to empower us to survive it. Depending on the circumstances, some of those responses are helpful, some are counterproductive. When our bodies dump a large load of adrenaline into our bloodstream our emotions tend to dominate our actions rather than allowing our rational thinking to dominate our actions. That can save our lives in an extremely dangerous situation, but it can also get us into a lot of trouble in other circumstances.

This is a simple breathing exercise that will help us to manage our emotional state. Don't breath too slow or too fast, pace yourself so that you do not pass out or hyperventilate. It's simple:

- Take as deep a breath in as you can through your nose for the count of four. Expand your stomach as you do this.
- Hold your breath to the count of four.
- Exhale completely through your mouth to the count of four. Relax your stomach as you do this.
- With your lungs empty, hold your breath for the count of four and repeat the cycle.
- Repeat this for a minimum of four times or longer as needed until the stressful situation subsides.

As you work through the stressful situation work on flexing and relaxing your muscles throughout your body with each cycle to further release all of your tension. As your thoughts relax the stress being lived out in your body will dissipate too. By doing this exercise you are managing your emotions in a healthy way and choosing how you will react to the stress in your life

Lord God, in our earthly journey we find that there is much that comes our way that is beyond our ability to manage. Aid us and guide us so that we will always turn to you when we are anxious and under stress.

Help us to manage our emotions, help us to manage what we might do and say. May our lives always be a reflection of the life of your son Jesus Christ who gave himself on the cross for our salvation. In his name. Amen

From Glory to Glory Transformation

But we all, with unveiled face,
beholding as in a mirror the glory of the Lord,
are being transformed into the same image from glory to glory,
just as from the Lord, the Spirit.
2 Corinthians 3:18 NASB

As disciples of Jesus Christ, we care called Christians. Our name, *Christian*, means *little Christs*. We were first called that in the city of Antioch in the first century.[83] We were given that name because we resemble our Lord by our conduct in life. We know our Lord, we love him and we have a relationship with him. Because of this we continue to be transformed, from being fallen in sin and active in addiction, to saints of God who by our lives reflect the greatness of the power of our God.

For us in recovery from addiction we know something of the greatness of God and his glorious reputation. Many of us had given up the hope that somehow we might be able to quit. We were fallen into deep despair, some of us had even given up living and tried to end our lives. Our recovery was made possible solely by the glorious reputation of what God has done and continues to do in the lives of addicts everywhere.

The resurrection of Jesus Christ was accomplished by the power of God's Holy Spirit which brought him back from the dead and gave life to him again. This is the same power that is at work in us, to deliver us from the strangle hold of addiction and bring us into freedom from drug addiction. This is transformation by the great and glorious power of our God.

God, you have called us to be your people and given your name to us. Transform us and use us for your purposes. Let others see your greatness in what you have done in our lives. This we pray in Jesus' name. Amen

---

[83] Acts 11:26

The Group Process I

**And let us consider how to stir up
one another to love and good works,
not neglecting to meet together,
as is the habit of some, but encouraging one another,
and all the more as you see the Day drawing near.
Hebrews 10:24-25**

In 12-step programs there is a strong emphasis on attending meetings. At the meeting there is commonly a review of the 12-steps and the 12 Traditions, a reading or two from a daily meditation book, along with other recovery related literature. This program works to get us into recovery and keep us in recovery too. This format was modeled after the Oxford Group's Bible study meetings from the early 20th century. Another type of meeting is the speaker meeting. These are typically large group meetings and someone shares their story of addiction and recovery.

The reason these meetings work in supporting us in our recovery is because they are modeled after an active faith life in the fellowship of the Christian church. In that setting a Christian goes to worship on Sunday, which compares loosely to the speaker meeting. The 12-step meeting is modeled off of a Christian prayer or Bible study meeting.

We all need to know that no one recovers in isolation. There is an indispensable need for interaction. The group process has a refining quality to it like nothing else. In the group we hear from others with identical issues that we are having. We find courage that they are being open about their experiences. It is a safe place to gather and we find help in all that is done and said there. It was King Solomon, who was undebatably the wisest man who ever lived, who said this about the benefits of fellowship, "Iron sharpens iron, and one man sharpens another."[84]

Heavenly Father, may the body of Christ, which is your son's church on earth, be blessed by you so that all of us may grow in faith, love, and Christian hope throughout our lives. Use all of us and empower all of us to build each other up in love. Through Christ our Lord we pray Amen

---

[84] Proverbs 27:17

Fellowship

**Whoever trusts in his own mind is a fool,
but he who walks in wisdom will be delivered.
Proverbs 28:26**

In our own heads and in our own thoughts, we can imagine just about anything. We are, like our Maker, creative beings. For the addict that becomes a problem. Our addiction takes license with this and runs with it in the wind. It gets us thinking and believing all kinds of lies. Our imaginations conjure up the wildest of ideas for us. On drugs we got to a place where we were not grounded in reality but in a fantastical world of our own making. For some, because of the addiction, and because of the drugs that we used we might have resembled someone who was insane. In some cases, we did enough damage to our brains that we develop a mental illness. If we isolated ourselves, either by living only among other addicts or living alone, we could have become very delusional.

In recovery we need to seek out the help that we need which includes the fellowship of other solid Christians in recovery. We do need to interact with them and allow them to have a good influence on us. We need to attend 12-step meetings, worship on Sundays, a Bible study and prayer group. We need to receive spiritual counseling from a competent pastor or maybe from a professionally licensed Christian counselor who is trained in addictions. We need to just hang out for coffee with other Christians and enjoy their fellowship. These interactions can all have a normalizing and refining effect on us, bringing us back from the craziness of addiction. While we will always be addicts, we do not have to continue living like one in any fashion. We also do not get into recovery by living in a vacuum. The group process is necessary.

Heavenly Father, restore our lives and our thoughts to sanity. Deliver us from our crazy and sometimes dark thinking. Give us clarity and center our minds on you, through Christ our Lord we pray. Amen.

The Reformation of Faith

**My little children, for whom I am again
in the anguish of childbirth until Christ is formed in you!
Galatians 4:19**

It was in the fifteenth and sixteenth centuries that the Reformation of our faith took place. It was a return to true faith, based on the Holy Scriptures of the Bible written by the prophets and apostles. It was a clearing out of the false doctrines and practices that had come into the church which were corrupting true faith. Martin Luther was perhaps the chief and most vocal of the many who worked for the restoration of the church to its true faith. He stressed that we are saved by grace alone, by faith alone, and the Bible alone is our sole authority in all matters of life and faith.

Luther also believed that the Reformation needed to come to every generation. What he meant by that was that each up and coming generation needs to be raised in the faith from childhood on up. Parents need to nurture their children in our faith by bringing them to church so they can be nurtured there as well. That is the first part of faith formation.

The second part of faith formation takes place when our children come into their teen and early adult years. It is then that their minds are able to process all that they have been told and have believed in. The hope is that they in turn accept it for their own. Their faith, hopefully, becomes one that is not just there because they were raised in a Christian home, but because they have accepted Christianity for themselves as an individual.

Beyond this, as maturing adults, as our lives unfold and we face the challenges of life our faith continues to mature. The hope here is that as our life moves forward, our faith grows with us and is being refined and reformed into a deeper, richer, and truer faith. In that processes the ideals and generalizations are made, the misconceptions and mistaken ideas are refined and reformed by the active Christian lives we live.

Heavenly Father, keep us in true faith in you and aid parents as they raise their children in our faith as well. In Jesus Christ's name. Amen

One Life and One Master

**Jesus said,
No one can serve two masters, for either
he will hate the one and love the other,
or he will be devoted to the one and despise the other.
You cannot serve God and money.
Matthew 6:24**

While this text refers to serving God or money, the principle is equally applicable in our lives as addicts in recovery. Jesus stated the obvious, we cannot have two masters. We cannot serve our addictions and expect that this will not adversely affect our relationship with God. In the case of our addiction we know first-hand how consuming this is in our lives. Our addiction to drugs wants us for its own and will leave nothing of us to spare when it is done ravaging our lives. On the other hand, God has said he is a jealous God and therefore he does not want to share us with anyone else, or in this case with anything else, such as drugs.[85]

As addicts we know the great guilt that we came under as we used drugs and compromised ourselves before God. We knew and experienced the agony of being torn in two as we were drawn to our loving God, but were also ensnared by our addictions. We knew that there were things about our addiction that we were not ready to give up because we still liked some parts of it. In some of our lives we kept using because we feared the terrible pain of going through physical withdrawal. This contributed to our growing sense of guilt that we tried to mask with more drug use.

Finally, with the intervention of the Lord we were freed of our active drug using. As we moved forward in our recovery our desire and the temptation to use continued to fade daily. We felt great relief in having just the one Master, our Lord Jesus Christ. Our love of God grew and we came to thoroughly hate the drugs for what they had done to us. We found ourselves rejoicing at the renewal he brought to us and rested securely in his all-consuming love.

Heavenly Father, free us from all that keeps us from a full life in you. Restore to us the lives that you have planned for us from the beginning of time. Through Christ our Lord. Amen

---

[85] Deuteronomy 5:9

Restoration

**I will extol you, O LORD, for you have drawn
me up and have not let my foes rejoice over me.
O LORD my God, I cried to you for help, and you have healed me.
O LORD, you have brought up my soul from Sheol;
you restored me to life from among those who go down to the pit.
Psalm 30:1-3**

We share in a mystical bond with our forebearers in the faith. Therefore, we are able to share in their experiences in our lives while using their words. In this psalm we hear the words of King David who is praising God for salvation from his foes who meant to do him harm. He called to God for help and he was helped. He was in a very dire situation, he referred to his soul as being in Sheol, meaning hell. He praised God for lifting him up from his distress and restoring his life from a pit. Our God is a miracle working God.

In recovery it is not hard for us to recall our times of distress. These words are easily transferable to our past when our addictions were active. The Lord proved himself faithful to us as he did with David. David God's brought healing to him, something we all need a lot of. We can recall similar times in our own lives. It would not be wrong, unless it causes us too much distress to do this, to remember times in our lives that were difficult for us. The words of David remind many of us of own past. We can believe in our hearts that just as God heard his prayer, he will be faithful to hear our prayer. We take hope because just as God delivered David from the hell of his life, he will also deliver and safeguard us. The hope for our healing is that we can recall those hard times for what they were, but that they will no longer be distressing to us anymore.

Heavenly Father, our past sometimes still haunts us and brings us distress. Comfort us with your presence and bring healing to our minds, memories, and hearts in all that our past holds. Through the name of him who died and rose again, Jesus Christ our Lord and Savior we pray. Amen

Maturity: Growing Up

**Brothers, do not be children in your thinking.
Be infants in evil, but in your thinking be mature.
1 Corinthians 14:20**

In most cases, when we began to use drugs, our natural abilities to mature as a person stopped functioning. If we were fourteen years old and our use was significate enough, we remain, at best a fourteen-year-old in our maturity until we got into recovery and we started to mature again. It is even possible that we regressed significantly as a result of using, and it doesn't matter what drugs we were using. Other factors can further slow or complicate our maturing, such things as:

Being raised with or by an addict, or an alcoholic.
Having had poor relationships with our siblings.
Significant losses in death or complicated grief.
Abuse: sexual, physical, emotional, social.
Being involved in crime.
ADD/ADHD.

In recovery from drug use things can change, but merely abstaining alone is never enough. We needed to get a jump start for our lives to get us moving forward into maturity again. We may need to find significant healing from past abuse that we were subjected to. We need to actively seek out help, things like meetings, inpatient or outpatient treatment, a Christian mental health counselor, spiritual connectedness with the church and resuming the pursuit of our lives.

Heavenly Father, fill us with your love and help us to restart our lives anew in you. Help us to grow in maturity and continue with normal lives again. Where there has been abuse in our lives, bring healing, and lead us in the way that is everlasting. Through Christ our Lord. Amen

Spiritual Practices: Meditation and the Breath-of-Life

And the LORD **God formed man of the dust of the ground, and breathed into his nostrils the breath of life; and man became a living soul.**
Genesis 2:7 KJV

Spend a few minutes preparing for this exercise by laying down, closing your eyes, and listening to some soothing music with a slow rhythm. If you won't be too cold have an electric fan blowing over your face. Then recite out loud the verse from Genesis 2:7. Imagine that you are newly formed by God from the dust of the earth, but not yet alive. Exhale and don't inhale for a short time. Wait until you feel slightly uncomfortable with not breathing. Then turn your face directly into the flow of the air from the fan and inhale deeply through your nose. As you do this image that it is God himself who is breathing directly into your nostrils the breath-of-life .

Imagine that now your heart has just started beating. With each slow and simple breath that you take imagine that they are your first few breaths. Wiggle your fingers as if for the first time, then wiggle your toes again as if for the first time. Take several deep breaths in your nose and out your mouth. Move your shoulders slightly, then your arms, right and then left. Move your legs in the same way. Pause and take several more deep breaths in your nose. Hold them for the count of five and then just relax and let your falling chest simply push the air out of your mouth. As you inhale imagine it is God breathing into your nostrils and filling your lungs with his power. As you near the end of your meditation imagine that God has instilled in you everything you need to know to begin your new life with him. As you open your eyes imagine you are seeing God and his son for the first time and how wonderful that is.

Heavenly Father, by your almighty power you created the world, the universe and all that there is. You made mankind for your glory and have breathed into our lungs the breath-of-life. By your life-giving-spirit in us, enliven us to journey free of drug use and in all that we do may we live for your glory. Through your son's name, Jesus Christ our Lord and Savior we pray. Amen

Spiritual Practices: Our Prayer Life

**But you, beloved, building yourselves up in your
most holy faith and praying in the Holy Spirit.
Jude 20**

Our prayers are especially important to our spirituality. Through our prayers God includes us in his work. Someone once said that prayer moves the hand of God, and they were right too, our prayers make a difference. There is also much to pray for. We need to pray on a daily basis, maybe even several times a day. This is a list of common things that need our attention in prayer:

> For support in our own recovery from addiction.
> For addicts everywhere who need to find recovery.
> For those in recovery, that they may continue in recovery.
> The sick and needy, the homeless and the hungry.
> Our military men and women and their families.
> The world, our nation, and our community.
> Our home church and the church throughout the world.
> Sunday School, church workers, ministers, pastors, priests, volunteers, worshipers.
> For our own family and relatives.
> Our neighbors.
> For those in Government.
>> For our president and our national leaders.
>> For our governor and our state leaders.
>> For our county and local governments.
> Law enforcement, fire, paramedics, and emergency workers.
> Schools and colleges and students everywhere.
> Prosperity in commerce in our land.

Summer-Time Prayers
> For the safety of our children on summer vacation and for travelers.
> For farmers and their lands, for rain and sunshine, crops, and livestock, so that the world may receive their daily bread and be fed.

In Fall
> For children returning to school.
> For the harvest, for safety and protection.

In Winter
    Safe travel.
    Favorable weather.

In Spring
    For graduates.
    For farmers and the planting of crops.
    The birth of new farm animals.

    Heavenly Father, enrich our prayer life and help us to grow in our skills as intercessors for all that is needed. Reveal to us those people that need our prayers and aid us in lifting them up to you. Remind us throughout the day to turn to you in prayer and give us the words to say as we pray for the needs of others. In Jesus' holy name. Amen

By the Grace of God Alone

**Therefore let anyone who thinks that he stands take heed lest he fall.
1 Corinthians 10:12**

Too often we have heard someone say that they quit on their own. Sometimes they even say it was easy, "I know what to do. I did it before. I was clean then, I can do it again." There are several problems with what they are saying. If they are addicted, which is likely, they cannot quit on their own, it is the nature of the beast. They may have surrendered to God and gotten his help, and that was why it worked for them. If that is the case then they have failed to give credit to God and acknowledged the major role he played in their clean time. Or, they may have summed up some wimpy amount of will-power and gotten "clean" for a short time. While they did it entirely on their own, it was already certain that they could not sustain it for long, as is always the case when it comes to our feeble will-power.

It is essential, call it what you will, it is critical that we get God's aid in quitting. We cannot do it on our own. We can choose to take the drugs, but we cannot merely choose to not take them, there are no two ways about it in the universe. We need to know that it is not a combination of God and us working together to quit. It is entirely God's action on us without our contributing anything additional that gets us clean. To take credit even in part could easily undermine and weaken our recovery. We are not able to quit and get clean on our own in part or whole.

In recovery we have God working in our lives. He is the Almighty. Our part in recovery is the addiction part, and we cannot afford to get confused about that. In all that we do in life we need to acknowledge his grace to us, that he has put his spirit in us and he is the one that sustains us in our lives.

Heavenly Father, thank you for all that you have done and are doing for us. You are awesome! In our weakness be the One who sustains us, in our foolishness bring us wisdom and in our time of need rescue us and hold us close to your heart, through Christ our Lord. Amen.

The Love of God Wins our Hearts Over

We Love Because He First Loved Us
1 John 4:19

In addiction we lived to use and used to live.[86] We might have started out loving our friends and using drugs, but in the end we all ended up loving drugs and using our friends. Our recoveries were made possible by the love our Savior has for us in his heart. For love Jesus endured the shame, endured the cross and died to save us from our sinful selves. In response we love our Lord and it is a love relationship that results in obedience, rather than a relationship of obedience out of fear because of the threat of being punished. In recovery we can admit that while we once love our drugs; now we love God more, much more.

There are qualities about using drugs that many of us liked. Over time the upside of using had its downfall in our lives. Some of us hit rock bottom and then turned to God for help and recovery. Some of us didn't hit rock bottom, we didn't need to do that to see how our lives would end. Of course, our addictive nature lies to us, telling us that we are now able to return to occasional drug use without falling back into full blown addiction again. We need to remind ourselves that our addiction would like to only nostalgically remember our drug using days. We know that to use again would be to our ruin. We turn our former love of drugs down because we have come to desperately love the Lord who brought us into recovery.

Lord Jesus, we love you more than all things in life. Fill us always with the Holy Spirit and keep us growing in our recoveries. Thank you for your never ending, never failing love for us. Amen

---

[86] Who, What, How and Why, White Booklet, Narcotics Anonymous World Services, Inc., 2000.

Progress Not Perfection I

Not that I have already obtained this or am already perfect, but I press on to make it my own, because Christ Jesus has made me his own. Brothers, I do not consider that I have made it my own. But one thing I do: forgetting what lies behind and straining forward to what lies ahead, I press on toward the goal for the prize of the upward call of God in Christ Jesus. Let those of us who are mature think this way.
Philippians 3:12-15a

Even before the addiction started, there was a good chance some of us had set our standards in life too high. We strove for a perfection in life that didn't exist and because it didn't exist we never arrived at it, nor could we. In addiction we found some short lived relief for this false sense of failure because being high gave us good feelings. The drugs lied to us and told us we had achieved greatness because of how they made us feel. When we weren't high, because we did not reach our false ideal of perfection in life, we felt like a failure and that led us to get high again.

In recovery we adopted a new way of living that included the phrase, *progress not perfection.*[87] Because this became one of our values we gave up the false notion that we could do something perfectly. We gave up believing that we needed to be perfect. We came to believe that being good enough the way we were was simply fine. This took a great load off our shoulders, and as we applied it to other people we were able to see them in a new and more healthy way.

In our faith life we found that we did not need to measure up as perfect Christians. We realized that there is no such thing as a perfect Christian. We were able to accept our sinfulness and confessed our sins to God and received his forgiveness because Jesus died for our sins. We found we were accepted by God because he loved us and for the sake of his son he accepted us.

Heavenly Father, thank you for loving and accepting us, sinners that we are. Help us to journey in this life and to grow in faith, love, and hope, through Christ our Lord we pray. Amen

---

[87] From N.A.'s list of Phrases.

More Than Meets the Eye

**Jesus said,
"Therefore be as shrewd as snakes and as innocent as doves."
Matthew 10:16**

Our common enemy, addiction, has been described in many words. It is cunning and baffling to name just a few.[88] Because of these qualities that it possesses we found that in recovery we needed to wise up and fast. Unfortunately, as addicts, even in recovery, we don't necessarily wise up fast, but we do wise up. We found that we needed to get to our meetings, several a week in fact, which was wise. We found that we needed help to not revert into believing in the lies again. For that we saturated our lives with the truth. We told ourselves the same things over and over again, I am an addict and cannot use again, not even just once. If I do, one is too many and a thousand is never enough.[89] We looked to the collective wisdom of the groups we attended, the program we worked, our counselors, our recovery friends, and most of all the Lord. By the grace of God we were in recovery and by the grace of God we will be staying in recovery.

As Christians in recovery we have a certain advantage. We have a personal relationship with God, commonly referred to as our higher power in some of the recovery literature. For us it is not an impersonal relationship with an impersonal deity. In our personal relationship with God through Jesus Christ we are able to call on his name for the help that we need. We have the indwelling of the Holy Spirit, who is always present and able to help us spiritually in supernatural ways. We need to turn to God daily, often and in the confidence that he will lead us, guide us, and come to our rescue as often as we need him.

Heavenly Father, thank you for all the spiritual gifts you have given us. Most of all, thank you for the gift of your Holy Spirit and your son in whose name we pray. Amen

---

[88] Michigan, Fletcher R., "Never Alone ... Never Again." *The NA Magazine* July 2001: 9.
[89] Who, What, How and Why, White Booklet, Narcotics Anonymous World Services, Inc., 2000.

Progress Not Perfection II

Not that I have already obtained this or am already perfect, but I press on to make it my own, because Christ Jesus has made me his own. Brothers, I do not consider that I have made it my own. But one thing I do: forgetting what lies behind and straining forward to what lies ahead.
Philippians 3:12-13

Our modern day ideal of perfection is an illusion, and it can be a dangerous one for us in recovery. Perfection as we might imagine it to be does not exist in this world for us, even though the Apostle Paul makes mention of the word. The word that he used for perfect is the Greek New Testament word *telos*. It might have better been translated *mature* because that is our goal in life, to become mature people as we get older. Paul's goal was to press on into all that his Christian life held for him. He let go of all his many outstanding achievements even though he was a growth oriented man. He considered them as trash as he reached forward to what God had in store for him.

For us in our recoveries we have that saying, *progress not perfection*. If we think for any reason that we can somehow obtain to perfection we are only fooling ourselves. God is perfect, and he alone is perfect. If we thought we were perfect, or even near to it, it would become a sinful self-righteous burden around our necks that would soon be proven to be false.

God has a plan for our maturity in recovery and it isn't that we won't be making any mistakes in life. His plan is that when we do screw up, we get help from him. When we screw up we admit to it and make apologies to whoever we might have hurt or offended. As maturing Christians we can accept our imperfection and allow it to be seen by others without feeling overly vulnerable. We can admit to our imperfect nature and trust God to guide us in our imperfection.

Heavenly Father, you sent your only son to find us when we had gone astray. Thank you for saving our lives from sin and the destruction of our drug addictions. Grant to us a certain calm assurance that in all things you will be there for us. For the sake of your son, Christ Jesus our Lord. Amen

Laugher is Good Medicine

When the LORD **restored the fortunes of Zion,**
we were like those who dream.
Then our mouth was filled with laughter,
and our tongue with shouts of joy;
then they said among the nations,
"The LORD **has done great things for them."**
The LORD **has done great things for us; we are glad.**
Psalm 126:1-3

For many of us our pasts hold a world of hurt that we suffered under, as well as a world of hurt that we may have inflicted on others by our addiction. Many of us suffer from depression and anxiety. We live somber lives because we are free and clean, but sometimes we are too somber in our general dispositions. Not that it is all bad, there is an upside to it, it can help us to be this way in order to maintain our recovery.

Along with our serious nature we need to be actively enjoying humor too. There have been scientific studies done that show laughter is incredibly good for us. To get a good belly jiggling laugh in has many personal benefits:

Reduces stress	Decreases pain
Relaxes muscles	Reduces blood pressure
Reduces anxiety	Prevents heart disease
Boosts immune system	Lifts our mood
Boosts cancer fighting cells	

There are also benefits to laughing in a social gathering too. It strengthens the ties that bind us together, builds teamwork and it soothes conflict. Because we are in recovery we need to enjoy clean humor that is not at the expense of addicts or that glorifies using either.

Heavenly Father, help us to enjoy our lives in recovery and bless us with the gift of laughter. Help us to find joy in all that you have done for us and lead us in the way that is everlasting. Through Christ Jesus our Lord and Savior. Amen

Jesus Was Tempted

And they offered him wine mixed with myrrh, but he did not take it. And they crucified him.
Mark 15:23-24

Perhaps this does not get shared enough in our recovery community of addicts. We all need to know that our Lord was indeed himself offered drugs to use. It was at the time of his crucifixion. He had already been severely beaten by a Roman soldier. He was severely whipped and according to tradition he received 39 lashes. History tells us that this was so harsh a punishment that many prisoners died from it before their sentence of execution could be carried out.

Jesus was suffering from severe pain. The *myrrh* that they offered him was likely a compound that included a narcotic strength pain killer. Gospel writer Matthew calls it *gall*.[90] This drug is referred to in the ancient world as being produced from a berry producing plant, which could have been the poppy. The opium poppy seed that opioids come from was well known in the ancient world from at least the fourth century BC. It is possible that this was included in the compound that was offered to him, but its exact makeup is uncertain. What is certain is that myrrh alone is a sedative that dulls the senses and it acts on the opioid receptors in the brain to kill pain. Jesus tasted the compound but then would not drink it. Our Lord would have been well justified in taking it given the severe pain he was in, however there were significant reasons for his rejecting it. He needed to experience the immeasurable agony and torture of the cross in order to join in humanities suffering from all the eons of time past and yet to come.

This example does not mean that we should not take pain medicine if we are properly prescribed one by a physician who knows about our addiction in advance. If we are in that much pain from an accidental injury or perhaps surgery then it is necessary for a short time under the correct circumstances and supervision. Equally true, to use over the counter pain relievers can be very appropriate when we take them for a legitimate reason and use them according to their directions.

Jesus' reasons for not accepting the myrrh included the fact that he was sent here by the Father to die on the cross for our sins. The medicine could have prevented him from dying because of crucifixion. Rather, he could have succumb to a combination of his injuries and the compound. The drug could have hastened his death by crucifixion. This would have cut short God's plan for our salvation through Jesus' suffering and death

---

[90] Matthew 24:34

not just on the cross, but his death because of the cross. That would have compromised and made null his death's redeeming qualities. By rejecting the medicine and the relief it would have brought him, he has shared in all of our endless suffering and he experienced a human death in all of its fullness. Therefore, he has completely shared in our experiences when we were tempted to use.

    Heavenly Father, your son has truly joined with us in life and all of its difficulties. We know that he was tempted in all things including the temptation to use drugs. As he rejected drug use let us join in with him and also find strength by his example to resist temptation. Lead us and guide us by his example in life, that we may lead peaceable and holy lives in all that we do and say. In his holy name we pray, Jesus Christ our Lord and Savior. Amen

> **Since then we have a great high priest who has passed through the heavens, Jesus, the Son of God, let us hold fast our confession. For we do not have a high priest who is unable to sympathize with our weaknesses, but one who in every respect has been tempted as we are, yet without sin. Let us then with confidence draw near to the throne of grace, that we may receive mercy and find grace to help in time of need.**
> **Hebrews 4:14-16**

We Shall Also Bear the Image of The Man of Heaven

**As was the man of dust, so also are those who are of the dust,
and as is the man of heaven, so also are those who are of heaven.
Just as we have borne the image of the man of dust,
we shall also bear the image of the man of heaven.
1 Corinthians 15:48-49**

After the fall God told Adam, and his wife Eve heard it too, that as a result of his sin, since he was taken from the dust, then to the dust he would return at the time of his death. We, like him, are people of the dust. We bear the image of the man of the dust, it is our mortal nature. As people of the dust, who are mortal and finite, we are subject to lead a life of sin. We have fallen and there is nothing we can do to contribute to our redemption. Likewise, there is not enough that we can do to regain our lives when drugs have overcome us. We are addicts.

In our redemption from sin we are changed, day by day. We were born-of-the-Spirit and are made in the image of Jesus Christ, we are Christians. However, in our addictions we did not resemble the image of our Lord. We resembled the man of the dust, mortal, enslaved to sin, and the life of an addict using drugs. Whether our using days were over at the time of our conversion, or if they continued on afterward, God's plan for our freedom was unchanged. Just as Jesus guided and taught his disciples for three years, so also we need his help and the help of others so that we can be free from addiction. In surrendering our lives to God we also accept the changes that he wants to bring to us. We accept the inpatient or outpatient treatment that God provides for us through others. We accept that we need to go to 12-step meetings and that we need to die to self-daily, picking up our crosses and following him.

Heavenly Father, by the blood of your son you have washed us clean from all of our sins. By the power of your Holy Spirit, help us to submit to your will and to walk in your ways day by day for all the days of our lives. This we ask in the name of Jesus Christ your dear son. Amen

Becoming What We Hate

For as he thinketh in his heart, so is he.
Proverbs 23:7 KJV

By a strange twist of circumstances we sometimes become like the very things we hate. For example, we might have grown up in a home where the discipline was unreasonable and the punishment was harsh, or even abusive. We may have vowed in our youth that we would never, never do that to our own children. Yet, in adulthood we found ourselves acting in the same ways. The dynamics of how the things we hated became part of our life happens in two ways. First, we were trained how to be a parent by our parents when we were in childhood, so we live in their example. Second, this was reinforced by our vow to never act the way they did. Odd as that may sound it is true. We spent too much time hating their behavior. We reminded ourselves of it and relived it by remembering our suffering. Through these long held preoccupations we gravitated towards what our mind had been intensely focused on for such a great length.

In recovery we need to take stock of our lives and make amends. We need to reconsider our ways and make changes where changes are needed. We need to uncover the source of our unhealthy ways in life, and look to God to dismantle and remove them from our lifestyles. The primary focus of our minds should not be on what we don't want to be like, but on what we do want to live like. We need to find healing from God for the abuses we were subject to so that they are not weighing us down in bondage. In Christ we have become new people and we want to live in the freedom he won for us on the cross.

God in heaven, aid and guide us in our recovery so that we may abandon our unhealthy ways and take on new and better ways to live. Free us from the weight of our past that hold us down in bondage and lift us up in Christ so that we may bring glory to your name. This we ask through Christ Jesus our Lord, who lives and reigns with you and the Holy Spirit, one God now and forever. Amen

The Love of Christ Controls Us

**For the love of Christ controls us, because we have concluded this:
that one has died for all, therefore all have died;
and he died for all, that those who live might no
longer live for themselves but for him who
for their sake died and was raised.
2 Corinthians 5:14-15**

Once we were tempted to use drugs on an occasional basis. This gave way to using them more often. Monthly use lead to weekly use, weekly use gave way to daily use. At that point we were controlled by our addictions. We lost jobs, friends, family, our self-respect, and all that we owned to the addiction. We were enslaved by it, living homeless and on the street, we were used by it and even left for dead by it. There was no escape, we were unable to control ourselves, we failed time and time again to quit on our own. We had passively resigned to let it rule and reign in our lives.

In recovery we came to know of the great power that God has to deliver us from this terrible evil. As a result, we came into a new, or perhaps a renewed, relationship with our Savior. We found strength in surrendering to him and our love for him grew in ways that we had never imagined possible. So grateful we became that it was not even a forethought that we should owe our lives to him. Willingly in our surrender to him we knew that our lives had become infinitely woven into his. In his death we found that our sinful nature and our addiction was also put to death with him on the cross. Because he suffered for us we found strength in our trials. Because he rose from the dead we found victory in his resurrection.

It is a special love for our Savior that grows in our heart. With this love we live for him, to serve him and bring him glory by our lives. This love surrounds us, persuades us, and compels us in all that we do. We know that he delivered us from death and the chains of enslavement. We love him freely for all that he willingly did for us.

God, you have given us hope that because your son died for our sins and rose, we too can die to sin, self and our addictions and rise with Christ to live for you. In Jesus' name. Amen

Forensic Righteousness

**For what does the Scripture say?
"Abraham believed God, and it was counted to him as righteousness."
Romans 4:3**

In addiction many of us suffered with self-condemnation over our lifestyle. We also suffered from an extremely poor self-image, which was one of the reasons we used in the first place. The former and the latter both kept us using and consequently we rode a downward spiral of self-hate and condemnation. In recovery getting through those terrible feelings about ourselves was not easy. It was a problem so overwhelming that only God could help us and thankfully he did.

The Scriptures give us Abraham as an example in the faith. He was a pagan and as such he worshipped many false gods. He was a sinner and far from good or righteous. Then one day God revealed himself to Abraham and the man came to believe in the one and only true God. Because of his faith in God, God counted him *as if* he was righteous. This is called forensic righteousness. God *counted* him as if he was righteous, which is an accounting term. His debt was wiped out and the books were balanced in Abraham's favor.

It works the same way in our own lives. As Christians in recovery we came to believe that God could restore us to sanity and to a healthy lifestyle. We might not feel like we are cleansed of our sins and from our drug use in particular, but by God's declaration we have been made righteous in Christ. By the power of Jesus' shed blood God has washed us clean and made us his very own people. We may wonder if that is enough but then we need to be reminded of the power of God's spoken word. By his Word God spoke all things into existence in the days of creation. By this same power we are cleansed and made to be righteous saints.

God, thank you for declaring us righteous by the blood that your son shed on the cross of Calvary. Thank you for moving in our lives and redeeming us from not only our sins but also from our addiction to drugs. Aid us in living solely for you. Through Christ Jesus we pray. Amen

Higher Power Verses God through Jesus Christ our Savior and Lord

**For while we were still weak, at the
right time Christ died for the ungodly.
Romans 5:6**

Jesus of Nazareth is not just the Savior of our sins, he is absolutely the Savior of our recovery. It could even be said, *while we were still in bondage and addicted to drugs, Christ died to free us from slavery to drugs.* Not to minimize salvation from our sins, that is the first and foremost reason for his redeeming death. For us as addicts we benefit from knowing and believing that the Lord is our Savior from addition too. We need to include this often in our daily thoughts and give him thanks and praise throughout the day for being our Savior from addiction too.

This title *savior* was used in the ancient world when a kingdom was under the threat of war. A champion fighter would rise up, gather the fighting men, and lead them out of the city to the battlefield and hopefully defeat the enemy who had threatened them. When he won the battle, he would triumphantly ride back into the city on his horse to an ancient version of a tickertape parade. He was hailed as the savior of the city because he saved them from domination. This term was then applied to Jesus who took up the fight against the devil, sin, death, and the grave, and won victoriously. Needless to say, he took up the fight against addiction and also won there for us.

Jesus himself rode triumphant into the city of Jerusalem too. The people welcomed him as their victorious Savior saying, "Hosanna![91] Blessed is he who comes in the name of the Lord, even the King of Israel!"[92] They most likely had the thoughts that he would reestablish the ancient Kingdom of David. Instead he established a new Kingdom of his own and in it he is the Savior of our souls from sin and the Savior of our recovery from drug addiction.

Lord God, your son is the Savior of our addiction and recovery. We bless you and give thanks for all that he has done for us in delivering us from bondage. In his name we pray. Amen

---

[91] Hosanna means *save us now.*
[92] John 12:12-15

Pity Parties Don't Happen Anymore, Right?

We rejoice in our sufferings, knowing that suffering produces endurance, and endurance produces character, and character produces hope, and hope does not put us to shame, because God's love has been poured into our hearts through the Holy Spirit who has been given to us.
Romans 5:3-5

    As addicts we have all known our share of suffering. Most of us have a common reason for using, to numb the pain of trauma in our lives. We suffered emotionally and physically, mentally, and socially, sometimes unbearably from past and present abuse. The high brought us momentary relief and for that we kept coming back to use again. Our addictions added to our suffering as well. From getting infected with something like hepatitis or HIV. From drinking alcohol, having a blackout, and waking up next to a stranger and not knowing what happened the night before. Our relationships with everyone suffered and there was no end to it. We ached and cried inside but our exterior was typically the best one we could put on even though it was fake. The suffering that Paul is taking about in this passage includes an addict's suffering. Much of our suffering needed healing and with that we hoped that the painful memories would stop being painful.

    In our recovery we sometimes suffer with wanting to return and get high again in the hopes that it will bring us some relief and that we might enjoy it too. As the passage says, suffering, which for us means struggling to fight off the temptation to use again, will produce endurance for us, which produces character. We need help with our character traits, to shed the old addiction lifestyle and take on a new redeemed and Christ-like character. This brings us into hope which tells us substantially that we are being renewed and transformed. We see the changes that brings us joy and patience knowing that our perseverance is being rewarded.

    Heavenly Father, by your grace we have been redeemed and translated into the Kingdom of your son, Jesus Christ our Lord. Continue this work of deliverance in us and purge our minds and hearts of all drug related thoughts and behaviors. In Jesus' name we pray this. Amen

Healthy Boundaries

**Whoever belittles his neighbor lacks sense,
but a man of understanding remains silent.
Whoever goes about slandering reveals secrets,
but he who is trustworthy in spirit keeps a thing covered.
Proverbs 11:12-13**

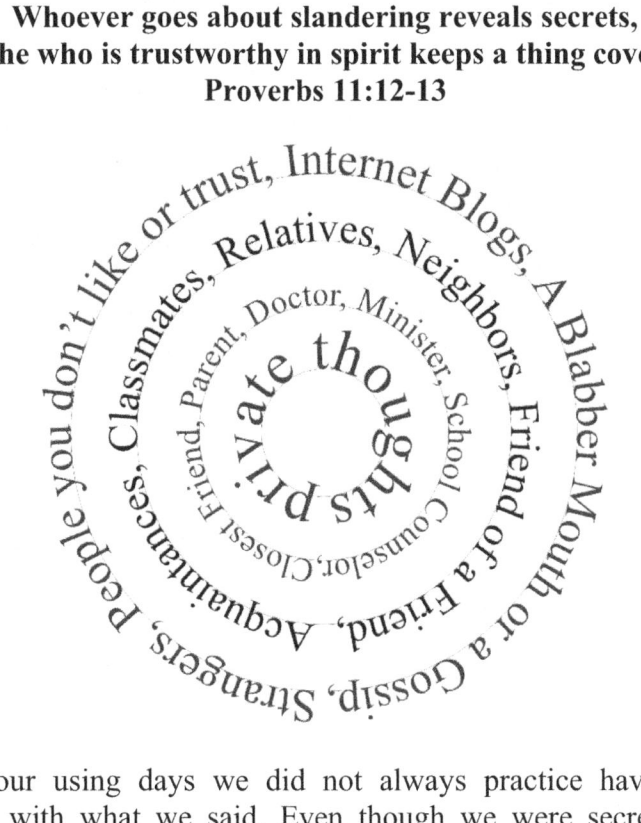

Concentric circles diagram (from innermost to outermost): Private thoughts; Doctor, Minister, School Counselor, Closest Friend, Parent; Classmates, Relatives, Neighbors, Friend of a Friend, Acquaintances; People you don't like or trust, Internet Blogs, A Blabber Mouth or a Gossip, Strangers.

    In our using days we did not always practice having healthy boundaries with what we said. Even though we were secretive in our addition, we also misspoke and spilled our personal secrets to someone we normally would not have. We may have told others things about ourselves that would have better been left unsaid. In our selfishness we might have revealed other's secrets and disrespected them in this way too.
    In recovery our heads cleared from the fog of drug use. We started to think straight again and along with it we realized that we needed to be selective about who we disclosed information to about our lives. The multi-circular image shows how our most private inner secrets are only revealed to those most trusted of people, such as our personal doctor, pastor, school counselor, parent, or closest friend. In the next ring moving outward is our common social circle of friends, relatives, neighbors, classmates, and acquaintances. In these relationships we shared things that were not sensitive or indiscreet. Furthest out is the most public places where anyone can access information about us, strangers, people we don't like or trust, internet blogs or even a blabber mouth or gossip. There we

shared things that were not personal or sensitive. There it is okay to share things that speak well of us.

In recovery we learned to be open but in appropriate ways. We may not have grown up in a family that kept secrets very well. From our family of origin we may or may not of had the best of examples of these two things, being appropriately open and of keeping secrets. In recovery we needed to either relearn them or learn them for the first time.

We know that addictions thrive in too secretive of a setting. We also know that recovery is best supported in a setting where we can share with some selective people about the disease we have. By our openness about our addiction and recovery we can also bring our message of hope to other who are still suffering.

Heavenly Father, guide us in the use of our tongues so that we do not misspeak ourselves or practice unhealthy boundaries. Help us by the indwelling of your Holy Spirit. Speak to our hearts and guide us in all that we do, that glory may be given to your holy name, through Christ our Lord we ask this. Amen

Trials: Testing and Temptation

Let no one say when he is tempted, "I am being tempted by God," for God cannot be tempted with evil, and he himself tempts no one. But each person is tempted when he is lured and enticed by his own desire. When desire when it has conceived gives birth to sin, and sin when it is fully grown brings forth death.
James 1:13-15

There are a few things about the trials we go through that we must know. *Trials* come in two forms: *testing* and *temptation.* Testing and temptation are like inseparable conjoined twins, one doesn't come without the other. A test is from God and his goal is to get us to do the right things and succeed. When we are tempted to sin its goal is always to get us to fail and fall.

Regarding temptations Jesus said they must come but woe to our fallen world for that reason.[93] Temptations can come from any number of sources: our own sinful self's heart or mind, from someone else, and from the devil or his crew.

God has made his creation in such a way that we are tested by it throughout our lifetime. He gives us tasks to complete, many of them are incredibly challenging. They are the things that help us to mature and grow. The tests are like bench-markers that tell us when we have succeeded, and they give us a sense of accomplishment. With maturity what might have been a temptation in the past is quickly passed over. However, we need to be reminded of what the Apostle Paul said about himself, "when I want to do right, evil lies close at hand."[94] Therefore we must be aware that we always are at risk of succumbing to temptation. Remember our ultimate victory comes from our Lord who gives to us his victory over temptation, sin, death, the grave and the devil.

Heavenly Father, the temptation to sin comes up often. Remind us that you truly are everywhere and will support us in our faith in every way. Through Christ our Lord. Amen

---

[93] Matthew 18:7
[94] Romans 7:21

The Lord's Prayer / The Our Father

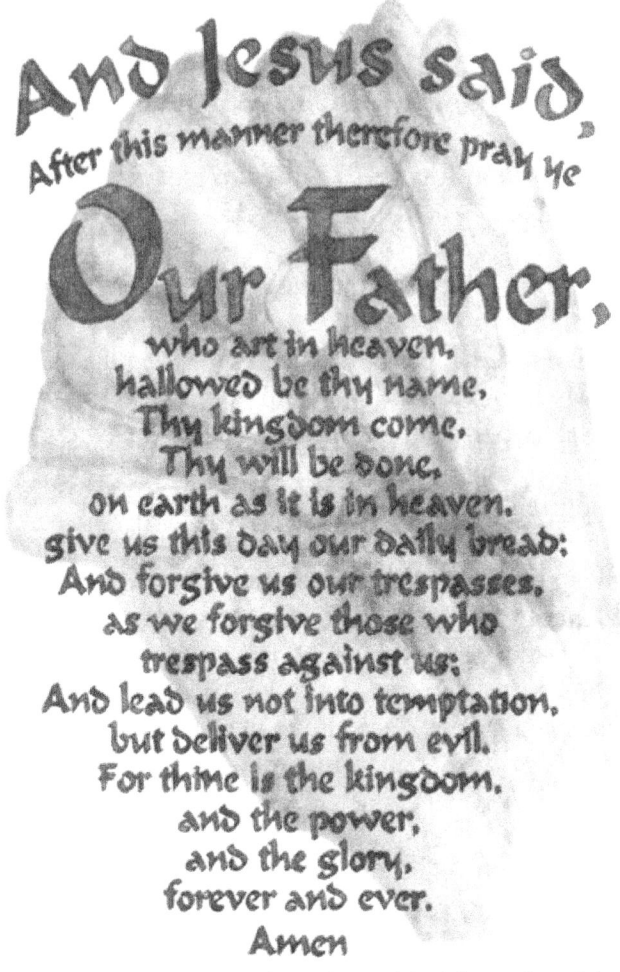

And Jesus said, After this manner therefore pray ye

Our Father,
who art in heaven,
hallowed be thy name,
Thy kingdom come,
Thy will be done,
on earth as it is in heaven.
give us this day our daily bread:
And forgive us our trespasses,
as we forgive those who
trespass against us;
And lead us not into temptation,
but deliver us from evil.
For thine is the kingdom,
and the power,
and the glory,
forever and ever.
Amen

    This prayer that we say has the added benefit of being from the Scriptures. We know that the Word of God is living, active and powerful. When we pray it we should fully understand its meaning for us. This is a wonderful explanation of its meaning as told by Martin Luther.

Our Father who art in heaven.
>What does this mean?
>Answer: God would thereby tenderly urge us to believe that He is our true Father, and that we are His true children, so that we may ask Him confidently with all assurance, as dear children ask their dear father.

The First Petition.
Hallowed be Thy name.
>What does this mean?

Answer: God's name is indeed holy in itself; but we pray in this petition that it may become holy among us also.
How is this done?
Answer: When the Word of God is taught in its truth and purity, and we as the children of God also lead holy lives in accordance with it. To this end help us, dear Father in heaven. But he that teaches and lives otherwise than God's Word teaches profanes the name of God among us. From this preserve us, Heavenly Father.

The Second Petition.
Thy kingdom come.
What does this mean?
Answer: The kingdom of God comes indeed without our prayer, of itself; but we pray in this petition that it may come unto us also.
How is this done?
Answer: When our heavenly Father gives us His Holy Spirit, so that by His grace we believe His holy Word and lead a godly life here in time and yonder in eternity.

The Third Petition.
Thy will be done on earth as it is in heaven.
What does this mean?
Answer: The good and gracious will of God is done indeed without our prayer; but we pray in this petition that it may be done among us also.
How is this done?
Answer: When God breaks and hinders every evil counsel and will which would not let us hallow the name of God nor let His kingdom come, such as the will of the devil, the world, and our flesh; but strengthens and keeps us steadfast in His Word and in faith unto our end. This is His gracious and good will.

The Fourth Petition.
Give us this day our daily bread.
What does this mean?
Answer: God gives daily bread, even without our prayer, to all wicked men; but we pray in this petition that He would lead us to know it, and to receive our daily bread with thanksgiving.
What is meant by daily bread?
Answer: Everything that belongs to the support and wants of the body, such as meat, drink, clothing, shoes, house, homestead, field, cattle, money, goods, a pious spouse, pious children, pious servants, pious and faithful magistrates good government, good

weather, peace, health, discipline, honor, good friends, faithful neighbors, and the like.

The Fifth Petition.
And forgive us our trespasses, as we forgive those who trespass against us.

What does this mean?
Answer: We pray in this petition that our Father in heaven would not look upon our sins, nor deny such petitions on account of them; for we are worthy of none of the things for which we pray, neither have we deserved them; but that He would grant them all to us by grace; for we daily sin much, and indeed deserve nothing but punishment. So will we verily, on our part, also heartily forgive and also readily do good to those who sin against us.

The Sixth Petition.
And lead us not into temptation.

What does this mean?
Answer: God, indeed, tempts no one; but we pray in this petition that God would guard and keep us, so that the devil, the world, and our flesh may not deceive us, nor seduce us into misbelief, despair, and other great shame and vice; and though we be assailed by them, that still we may finally overcome and gain the victory.

The Seventh Petition.
But deliver us from evil.

What does this mean?
Answer: We pray in this petition, as in a summary, that our Father in heaven would deliver us from all manner of evil, of body and soul, property and honor, and at last, when our last hour shall come, grant us a blessed end, and graciously take us from this vale of tears to Himself into heaven.

Amen.

What does this mean?
Answer: That I should be certain that these petitions are acceptable to our Father in heaven and heard; for He Himself has commanded us so to pray, and has promised that He will hear us. Amen, Amen; that is, Yea, yea, it shall be so.[95]

---

[95] https://en.wikisource.org/wiki/Luther%27s_Small_Catechism

The Temptation of Christ

And Jesus, full of the Holy Spirit, returned from the Jordan and was led by the Spirit in the wilderness for forty days, being tempted by the devil. And he ate nothing during those days. And when they were ended, he was hungry. The devil said to him, "If you are the Son of God, command this stone to become bread." And Jesus answered him, "It is written, 'Man shall not live by bread alone.'" And the devil took him up and showed him all the kingdoms of the world in a moment of time, and said to him, "To you I will give all this authority and their glory, for it has been delivered to me, and I give it to whom I will. If you, then, will worship me, it will all be yours." And Jesus answered him, "It is written, "'You shall worship the Lord your God, and him only shall you serve.'" And he took him to Jerusalem and set him on the pinnacle of the temple and said to him, "If you are the Son of God, throw yourself down from here, for it is written, "'He will command his angels concerning you, to guard you,' and "'On their hands they will bear you up, lest you strike your foot against a stone.'" And Jesus answered him, "It is said, 'You shall not put the Lord your God to the test.'" And when the devil had ended every temptation, he departed from him until an opportune time. And Jesus returned in the power of the Spirit to Galilee, and a report about him went out through all the surrounding country.
Luke 4:1-14

Remember how under the best of conditions Adam and Eve fell into sin? They lived in an ideal place, the Garden of Eden. They had been instructed directly by God not to eat that fruit of the tree of the knowledge of good and evil. They had each other to rely on having been made perfect mates for each other by their Creator. They were in an unfallen state. Still, they fell.

Now, here Jesus our victor is in the one of the worst places under absolute horrible circumstances. He is in a desert wilderness and all alone. He is hungry having fasted forty days and nights. The devil tempted him where he was weakest. First, he was hungry and he was tempted to make bread out of desert stones. This temptation came with a twist. The temptation was to do it "if" he was the son of God, as though he had something he needed to prove, which he didn't. Jesus successfully resisted and used the Word of God in the process. That is something we need to remember and practice ourselves, using the Word of God to resist temptations that come our way.

The second temptation that the devil brought to him was interesting. The devil offered him authority over all the kingdoms of the world. Jesus came as the King of kings and Lord of Lords over all the earth. Giving into this temptation would certainly have seemed to be in line with this. The catch, and there is always a catch, was that Jesus would first have to worship the devil. That does not happen of course. Note here too that there is no trusting the devil at his word, ever. The name devil means deceiver and he is the father of lies.[96] Again, Jesus relied on the Word of God, which is the absolute authority.

There was a third and final temptation in this encounter. There are holy places that have been set aside and dedicated for the purpose of serving God. The devil is no respecter of God or holy places. The devil and Jesus were at the pinnacle of the holy temple in the city of Jerusalem. The temptation came in the form of a dare. "If you are the Son of God…" prove it. Again, Jesus did not have to prove anything, they both already knew the truth, he is the Son of God.

In the end Jesus walked out of the desert wasteland victorious. It is also especially important that we learn from this that the devil was defeated by a human being which created a precedent for all of mankind. Not that we can believe that with our will-power we can resist temptation, we always need God's help. We know that our ultimate victory comes to us through Jesus' victory that he shares freely with us as his disciples.

God in heaven, we have been tried and we have failed, we have been tempted and we fell in sin. Forgive us for our shortcomings and our sins. Guide us to trust not in ourselves, but in you and your son who has been victorious in all things. We give you thanks that he shares with us his victory over temptation, sin, the devil, suffering, death, and the grave. Thank you that by joining with our Lord by faith we too can share in his glorious victory over temptation and the devil. Bless us and strengthen us for our journey. This we ask in Jesus' name. Amen

---

[96] John 8:44

One Day at a Time[97]

**Jesus said, "Therefore do not be anxious about tomorrow,
for tomorrow will be anxious for itself.
Sufficient for the day is its own trouble."
Matthew 6:34**

Beginning in the book of Genesis with the days of creation and their never-ending cycle, there has always been something spiritual about the pattern of how time passes that God set in place. It is like a metrical drum beat with a tone that we simply cannot get out of our heads. We live our lives day by day, with each day being separated by the night.

This pattern of days and nights is called the *circadian rhythm,* meaning *around the day*. Every living thing, including plants and animals live in accordance with its patterns. According to God's design plants follow the sun with their posture as it rises in the east and sets in the west. Even our own sleep and awake times are influenced by it. In the summer we sleep less because of the increase in daylight. In the winter we tend to sleep more because there is less daylight.

In our addiction our sleep and wake cycles were disrupted by the drugs. Some of us used meth to energize our lives and avoid sleeping for days at a time. Consequently, and regardless of our drug of choice, our sleep and wake times were out of synchronization with God's creation. Our sleep and wake periods followed the rhythm of the chaos and the insanity of addiction.

In recovery our bodies began to return to normal, our sleep and wake patterns included. As we lived one day at a time we recovered our sanity and by God's grace we could sleep peacefully and wakeup refreshed under the promises of God that gave us the courage to live clean and free.

Heavenly Father, by your grace we are now walking to the rhythm of the beat of your creation. Help us to also walk in the footsteps of our Lord as we seek to live like him. In the name of Christ our Lord we pray. Amen

---

[97] From N.A.'s list of Phrases.

This Too Shall Pass

**The end of a matter is better than its beginning,
and patience is better than pride.
Ecclesiastes 7:8**

Patience is not something that we as addicts were accustomed to accommodating. We might have acquired a measure of it in the days before our addictions, but that was lost with the onset of drug use. In our addictions we wanted relief and we wanted it right now. No longer did we have the patience to find relief by suffering through our trials and coming out on the other end of them with a sense of serenity and accomplishment. For some of us who were physically abused we came to know the torture of the helpless. Physical pain was inflicted on us. When it became unbearable we screamed in torment, but we found no relief for its endless, and merciless pangs. This created in us the need to seek immediate relief in life. Drugs seemed to help, at first, then less and less, and our addiction to them became the source of shame and additional pain for us. In addiction we had no way out because our solution, getting high, was also the problem.

While some of us continued to suffer physical abuse, those among us who did not were still stuck with the traumatic memories of the impossible torture we suffered under. We felt worthless, rejected, and hated. We wanted acceptance, affirmation, and to be loved. When we could not find any of these we used drugs to numb ourselves from the pains that would not heal. We used drugs to have feelings because we were otherwise numb to the world we lived in. We used drugs to create an alternative world of pleasant feelings, of relief, soothing and comforting, because we could not feel that way otherwise.

In recovery we opened up about our past and all of its trauma. We found healing in the groups, treatment, and counseling. We found help from God our Father who loved us as no other could. God mysteriously moved in our lives and we found healing and wholeness had come to us.

Heavenly Father, bring us comfort through the relationship that we have with you through your son, Christ our Lord, in whose name we pray. Amen

Judgement and the Word Game

**Those who are spiritual discern all things,
and they are themselves subject to no one else's scrutiny.
1 Corinthians 2:15 NRSV**

In recovery we have needed to wise-up and grow in maturity because as addicts we had been frozen in time and were not maturing as we aged. One area that we need to be wise in is how the word *judge* gets thrown around in a conversation. The worry is that someone might try to lure us into a spiders trap of deceit with their web of lies. The truth is that if you haven't noticed yet in life, there is more than one meaning to the word judge. In fact, if you were to do a study of how this word is used in the Bible, you might come away very confused.

Jesus himself said, "Judge not, that you be not judged. For with the judgment you pronounce you will be judged."[98] Then again he also said, "Do not judge by appearances, but judge with right judgment."[99] While these two references on the surface seem to be in contradiction of each other, they are not when examined closer. In the first instance Jesus is referring to being of a critical mindset. Judging in this way is the practice of destructive fault finding from a condescending and condemning viewpoint. In the second reference the meaning of judging is vastly different than that. In this case it is calling for us to make correct and accurate decisions and discernments about something.

It is not uncommon for us to have both a critical mindset about something, while at the same time correctly judging it as something negative, bad, or even sinful. Having a negative attitude about something does not disqualify us from also correctly discerning it for what it is. However, if we have a prejudice or a bias about it, we are wise to spend a little time in self-examination before coming to a conclusion so that we are accurate in our assessment of what it truly is.

In addiction, our thoughts were blurred by the lies that we had bought into. Our minds were compromised by the chemicals at work in them. Our logic and perceptions were skewed and unreliable. We were not able to rely on ourselves as we might have if our minds were drug free. Our judgements were prejudiced toward using and believing whatever we needed to in order to rationalize our addictive behavior. We may very well have found ourselves going between the extremes of rationalizing away and self-justifying our drug use, and also shaming and condemning ourselves for doing it.

---

[98] Matthew 7:1-2
[99] John 7:24

As we neared the point of surrendering our lives to God to get clean we had glimpses of the truth regarding our lies and deceit. We might not have known much about the truth of addiction, but we could see more clearly the lies of our addiction. We saw things that other active addicts had told us to believe were also lies. In recovery we abandoned the lies for the truth, and came to believe that our lives had become unmanageable and only God could save us from our path of drug laced destruction.

In our recovery journey we came to see and judge that we were truly addicts and were powerless over our drug use. We eventually came to have a critical and negative attitude toward drug use. This was not a bad thing given the fact that we had also grown enough to correctly judge and discern that drug use was always a dangerous practice.

In our growing maturity, when we encountered others of a differing mindset, we were able to fend well for ourselves. They may have wanted to play word games with us about drug use and addiction. They may have told us to not judge others for their drug use. Only they meant that we shouldn't have a bad attitude about drug use, but we knew we were speaking from a healthy and discerning point of view. In our maturing skills at being assertive we were able to make our point of view known to them, whether they wanted to hear it or not.

Heavenly Father, give us wise and discerning hearts and minds to make correct judgements in our lives. Keep us from having critical attitudes and judgmental mindsets where it is not justified. Give us a hunger and thirst for righteousness and help us to deal with others out of kind hearts. This we ask in the name of your beloved son, Jesus Christ our Lord and Savior. Amen

Strength in Weakness

For the sake of Christ, then, I am content with weaknesses, insults, hardships, persecutions, and calamities. For when I am weak, then I am strong.
2 Corinthians 12:10

It was the Apostle Paul who said these words, that when he was weak then he was strong. He was talking about his personal struggles, which were significant, and their effect on him. He found that in his greatest struggles he was forced into a state of utter desperation. It was from there, that in his dire need, he was forced to earnestly cry out to God for the help he needed and only God could provide. Should he for any reason not look to God for his help, he would have been overwhelmed and consumed by his problems. He did not tell us specifically what his problems were, but we can believe that they were severe as he referred to them as a thorn in the flesh and as a messenger from Satan.[100]

As addicts in recovery we have this certain thorn in our flesh, which is of course our addictions. None of us can simply throw our hands up and walk away from it. If we did, our additions would still be with us, we cannot escape them in that way. We personally know what their tenacious and obstinate nature is like. We are dogged by them day and night. For us there are a countless number of landmines in our lives that we could step on at any time that can trigger us into a relapse. We know how much we need God's help, and help he does.

In recovery we are much like the apostle who recognized that his strength in life came from God. Like him, we know that from our desperate state we are able to sincerely call on God for strength in our weakness. Then we are able to know strength from God. Like the apostle we need to become content with our weakness, then we will rest in our Savior's strength.

Thank you God helping us to be content in our weaknesses and reliant on you for our strength. This we pray in Jesus' most holy, most precious, and glorious name. Amen

---

[100] 2 Corinthians 12:7

The Whole Armor of God

**Finally, be strong in the Lord and in the strength of his might. Put on the whole armor of God, that you may be able to stand against the schemes of the devil. For we do not wrestle against flesh and blood, but against the rulers, against the authorities, against the cosmic powers over this present darkness, against the spiritual forces of evil in the heavenly places. Therefore take up the whole armor of God, that you may be able to withstand in the evil day, and having done all, to stand firm. Stand therefore, having fastened on the belt of truth, and having put on the breastplate of righteousness, and, as shoes for your feet, having put on the readiness given by the gospel of peace. In all circumstances take up the shield of faith, with which you can extinguish all the flaming darts of the evil one; and take the helmet of salvation, and the sword of the Spirit, which is the word of God, praying at all times in the Spirit, with all prayer and supplication.
To that end, keep alert with all perseverance,
making supplication for all the saints.
Ephesians 6:10-18**

Paul was held a prisoner of the Roman Empire in the final years of his life. For much of that time he was guarded by the elite Praetorian Guard who also provided security for many government officials and the emperor's palace. He was able to share the gospel with these soldiers, and many of them converted to Christianity. There is no doubt that all the time he spent with them was influential in his writing this text.

We are instructed to be reliant on the Lord for strength. Our measly strength and abilities are worthless in this area. We need to guard against taking on a fortress mentality of our own. This means that we should not imagine that we are strong and resilient, because we aren't. The Lord is the Almighty God and we must live in the shadow of his might and have no confidence in our flesh. Our enemies are powerful foes starting with the devil, and we need to recognize that our drug of choice is also a fierce enemy of ours.

All of the elite Praetorian Guard's armor has a spiritual equivalent that Paul recognized and advised the church to take full advantage of:

- o The belt of truth.
- o The breastplate of righteousness.
- o Shoes for the gospel of peace.
- o The shield of faith.
- o The helmet of salvation.
- o The sword of the Spirit, which is the Word of God.

We need to give special attention to the final words of this passage. Paul makes four references to the need for us to pray. This is not to be underemphasized either. Someone once said that when the saints form up committees to get something done the devil laughs. When we startup Bible studies he snickers, when we hire a new pastor he thinks it is hilarious, but when we get together and pray he shrieks and flees.

Prayer moves the hand of God. Prayer is how God includes us in his work. Prayer is how the needs of our lives, and the needs of others are lifted up to his attention. Prayer is how we talk with our Heaven Father and participate in our personal relationship with him.

Heavenly Father, thank you for coming to us in the life of your son, Jesus Christ. Thank you for sending your Holy Spirit to us who lives inside of us, who talks to us and guides us daily in our lives. Thank you for all the gifts that you have given to us. Empower us by the spiritual armor you have provided. Most of all, let us share in your work through prayer and good works done in your son's name, Jesus Christ our Savior and Lord. Amen

Spiritual Signs and Wonders

And they devoted themselves to the apostles' teaching and the fellowship, to the breaking of bread and the prayers. And awe came upon every soul, and many wonders and signs were being done through the apostles.
Acts 2:42-43

What makes the program a spiritual recovery program, and what makes it work, is that we are doing what the Bible says a Christian ought to being doing all along. As addicts it is critical that we are more intentional about our devotion to the Lord in order to recover and stay in recovery.

Our addiction was a toxic, poisonous form of spirituality or religious faith. There were rituals that we went through when we got high and we had a language with words and phrases that belonged only to it. Being high was a false form of pseudo-spiritual transcendence. We were devoted to it and it had the grip of an almighty god over our very souls. It was transforming us, but not for the better. It had the power of death over us. It was a consuming fire in our lives.

For some of us in recovery we came into Christian faith after we got into recovery. For others of us, we had fallen away from our faith only to return to it in recovery. In our new lives we gave ourselves over to the care of God through our Lord Jesus Christ. God Almighty delivered us and now he keeps us in his care. We respond to him with our daily devotions of prayer, Bible reading, mediation, maybe a song or some music, perhaps incense, and lighting a candle. Our thoughts throughout the day return to him, to his Word and we think about his love for us and our love for him. Let important or urgent needs come up, let our schedules fill up, but let nothing come between us and our daily devotions, they are our lifeline to God. We are challenged and at times overwhelmed. We might be tempted and think about the relief we might find by getting high, but our thoughts do not stop and stay there. We turn to God and say a silent prayer, asking for the help we need and his strength to carry us through the situation and keep us in recovery.

Gracious God, you have delivered us out of darkness and brought us into your son's Kingdom on earth. May we abide closely with him all of our days. In Jesus' name. Amen

Dope Made Us Stupid

**But it is the spirit in man,
the breath of the Almighty,
that makes him understand.
It is not the old who are wise,
nor the aged who understand what is right.
Job 32:8-9**

Job was an elder in his community. He was an older man with adult children. He knew a thing or two about life. This text is what he said in the midst of his greatest tribulations, that understanding comes from having the life-giving-spirit of God in us. This can also be seen in the practical example of young King Solomon, who was just a child when he began ruling ancient Israel. He prayed for wisdom to rule his nation with and it was granted to him by God. His gift of wisdom is unsurpassed to this day throughout all the earth.

In our addiction when we got high on the smoke of meth, marijuana or whatever our drug of choice was our eyes were blinded to what others could easily tell. The smoke not only clouded up the room we were in, but it also clouded our souls and the spirit within us like a thick fog. When we were high our using friends said, "Be cool," meaning that we should act straight. We couldn't fool anyone other than ourselves on that count. Things progressed in this direction to the point where we didn't even need to be high for people to see by our behavior and appearance that we were a drug user and that we were pretty bad off.

In recovery our eyes began to open up again. We began to take notice of those things that we had neglected. We also worked the steps and we had to open our eyes further. We had to see the insanity we had been in the midst of, we had to open our eyes to the hopelessness that had been ours. We had to look to God for the help that only he could provide.

Heavenly Father to all of us, continue to open our eyes to the truth. Let us see the world as you see it and our lives as you see us, and let us see others with the compassion you have for all mankind. Fill our lives with your special love to overflowing so that others can see the miracles you have worked in us. This we pray in the name of your only son, Jesus Christ our Lord. Amen

The Occult IV

**As we were going to the place of prayer,
we were met by a slave girl who
had a spirit of divination and brought
her owners much gain by fortune-telling.
She followed Paul and us, crying out,
"These men are servants of the Most High God,
who proclaim to you the way of salvation."
And this she kept doing for many days.
Paul, having become greatly annoyed,
turned and said to the spirit,
"I command you in the name of
Jesus Christ to come out of her."
And it came out that very hour.
Acts 16:16-18**

While the majority of the modern world may not believe that the occult has something genuine to offer, we cannot afford to be so ignorant. The world of drugs holds within its powers a gateway into the dark world of Satan and his minions. Drug use is sorcery. Getting high opens the soul to the underworld of demons and they love to work their evil on vulnerable minds on drugs. The evil that they work will rear its ugly head gladly, but more often they will simply try to creep subtly into our lives. We need to absolutely avoid all forms of the occult and witchcraft. This includes such things as the zodiac and horoscopes, palm readers, Ouija boards, magic eight balls, parapsychology, the paranormal, tarot cards, mediums or psychics and anything such as these.

Our recovery from drugs may also need to be a recovery and deliverance from evil in all its forms. If any of us have ever been involved in any of those things mentioned or anything related to it, we need to talk to our pastor or a minister with experience in freeing people from these practices. In our recovery we need to be solely dedicated to the Lord. Our loyalties cannot be divided, that would open us up to the risk of a relapse. Our lives are free of drugs for the reason that we are servants of God and live holy and peaceable lives dedicated to him who died for our sins.

Heavenly Father free our lives from all of the evil that our past once contained and lead us in the way that is everlasting. Purge us and make us fully your own. This we pray through Christ our Lord. Amen

Smoke and Fire

**Then Moses brought the people out of the camp to meet God, and they took their stand at the foot of the mountain. Now Mount Sinai was wrapped in smoke because the Lord had descended on it in fire. The smoke of it went up like the smoke of a kiln, and the whole mountain trembled greatly. And as the sound of the trumpet grew louder and louder, Moses spoke, and God answered him in thunder.
Exodus 19:17-19**

Fire has long been a fascination of mankind's for a long, long time. It seems like everyone enjoys a warm fire in the fireplace on a cold winter day. In the summer who doesn't like to sit around a campfire and eat s'mores? Starting a fire has come a long way in the last few centuries. No longer do we need a flint stone to make sparks with. Just put your thumb to the lighters switch, flip it, and there you have it, wallah, fire!

Some drugs you can cut up with a razorblade, make them into a fine powder and snort them. Many drugs you have to light-up and smoke. The act of preparing the fix, rolling it into a joint or putting it into a pipe is very much a part of the addiction. As that was going on there were thoughts of anticipation about how we were going to feel from the high and it was only moments away. Striking up the fire, blazing up the fix and inhaling its smoke was all part of the excitement. Then came the amazing rush, the throbbing pulse, and we were off and flying high again. Some say their highs were more intense and fulfilling than sexual orgasms. Many of us were also mesmerized by the trail of smoke the fix made or were captivated by the cloud of smoke that we exhaled.

In recovery we find out about the sacredness of some fires. There is the lighting of two candles on the altar at church. One represents Jesus of Nazareth the man, the other represents Jesus the son of God who is also divine. There is the eternal candle light at the front of the church. In some churches there is the burning of incense that permeates the sanctuary. At weddings there is the unity candle the couple lights. On Memorial Day Sunday and All Saints Day Sunday there may be the lighting of candles for the remembrance of loved ones who are now with the Lord.

In our recovery we can enjoy the recreational use of fire, in our fireplace, or in an outdoor campfire. In church we can volunteer to assist with the lighting the candles or aiding the Acolytes who do that task. At home we can light a candle or some incense in our personal devotions. We can light a candle at home in remembrance of a loved one.

We need to remember that all that God has created is good. It is only when the things that he has made are abused in one fashion or another, like drugs, that they take on an evil nature. In recovery we can discover the sacred stories of the Bible and how fire was used by God in some amazing and miraculous ways. By reading and studying these kinds of texts we can see in our minds eye's what things looked like to our forefathers in the faith.

    Gracious God in heaven, you have given to us the life of your son so that we could be freed from our sins and our addictions to drugs. As he rose victorious over death and the grave, so also raise us up with him so that we can walk in newness of life. This we pray in his holy and precious name, Christ Jesus our Lord, our Savior, our all in all. Amen

Case Study: Through many Tribulations

**When they had preached the gospel to that
city and had made many disciples, they returned
to Lystra and to Iconium and to Antioch,
strengthening the souls of the disciples,
encouraging them to continue in the faith, and saying that
through many tribulations we must enter the kingdom of God.
Acts 14:21-22**

Relatives had gathered for a holiday. The parents were well to do. Their adult children were just getting started in life. One child complained that life was hard. All the young adults thought that the older generation had it easy with their houses paid for, nice cars, and a cushy retirement in sight. To their surprise one of their mothers agreed, life was hard. It was not just hard for the young adults, it was hard on the older adults too. That bit of truth dispelled the illusion that life was hard on them but not on their parents. The truth is that life is hard most of the time. Do not be discouraged by that. There are times when all goes well. Life is good after payday, bills get paid and there is enough food in the house for a week. Then we can kick back and feel successful, even if it is only for a day or two. This is payday success. That is the pattern of things for most of us.

In addiction we turn away from the reality of our lives and turn to drugs to regulate our emotions. This is living the lie. Sometimes we don't have a life that lets us pay all the bills on time, which leads to distress. Sometimes we are dissatisfied with only feeling like we made it through to another payday and that we need more than this life has to offer to help us feel good about ourselves. In recovery we need to adjust to reality and when another payday success comes to us, or any success for that matter, we need to relish the moment. It is time then to put our feet up and breathe in and out in a giant sigh of relief. We need to savor its flavor while it's around because it won't last, which is normal. As its newness fades into the recent past we need to apply ourselves to make it happen all over again. We need to recall it when we need a bit of encouragement and remind ourselves of that day and the good feelings it brings will come to us again.

Dearest God, help us to apply ourselves to leading fruitful lives and serving you. Encourage us in our hardships and help to celebrate in our successes. In Christ's name we pray. Amen

Celebrate

**You have turned for me my mourning into dancing;
you have loosed my sackcloth and clothed me with gladness,
that my glory may sing your praise and not be silent.
O Lord my God, I will give thanks to you forever!
Psalm 30:11-12**

We had been living hedonistic lifestyles and wanting to enjoy only the pleasures of life. At first drugs enhanced this pursuit of ours and gave us more of what we enjoyed. Over time things changed and we were not getting the same effects. To compensate we had to use more and more to get a better high, but that had a diminishing effect on us too. Over time the low periods of our lives slipped continually lower. What was once a great time for us now took on an entirely new role, we were using just to not feel so low and not really getting a high out of using anymore.

In recovery we discovered a new normal for ourselves. At first we might have had dramatic mood swings as our bodies and minds adjusted. We worked to get in touch with our emotions and what they meant for our lives. We found out how to recognize our emotions, put names to them and to understand why they were occurring. We learned how to do something about our thoughts and the emotions they generated. We learned how to do something healthy about our lives and the emotions that our lifestyles created. We were able to smile and enjoy our lives again without the manipulating influence of drugs pulling and pushing us around emotionally.

In our new lives we found a growing joy that we had never experienced. We were ready to celebrate what our lives had become, and rejoice in all that God had done for us. We were free from the weight of drugs bondage and felt like dancing in celebration over how wonderful it was.

Heavenly Father, you have given to us wonderful lives and brought us into the glorious freedom of your son's Kingdom on earth. Help us to throw off every weight that hinders us in living for you and give us joy overflowing. We praise and thank you, we give you glory and worship you, through Christ Jesus our Lord. Amen

Miserable, Desperate and Hopeless

Wretched man that I am!
Who will deliver me from this body of death?
Thanks be to God through Jesus Christ our Lord!
So then, I myself serve the law of God with my mind,
but with my flesh I serve the law of sin.
Romans 7:24-25

The Apostle Paul who wrote this Scripture passage wrote from his heart. He described what had become an impossible and horrifying life for him. This was because of his dilemma over his sinfulness. Try as hard as a person could, and he did, he could not rid himself of this problem in his life. Paul explained that he had the Word of God and the Law to follow, but he by nature, even when empowered by the Law, could not follow it. Sin in his life was a very tenacious problem. In his struggle to overcome his sinful nature he found that there was nothing he could do to escape sinning. He came to his wits end and admitted to what a wretch he was. At that point he looked for help outside of himself. His answer came in the person of God's son, Jesus Christ.

For us in recovery, it is a valuable thing for us to always remember how bad off we were in our addictions. We should never forget how terribly miserable we were and desperate for the help we needed to get off drugs. We may have felt like help would never come or maybe that it didn't exist in the first place. These desperate memories can be a strong motivating factor in helping us stay in recovery. By remembering our misery, our inability to quit and our sick dependence to drugs we are motivated to never go near them again.

Paul learned that he could not find the solution to his sins on his own. He came to know that he needed a deliverer, Christ the Lord. We too needed a deliverer, Christ our Lord. Our indebtedness to him for freeing us from addiction is something we must remember daily.

Dearest Father, you have redeemed us and given us new lives and new purpose to live for. Ever keep us in your grace and remember us according to the love you hold for your son Jesus, in whose name we pray. Amen

Anselm of Canterbury: Religion Is Faith Seeking Understanding

**And so, from the day we heard,
we have not ceased to pray for you asking that
you may be filled with the knowledge of his will in
all spiritual wisdom and understanding, so as to walk
in a manner worthy of the Lord, fully pleasing to him:
bearing fruit in every good work and
increasing in the knowledge of God;
Colossians 1:9-10**

There is a modern line of thinking that says Christianity is not a religion, it is a relationship. Christianity is a religion and it is about having a relationship with God through Jesus Christ, who mediates it. The Bible refers to our faith as a religion. It is best not to get hung up on private interpretations of how to describe our faith. Of late religious faith has been called our spirituality.

There are, in this world, more definitions to spirituality than imaginable. It is in Christian faith where the only true spirituality exists, all else is counterfeit. Outside of Jesus Christ people do know about God, but not very well. It is in the life of Jesus that we have the best revelation of God. Some people say they commune with God through nature, but that is by definition idolatry. While God is evident in what can be seen in his creation it is Jesus alone who is the mediator between us and God, not his creation.

There was a Christian man in the eleventh century named Anselm of Canterbury who described religion as faith seeking understanding. Our religion is very experience oriented too. We have encounters and experiences with God. We pray to him, we receive communion, we worship him in church, we hear him speaking to our hearts and minds.

For us as addicts it is essential that we come into a deeper understanding of faith. For the success of our recovery we need a good understanding of the Bible and what it says. We need to live as active Christians based on the Holy Scriptures. It is vital that we don't merely go through the motions, but that we are growth oriented, and seek to apply it in practical ways to our lives. It is by being active, knowledgeable, and practical in our faith that we maintain ourselves in recovery.

Heavenly Father, may we grow to know you more closely every day. Through your son enrich our relationship with you and reveal yourself to us more and more. In Jesus' name. Amen

Living in Remembrance

This day shall be a day of remembrance for you. You shall celebrate it as a festival to the Lord; throughout your generations you shall observe it as a perpetual ordinance.
Exodus 12:14NRSV

One of the spiritually mystical things that we do is to live in remembrance of our ancestors in the faith. In the Old Testament they observed the Passover Feast which was done in remembrance of our spiritual ancestor's days of slavery in Egypt and their deliverance from there by the mighty hand of God. To observe the Passover Feast was more than just remembering what happened. To do it in *remembrance* was to spiritually transcend time and place and be joined with them in the mystery of our faith. This meant they shared what their forebearers went through and were there for it all. In this spiritual state of remembrance they recalled as though they were there for the bitter suffering their ancestors endured: as slaves, the murder of their male infants, the mighty signs God worked through Moses to humble Pharaoh, their flight from Egypt and the miraculous parting of the Red Sea when Pharaoh sent his army to bring the nation of Israel back.

For us in recovery just as God delivered the Israelites from bondage and brought them to the promised land, so also he has freed us from addictions. It can be an enormously powerful experience to imagine that our bondage was similar to the Israelites bitter slavery. We can also see the similarities of how they were delivered from their taskmasters clutches and how the Lord also delivered us from the bonds of addiction. By living in remembrance of their experiences we can be strengthened in our faith and our recoveries, knowing as God was for them, so also he is for us.

God of Abraham and Sarah, Isaac and Rebecca, Jacob and Rachael, you delivered our ancestors in the faith with a mighty hand from their bitter enslavement in the ancient land of Egypt. You were faithful to bring them into the land promised to them. Continue to deliver us from the drugs that were taskmasters over us and enslaved us in bitterness. Just as you brought them into the promised land, bring us also into all that you have planned for our lives. This we ask in Jesus' holy name. Amen

Free Will

For I do not understand my own actions. For I do not do what I want, but I do the very thing I hate. Now if I do what I do not want, I agree with the law, that it is good. So now it is no longer I who do it, but sin that dwells within me. For I know that nothing good dwells in me, that is, in my flesh. For I have the desire to do what is right, but not the ability to carry it out. For I do not do the good I want, but the evil I do not want is what I keep on doing. Now if I do what I do not want, it is no longer I who do it, but sin that dwells within me.
Romans 7:15-20

When it comes to the discussion on free will and addiction it seems to come down to a few simple things. In addiction and recovery we had control over one thing. We could choose to, or choose not to take the very first hit. If we did decide to use we could not control ourselves after that. At that point our lives became unmanageable because we were powerless over our addiction.

In recovery, we can decide to quit but it takes God to make that happen. We might find ourselves despising and swearing them off with all fervency. All that and anything else we could muster did us no good. That is the nature of addiction, we could not quit on our own.

We all know that we needed God's intervention to begin and sustain our recovery. Even that is something that has a twist to it. The Scriptures say that we need to receive Jesus into our lives, which is a passive act.[101] In receiving him we are given the power to become children of God. In all of this, God is the one acting in our lives, we are in the role of passive recipients.

Heavenly Father, you sent your son into the world to save us from our sins. We believe in the one that you sent, who is Jesus and he has saved us from our sins and delivered us from our addictions. Empower us to live as your holy children according to the Scriptures. Reveal your will for our lives to us and provide for our daily needs, day by day, in Jesus name. Amen

---

[101] John 1:12-13

Spirituality

**As you come to him, a living stone rejected by men but in the sight of God chosen and precious, you yourselves like living stones are being built up as a spiritual house, to be a holy priesthood, to offer spiritual sacrifices acceptable to God through Jesus Christ.
1 Peter 2:4-5**

The world seeks to offer a variety of spiritualities but there is only one true spirituality, Christianity. The other religions are nothing more than phony. Anyone in the world can call anything they want spiritual. The truth is there is only one God and his son is Jesus Christ.

Some deceived souls have erroneously claimed to have had spiritual experiences with marijuana, LSD, mushrooms, or other substances. They may have had a spiritual experience but it had nothing to do with the true and Living God. They very well may have been deceived by lying spirits who are fallen angels and serve their master who is the devil. As Christians in recovery we should never think as they do or appear to give credence to their claims.

For us as believers the highlights of our spirituality include being in touch with God though his son Jesus. Jesus is the mediator of our covenant relationship with our Heavenly Father. We believe that we are sinners by nature and that we can only be forgiven by the blood that God's son shed when he suffered and died for the sins of the world.[102] We believe that God empowers us to live as his faithful people.[103] Our spirituality supports us fully in our recovery and through it we are kept in God's care in all that we do.

Heavenly Father, you have made us your own and given to us the forgiveness of our sins. You have made us to be holy priests to serve you and to bring you glory. Build us up in our faith and give us ever deepening revelations of who you are through Jesus Christ our Lord. Amen

---

[102] Ephesians 1:7
[103] Philippians 4:13

Loving God Entirely

**"Teacher, which is the great commandment in the Law?"
And he said to him, "You shall love the Lord your God with
all your heart and with all your soul and with all your mind.
This is the great and first commandment.
Matthew 22:36-38**

In our addiction, when we were at our worst, there wasn't anything we wouldn't do to continue in our habits. Even if we no longer enjoyed any part of it, we still did it because we were enslaved to do it by this impersonal master of our lives. Our devotion to it was extreme, and there was nothing we could do about it. We might have lost all hope and lived in passivity to it. As a slave who had no rights or will of our own we lived out this tyrants desire for us. It wanted everything, our family, our home and money, career, and our very lives. We were enslaved to it with all that we were.

In faith and recovery our loyalties shifted. We might have received a miraculous deliverance and been freed from going through withdrawal. We might have struggled greatly with temptation to return to serving our former master. Day by day we did what we needed to do: we went to meetings, outpatient treatment, counseling, read our devotional books, and talked to our sponsor. Over time our desire to use faded and we came to feel very free again. We dumped our old using friends and got new friends. The importance of our Christian faith to us grew by leaps and bounds. Our faith blossomed and grew deep as we matured. We realized that our faith in Jesus Christ was becoming more than we ever imagined it could be. In our personal relationship with our Heavenly Father and his son, Jesus Christ, we felt loved and very well cared for. We could talk with others, who to our amazement, had the same things to say about their lives and recovery. We came to feel very secure in God's care.

Heavenly Father, you sent your son to redeem our lives from sin and the grips of addiction. We love you so much and are so grateful for the lives that you have given to us. Help us to grow and mature, and bring us into the fullness of life, through Christ our Lord we pray. Amen

The Sabbath Rest

Thus the heavens and the earth were finished, and all the host of them. And on the seventh day God finished his work that he had done and he rested on the seventh day from all his work that he had done. So God blessed the seventh day and made it holy, because on it God rested from all his work that he had done in creation.
Genesis 2:1-3

Big cities are running 24/7 and more and more small towns are edging that direction. Many careers and educational events require us to work on weekends and evenings, not to mention all those who work the night shift. Maybe a hundred years ago life allowed most people to take Sunday as a day of rest, but that is very much a thing of the past. While the Bible does not require us to take Saturday off as a day of sabbath rest anymore, or to rest on Sunday because it is the Lord's day, it is a good idea to observe a day, or at least part of one, as a day of rest every week.

The benefits of having time to rest are clear. By resting we can avoid the dangers of burnout in our jobs and in our relationships. By taking vacations we also break up the monotony and boredom of life. By taking a trip and doing some extraordinary things we can bring some excitement into our lives. The caution for us is not to take a day off, or a vacation, only to be so active that we return from it more tired than when we started.

In practicing our faith it is a good and wise practice to take breaks to be spiritually refreshed. We benefit by setting aside time daily as well as weekly to physically rest and devote our time to reading the Scriptures, praying, and meditating. This is especially true after we complete a significantly big or busy project that has wearied our souls.

Heavenly Father, help us to enter into your rest so that we may honor you for all that you have done in our lives. Refresh us often in your love and restore our weary bodies to health and strength. This we ask through Jesus Christ our Lord and Savior most beloved. Amen

Grace and the Gift of Faith

**For by grace you have been saved through faith.
And this is not your own doing; it is the gift of God,
not a result of works, so that no one may boast.
For we are his workmanship, created in Christ Jesus for good works,
which God prepared beforehand, that we should walk in them.
Ephesians 2:8-10**

These three verses were a great turning point in the history of the church. There was a time when it was incorrectly taught that we needed to do good works to try and earn God's forgiveness. In the Reformation the church returned to the faith of the apostles and prophets as recorded in the Bible. It was the Apostle Paul who taught that we are saved and forgiven by the free gift of grace from God. This is given to us through the gift of faith that God has freely given to us.

Recovery also came to us in much the same way. We needed to turn from our addiction and turn to God in faith, and ask him to deliver us from our addiction. We also need to be renewed in our faith, turning again to God for the needs of that day, day by day. By his grace in our lives we are able to live for him, clean and free from drug use and empowered to fulfill his will in our lives.

Good works do play a role in our lives. They are not required for salvation or for our deliverance from addiction. God has already prepared good works for us to do from before the creation of the world. Learning from him what his will is for us and carrying that out is to carry out the good works he has prepared for us to do. This should never be confused or mixed with the gifts of his saving grace to us and the faith we have in him.

Heavenly Father, you have come to us in the life of your son Jesus Christ. His life serves as the example we need to live by. We pray that you will day by day reveal your will to us and strengthen us for service in his Kingdom on earth. For your grace in our lives and for revealing yourself to us so that we may believe in you we give you thanks and praise, in Jesus' name. Amen

Winning by Losing

**Then Jesus told his disciples,
"If anyone would come after me, let him deny
himself and take up his cross and follow me.
For whoever would save his life will lose it,
but whoever loses his life for my sake will find it.
For what will it profit a man if he gains
the whole world and forfeits his soul?
Or what shall a man give in return for his soul?
Matthew 16:24-26**

In recovery we are required to admit that we are addicted and cannot stop using. We are required to turn over our lives to the care of God. As Christians, this means that we turn our lives over to the care of God our Father, through our Lord Jesus Christ. The level of surrender is complete, it is an absolute denial of ourselves. At this level of self-denial we have to pick up our own cross, die to ourselves and continue on in death to ourselves as we also follow after our Lord. The totality of it is fully encompassing. In addiction we thought that drugs were what we needed to enhance our lives and make them full. In recovery we found that we could only be fulfilled by giving ourselves over to God.

Ours is a spiritual recovery that requires us to live as dedicated Christians whose first objective in life is to serve God with all of our heart, soul, mind, and strength. Our relationship with God our Father is mediated through the life of his resurrected son, Jesus Christ. In order to have a life that is free and clean of drug use our first priority isn't to be free and clean of drugs. To do that, important as it is for us in addiction, would be falling short of God's design for our lives. Our lives must be lived for God. By living in this way we are able to live in sustained recovery.

God, we live to serve you and in serving you we have our lives. We pray that you will keep us through the day and through the night, one day at a time, through our Lord Jesus Christ. Amen

Spiritual Practices: The Home Altar and Daily Devotions

**Send out your light and your truth; let them lead me;
let them bring me to your holy hill and to your dwelling!
Then I will go to the altar of God, to God my exceeding joy,
and I will praise you with the lyre, O God, my God.
Psalm 43:3-5**

As part of our spirituality and recovery consider having a home altar. It does not need to be anything fancy. It could simply be part of your kitchen, or the top of a chest of drawers in your bedroom. It is best if it is where we practice our daily devotions. Suggestions for what to put on it include our Bible, a candle, an incense burner if we are so inclined, and a cross.

For a routine of devotions done on a daily basis it is best to read our Bible. If we haven't read through it in its entirety, set that as a goal for ourselves. Then re-read the books that spoke to you the most, such as the books of the New Testament and the Psalms. If we want, we can read through the entire Bible in about a year by reading about four chapters a day. The Gospel of John is a wonderful place to start and then go on to the entire New Testament. Additionally, it is a good idea to study in depth the most important books of the Bible beginning with the four Gospel stories, Matthew, Mark, Luke, and John. Consider reading commentaries about the books of the Bible to get more out of them. Many churches have these kind of books in their libraries.

In our daily devotions we should spend time in prayer. Keep a list or a diary of things to pray about, such as prayers for each member of our family, our friends, our church and pray also for ourselves. Prayers include requests as well as praise for who God is, and prayers of thanks for what he has done, and especially give thanks for answered prayers.

Heavenly Father, we give you thanks and praise for all that you have done in our lives. You have redeemed us from our sins and delivered us from our addictions. Be with us this day so that in all that we do and say we can bring glory and honor to you. Through the name of the one who suffered, died and rose, and is seated at your right hand, Jesus Christ we pray. Amen

The Group Process II

**As iron sharpens iron, so one person sharpens another.
Proverbs 27:17 NIV**

When we were enslaved to drugs we cared little for anyone or anything other than ourselves and our drugs. Under their influence our social skills suffered greatly. We abandoned the habits that make for good conduct and took on behaviors that were rude, selfish, and even hostile.

Being free and clean of drugs gives us the opportunity to recovery our social life. It is not until we are out and about and interacting with others that we can truly see what we are like. It is in the face of fluid interactions with others that we see ourselves in a more true light. We can see how we handle ourselves emotionally and mentally when faced with other people's opinions. We can see where our thoughts take us when we are challenged with other ideas. We can find out if we are able to be true to ourselves or will we cave under the slightest pressure. For us in recovery we need to be active in a safe group process in order to mature and be strengthen in our recovery.

We will always be addicts for life, though we do get clean and recover. We do not get into recovery by living in a vacuum, it takes God and others to help us. The fellowship of the group process is necessary. What happens in the meetings is spiritual. In our 12-step meetings we gather together to pray, and hear, and share about each other's recovery. It is the most successful format of its kind in treating addictions. This process in its beginnings was entirely based on the Holy Scriptures and its rudimentary form was started up by the Oxford Group. As Christians in recovery we also need to include Bible readings, meditation, and worship with God's people. All of this working together in the recovery community and in the church leads to a sustained, growing, and strong life lived clean and free of drugs through God's grace.

Dearest Father, you have made us to be the body of Christ which is the church. Grant to us grace so that we may share fully in the fellowship of all believers and by it be refined and grow in our maturity. Build us up so that we can contribute to the good of the body and use us according to your designs. This we ask through the name of Jesus Christ who is the head of the church. Amen

What Are Your Red Flags?

**I am astonished that you are so quickly deserting him who called you in the grace of Christ and are turning to a different gospel— not that there is another one, but there are some who trouble you and want to distort the gospel of Christ. But even if we or an angel from heaven should preach to you a gospel contrary to the one we preached to you, let him be accursed. As we have said before, so now I say again:
If anyone is preaching to you a gospel contrary to
the one you received, let him be accursed.
Galatians 1:6-9**

Once an addict, always an addict. The only thing that makes a difference for us is that we are in recovery. We are in recovery because we have a right relationship with God through our Lord Jesus Christ. When this relationship is healthy and strong our recovery is secure. When our relationship with the Lord suffers, we are at risk. Any number of red flags could be the warning sign that we need to take seriously and when they occur, we need to do something to fix it:

> Not doing our daily devotions ... Not living in our normal routines ... Not worshipping and fellowshipping on a weekly basis ... Anger outbursts ... Minimizing the dangers of our past using or glorifying it   ... Lying ... Having mood swings or emotional extremes ... An increase in our stress level ... Visiting locations where we once used ... Not going to meetings ... Not following the program ... Spending time with old friends that use ... Isolating ... Not taking care of ourselves ... Not eating right ... Not getting enough sleep ... Not caring for our personal hygiene...

Heavenly Father, by your grace we follow you and have our lives of recovery. Help and aid us to live daily in accordance with your divine will for our lives. In Christ's holy name. Amen

Our Purpose in Life

For you have died, and your life is hidden with Christ in God. When Christ who is your life appears, then you also will appear with him in glory.
Colossians 3:3-4

Sometimes in our pursuit of life we thought that our career was the thing. If we could get the right job, then life would be fine. For as important as they are, neither can our families be the central most thing. The thing that needs to be the most central part of our life is our relationship with God and that is doubly true for us in recovery. The Scriptures tell us that our life is hidden with Christ in God. We can have all the success we can imagine in life, with our family, career, sports and whatever, and still be completely unfulfilled. We can "have it all" as the saying goes, and still feel empty and lost if we don't have a healthy relationship with our Lord.

God our Maker designed life so that we need to be in a covenant relationship with him. The thing that makes the difference in life is our relationship with God. Everything can look right on the outside but on the inside we can have a certain restlessness that gnaws away at our souls. Our quick fix to this was to turn to drugs. Only the drugs didn't fix anything. Using drugs was like drinking salt water when we were dying of thirst. That water only makes us more thirsty and draws us into a cycle of drinking more and more to quench a thirst that it can never satisfy. Drugs do the same thing to us. We got high to try and feel fulfilled only to find ourselves feeling even less fulfilled. Our addiction grew larger and our lives felt more and more empty day after day.

In recovery we had to work hard to repair the damage the drugs did. At first it was extremely hard but as we made gains we began to get a taste of fulfillment from God. We found a new sense of purpose and rediscovered ourselves through our relationship with God.

Heavenly Father, restore unto us the lives that you have planned out for us. Help us to see that in all our relationships you are to come first and are to be included in all of our relationships with others. Bless us this day in our recoveries and strengthen us for service in your son's Kingdom on earth, through Christ our Lord. Amen

Uncover, Discover, and Recover

**The way of the wicked is like deep darkness;
they do not know over what they stumble.
Proverbs 4:19**

In getting clean we needed to do more than just stop using. If that was all we did, we became the addict's equivalent of a dry drunk. Among other things we needed to understand how and why we became addicts. We needed to take a serious and thorough look at ourselves introspectively, hard as that may have been. By searching our memories we could recall and could see what our actions had been. We may have been tempted to forget them or deny them, but we needed to put words to what we had recalled. Following this uncovering of memories we needed to discover how our actions had not only affected ourselves but others as well. The weight of our past can be formidable, but it was essential that we did this and where appropriate we need to seek to bring healing to those we had hurt and healing to ourselves for the woundedness we had created in our own lives.

In recovery we needed to move forward and find the life that we would have had if it had not been for our addiction. With our friends and family, having worked to heal and restore those relationships, we needed to move forward with them in normalized relationships. Healthy friends needed to replace the people we bought drugs from and used drugs with. We needed to return to the pursuit of our educations, our careers, and all of our ambitions. These healthy activities in recovery were there to replace our addictive behavior and they need to fill up our days because too much idle time can bring with it a danger for relapsing.

Heavenly Father, your son came to bring us abundant life. We pray that in our recoveries we would be able to come into the lives you have planned for us. Help us to live faithfully for you, may we know your will for our lives and live that out to the fullest, though Christ our Lord we pray. Amen

Ah,… Ah,… Ah Choo

**Beloved, I pray that all may go well with you and
that you may be in good health, as it goes well with your soul.
2 John 1:2**

There was an old-world folk belief that when you sneezed it could expel your soul right out of your body. The fear was that in that awkward spiritual state it opened you up to being overcome by the devil or an evil spirit. It was also believed that by sneezing it might be the body's way of trying to forcefully expel an evil spirit. That is why when someone sneezes, we say, "God bless you".

When we were using, whether we smoked it, snorted, swallowed, or injected it, we took the drugs into not only our physical bodies, but we also took them into our souls. Our souls are housed within our body and are especially prominent in our brains, heart, lungs, and abdomens. Our soul is a very spiritual part of us. While it is located in our physically tangible bodies, it also has in its spiritual nature, an intangible quality, just like a gentle puff of air. When we take drugs, they have an effect on us and on our souls. The drugs that we surrendered to as we used them took over a part of our soul for its own and the drugs, impersonal as they are, don't give back our souls without a struggle.

In our attempts to quit we may or may not have realized that our soul works both for and against kicking the addiction. We know that we sabotage our own efforts and it is quite easy for a saboteur to bring us to ruin. Clearly, we cannot quit on our own when it is our own souls that are both trying to live clean and also not willing to give it up. For this reason alone we need God.

Heavenly Father, purge and purify our souls by the blood that was shed by your son when he died for our sins on the cross. Fill us with your Holy Spirit and enliven us to pursue recovery in every area of our lives. We have life because you gave us life. Let us live fully for you and bring glory to you for all that you have done to bring us into recovery. In Jesus' name. Amen

Our Purpose in Redemption

**Train up a child in the way he should go,
even when he is old he will not depart from it.
Proverbs 22:6**

  A child is born and the parents wonder, what will their child aspire to do? They may have high hopes that some of the children will follow one of them into their career field, teaching, healthcare, the family business, whatever. They also wondered what about faith and what will their religious practices be? Recent trends in the world have included parents not giving their children religious upbringings so they can decide for themselves later in life what they will believe. That is a recipe for ruin in a person's life. We have to ask, why in the world would anyone do that? For as important as salvation is for our sinful souls, why would we not lead our children into a saving relationship with our Maker? For as important as it is to know how to pray to God, to rely on him for all that we need, why would parents forgo telling their children about the Savior?

  From their earliest days we need to implant in our children the memories of attending church worship on Sunday mornings. They need to see us reading our Bibles, praying in our homes, listening to Christian music, and blessing the Lord for the food we eat. As our children grow we need to put the Bible into their hands and instruct them in what it says. As addicts in recovery we need to let them know about our lives and these struggles that we have. For all we know, our children may also go on to have the same struggles. When they are young and receptive we need to instill deeply in them what we know, that we are all sinners and the only saving grace that there is, is through our Lord Jesus Christ, God's only begotten. We need to teach our children how to pray to God. Lastly, we need to let them know what to do if addiction occurs in their own lives too.

  Heavenly Father, make us good parents and grandparents. Help us to share our faith with our children and grandchildren. Let us lead them by our example. Through Christ our Lord. Amen

The Transforming Power of the Word of God

**So Jesus said to the Jews who had believed him,
"If you abide in my word, you are truly my disciples,
and you will know the truth, and the truth will set you free."
John 8:31-32**

When we encounter the Word of God, the Bible, one of two thing happen. First, if we don't like or accept what it says we downplay its importance and we reject it, all because we don't want to change our ways. Or second, we see that it can transform us and we accept what it is saying.

The Bible says of itself that its Word is living and active.[104] We need to know that by the power of his spoken Word, Jesus brought again from the dead his friend Lazarus, who had been dead four days. We need to remember how by the power of his Word God created the heavens and the earth. Then given the power of God's Word to create all that is and to raise the dead, we need to take confidence that his Word can and will transform us in our recoveries.

Our surrender to the drugs changed us. An important boundary in life was trampled down by us when we crossed over it and got high. We were held captive by them, enslaved and brutalized by them. We might not have liked being addicted to them, we might not have liked what they did to us, but we cooperated with them. We defended our behavior, justified our actions, and rationalized our reasons for continuing in addiction.

In surrendering to God in order to find recovery we had to put our faith in him. We had to take him at his Word. We found his promises to us recorded in the Bible. In our greatest desperation he was true to his Word. No one else could do for us what he did for us. God's Word is our lifeline, it is our salvation now and every day, one day at a time.

Heavenly Father, by the power of your Word you freed us from Satan's domain and enslavement to addiction. By the power of your Word keep us in your grace, lead us to live faithfully for you, through Christ Jesus our Lord. Amen

---

[104] Hebrews 4:12

Parallels

**So Jesus said to the Jews who had believed him,
"If you abide in my word, you are truly my disciples,
and you will know the truth, and the truth will set you free."
John 8:31-32**

The drug culture and using are very toxic and poisonous forms of spirituality. Emphasis must be made that these are false forms of spirituality and not true spirituality. In our recovery we need to see them for all the evil that they are in the light of God. This will strengthen us in our walk with God.

We need to know that the devil has no creative power or abilities of his own whatsoever. All that he can offer is a counterfeit based on the real thing. Not being a creative person, he is limited to using what God has already made. For that reason, there are significant parallels between the Christian life, and the life lived in addiction. Just think back to the days when we used and the ritual like patterns we followed so closely as we cooked, snorted, shot up or smoked our drug of choice. That ritual of preparing and consuming hardly ever varied, and the reason for that was it was part of a toxic ritual that mimicked what God has for us in the true faith. The devil used drugs to lure us in, ensnare us, and then imprison us. Through drug use and addiction, through the occult, and other deceptions, he worked to keep us from God's purpose for our lives. On the other hand, God offers us forgiveness, freedom in Christ and eternal life because he died for our forgiveness.

When we came into the truth about our addiction we had to admit that we were addicted and could not free ourselves. We knew that without God delivering us from using it was never going to happen. In recovery we devote ourselves to a new way of life. Drugs demanded our devotion and enslaved us. God welcomes us and offers us freedom and forgiveness but nothing is forced. Unlike with drugs, we are free to follow his son as our Lord.

God, thank you for revealing yourself us to and freeing us by the truth of your Word. Give us this day your grace so that all we do and say will bring you glory, in Jesus name. Amen

The Oral Tradition of the Word of God

Such is the confidence that we have through Christ toward God. Not that we are sufficient in ourselves to claim anything as coming from us, but our sufficiency is from God, who has made us sufficient to be ministers of a new covenant, not of the letter but of the Spirit. For the letter kills, but the Spirit gives life.
2 Corinthians 3:4-6

In our modern society there is something from the ancient world that has been all but forgotten. That is the oral tradition. In the ancient world even with the invention of writing they still relied heavily on the spoken word. The written word was not viewed as being the same as the spoken word. In the Greek language of the New Testament there are actually two different words used for the written and the spoken word. *Logos* refers to the written word and *rhema* refers to the spoken word.

Our common modern-day understanding of the written word or letter verses the spirit of the word is that the letter of the word is being applied to life in a strict manner. Whereas applying the spirit of the word is to apply its intent which allows for a more practical application. We need to know that the ancient people of faith viewed the letter and the spirit of the word very differently. The spoken word was something that was alive, whereas the written word was something that killed. The spoken word was living because it was given life by our breathing it out loud and giving it our breath. This compared to the written word that had not been given life by someone speaking it aloud and giving it life with their own breath. This is why the written letter of the word killed.

We also need to know that prior to the fourth century, silently reading to yourself had not been invented yet. One day someone noticed that Saint Ambrose had a book in front of him but he was not reading it out loud. He was reading, but only in the sense that it was silent reading in his head alone. From that time silent reading to yourself began to take over as the common practice.

When we read to ourselves there is a specific neuropathway in the brain that is activated. Likewise, when we hear our own voice read aloud the word it is yet another neuropathway. Still again, when we hear the spoken Word of God and listen to it being read aloud to us by someone it is different neuropathway.

This is important for us to know this in our recovery because our old sinful and adamic nature is so resistant and hostile to God and his Word. We need to overcome our sinful old-nature by not only reading the Word but also by hearing the Word. Therefore, take time to read aloud from the Bible to yourselves. Also, consider purchasing an audio Bible to listen to and use it often. We benefit by hearing the Word of God read aloud in worship and in Bible studies too. We need to let the Word of God dwell in us richly from these sources so that it may have its full effect on our lives.

    Heavenly Father, thank you for your Word that sustains us in our lives. By your living Word lift us up and guide us in all that we do, empower us to fulfill your will in our lives and to bring glory to your holy name. Through Christ our Lord we pray. Amen

Morning Prayer

**But I, O Lord, cry to you;
in the morning my prayer comes before you.
Psalm 88:13**

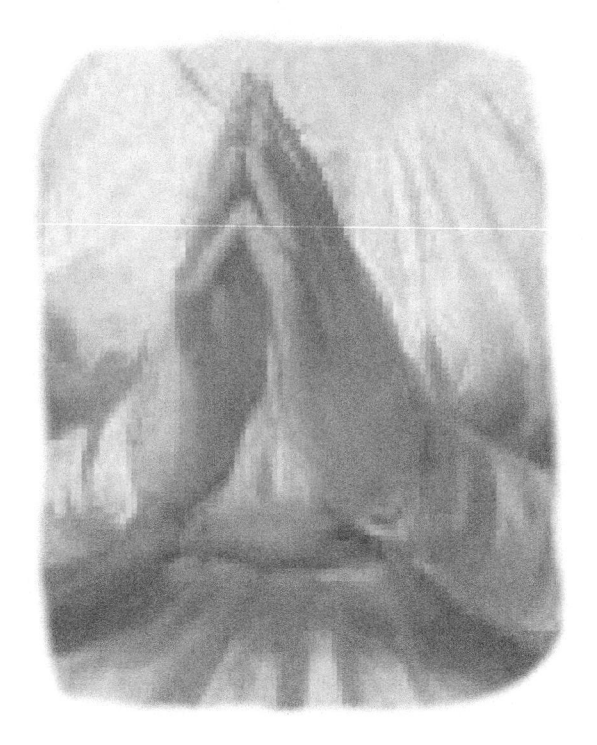

From the Great Reformer, Martin Luther, as stated below is his prayer for us to say when we rise from our sleep. To this we should also remember to pray for our continued recovery and all the things we hope to accomplish this day. In giving God our thanks and praise we remember to intercede for all who need to find recovery, for those who are struggling with the temptation to use again and for all who are in recovery, that the day will go well and that they will receive God's continued blessings in their lives.

I thank Thee, my Heavenly Father, through Jesus Christ, Thy dear Son, that Thou hast kept me this night from all harm and danger; and I pray Thee to keep me this day also from sin and all evil, that all my doings and life may please Thee. For into Thy hands I commend myself, my body and soul, and all things. Let Thy holy angel be with me, that the wicked foe may have no power over me. Amen.[105]

---

[105] https://en.wikisource.org/wiki/Luther%27s_Small_Catechism

Evening Prayer

**Then I turned my face to the Lord God, seeking him by prayer.
Daniel 9:3**

    I thank Thee, my Heavenly Father, through Jesus Christ, Thy dear Son, that Thou hast graciously kept me this day, and I pray Thee to forgive me all my sins, where I have done wrong, and graciously keep me this night. For into Thy hands I commend myself, my body and soul, and all things. Let Thy holy angel be with me, that the wicked foe may have no power over me. Amen.[106]

    By bringing the day to closure in prayer we are crediting God with all that we have to be grateful for and for all that we accomplished and for all of his blessings that we have received. This example of a bedtime prayer by Luther guides us in what to say and think about. The greatest things for us as addicts are of course the salvation of our souls from sin by Jesus's atoning death on the cross and for our recovery from drug addiction that had once enslaved us.

---

[106] https://en.wikisource.org/wiki/Luther%27s_Small_Catechism

Troubling Things Will Happen

**Jesus said,
"Let not your hearts be troubled.
Believe in God; believe also in me."**

On the night of our Lord's betrayal he spoke these very words to his disciples. He told them that very disturbing things would happen to him. That he would be betrayed, treated abusively by their countries leaders, and be unjustly executed. He said troubling things would happen, but that they should not be troubled by any of it. The disciples may have wondered, how can we not be troubled by all this, it is the very thing that major catastrophes are made of. Yet our Lord made it very clear to them not to be troubled by any of it. How can they avoid being troubled? For the simple reason that they believed in God and that they believed in Jesus Christ our Lord.

In addiction we have very skewed perceptions of things sometimes. On the whole, we tended to either underreact or overreact to things because of our using. If we under reacted it might have been because we didn't care or because we were too out of it from the drugs. If we overreacted it might have been because of the drug's effect on us or because we were already living our lives on the edge of survival and any little thing would set us off. Over reacting has been called catastrophizing. That means that we make something that is a mole hill into a mountainous problem.

In our recovery our minds began to return to a normal state and continued to progress as we applied ourselves to the program. We found that in the midst of the trials of our lives that we could find a supernatural sense of peace from God through our Lord Jesus Christ. We found that God aided us in everything from the smallest to the greatest of needs that we had. We came to know that we did not have to face the burdens alone anymore.

Dearest heavenly Father, thank you for your grace in our lives, that you sent your son to redeem us and who abides with us always. Thank you for all the help you give us in sustaining our recovery. Through Christ our Lord we pray. Amen

Peer Pressure

**Jesus said to Simon Peter,
"Simon, son of John, do you love me more than these?"
He said to him, "Yes, Lord; you know that I love you.
John 21:15**

  Peer pressure was not friendly to us. It was the thing that tilted the scales off the deep end for many of us. We wanted friends, we wanted to belong, and we were desperate not to be excluded from joining a social circle. In our adolescent years having personal friends was more important to us than family. If using drugs with them was the cost of belonging, then so be it, we joined with them and used drugs. We yielded ourselves, and our identities to them. We kept the things we did with them secret and that tightened the bonds we shared with them. As we got high with them we gave up our individuality, our self-identity, and the group consciousness took over. As our personal boundaries were worn down so was our ability to say no to anything. As the grip of drug use grew tighter we slipped further and further into addiction. We knew that if we quit using the group would shame us and try to get us to use again. If we did quit they would reject us, which would leave us without friends. We felt trapped and the truth was we were trapped in a sick addiction that came with sick relationships with sick friends.

  In recovery we had to dump virtually every friend we had. It made us feel lonely. We worried if we would ever have friends again. We worried that our new friends might not be capable of being good friends to us. We had to realign our lives to maintain being clean, there was treatment, there were meetings to go to and counselors to talk with. We had trust issues and didn't open ourselves up to many others in those days. We feared relapsing or that someone else newly in recovery would drag us down with them into a relapse. Over time we came to have new friends, none of whom used, some of whom were in recovery too.

  Heavenly Father, thank you for accepting us and making us to be members of your son's church on earth. Bless us with sweet fellowship and warm friendships. In Jesus' name. Amen

We Are the Temple of the Holy Spirit

Or do you not know that your body is a temple of the Holy Spirit within you, whom you have from God? You are not your own, for you were bought with a price. So glorify God in your body.
1 Corinthians 6:19-20

When we use drugs in any form their smoke and our soul co-mingled together. Then the drugs competed hostilely for our lives to keep us from God. When we were using drugs we were unavailable to fellowship with God. We know that life first came to Adam when God breathed into his nostrils the breath-of-life. His body was alive because God's life-giving-spirit was in him. When we, the sons and daughters of Adam, inhaled the toxic smoke from our drug of choice it mixed with our souls and blurred who were we, taking over major parts of who we were at the most basic and fundamental level. It was a very unholy thing that we did to ourselves and it resulted in us being re-created into addicts. Spiritual birth came to us when our Heavenly Father and his son, our Lord Jesus Christ gave us the Holy Spirit. This made us to be a temple of the Holy Spirit.

When as a Christian we shared our bodies with the smoke of meth or marijuana, snorted coke or something else, we were deeply grieving the Holy Spirit who lives in us. The two, what is Holy and what is entirely unholy, by nature have nothing in common with each other. When we are host to both of them in our physical body we are sabotaging ourselves in our recovery and sabotaging ourselves as Christians as well. There is no living halfway in between or living partially in both lifestyles, drug use compromises us completely. In using we return quickly to all the old and terrible behaviors. Our thinking becomes corrupt, our emotions are volatile and we return to our old lifestyle at its worse and progress downward from there.

Gracious God in heaven, we give you thanks this day for our redemption from sin and our deliverance from drug addiction. Guide our thoughts that they might be entirely about you and how we can live to do your will. In Jesus's holy name we pray. Amen

Slaves of God

**But now that you have been set free
from sin and have become slaves of God,
the fruit you get leads to sanctification and its end, eternal life.
Romans 6:22**

Once we were enslaved to drugs. We welcomed them into our lives and they took over, ruling and reigning over us without mercy. Maybe we had short periods of clean time. We may have told ourselves that we could quit if we wanted to. The truth was in all of our lives that we had no control over our use and we had no control over quitting. We were enslaved and we told ourselves lies like, I'm not ready to quit, and I'm enjoying it too much for now. Underneath our façade of not being ready, we were scared and did not want to think about what we could not do. We did not want to think about the hopelessness of our addiction.

When God delivered us from our enslavement to drugs we became indebted to him. We had in fact exchanged one terrible taskmaster for a new but kind and benevolent master. We were freed from a taskmaster who was working us to our deaths by slowly destroying our lives through addiction. It was a slow death that took our money, our homes, our families, and friends. Our new master was also our Creator. Being enslaved to him was different. Our indebtedness to him was a new kind of freedom. We were free from drugs and that lifestyle. With drug addiction we had an impersonal relationship with drugs. With God we came to have a warm and loving relationship with our Heavenly Father and our Lord Jesus Christ. We were now able to enjoy our lives again, with choices about how we would live for him. We were free to live in accordance with God's will for our lives.

Gracious Father in Heaven, thank you for making a way for us to be redeemed from drug addiction. Thank you for sending your son to die for our salvation. We love you with all of our hearts, souls, minds, and strength. We live to bring you glory, for you alone are worthy. This we pray through our Lord Jesus Christ. Amen

Life Got You Down?

**About midnight Paul and Silas were
praying and singing hymns to God,
and the prisoners were listening to them,
and suddenly there was a great earthquake,
so that the foundations of the prison were shaken.
And immediately all the doors were opened,
and everyone's bonds were unfastened.
Acts 16:25-26**

Paul and Silas had been attacked, arrested, publicly beaten, thrown into prison, and placed in stocks. And it was all done illegally in their case. They were Roman citizens and their rights had been violated. They were innocent of all that they were accused of. In prison they did not have a pity-party or make threats to anyone who mistreated them. They accepted their misfortune, praying and singing hymns to the praise of God. Amazing! Even more amazing was the fact that God sent an earthquake just then that opened the prison doors and released everyone's restraints. Still more amazing was the fact that no one left even though they could have escaped. They wanted to stay and find out about the message of salvation that Paul and Silas were preaching.

Our God is a miracle worker. We were in bondage to drugs and the lifestyle that came with it. We were addicted, manipulative, egocentric, untrustworthy and devious. Their prison had walls that could be touched; our prison was intangible and even more impossible to escape from. We were ensnared with fetters that could not be seen. We were without a solution to our problem.

When we came to our end, we turned to God for help. He miraculously freed us from our prisons and all the bonds that held us in addiction. Then we were able to sing his praises and pray to him without ceasing. Therein laid our sustained recovery.

Heavenly Father, we love and adore you, praise and worship you, for you have done great things for us and worthy is your name. Through Christ our Lord we pray. Amen

Transcendence

**Oh, that I had wings like a dove!
I would fly away and be at rest.
Psalm 55:6**

Here in this Psalm David wishes for a miracle of transcendence, then he could be above his problems and could find some rest for his weary soul. He was the king of a very great nation, but that position of wealth and power did not alleviate his problems, it multiplied them. He wished, longed for, and dreamt about this solution, but he never did sprout wings to rise above anything.

In the Old Testament days the Holy Spirit would come upon the people of God on a temporary basis. The prophets would have this special experience and by it they would preach the Word of God and foretell the future. It wasn't until the days that followed Jesus' resurrection that the permanent indwelling of the Holy Spirit happened for all believers.

Like weary King David we will not be sprouting wings either, but we do have this advantage. We can find rest for our souls because of the constant abiding and indwelling of God's presence through the Holy Spirit. Jesus said he would send it to us in his own name and it would be a Comforter in our lives.[107] There we can find rest for our souls, by turning to God and relying on the Holy Spirit. When we pray, worship and sing, meditate and read his Word, we can find renewal in our physical bodies, peace for our minds, rest for our hearts and become energized in our spirits.

Heavenly Father, we carry many burdens in our lives as addicts in recovery. We pray that you will bring us times of relief and freedom for the worries and fears that we alone know. May we find peace and rest in you through your constant presence in our lives through the Holy Spirit. This we pray to you in Jesus' name, our Lord and Savior. Amen

---

[107] John 14:26 KJ21

We Are Never Alone

**For he has said, "I will never leave you nor forsake you."
So we can confidently say, "The Lord is my helper;
I will not fear; what can man do to me?"
Hebrew 13:5-6**

There is a peaceful calm in knowing that no matter what happens in this life God is there with us and he is for us. He has promised to never leave us or forsake us. No matter what man may do to us, or what calamity may come, the Lord is present in our lives. He will heal us, sustain, and uphold us.

In our addiction we may go where we shouldn't go, we may even do things that we shouldn't do, but God is there with us. We need to know that God may not like what we are doing and this does grieve him deeply. Also, God may not like where we go and this too grieves him deeply. We may compromise ourselves, but God's promise is uncompromising, he will never, no never, leave us or forsake us.

We also need to be reminded that we should not use this promise of God as an opportunity to sin as some have. We hear from others who returned to their former life of using or some other major sin. They all seem to say the same thing, it was not the same this time. I did not enjoy it as before, and I know that is because I am a Christian and I was convicted of my sin the whole time.

In recovery there is a boldness that is ours and it comes to us in a unique way. It is the fruit of our surrender to the Lord. We know that we are in his hands and there is nothing that he cannot handle for us. Our place is to have faith and trust in him. He is present with us in all of the troubles we face, he will protect us and guide us supernaturally.

Heavenly Father, you have given us your all to provide for and sustain us in our recoveries. We give you our thanks and praise because you have made it possible for us to live clean and free from drug use. Reveal your will to us and empower us to live it out in our daily lives. This we pray through Christ Jesus our Lord, who lives and reigns with you and the Holy Spirit. Amen

Come, Thou Fount of Every Blessing

Oftentimes with the passage of time hymns and songs lose their popular appeal. This is not the case with this beloved hymn of praise. Whether it is played on a pipe organ, on a guitar or sung A Capella, its beauty is timeless. Written by Robert Robinson (1735-1790) its words reveal something of its author. He was a British Baptist and a barber's apprentice who was taken by the preaching of George Whitefield. In his younger years he had been part of a street gang and lived an immoral and self-indulgent life. He was saved in 1755 and preached in the Methodist church and founded a Baptist church a few years later. He was remarkable in that he had no formal education by those day's standards but he rose to become an exquisite preacher and scholar. His reference to raising his *Ebenezer* in the fourth verse is not universally understood. It is a reference to 1 Samuel 7:12 when the Prophet Samuel set up a stone marker and named it Ebenezer as he declared that *the Lord had helped him this far*.

Take time this day to play the tune on a CD or the internet and sing along with it as part of your devotions. Consider setting it to memory and including it in your spiritual practices on a weekly basis.

Come, Thou Fount of Every Blessing

Come, thou Fount of every blessing, tune my heart to sing thy grace; Streams of mercy, never ceasing, call for songs of loudest praise. Teach me some melodious sonnet, sung by flaming tongues above. Praise the mount, I'm fixed upon it, mount of Thy redeeming love.

O to grace how great a debtor daily I'm constrained to be! Let that grace, Lord, like a fetter, bind my wand'ring heart to Thee. Teach me, Lord, some rapturous measure, meet for me thy grace to prove, While I sing the countless treasure, of my God's unchanging love.

Prone to wander, Lord, I feel it; Prone to leave the God I love: Take my heart, oh, take and seal it with Thy Spirit from above. Rescued thus from sin and danger, purchased by the Savior's blood, May I walk on earth a stranger, as a son and heir of God.

Here I raise my Ebenezer. Here by Thy great help I've come. And I hope, by Thy good pleasure safely to arrive at home. Jesus sought me when a stranger wandering from the fold of God. He to rescue me from danger interposed His precious blood.

Oh, that day when freed from sinning I shall see thy lovely face. Clothed then in the blood washed linen how I'll sing thy wondrous grace. Come, my Lord, no longer tarry take my ransomed soul away. Send thine angels now to carry me to realms of endless day.

Robert Robinson 1758

Spiritual Practices: Breathing and Meditation

**The Spirit of God has made me,
and the breath of the Almighty gives me life.
Job 33:4**

You may ask, "How important is this matter of breath and breathing?" It is vitally important to us and to our sustained recovery. We know that we must breathe in order to live and we can only hold our breath for so long. Without air we will die in as little as four or five minutes, but there is more to it than that. How often do we remember that our lives came to us as a gift, from our parents and more importantly from God himself. We have in us the breath of the Almighty which gives us life.

This verse is one that we would do well to meditate on. Take time today to lay down or sit in a comfortable chair and focus on it. Rehearse this verse over and over in your mind and say it aloud as well. Speak with emphasis each word in a pattern like this until you have completed saying it with emphasis on each word to its end:

The Spirit of God has made me, and the breath of the Almighty gives me life.

The **Spirit** of God has made me, and the breath of the Almighty gives me life.

The Spirit **of** God has made me, and the breath of the Almighty gives me life.

The Spirit of **God** has made me, and the breath of the Almighty gives me life…

As you go through the verse meditate on knowing that our lives are being held in God's very own hands. We are his children and he lovingly cares for us. Our lives are not our own, they are gifts from God for us to live for his glory.

Heavenly Father, thank you for the gift of our lives. Thank you for your love that you bear for us. Aid and guide us that in all that we do, in all that we say and think, we may bring all glory to your name, for Christ's sake we ask this. Amen

We Can Decide Not to Use Anymore, but It Takes God to Get Us to Quit

But to all who did receive him, who believed in his name, he gave the right to become children of God, John 1:12

We lied and told ourselves we would quit, but that didn't happen, we didn't even try. Then when we tried to quit, we failed time after time, every time. We were very discouraged and because of our failure we used again to pick up our wounded spirits. Then, finally, in desperation we turned to get help and that help came from God. We asked and he answered. He was the one reason we were able to quit. It wasn't a partnership, it was him 100% all the way. Day by day we felt like we were getting the hang of it, of letting go and letting God care for our lives.

We were incredibly grateful for God's intervention in our lives. We were feeling renewal and hope for our future. We came to understand that we needed to turn to God for help for each new day. We sought to know him better and to know his will for our lives so that we would have direction and the conviction that we were fulfilling his purpose for our lives. We found assurance and security in the steps of our new recovery routine. We continued to be so incredibly grateful for God's aid in living a clean and free life.

We attended meetings and there we learned about ourselves by hearing others sharing about their lives. As it turned out, we have a lot in common with other addicts. We found strength knowing that we were not alone in what we experienced in our addiction. We felt a growing bond with the others and felt secure in sharing openly about our own experiences.

Heavenly Father, when we were without a hope you came and delivered us from using drugs. You sustain us day by day, keeping us in your will and empowering us to live according to it. Abide with us still, lead and guide us, and may we live in your grace day by day, one day at a time. Through Christ our Lord, who lives and reigns with you and the Holy Spirit, one God, now and forever. Amen

The Lament Rather than a Pity-Party

**Do not remember against us our former iniquities;
let your compassion come speedily to meet us,
for we are brought very low.
Help us, O God of our salvation,
for the glory of your name;
deliver us, and atone for our sins,
for your name's sake!
Psalm 79:8-9**

In contrast to our tendency as addicts to want to wallow in pity there is a spiritual alternative for us to practice. In Hebrew it is called *saphad,* which means to *lament*. There are five types of Psalms in the Bible, praise, wisdom, royal, thanksgiving and lastly the laments. The lamenting Psalms include 44, 60, 74, 79, 80, 85, and 90. There are other examples of laments throughout the Bible. A lament is a prayer to God that passionately expresses our grief and sorrow over life's events. Jeremiah the Prophet was known as the weeping prophet because he lamented so greatly over the coming fall of Judea and Jerusalem to the Babylonians.

The lament is a very heart felt complaint that we lift up to God to express our feelings over the way life has been for us or is unfolding. It doesn't have to ask for a solution to what is going on, it can simply be our way of bringing it to God's attention. Of course we can ask for a solution too if we want to.

Heavenly Father you know more than we do about how difficult life can be. Of all the people on the earth, we have the additional burden of trying to live in recovery in a world where that is not always supported. Our frames are but of flesh, and we are weak and weary. We call upon your Name because you are great and awesome. Fill us with your love and by your Holy Spirit living in us, sustain us day by day, and bring us relief from our burdens. In Jesus' name. Amen

Covenant Relationships: Codependency and Interdependency

**Then the man said,
"This at last is bone of my bones and flesh of my flesh;
she shall be called Woman, because she was taken out of Man."
Therefore a man shall leave his father and his mother and hold
fast to his wife, and they shall become one flesh. And the man
and his wife were both naked and were not ashamed.
Genesis 2:23-25**

Someone once shared the example of these two images to portray healthy and unhealthy relationships. Image a marriage relationship as if the couples are characterized as simply leaning against each other. As long as neither of them moves or changes position they remain standing. However, if just one of them moves a little they both will fall over. This is a simple depiction of a codependency in a marriage. Now, imagine that the couple are two coils, or spring like strands. They each have a stable round base to stand on. They are both able to interwind into the other's life and if one or both of them move or change something in their lives, they are still able to stand on their round base and interwind into the other's.

In drug use addiction and codependency go hand in hand. Because we are addicts we are automatically codependent. If we are in a marriage or a relationship with an addict, we might as well consider ourselves codependent. In recovery it is important to work together to also recover from codependency. This can be helped by attending 12-step meetings. Co-Dependents Anonymous, or CoDA meetings are specifically designed to help with recovery from codependent relationships. Once a couple has a taste of the flavor of what drug free, healthy lifestyles are, they commonly strive for more and cannot get enough of what makes for a healthy relationship.

Heavenly Father, you designed us to be in relationships, with you and with others. Bless us in our marriage relationships, with spouses, family and with friends. Help us to be healthy contributors in the give and take of lives lived with others. Lead us out of codependency and into better, healthier relationships with all. Through Christ our Lord we pray. Amen

Unconditional Positive Regard

**"Teacher, which is the great commandment in the Law?"
And he said to him, "You shall love the Lord your God with all your heart and with all your soul and with all your mind.
This is the great and first commandment.
And a second is like it: You shall love your neighbor as yourself.
On these two commandments depend all the Law and the Prophets."
Matthew 22:36-40**

Sometimes you can see in a person's eyes or on their face the signs that they are suffering in brokenness. Though not everyone is so easy to read, it is universally true among addicts that we are all suffering with very tender hearts. We have at our core a very wounded and low self-image. Many of us hide it well but it is there and that is without exception. The causes for this vary. For some it is because we have been overcome by the addictions that lured us in with the wonderful feelings it first gave to us. For others of us we came into addiction already suffering. We found that drugs gave us the feelings that we were someone and with them we could feel good about ourselves for a while, until their affects wore off.

In our faith we learned that one of our most valued and important tenents was to love our neighbor as ourselves. In addiction we may have actually hated ourselves which made it hard for us to imagine what it was like to love others. Our needs for affection and affirmation in our developmental years may not have been met. Worse, we may have been maltreated in those early years of our lives. For this we needed to, or maybe even still need to, find deep healing. Among the most healing actions that we can pursue is in loving God. By embracing him, by going to God we can be healed of our countless wounds and made whole.

Dearest God, help us to love you fully and empower us to love our neighbors as ourselves. Bring healing to our lives for all that we suffer with and use to show your great love to others as well. In the name of Jesus Christ our Lord. Amen

Seeking the Lord

You will seek me and find me, when you seek me with all your heart. I will be found by you, declares the LORD, and I will restore your fortunes and gather you from all the nations and all the places where I have driven you, declares the LORD, and I will bring you back to the place from which I sent you into exile.
Jeremiah 29:13-14

Adam and Eve abandoned their relationship with God when they tried too much to be like him by coming into the knowledge of good and evil. That is called original sin. They attempted this by eating the forbidden fruit. Following their missed attempt at being something greater than they were, they did not go to God, rather he came to them. So it is with all of us, God has come to us in the life of his son, Jesus Christ. The problem for us is that in our addictions we had turned our backs on God and eaten of the forbidden fruit of another kind. We used drugs in the hopes that they would do something great for us. Just like with Adam and Eve, it all backfired on us. Our addiction caused us to run from God and hide. In our recovery we had to quit running from God, we had to quit hiding from him and call on his name for salvation from our sins and for our recovery from our addictions.

God offers us many promises when we live for him. First and foremost is the forgiveness of our many sins through the blood of the new covenant that he established by the suffering and death of his son. For us as addicts, perhaps the next most important one is deliverance from drugs. This happened because we entered into a covenant relationship with God, which is meant to be an enduring, daily, and lifelong relationship. God spoke through his prophet, Jeremiah saying we need to seek him with our whole heart. That is because our hearts had divided desires and loyalties. As addicts we wanted to get clean but not give up the high feelings we got from using. We wanted God in our lives, but only on a limited basis because we wanted to control what he would do with and in our lives.

God's plan for us is that we surrender our hearts completely to him. Jesus himself said we cannot serve two masters.[108] We cannot have it both ways with God. Our addiction made us want to believe in a god, but it was a false god that we wanted who was made in our image according to our will who would serve us. Addiction in our lives appeared to be willing to compromise a little, in an apparent cooperative effort with faith in God. That way we could continue using and with the god of our imagination we could cut down using and keep it under our control. That of course never

---
[108] Matthew 6:24

happened, and the addiction continued to dominate us more and more until it took all that we had.

God does not work in our lives that way, he works for our good and he will not share us with the demigod of addiction. He tells us that he is a jealous God and will not share us in that way.[109] This is why in the words of the prophet we need to seek him with all of our hearts, with a singularity of purpose, with no reservations whatsoever. In this context, of complete surrender, one that has an immeasurable depth to it, we can turn our wills and lives over to him, and be in his care for our recovery.

God promises to be found by us, and he made this promise to us even before we were willing to seek him. Along with that promise God tells us that he will restore our lives to us. Addiction is never satisfied, and it wants all of us. Beyond that, addiction also robs our families and our friends of what we should have been for them. In recovery God aids us to be the person he wants us to be. In recovery we are able to fulfill his purpose in our lives and over time he restores the fullness of our lives to us.

God, we have sinned against you. We used drugs and surrendered ourselves to them. We continued to use and abandoned our entire lives over to their raging dominance. As Adam and Eve failed to seek your help when they fell in sin, we followed in their footsteps and failed to turn to you for the help we needed. Forgive us according to your grace and cleanse us from our sins with the blood of your son, Jesus Christ our Lord. Help us to seek you daily, day by day, and sustain us by the power of your eternal Word. Amen

---

[109] Exodus 20:5

Spiritual Practices: Breathing and Envisioning

**When the day of Pentecost arrived,
they were all together in one place.
And suddenly there came from heaven a
sound like a mighty rushing wind,
and it filled the entire house where they were sitting.
And divided tongues as of fire appeared to them
and rested on each one of them. And they were all filled
with the Holy Spirit and began to speak in
other tongues as the Spirit gave them utterance.
Acts 2:1-4**

There are, and perhaps there has always been, those parts of the church that really emphasize the work of the Holy Spirit. In our times that includes the Pentecostal churches and also others that identify as Charismatic churches. In the days of the Reformation they were known as the Enthusiasts. This word, enthusiasts, means "in-God-breathed." Its modern day meaning has lost its religious connotation and to be enthusiastic about something has come to mean someone who is really fired up, or passionate about something.

In our day there are occasions when people have very vibrant experiences with the Holy Spirit in their lives. There are valid experiences of people speaking in tongues and having other signs of the Holy Spirit in their lives. The many gifts of the Holy Spirit include among other things miracles and healing of course. Also, applications of knowledge and wisdom, prophecy and preaching, discernment, and faith.[110]

We need to know that all of us as Christians have the Holy Spirit living inside of us. We received the Holy Spirit when we were first saved. It is God's Spirit that works in us and sanctifies our lives. By it we are inspired, empowered, and guided by it in our lives.

Heavenly Father, you live among us and in us through your Holy Spirit. Thank you for this wonderful gift. Teach us how to listen to your Spirit and to be guided by your Spirit in all that we do. Through Christ our Lord we pray. Amen

---

[110] 1Corinthians 12:8-11

Being of Two Minds

For as he thinketh in his heart, so is he.
Proverbs 23:7 KJV

Our deepest thoughts concerning ourselves can reveal what secrets we are keeping about what we genuinely believe about ourselves. The problem is that we were of two minds. We have lived in the middle of lies that we had been telling ourselves so that we could survive in the world. On the one side of our mind we knew at heart that we were in trouble because we were addicted. We knew that our addiction kept us in a world of danger. We could be busted at any time, overdose, loose our jobs, have a bad trip or any number of terrible things could come upon us suddenly. On the other side of our minds were the others lies that we told ourselves. That all we had to do was hang on until the next high and that would make all of our worries disappear. Then we would feel on top of the world and be happy again. All the while our lives sank deeper into despair as we lived on the edge of impending disaster.

Finally, we were in recovery and getting better because we were making progress. It wasn't easy, but we were on our way to better days. In our recovery we knew that we needed to attend to our thoughts about how we viewed ourselves. We needed to be honest and admit that we were addicted to drugs and that by God's amazing grace we were now clean. Among the thoughts that we needed to change was the lie that our drug use days were good old days. We caught ourselves glorifying how wasted we had gotten, how dangerously we had lived and the risks we took. So we now tell ourselves and others about those days referring to them as the bad old days. We admitted to ourselves and others how detrimental and harmful our actions had been. We rethought everything and saw our old lifestyle in a new light, the light of God that removed the lies and showed them for what they were. We saw ourselves in a new and healthy light, as now in recovery.

Heavenly Father, thank you for redeeming us from our sins and our addictions. Continue to reveal to us the truth of your Word so that we may live according to all that you have said. In Jesus' most holy name. Amen

The Blind Leading the Blind

**Jesus said,
"Let them alone; they are blind guides.
And if the blind lead the blind, both will fall into a pit."
Matthew 15:14**

In addiction we were counted among the blind leading the blind. We were both blind being led by the blind, and we were the blind leading the blind. We were in a rut in life, we were in bondage and couldn't get out. The drug of our choice was a demigod that we worshiped and it had blinded our minds to the truth of our addictions in order to keep us in its deadly grip. The problem with being blind was that we didn't even know that we were blind, we didn't know that we were believing in lies, we just didn't know.

In recovery our eyes began to open, like a newborn the world around us looked strange. We needed to learn to focus again on the reality of the world. It was hard for us because of how consumed we were by our addiction, its grip went to the core and bedrock of who we are. Because we had gotten a taste for recovery and what our lives could be like we pushed onward. We got help from many sources that assisted us in regaining our lives. We looked, we listened, we thought for ourselves and we struggled to overcome the deep damage that our addiction had done to us.

In recovery we looked to God daily, for the supernatural and spiritual help that we needed. We had dropped out of society, stopped maturing and were frozen in place for a long time. We needed to get back into the fullness of life. We needed to fast track to get us back to where we should have been had it not been for our drug use. God came to us and delivered us from drugs, from sin, the devil, death, and the grave. He did not stop there either, God continues to be with us daily, one day at a time, leading us, guiding us, and sustaining us in our life-long recovery journey.

Heavenly Father, thank you for opening our eyes and by your grace saving us from addiction. Help us to grow and participate in all of life, to contribute to the good of our society and to be living witnesses to the power of what your grace can do for people in the greatest of needs. Through Jesus Christ our Lord and Savior we pray. Amen

Healthy Boundaries: Bridges, Fences and Gates

**Violence shall no more be heard in your land,
devastation or destruction within your borders;
you shall call your walls Salvation, and your gates Praise.
Isaiah 60:18**

In our addiction everything we did came to be centered around using drugs, getting more drugs, and then using again. Because of this cycle we compromised ourselves a great deal. Some of the people we came to be around were not safe people, and we ourselves were probably not safe to be around either. We might have even been running from arrest warrants. What mattered for us in addiction wasn't being good and law-abiding citizens, it was the restless cycle of getting high and getting more to get high with.

Addiction compromised all the social boundaries we had practiced in our earlier lives. Now in recovery we needed to reestablish new, healthy boundaries. In some cases we wanted no contact with certain people who were dangerous to our recovery.

An actor from the last century named Will Rogers said, "Fences make good neighbors," and so they do. Having an imaginary fence between us and the people we used to get high with, who are not in recovery is a good and sometimes necessary thing. Once we are far enough along in our recovery and stronger in it, maybe then the fence could include a gate so that we can share with our former using friends that they could benefit by getting clean too. If there is someone we feel especially vulnerable to, a dealer, a former boyfriend or girlfriend, we might need to take more dramatic action. We might need to burn down the bridge between them and us, or at least burn it down temporarily. This way, by having no contact and no means of contact, we are safeguarding our recovery until we have made more progress.

God in heaven, protect us from those people that might drag us down and back into active addiction. Help us to maintain safe and secure boundaries in our lives so that no one can come between us and our relationships with you, through Christ our Lord we pray. Amen

Maturity: From Childhood to Adulthood

**When I was a child, I talked like a child, I thought like a child,
I reasoned like a child. When I became a man,
I put the ways of childhood behind me.
1 Corinthians 13:11**

For many of us our childhood held some traumatic events. We were neglected and abused in different ways. We grew up in highly dysfunctional homes, but what did we know? We didn't like any of it, but we thought all that was normal for all families and why wouldn't we? We did not have many choices in our young life, we simply had to try and survive our way through it. This took a toll on us too. We thought that this is the way we should live in our adult lives. Many of us had parents and even grandparents who were using drugs or drinking. This affected us adversely. It made us much more likely to do the same thing with our lives in adulthood.

As adults we found out that we could choose how we wanted to live. We realized that we did not have to follow in the footsteps of our dysfunctional parents. We made choices of our own. Sometimes our parents wanted to continue to be too influential in our lives and we were tempted to idly stand by and let them continue to domineer over us. We were like children trapped in adult bodies but had not yet attained to adulthood.

In recovery we could choose not to use but it took God to free us and make that happen. Independence from our parents is an important step in living the lives God has in store for us. That does not mean we cannot be connected to our parents, it does mean that there are boundaries that we need to set up and enforce. In recovery we need to decide for ourselves what our lives will be like. In all of our choices we need God to aid us fully to bring it about.

Heavenly Father, help us to fully grow into the lives you have held for us since before time began. Help us by our lives to bring glory to your name and to share with others what all you have done for us. We give you thanks and praise, and magnify your holy name. Through Christ Jesus our Lord we pray. Amen

God's Amazing Grace

John Newton was a reprehensible man. His mother was a devout Christian, his father was a pagan. Newton was a sea captain who owned his own ship. The cargo he carried was slaves from Africa. He had no regard for them other than for the exceptionally large profits he was making from selling them. His mother prayed for him constantly, for his repentance from sin and his conversion. Then came the day when his death was looming near. He was at sea and there arose such a terrible storm that he was sure all would be lost. At that point what most ships do is throw their cargo overboard in an attempt to save the ship and the crews lives. Newton was ready to do that very thing and send those innocent people to their deaths. Then God convicted him of his terrible sins and he got down on his knees and repented. God spared his life, the lives of the captives he held, the lives of his crew and his ship. Newton turned his ship around, returned to Africa and let everyone go free.

Years ago in a treatment center in the Midwest a preacher shared this story with those who had gathered to worship. One woman who was there became dangerously angry as she heard the beginnings of the story. She was so angry that she was ready to jump over the chairs in front of her and beat that preacher to a pulp. The preacher was able to discern in the spirit that she carried the anger and resentments of her ancestors who had been subjected to the brutal treatment given to slaves so many decades ago. As he continued telling the story he reached the part about the storm and Newton's repentance. The woman's anger began to melt away. He shared how the slaves were returned to their homeland and given their God given right to freedom. The woman continued to relax and it was visibly clear that she found great healing in hearing the entire story. Her face grew warm and relaxed. Then as the group sang this hymn she was able to join with them fully and in grateful praise to what God had done in Newton's life as well as what God was doing in hers.

Take time this day to play the tune on a CD or the internet and sing along with it as part of your devotions. Consider setting it to memory and including it in your spiritual practices on a weekly basis.

Amazing Grace

Amazing grace! How sweet the sound that saved a wretch like me! I once was lost, but now am found; was blind, but now I see.

Through many dangers, toils and snares, I have already come; 'Tis grace hath brought me safe thus far, and grace will lead me home.

The Lord has promised good to me, his Word my hope secures; He will my Shield and Portion be, as long as life endures.

Yea, when this flesh and heart shall fail, and mortal life shall cease, I shall possess, within the veil, a life of joy and peace.

When we've been there ten thousand years, bright shining as the sun, We've no less days to sing God's praise than when we'd first begun.

John Newton 1725-1807

Spirituality

**Jesus said,
"The wind blows where it wishes, and you hear its sound,
but you do not know where it comes from or where it goes.
So it is with everyone who is born of the Spirit."
John 3:8**

In the recent past, in the change of one generation to the next, the word religion has in part fallen out of popular use and is more and more being replaced by the word spirituality. Now every Christian knows, or should know, that Jesus said we must be born-again. In that same text our Lord also said we must be born-of-the-Spirit, which is just another way of saying the same thing. As Christians we are born-of-the-Spirit and our spirituality is the Christian faith. Jesus describes our nature as having some of the mysterious qualities of the wind. The wind is invisible, we feel it blow against our cheeks, but where it came from and where it disappears to is a mystery.

What this means for us in recovery is important. It does not mean that we are all going to become mystics and prophets who can foresee the future. It does mean that we have the fruit of the Holy Spirit in our lives. We may even have some of the gifts of the Holy Spirit at work in our lives from time to time. We also have the Holy Spirit living in us and speaking to our hearts. We might even have some great times of spiritual insight into life. As people who are born-of-the-Spirit of God we remain grounded in reality and we are blessed to have the Lord in our lives.

In our addiction we were flighty and impulsive, unpredictable, and unreliable. We lived according to our whims and under the mind altering influence of drugs. In recovery God began to restore us to sanity. As we continued in our new lives we recovered even more of what our lives should have been like and we came to enjoy living as Christians who were born-of-the-Spirit.

God in heaven, you came to us in the life of your son, Jesus Christ. In him we found ourselves and recovered our sanity. Help to keep us on the path of recovery and lead us into fuller lives in you, through Christ our Lord we pray. Amen

Natures: Our Old and New Natures

**Therefore, if anyone is in Christ, he is a new creation.
The old has passed away; behold, the new has come.
2 Corinthians 5:17**

Being born-of-the-Spirit creates us into a new person, a person who is Christ-like. Being in Christ also puts to death our old and sinful nature. The Bible describes these two natures of ours in several different ways. Our old-nature is called our old Adam or our sinful-self. It cannot submit to God, it must die with our Lord on the cross. Our new-nature in Christ is sinless and incapable of being addicted to drugs. Remember, when we sin the blood of Christ cleanses us from our sins.

Because our old sinful nature cannot be made holy, our old sinful-self has to be put to death, as Jesus said, "If anyone would come after me, let him deny himself and take up his cross daily and follow me. For whoever would save his life will lose it, but whoever loses his life for my sake will save it."[111] Our old sinful nature would be happy to put on a highly polished spiritual veneer and try to look the part, to save its own life. There is only one solution for it, crucifixion, and death. In sharp contrast to this is our new-nature. It is sinless and it is Christ-like

Having these two natures in us also creates a certain dilemma for us. Our old sinful self struggles within us and works against our new Christ-like-nature. When we are tempted to sin, it is our old fallen nature that agrees and would be happy to go along with temptation and give in to sin. Our new Christ-like nature resists temptation and wants us to do what is right. Together these two natures war against each other within us. Thankfully, the war is not always raging. As God's faithful people we do find victory in that struggle when we seek to do his will.

Dear God, help us to die to ourselves daily and pick up our crosses following after our Lord. Strengthen our new-nature and help us to live and walk in the Spirit. This we pray in the name of your son who died and rose for our redemption, Christ Jesus our Lord. Amen

---

[111] Luke 6:23-24

Natures: Old and New

But I say, walk by the Spirit, and you will not gratify the desires of the flesh. For the desires of the flesh are against the Spirit, and the desires of the Spirit are against the flesh, for these are opposed to each other, to keep you from doing the things you want to do. But if you are led by the Spirit, you are not under the law. Now the works of the flesh are evident: sexual immorality, impurity, sensuality, idolatry, sorcery, enmity, strife, jealousy, fits of anger, rivalries, dissensions, divisions, envy, drunkenness, orgies, and things like these. I warn you, as I warned you before, that those who do such things will not inherit the kingdom of God. But the fruit of the Spirit is love, joy, peace, patience, kindness, goodness, faithfulness, gentleness, self-control; against such things there is no law. And those who belong to Christ Jesus have crucified the flesh with its passions and desires. If we live by the Spirit, let us also keep in step with the Spirit.
Galatians 5:16-25

In our salvation we are given new spiritual birth. Old-nature and sinful self was put to death and because of our spiritual birth we take on a new Christ-like nature that is referred to simply as our new-nature. Our old-nature is sinful, our new-nature resists the temptation to sin. We live with dual natures, one sinful, one Christ-like. The old-nature loves to tempt us with the idea of using again. Early in our recovery the temptation is the greatest, but over time with sustained recovery that temptation to use again fades. Our sinful-self wants us to have selective memories that leave out all the terrible things that went on and only recall what it presents to us as good times. Our new Christ-like nature calls to us, resisting temptation and working to bring the light of Christ into our lives. In the light we can see the lies of addiction for what they are. In Christ we are able to resist the temptation to use successfully. In our new-nature we are able to fulfill God's calling for us.

Father in heaven, as you raised your son to life on Easter morning so also you have given new life to us. Because our Lord lives again we too have new lives so that we can live clean and free of drugs. We praise you for the redemption of our lives. In Jesus' name. Amen

Sorcery: Recreational Drug Use

**Now the works of the flesh are evident: ... sorcery ...
I warn you, as I warned you before, that those who
do such things will not inherit the kingdom of God.
Galatians 5:19-21**

All drug use is sorcery by the Biblical definition. All recreational drug use is drug abuse. The word recreation has two meanings. First it means doing exercise, having fun, amusing ourselves or playing. It also means rebirth, as in re-creation. Using drugs for recreation, meaning using them for amusement has a re-creation-al effect on a person. That's right, using drugs gives the person using them a rebirthing experience and it is not good. They turn us into addicts.

God formed up what would become the body of Adam from the dust of the earth and breathed into him the breath-of-life. With that the dust became a living-soul with a body of flesh and blood. It was clear that he was made in God's image and likeness. With recreational drug use we, the sons and daughters of Adam and Eve, inhaled drugs and got high. The action of inhaling drugs is a parallel action to the action that brought life to Adam. God's life-giving-spirit entered his lungs and he became a living-soul. Then when we got high, we inhaled the drug's poisonous smoke and it mingled with our bodies and with our souls. This had a profound life altering effect on us. We became living-addicts inwardly and outwardly and our lives came to reflect the effects of the drugs on us.

In recovery we were born-of-the-Spirit and as a result of our spiritual birth we become Christ-like. With that we became inheritors of the Kingdom of God. We did not retain our original nature in life because of our addictions. By being born-of-the-Spirit we took on a new and redeemed nature that freed us from addiction.

Great God in heaven, forever we are in your debt for the forgiveness that we have received. By the blood of your son you have redeemed us and made us your children. Help us to live faithfully as your Kingdom subjects, through Christ our Lord. Amen

What to Do with Anger

**A hot-tempered man stirs up strife,
but he who is slow to anger quiets contention.
Proverbs 15:18**

Everyone experiences anger. Anger is not really so much a problem, it is what we do with it that matters. It is better not to stuff it away hoping it will go away, it doesn't. It is likely to grow and fester until it becomes a hotbed of emotions that will erupt like a volcano. It is best not to react too quickly to the emotion of anger because it should not rule over us, but us over it. We need to know that it is considered to be a secondary emotion which means that we felt a primary emotion first, such as fear that led us to become angry. Anger generates emotional energy that is like high octane fuel for a jet fighter airplane. Anger sometimes arises to give us the energy we need to do a difficult task, like confront someone about an injustice to our lives.

In addiction we were out of touch with our true emotions. What we had on drugs was a discombobulation of mismatched, confused and chemically induced emotions that were not reliable. In recovery our bodies worked hard to return to normal. Our emotions might have been frightening, confusing to us, and overwhelming. We needed to find out about ourselves again, who we were and what we were like. As we processed our past we might have had anger issues that surfaced. We needed to work on admitting to them and then trying to resolve the anger we felt. We needed to learn how to harness our anger and bring it to heal. If we have too strong an expression of anger we were seen as hotheads. As the proverb advises, we need to be slow to anger. That is so it can be matched with our rational thought processes. Who knows we might be in the wrong, we might be mistaken in what we were thinking that lead to our anger in the first place.

Gracious Father, free us from being anger bound, so that we are not controlled by it. Give us your grace so that by your wise guidance we can learn to manage our anger according to your righteousness. This we ask through the name of Christ Jesus our Lord and Savior. Amen

Our Lying Nostalgic Memories

**The way of the wicked is like deep darkness;
they do not know over what they stumble.
Proverbs 4:19**

Even in our recovery there were lingering effects from our addiction that continued on. One of them is the phenomenon of recalling our days of using with nostalgia. Specifically, we selectively remember what we thought were the best of things from our active addiction. We might have minimized when we broke the law and drove while we were high. We might think it was funny that we stole money from someone. It might just be that we got really wasted and felt no pain on a Friday night. We were remembering things and putting them in a good frame of reference when there was nothing good about it at all. One reason we might have been doing this was to take something that was quiet serious and make light of it because we could not bear the thought of the danger we were involved in. Another reason we may have been remembering things this way was to fool ourselves into thinking we were healed from our hurtful and painful past when we weren't.

In our ongoing and maturing recovery we need to recognize when we are doing this and stop doing it. We really should try to recall the objective truth about what that memory actually was about and let it be cemented in our minds. We might find that our memories are holding somethings that we need to make amends for. We might find that our drug addiction, for as bad as we remember it being, was actually much worse than we have been allowing ourselves to remember. Additionally, we may need to see that we have been suppressing memories of painful feelings that need to be healed by God.

Heavenly Father, open our eyes to the light of truth in our lives. Help us to see our lives as you see us. Bring us to full recovery and help us to heal, help us to make all amends to those we have hurt. Through Christ our Lord we ask. Amen

Maintenance Work

**Now to him who is able to keep you from stumbling
and to present you blameless before the presence of his
glory with great joy, to the only God, our Savior, through
Jesus Christ our Lord, be glory, majesty, dominion,
and authority, before all time and now and forever. Amen.
Jude 24-25**

Once in recovery, having gone through treatment, attended 30 meetings in 30 days, or simply stopped using by the grace of God, we need to actively continue doing our part to maintain our living free of drug use. It is a rare day when someone who is going to meetings on a regular basis slides back into using again.

There is more to recovery than just the abstinence of drug use. We need to deal with our character flaws and our using behavior. Under the influence of drugs we used people, made bad choices, lost touch with our emotions, and were calloused to the people around us, to name only a few of our problems. Recovery is also about resuming a healthy life in every way. We need to be ever remindful that our recovery is entirely dependent on God's grace. That is the nature of addiction and recovery. We cannot quit on our own and to be certain, we will not be able to sustain our recovery without his continuing grace at work in our lives.

As people of faith we ought to be actively engaged in living out our faith in specific ways. As people in recovery this is especially true for us. Prayer is a daily practice for us, as is reading our Bibles. During the week we need to attend at least one 12-step meeting and we should be connected to a Bible study group or a Sunday school class that appeals to us. We also need to worship at a church where we feel at home. We should maintain our relationships with Christian friends who are supportive of our recovery-based lifestyles. Having a sponsor or mentor is also of great value.

Heavenly Father, in surrender we place our lives in your hands. By your grace you have saved us, by your grace you keep us in recovery. This we pray in Jesus' name. Amen

Natures: Our Old-Nature is Hostile Toward God

**For those who live according to the flesh
set their minds on the things of the flesh,
but those who live according to the Spirit
set their minds on the things of the Spirit.
For to set the mind on the flesh is death,
but to set the mind on the Spirit is life and peace.
For the mind that is set on the flesh is hostile to God,
for it does not submit to God's law; indeed, it cannot.
Romans 8:5-7**

Our old and new natures are very much opposites of each other. They don't live in harmony with each other, instead they oppose each other vehemently. Our old sinful nature is not re-formable, it must be crucified with Christ on the cross and put to death. It will do everything it can to survive, even to the point of putting on a paper-thin mask and acting as if it is religious or spiritual. For this problem Jesus instructed us to pick up our own cross and die to self daily.[112] Our new Christ-like

---
[112] Luke 9:23

nature is not capable of sinning, it fully submits to God and his will. Our new-nature comes alive when we are born-of-the-Spirit and become a Christian.

In recovery we need to recognize that it is our old sinful nature that tries to get us to relapse and fall back into our old lifestyle. Equally true, our new-nature in Christ is there urging us to resist temptation and remain clean. Over time our desire to use does fade, for some it even disappears.

Heavenly Father, you know the war that rages on in us. Our old-nature and our new Christ-like nature, our addiction, and our recovery both fight each other for the dominance of our lives. As your son rose victorious from death, may we also we live in his victory. In Jesus' name. Amen

Covenant Relationships: Near and Dear to the Heart of God

**But God, being rich in mercy,
because of the great love with which he loved us,
even when we were dead in our trespasses,
made us alive together with Christ—
by grace you have been saved—
and raised us up with him and seated
us with him in the heavenly places in Christ Jesus,
so that in the coming ages he might show the immeasurable
riches of his grace in kindness toward us in Christ Jesus.
Ephesians 2:4-7**

In most households there are a few special places that the heads of the household sit. It might be at the head of the dining room table, or in a special recliner in the living room. To be able to sit at their right side is also a place of great privilege. This is the case with our Heavenly Father and his throne in heaven. Jesus, his only begotten son, is seated at his righthand side, which is the ultimate in great places to be seated. Here in the Ephesians text we learn that because we are in Christ we too are seated with him at God's righthand side, a place of privilege for us as well.

In our addictions we may have hung out with some pretty seedy people, visited drug houses and been in some rather detestable places. We did that for the sake of getting high and acquiring more drugs. We compromised ourselves and may have been in some dangerous setting too.

In our salvation from sin God gave us by his grace the free gift of forgiveness. In our recovery God continued to lavish his grace on us. Like a prodigal son or daughter who had come home our heavenly Father placed us at his righthand side with his beloved son and welcomed us warmly into his presence.

Loving God and Father, we are unworthy to be called your children, but you have made us your children and welcomed us to sit at your side. Thank you for inviting us to be so close to you and to be in this relationship with you. In your beloved son's name we pray. Amen

The Mystery of our Faith

**Now to him who is able to strengthen you according
to my gospel and the preaching of Jesus Christ,
according to the revelation of the mystery
that was kept secret for long ages
but has now been disclosed and through
the prophetic writings has been made known
to all nations, according to the command of the
eternal God, to bring about the obedience of faith.
Romans 16:25-26**

In our lives as Christians there are certain things that we accept by faith. They are a mystery and will remain a mystery to us until we get to heaven. In our recovery program we understand that there are certain steps and we understand them in part. How exactly is it that as they are all applied in our lives do they keep us clean and free from drugs? That too remains somewhat shrouded in the mystery of our faith.

In the area of faith, one of the great mysteries that we fully accept is this: how does the blood of Jesus, that was shed two thousand years ago, across the ocean, on another continent get applied to our sins so that we can be forgiven? How do our sins get transferred from us to our Lord when he died way back then? We don't have those details other than to say that in the mystery of our faith God somehow does it for us. We accept and believe that this does happen based on faith alone, meaning that we trust that God does it for us.

In living in recovery and working the program things are a little more transparent but there are still parts that we do not fully understand. By working the steps we are able to achieve, by God's grace in action in our lives, clean and drug free lives. We can see how some of it works, but much of its dynamics are outside of our awareness and part of this spiritual mystery of faith.

Dearest God, through the blood of your son shed on calvary you have cleansed us of our sins and washed us clean. By the power of his blood also keep us free and clean of drug use. For this and for all our many blessings we give you thanks in Jesus' name. Amen

Following in the Example

Remember your leaders, those who spoke to you the word of God. Consider the outcome of their way of life, and imitate their faith.
Hebrews 13:7

How many of us as children heard contradictory things from our parents? Perhaps they smoked but then told us they did not want us to smoke because it was a bad habit. In essence they were saying, "Do as I say, not as I do." A lot of good it did us too because the odds were that we smoked anyway. In life we have this inherent tendency to follow in someone's example even though they may have said things to discourage us from doing this. That is because their lifestyle and their actions had a bigger impact on us than their words.

When it comes to drug use and addiction the same is equally true. When parents, grandparents, or others who have had significant roles in our lives, lived in a certain way or did certain things, we were naturally drawn to live out our lifestyle in similar, if not identical ways. No matter what they may have said to us, one thing is certain, we most likely did as they did, rather than as they said.

In recovery we have to break many of the bonds that are associated with our addiction. We may have been thinking, even telling ourselves: my parent smoked marijuana, their parent did too, so I do it too, it was that simple. The problem that can arise with following in someone's example is that they may have been a bad example to us. We need to dig beneath the surface and reexamine our lifestyle as well as theirs. Brutal honesty is sometimes necessary in recovery. We need to ask ourselves if there is anything about their life that influenced us in our addiction. Then we need to own up and take responsibility for our own actions and dispel our reasons for using. Doing this will strengthen us in our recovery and free us from the generational curses that are sometimes passed on to us.

Heavenly Father, help us to live free from the curse of addiction, and from generational curses. Let us live in the example of faith that has been provided, through Christ our Lord. Amen

Natures: Our Old Adamic Nature on Drugs

**For those who live according to the flesh
set their minds on the things of the flesh,
but those who live according to the Spirit
set their minds on the things of the Spirit.
For to set the mind on the flesh is death,
but to set the mind on the Spirit is life and peace.
For the mind that is set on the flesh is hostile to God,
for it does not submit to God's law; indeed, it cannot.
Those who are in the flesh cannot please God.
Romans 8:5-8**

Anabolic androgenic steroids, or steroids are used to build up muscles and to boost athletic performance. Body builders, athletes, fitness buffs, and others abuse them. They increase the size of muscles, burn off body fat and can greatly increase aggressive behavior. They are a drug that can be abused and they too can damage our minds and our bodies. Remember that our old adamic nature is sinful in every way. Imagine how our sinful self would behave under that kind of stimulation; what you would have is our old-nature on steroids. Everything would go from bad to worse and from wicked to pure evil. We lived a life of absolute ruin, using people, committing terrible crimes, trashing out our careers, destroying our friendships and our own families. We did things no one in their right minds would do. Sometimes it even seemed like it wasn't even us doing it, it was as though someone had taken over our bodies and were using them against our wills. That is like having our old sinful, adamic nature on steroids because of our drug use. Drugs increase the effects of the fall in our lives many times over.

In recovery we abstain from drugs. Once free of their influence we could make amends for the abuse we dished out to others. In recovery we could see what we had become without the fog of addiction blinding us to the truth of how far down we had fallen into sinful living. Now we can live as God meant us to, contributing in positive ways to the lives of others, our community, working and paying taxes, and serving him who redeemed us from the depths of hell itself.

Heavenly Father, may we always keep our minds on you. Let our sinful nature die daily so that we may be freed to live for you and live to fulfill your will. In Jesus' name we pray. Amen

Natures: We are Simultaneously Sinners and Saints

> For we know that the law is spiritual,
> but I am of the flesh, sold under sin.
> For I do not understand my own actions.
> For I do not do what I want,
> but I do the very thing I hate.
> Now if I do what I do not want, I agree with the law,
> that it is good. So now it is no longer
> I who do it, but sin that dwells within me.
> For I know that nothing good dwells in me,
> that is, in my flesh. For I have the desire to
> do what is right, but not the ability to carry it out.
> For I do not do the good I want,
> but the evil I do not want is what I keep on doing.
> Now if I do what I do not want,
> it is no longer I who do it, but sin that dwells within me.
> So I find it to be a law that when I want to do right,
> evil lies close at hand. For I delight in the law of God,
> in my inner being, but I see in my members
> another law waging war against the law
> of my mind and making me captive
> to the law of sin that dwells in my members.
> Wretched man that I am!
> Who will deliver me from this body of death?
> Thanks be to God through Jesus Christ our Lord!
> So then, I myself serve the law of God with my mind,
> but with my flesh I serve the law of sin.
> Romans 7:14-25

For all of us either suffering with an addiction, or in recovery, these words written by the Apostle Paul sound exactly like what we experience in addiction and recovery. If we didn't know better, we might think that this passage of Scripture was written by an addict. Using is, of course, a sin and therefore it fits very well into the context of what this text says about us and how sin affects us in life.

We know all too well of how while we were using our actions were ironically beyond our understanding. We wanted to quit, while at the same time we didn't want to quit, and in fact could not quit. No matter how we felt about using we were conflicted about. It did not matter if we vowed to quit or not. We could not quit no matter what we determined to do about it. Moreover, the closer we got to doing the right thing and quitting, the harder it was for us to carry that out in our lives. It was as if our determination to quit was being funneled in the opposite direction and fortifying our addiction to continue using all the more. We could admit that this great conflict existed in us. We could see that we were fundamentally flawed in that way, but even in understanding it we could not overcome it.

It was in complete exhaustion that the Apostle Paul thought this problem through to its end and his first conclusion was to confess how wretched a man he was. Isn't that the basis for step one when we admit that we are powerless over our addiction? We were unable to manage our addiction, we recognized that no matter what we tried it had just the opposite effect and our addiction continued on unhindered.

At that point in our lives we were ready to look outside of ourselves for the solution to our problems. If we had harbored any reserved notion that we could do it on our own, that would have been the destructive seeds that would later give way to a relapse back into using again. Our coming to thoroughly know and being completely convinced of our inability to quit was the key to getting the only help that would restore our lives to us.

As Paul says, "Wretched man that I am! Who will deliver me from this body of death?" and then came the answer. Jesus Christ will help. Just as he delivered us from our sinful selves, so also he delivered us from our addictions. In surrendering to him we found a victorious recovery. It is in giving up, first on our own ability to quit, and then in surrender to the Lord of creation that we find we are empowered by God to abstain from practicing our addiction. Furthermore, just as we are delivered from our addiction we are able to live out a sustained recovery by continuing to daily live in surrender to him. In recovery from addiction we will never arrive at a place of spiritual maturity where we can go it alone. We will never be mature enough, strong enough, or transformed to the point where we can rely on ourselves and not on our Lord, which is how it should be.

Dearest Savior, Christ Jesus our Lord, thank you for bringing us into your grace and delivering us from the power of sin and drug addiction in our lives. Forever we will serve you and carry out your will in our lives, day by day, and year by year. Amen

The Way of Cain: Toxic Relationships

As they were coming home, when David returned from striking down the Philistine, the women came out of all the cities of Israel, singing and dancing, to meet King Saul, with tambourines, with songs of joy, and with musical instruments. And the women sang to one another as they celebrated, "Saul has struck down his thousands, and David his ten thousands." And Saul was very angry, and this saying displeased him. He said, "They have ascribed to David ten thousands, and to me they have ascribed thousands, and what more can he have but the kingdom?" And Saul eyed David from that day on.
1 Samuel 18:6-9

David and King Saul started out as friends; before long they became enemies. Their nation was at war and under those conditions things were very polarized to the extremes. There had been a Philistine man named Goliath who was a giant. No one dared to fight him, until young David arrived and slew him with a rock and a sling. David became an overnight sensation. However Saul was very jealous of his quick rise to popularity over his own. From then on there was trouble between the two because Saul had homicidal intentions towards young David.

When we were using we were not always on peaceful terms with everyone else. Jealousies, grudges, and bitter feelings existed. We were not capable of being in healthy relationships and that was doubly true if they were using. Our ability to be honest, open, genuine, and work with others in good faith was not possible because we were ruled by our additions. Our minds and emotions were twisted inward on themselves and they too were untrustworthy.

It wasn't until we got into recovery that we started to become capable of having healthy relationships with others. Our minds needed to clear and heal. Our emotions needed to return to normal again. We needed to learn how to live all over again. In the fellowship of the church and the recovery community we regained our ability to live in healthy ways with others.

Dearest God, as David was victorious, by your grace make us victorious warriors day by day over our common enemy of addiction. This we ask through Christ our Lord. Amen

The God of Our Own Understanding

**Long ago, at many times and in many ways,
God spoke to our fathers by
the prophets, but in these last days
he has spoken to us by his Son,
whom he appointed the heir of all things,
through whom also he created the world.
He is the radiance of the glory of God
and the exact imprint of his nature,
and he upholds the universe by the word of his power.
After making purification for sins,
he sat down at the right hand of the
Majesty on high, having become as much
superior to angels as the name he has
inherited is more excellent than theirs.
Hebrews 1:1-4**

There is a revelation that often comes to many of us in our recovery. We learn that God is not always what we thought or imagined him to be. There is a reformation of our beliefs and even our faith in him that happens for us. We know that we were made in his image, however in many of our lives we may have passed on to him many traits that were not actually his. Too often he was seen as judgmental, harsh, cold, and distant. This kept us from turning to him for help, and kept us at a distance for fear of what might he do with us if we were to draw closer to him.

As Christians we believe in the God who has revealed himself to us. Historically, he spoke to our forbearers in the faith through his prophets. Then he sent his son, Jesus Christ, and it is through his words and his life that we best understand the true nature of God. By the life, suffering, death, and resurrection of Jesus we know that God will go to any length to save us from our sins. He actually went from the cross to hell and back for our forgiveness from sin and our deliverance from addiction.

Heavenly Father, Lord Jesus Christ, thank you for loving us and redeeming our lives. Live in us by your Holy Spirit and fill our lives with your love and truth. Lead and guide us day by day as we follow faithfully in your will for our lives. Amen

Natures: Our New Hearts

I will sprinkle clean water on you, and you shall be clean from all your uncleannesses, and from all your idols I will cleanse you. And I will give you a new heart, and a new spirit I will put within you. And I will remove the heart of stone from your flesh and give you a heart of flesh. And I will put my Spirit within you, and cause you to walk in my statutes and be careful to obey my rules.
Ezekiel 36:25-27

One of the most refreshing things to do after working at a grungy job like gardening or mowing the yard is to take a shower. We wash off all that sweat, grim, and dirt from our body and come out feeling so clean. Then we can put on a bathrobe and relax on our recliner or on the couch. That is a rough comparison to what it feels like when God cleanses and delivers us from active using. Whether it is for the first time or from a relapse, it is very refreshing, relaxing, and restoring.

When God works in our lives things happen. In our former way of life we lived as sinners being dominated our old adamic nature. Using drugs was like putting our sinful nature on steroids and we became ten times, maybe a hundred times more terrible. We were stuck in a powerful whirlpool of wicked debauchery that was knocking us off our feet and dragging us down to a deadly abyss.

In salvation from our sinful selves and deliverance from drugs we came into a new life in Christ. God made changes in us that we never could have achieved in a thousand lifetimes. Our cold and harden hearts were removed and we had new tender God centered hearts. We felt clean again and it was wonderful! God called us from darkness and led us into a whole new life filled with love for him. That was exactly what we needed and we wondered why didn't we turn to him sooner and ask for help.

Heavenly Father, thank you for making all things new again in our lives. You have redeemed and delivered us, cleansed us, clothed us, and given us new hearts. Praise to your holy name, for you alone are worthy of all glory and honor, majesty, and dominion for evermore. Through Christ our Lord we pray. Amen

Participating in the Continuing Work of God

**Then they said to him,
"What must we do, to be doing the works of God?"
Jesus answered them, "This is the work of God,
that you believe in him whom he has sent."
John 6:28-29**

When Jesus fed the five thousand[113] everyone recognized that he was a prophet. This was extremely exciting because it had been about five hundred years since they had last heard a prophet's voice. So great was their enthusiasm that they wanted to join with Jesus in what he was doing. They wanted to work the works of God. Jesus instructed them that what they needed to do to share in the doing the works of God was to believe in him because this was God's plan for them.

What that means for us is also extremely exciting. We know that when God created the earth he blessed Adam and Eve and said to them to be fruitful and multiply. In that way they would be continuing in the work that God had started in the days of creation and he was turning some of it over to them to continue with. Our role in our lives is one of complete surrender to God and to believe in his son who redeemed us from the curse of sin. This word believe in the New Testament Greek, *pisteuo*, means to have faith in God, and to put our trust in him. It is also a picture word and an example of this is when a leech attaches itself to a fish and sucks its blood for its survival. It is said that the leech is believing in the fish in this way. The leech is dependent on the fish for its life; it has committed itself to go where the fish goes and get all that it needs from the fish alone.

In recovery we need to see how our lives of faith are contributing to the continuation of God's work in the world. That does not require us to enter into public ministry, rather that we are contributing to society as Christians by working and involving ourselves in other activities too.

Gracious Father, we believe in your son for our salvation and we trust in you for all that will come our way in life. Grant to us ways to fulfill your will in our lives. This we ask through Christ Jesus our Lord and Savior. Amen

---

[113] John 6:1-15

Saved to the Uttermost

**Consequently, he is able to save to the uttermost
those who draw near to God through him,
since he always lives to make intercession for them.
Hebrews 7:25**

In addiction many of us had major trust issues. Our parents may have failed us in significant ways, others may have not been there for us as we needed them to be. We may have been blaming God for the way our lives had been unfolding. When we needed help we did not feel like we could go to others and ask for their support. We may not have known God, or known him very well. We may have been holding strong grudges against others, God included. We had our doubts anyone would be able to help us in life. Because of our addiction we likely alienated ourselves from others who were offended by our addictive behavior. It is possible we asked God to help us out of our addictions while at the same time we were unwilling to allow the change of recovery to come to us.

As we got further along in our recoveries we came to realize what all God was doing for us. As the fog cleared from our minds we came to understand how twisted our thinking had been. We saw how our self-deception and denial of reality had woven itself into our souls like a malignant cancer. As we worked through the tug of war for the domination of our soul against us we gradually lost our strong desire to use again. Our hunger for continued recovery was taking over and we felt more and more secure in the sustainability of our recovery. Most of all we saw how much our entire recovery was dependent on having God make it happen.

Heavenly Father, you worked miracles in our lives when you delivered us from the domain of drug addiction and into your son's Kingdom. By his life, suffering, death, and resurrection you have transformed us from addicts to saints. In his name we give you thanks. Amen

Discipleship and Life Skills

**Jesus said, "A disciple is not above his teacher,
but everyone when he is fully trained will be like his teacher."
Luke 6:40**

As Christians we are called to be *disciples*. This word means that we are *learners* of Jesus' teachings. The name Christian actually means *little Christ* because we resemble him. With discipleship there is a devotion we live by so that we are learning and growing daily. We want to reflect to the world that we are following a certain lifestyle that reflects our Lord. This is true for all Christians. Sadly for many, being a Christian in some people's minds simply means that they confess faith in the Lord, but it does not have a significant impact on their lifestyle.

When we were using our lives reflected that lifestyle. Maybe not so much at first, but as our addiction grew, so did the signs of our problem. Others could see that we were devoted to getting high and getting more drugs to stay high on. Landlords and employers, friends, relatives, even people we casually interacted with could detect something was going on with us. Though we worked to keep our using a secret, it was noticed by others more than we realized. The drugs had put our minds into a fog and lied to us, making us think that we were getting away with no one noticing our using.

In order for our recovery to work we needed to take certain steps to stop using. We needed to be very intentional about this. We needed to do our daily devotions, reading the Word, praying, seeking to do God's will in our lives. Discipleship for us is the foundation that brought us into recovery. It is the backbone that both keeps us from having a relapse and keeps us progressing forward in our recoveries. More than others, our following the program needs to be not just the 12-steps, we need to live the life of a disciple.

Dearest God, we lay our lives before you in complete surrender. We dedicate ourselves to living as disciples of your son. Teach us his ways and empower us to live by all that he has taught, that our recoveries may be strong and lifelong. This we ask in Jesus' name. Amen

Call for the Elders

Is anyone among you suffering? Let him pray. Is anyone cheerful? Let him sing praise. Is anyone among you sick? Let him call for the elders of the church, and let them pray over him, anointing him with oil in the name of the Lord. And the prayer of faith will save the one who is sick, and the Lord will raise him up. And if he has committed sins, he will be forgiven. Therefore, confess your sins to one another and pray for one another, that you may be healed. The prayer of a righteous person has great power as it is working.
James 5:13-16

One of the reasons addiction can thrive is because of the secrecy that typically surrounds it. One of the reasons recovery works so well is that the secrecy is gone and spiritual recovery is actively practiced. We share our story at our anonymous meetings which is safe and reasonable to do. Sharing with others who are significant in our lives, such as family, friends and church members should be done according to our comfort level with it. When we share with the pastor at our church or any of the elders there, if they have been appointed and are spiritually mature, we can count on them for their understanding, their prayers and support. They can also be helpful in holding us accountable to continue in our recovery, which can aid us in avoiding a relapse.

Asking for prayers from our pastor or elders is valuable. Recovery is also a spiritual battle against the forces of darkness that wage war for the control of our souls. Having spiritually mature people praying for us, laying hands on us in prayer and anointing us with oil is particularly good for us. Confessing to our pastor our involvement with drugs and our addiction is also exceptionally good for us. Our pastor will keep things very confidential if that is what we want, he is a trustworthy servant of God. Pastors frequently have some training in how to help church members get help for our addictions too. Their support in these areas is invaluable.

Heavenly Father, thank you for our pastors and the spiritually mature men and women who help care for us and support us in our addictions. Bless them in their callings so that they may be the blessing to us that we need in our recoveries. In Jesus name we pray. Amen

The Spiritual Time of Day

Now there was a man of the Pharisees named Nicodemus, a ruler of the Jews. This man came to Jesus by night and said to him, "Rabbi, we know that you are a teacher come from God, for no one can do these signs that you do unless God is with him." Jesus answered him, "Truly, truly, I say to you, unless one is born again he cannot see the kingdom of God." Nicodemus said to him, "How can a man be born when he is old? Can he enter a second time into his mother's womb and be born?" Jesus answered, "Truly, truly, I say to you, unless one is born of water and the Spirit, he cannot enter the kingdom of God. That which is born of the flesh is flesh, and that which is born of the spirit is spirit. Do not marvel that I said to you, 'You must be born again.' The wind blows where it wishes, and you hear its sound, but you do not know where it comes from or where it goes. So it is with everyone who is born of the Spirit."
John 3:1-8

Early in Jesus' ministry the leading rabbi of that day came to him by night. Some have speculated that Nicodemus came at this time of day in order to keep his visit a secret. While that is a possibility, there is a more likely explanation that is much more fitting in view of the fact that both of these men are rabbis.

Going all the way back to the beginning of time, when the earth was young and Adam and Eve still lived in innocence there was a very spiritual time of day that occurred in the evenings. It is simply referred to as *the cool of the day* in a Genesis text.[114] There is much more to these words than meets the eye, however its deeper significance is lost in translation. At sunset, with the disappearing of the sun into the horizon the temperatures begin to drop. As the air cools it contracts which causes the wind to blow by drawing air in to equalize the atmospheric pressure. The blowing of the wind literally means the blowing of the *spirit* and it is considered to be a spiritual phenomenon. Added to that happening in the evening is the fading of the earth's blue sky and the appearance of stars in the night sky which reveal the greatness of God. The heavens are revealed then and it is a natural time for minds, such as those of two rabbis, to ponder the greater questions in life, such as eternity and the things of God. Many people consider this time of day to be an opportune time for deep thinking and reflection.

In our addiction some of our practices ran counter to God's designs for us. With occasional drug use it seemed like one of the more popular

---
[114] Genesis 3:8

times to get stoned was in the evening, particularly when we had the next day off, like Friday or Saturday evenings. This robbed us of what could have been a time of true spiritual reflection, prayer, Bible study and Christian fellowship.

In recovery, our lives returned to being lived around a more conventional timetable. The two most influential factors in our weekly activities being our work hours and our days off. These two time periods are directly related to fulfilling God's purpose for our lives. Our secular calling is God's purpose for our lives as we work to be fruitful in his creation. Our free time is ours to use as we please, but as Christians it can be a time to give extra devotion to our lives of faith, this can include Bible reading, prayer, meditation, and worship with God's church. Evenings especially can be a spiritual time for us to dig deeper into the questions we have of God and the Scriptures.

Dear Heavenly Father, you delivered us out of the domain of darkness and brought us into your son's Kingdom reign. Help us to grow in our faith and to be devoted to you and the church on earth. Let us take these days and make the most of them so that as they give way to the years that are to come we may be found faithful and true to you. Through Christ our Lord we pray. Amen

Accountability

The next day he saw Jesus coming toward him, and said, "Behold, the Lamb of God, who takes away the sin of the world!
John 1:29

Many of us have gotten into trouble with the law. We knew that when we were sentenced, we had to do the time that the judge ordered. Imagine for a moment what life would have been like if someone else willingly took responsibility for our crimes and spent time in lock up for us.

Things are vastly different in how God holds us accountable. In the centuries prior to Jesus' death on the cross for us, people needed to raise their own lambs to bring to the temple to sacrifice for their sins. The lambs had to be perfect, no broken bones, scares, or rashes. It was like a family pet that your children loved. Then the time came for you to journey to the temple with your family lamb. There the father went to the priest and placed his hand on the lamb's head to signify that the sins of the family were transferred to the lamb. He confessed their sins saying, "My son was caught with marijuana and coke, my oldest daughter with meth, and my wife got a DUI." Then the priest said, "What about your sins?" Your heart sank as you admitted, "I'm in drug court and outpatient treatment. I am addicted to heroin." The priest listened to you with a compassionate heart and you could see his genuine concern in his eyes. He nodded knowingly and another priest held the lamb as he sliced open its neck with a very sharp knife killing the lamb instantly. Your sins and the sins of your family had been transferred to the lamb and it was put to death as punishment for your lawless sinning. The penalty had been fully paid for you and your family by the lamb's death.

This is what had been done for thousands of years until Jesus, the lamb of God, came and died for all of our sins. Our Lord was punished for our sins, he suffered and then was put to a horrible death to take away our sins. As Christians we put our faith in him and his redemptive death for us, believing that he died to take away our sins as well as our drug use.

Heavenly Father, thank you for sending your son to redeem us from all of our sins. We love you because you have done so much for us. We pray in Jesus' righteous name. Amen

God Supports Marriage

Two are better than one, because they have a good reward for their toil. For if they fall, one will lift up his fellow. But woe to him who is alone when he falls and has not another to lift him up! Again, if two lie together, they keep warm, but how can one keep warm alone? And though a man might prevail against one who is alone, two will withstand him—a threefold cord is not quickly broken.
Ecclesiastes 4:9-12

The covenant relationship of marriage was created by God in the days of innocence before the fall and he continues to support marriage now in the time after the fall of mankind into sin. Solomon in his wisdom had something to say about how God is involved in the covenant relationship in this Ecclesiastes text. The Scripture begins with multiple references to the advantages of being a couple rather than being single. In his conclusion Solomon makes reference to a relationship of three, specifically a *threefold cord*. He speaks highly of it saying it is a strong bond that cannot be easily broken. He used this metaphor to imply that marriage is not just made strong by the commitments of the husband and wife to each other but it is further strengthened by the commitment that God has made to the married couple because God is the third strand in the cord.

Marriages suffer when one or both of the couple uses drugs. If addiction sets in it is disrupted further, sometimes very deeply. Sometimes in the chaos one or even both are unfaithful to each other, causing profoundly serious damage to the bonds that have held them together. Because of the addictive behaviors there may have been lies, deception, fighting, physical abuse, emotional abuse, and verbal abuse. Codependent relationships were created because of the situation and the relationship fell further. Financial problems arose, loss of jobs, losses of property such as cars and homes may have happened. Sometimes the marriage did not survive and other times it was repaired and the relationship was healed.

In recovery we were freed from the addictive habit of using drugs. That was only the beginning. As we pressed forward in recovery we found the courage to ask our spouses for their forgiveness. Because we were in a healthy place we were ready to accept whatever their answer was. Sometimes forgiveness was given; sometimes it wasn't. Regardless of their answer, we knew that we had done what we needed to do, which was to confess our wrongs and try to make our amends. From there we moved forward.

We did what we needed to do to stay in recovery for our own sake and as a secondary motive we did it for the sake of our marriage. If we needed outpatient, short-term inpatient, even long-term inpatient treatment. We received marriage counseling and worked to strengthen our relationships. When children were involved we also worked to bring healing to them and received family counseling.

    Heavenly Father, in the innocence of mankind you created marriage and you work to support it still. Strengthen and bless our marriages and marriages everywhere throughout the earth. Provide for all that is needed for housing, food, love, and safety so that our needs may be met. Nurture the love we have for our spouses, and empower us to live together in fruitful, productive, and harmonious relationships. This we pray through Jesus Christ our Lord and Savior. Amen

Spiritual Core Concepts: The Anatomy and Physiology of Circulation

**For the life of the flesh is in the blood, and I have given it
for you on the altar to make atonement for your souls,
for it is the blood that makes atonement by the life.
Leviticus 17:11**

As we breathe, air is passed in and out of our lungs. In our lungs oxygen from the air is absorbed into the blood. The oxygen is carried on a molecule in the blood called hemoglobin to every cell in our body where it is used for metabolism. Then carbon dioxide is produced in our bodies. It is carried by the hemoglobin away from our cells to our lungs where it is eliminated when we exhale.

This process works very efficiently, and it keeps us alive and well. The problem for us in addiction begins when the drugs we use are smoked. Our hemoglobin loves smoke more than it does oxygen. It will bind with it much more readily, and for a much, much longer time then it will with oxygen. This unfortunately means that our cells don't get all the oxygen they need. That is because the smoke and drugs circulated inside us for a prolonged time as they adversely affected every cell in our bodies.

Many of us have wondered why does addiction happen? For some of us who have had a particularly hard time finding a sustained recovery, we have tearfully struggled asking why it is so hard to stay clean? The answer to this can be best understood spiritually. Remember that the life-giving-spirit of God in us can also mean a powerful gust of wind, and that our soul can also mean a gentile puff of air? The marijuana, meth, heroin or whatever our drug of choice is, it is their smoke that we inhaled into our lungs. Their smoke was able to intermingle with our spiritual parts, our souls, and the life-giving-breath of God in us. Worse, when we use drugs for recreation, they had a re-creation-al effect on us. Worse still, the scriptures say that the life of the flesh is in the blood. For that reason, blood served as an essential element in establishing and maintaining the covenant relationship that we have with God. When the drugs entered our bloodstream through any route, they worked quickly to destroy whatever our relationship with God had been. Spiritually, when we took drugs in and they were carried throughout our bodies by our blood, it was as though we were establishing a covenant-like relationship with them. Consequently, by this we came into alignment with them as if they were our demigod and we were forced to serve them. In salvation, and living a life of active faith in God through Christ the damage of the drugs is reversed and their grip on our souls is weakened day by day.

Heavenly Father, we have sinned and gone far astray. Forgive us and renew us, strengthen us in our walk with you and in our recovery.

Equip us to bring glory to your name through the testimony of our recovery. Let us walk in newness of life and in the freedom that your son won for us by his suffering, shed blood, death, and resurrection from the grave. Amen

Hebrews 13:19-20
Now may the God of peace who brought again from the dead our Lord Jesus, the great shepherd of the sheep, by the blood of the eternal covenant, equip you with everything good that you may do his will, working in us that which is pleasing in his sight, through Jesus Christ, to whom be glory forever and ever.
Amen

The Golden Rule

**Jesus said,
"Do to others what you would have them do to you."
Matthew 7:12**

The need for us in recovery to follow the golden rule is essential. Early in our addiction we were happy to consider others and their interests, but that did not last. As our addiction worsened we no longer cared for anyone but ourselves and getting our needs met, even if it had to come at the expense of others. We did not trust others either. Our friends were only our friends because we could score more drugs through their contacts, or because we got high with them when we didn't want to get high alone. They took advantage of us and used us, which we didn't like, but we would put up with it if there was something in it for us. We also took advantage of them and used them, which was okay for us to do in our minds. It was a matter of every man for himself, we lived to put ourselves first and nobody second.

In recovery we were being transformed from this selfish person we had become into someone who could care about others. In working the steps we came to care about how we had hurt others and we worked to make amends. We no longer wanted to live selfishly and we considered how others might be affected by our words and by our actions. We were glad to share with others and even sacrifice to help them out. We had new friends and together with them we live in harmony.

The Golden Rule used to be universally known because it was taught in our schools, but it is not widely known anymore which is terrible. If we all lived by this simple message the world would be a much better place. It takes a certain amount of spiritual maturity to live by it. In our former way of life we were glad to take revenge on someone or be vindictive to them. Now in our new life we came to a place where by God's grace we were able to treat others with kindness.

Heavenly Father, you did not reward us according to our sins, but according to the love you bear for your son, Jesus Christ. Empower us to live by the golden rule. In Jesus name. Amen

Reviving the Soul

**The law of the Lord is perfect, reviving the soul;
the testimony of the LORD is sure, making wise the simple.
Psalm19:7**

Make no doubt about it, drugs did damage to us. They damaged our bodies and our minds. Sometimes the damage was serious and impaired our ability to carry out a normal life. In recovery their adverse short-term effects slowly wears off. With regard to the drugs long-terms effects and damage there is hope. King David spoke centuries before modern medical science recognized that our brains have the natural ability to heal themselves to some extent. He saw that the Word of God had a supernatural effect on us to make us wiser and more importantly, to revive our souls. Modern medicine refers to that quality as *neuroplasticity* which is the brains ability to repair itself by growing new connections between its cells. By making these new connections the brain can offset functions lost to brain damage due to injury or in our case addiction due to drug abuse.

What this means for us in recovery, in practical terms, is this: by reading the Word, by meditating on it, by studying it, by hearing it, and singing it in spiritual songs we can regain what has been lost, at least in part. We can retrain our brains by immersing ourselves in the Word of God. This practice helps to increase our attention span, it can reduce anger, anxiety, depression, irritability and more.

Thinking about the Word of God activates one neuropathway in our brain. Meditating on the Word is a different pathway, imagining what the Word is describing visually is also a different pathway, saying it out loud to ourselves is a different one, and saying it out loud to others is still a different neuropathway. We need to stimulate all of these pathways. These practices can speed the early stages of our recovery and help to solidify us in our long-term recovery.

God, may your Word dwell richly in our lives. Help our love for your Word to grow infinitely. Heal us from the damage the drugs did and restore our souls, for Christ's sake. Amen

Why We Cannot Recover on Our Own

For all have sinned and fall short of the glory of God, and are justified by his grace as a gift, through the redemption that is in Christ Jesus, whom God put forward as a propitiation by his blood, to be received by faith. This was to show God's righteousness, because in his divine forbearance he had passed over former sins. It was to show his righteousness at the present time, so that he might be just and the justifier of the one who has faith in Jesus.
Romans 3:23-26

Imagine an archer who is not particularly good at the sport. He carefully places his arrow on the bow's string and draws back. He looks at the target and adjusts his sights for distance and the wind. Then he releases the arrow which goes toward the target but always falls short of it. The archer continues to try harder and harder. He practices every day. He even asks others for help. Still he is never able to hit the target and always falls short of it.

This scenario sounds a little hard to believe but it is the very picture of how the Bible describes sin. The word for sin in the Greek New Testament is *harmartia,* and it means falling short of the mark, just as the archer always fell short of his target. Sin is described as falling short of God's glory meaning that we fail to live up to the standards he has set for how we are to live out our lives. We try, we fail. We try harder, we fail even worse. We try even harder and still we fail every time. We might make some improvements but ultimately, we fail every time.

There is another problem with our efforts too. Not only do we sin by our actions, which is our conduct, but we are by nature sinners which is who we are by character. We are sinners by nature. Now if anyone is not convinced that this is a problem that we cannot solve then read on. If for some reason we were able to live a life without sinning, which we cannot, it would still be a life lived in sin. No one has ever lived a life without sinning, except for one person, God's son Jesus Christ. In our case what WE would have done by living without sinning, by OURSELVES, is establish OUR OWN righteousness apart from God. Another name for this is *self-righteousness*, which is a very terrible sin. Just to make this matter worse in everyone's eyes we need to consider what the prophet Isaiah said about our righteousness deeds, that they are like wearing a, "polluted garment."[115] So it is in our recovery from addiction, we try but we cannot recover on our own.

---

[115] Isaiah 64:6

Some of us needed to hit rock bottom to be convinced that we could not do it on our own, others of us saw the handwriting on the wall early on. Ultimately, we all came to a place where we spiritually understood and had discerned that all our efforts were fruitless and we needed help from God.

At this point, when in humility and desperation we turned to God he was there for us. In fact, God has been there for us all along. He has been waiting for us to turn to him for help. In him we find forgiveness, we are justified for our sins and redeemed from our addictions. God transforms us, empowers us, and leads us in our recovery. God makes all things possible for us to live clean and free, he restores our lives to us and leads us forward into abundant life.

Gracious God, you make all things possible for us. We were enslaved to the drugs of our addiction, but you sent your son into the world to free us. By his death and resurrection you have made a way for us to live again as your children in your son's Kingdom on earth. We are forever and eternally grateful. We give you blessing, and honor, and praise. Be with us, we pray, in our recovery to sustain and uphold us for your glory, through Christ our Lord. Amen

Addiction Character Traits: Denial

**For if anyone is a hearer of the word and not a doer,
he is like a man who looks intently at his natural face in a mirror.
For he looks at himself and goes away and at once forgets what he
was like. But the one who looks into the perfect law, the law
of liberty, and perseveres, being no hearer who forgets but
a doer who acts, he will be blessed in his doing.
James 1:23-25**

The nature of denial is such that it hides the truth from us, then it hides itself from us too. It is something that we became experts at but because of its stealth-like qualities we were not fully aware of it. We had only occasional glimpses of the truth but because it was unpleasant to us we gladly forgot about it. This is the nature of addiction. In part this is driven by our sense of hopelessness, we could not stop using so we learn to tolerate all that comes with it because we had no choice. The mechanism of denial is self-reinforcing because of how drugs affected our minds.

In recovery we strove to overcome what had become a habit for us. Step four, to do our far-reaching inventory, is specially designed to counter the deep-seated denial character trait that came from using drugs. In our meetings we heard others share about their drug related behaviors and it woke up our memories for us. Because of the honesty of others we realized what we were like in our using days. Our unpleasant memories were no longer denied instead we worked to make amends and bring healing to those we hurt.

In our growing life of faith we found that the immeasurable weight of guilt that we carried was lifted from us by knowing that God in Christ had forgiven all of our sins and reconciled all things in the cross. Having had that wonderful spiritual experience we found it was inspiring us to live life on life's terms and according to God's will. No longer did we have to indulge in the elaborate scheme of denial that came with our addiction.

Heavenly Father, thank you for delivering us from addiction and all the terrible things that it did to our lives. Help us to grow and nurture us day by day. Help us to mature in Christ in whose name we pray. Amen

The Christ Hymn

Have this mind among yourselves, which is yours in Christ Jesus, who, though he was in the form of God, did not count equality with God a thing to be grasped, but emptied himself, by taking the form of a servant, being born in the likeness of men. And being found in human form, he humbled himself by becoming obedient to the point of death, even death on a cross. Therefore God has highly exalted him and bestowed on him the name that is above every name, so that at the name of Jesus every knee should bow, in heaven and on earth and under the earth, and every tongue confess that Jesus Christ is Lord, to the glory of God the Father.
Philippians 2:5-11

    Paul is talking about our thought life here in this text that is called *The Christ Hymn*. The first few words of this text could literally be translated, *think this way among yourselves*. This is about our Lord's nature and his way of thinking. Even though he could have righty thought very highly of himself and lived out a life of privilege, he humbled himself as a human and was born in a stable. He lived in obedience to his parents and his father in heaven. He served others and prayed in the garden of Gethsemane, "not as I will, but as you will."[116] He died as a condemned man even though he was entirely innocent. Paul says Jesus did not think of his equality with God as being a thing to grasped at. Jesus emptied himself of all privilege.

    This compares to the problem Adam and Eve had in the Garden of Eden when they wanted to have equality with God. They took of the forbidden fruit that they had been lied to about and believed it would give them divine power. The lesson that we need to learn is twofold. Don't try to do what we need to trust God for and two, we shouldn't try to get God to do for us what we need to do for ourselves.

    Heavenly Father, may we come to share with our Lord his same attitude of humility and servanthood. Grant us grace to follow after him in his example. In his name we pray. Amen

---

[116] Matthew 26:39

Case Study: A Generational Curse

**For I the Lord your God am a jealous God, visiting the iniquity of the fathers on the children to the third and the fourth generation of those who hate me, but showing steadfast love to thousands of those who love me and keep my commandments.
Exodus 20:5-6**

In the movie classic, *The Wizard of Oz*, Margaret Hamilton played the role of the Wicked Witch of the West. In taking the part she feared it would type cast her as something of an evil villain in the eyes of the American public and limit the types of roles she could appear in. She was correct in that assumption too, because in her acting career she was selected to play in the role of a witch in other movies as well. Just as murderous Cain was marked by God, Margaret Hamilton suffered second and third degree burns during one of the fiery scenes in The Wizard of Oz, which left her marked with facial scares. In her life prior to her acting career Margaret had been an exceptionally fine schoolteacher. She contributed to many worthwhile causes to further the interests of children and their education. In her real life, she was far from being any kind of an evil witch.

In sharp contrast to the life of Margaret Hamilton was Hollywood's glamor girl, Judy Garland, who wore the ruby slippers on her feet. Hollywood portrayed her as the all-American girl in many movies and she costarred with Micky Rooney, the most popular man in America in that day. Though she was depicted in roles as an ideal and well-rounded person, in her real life she suffered greatly with the disease of addiction. Though an extraordinarily talented actress and incredible singer she suffered greatly in her personal life with monumental problems. Because the disease of addiction is progressive, she continued to suffer to the point that she could no longer provide a stable life for her children and she lost custody of them. She was unable to secure work in America because she had offended so many people. She was forced to go abroad and found work in London for a while. It was not long before her out of control drinking and drug use lead her to offend her audiences there too. Sadly and tragically, she died from a drug overdose in 1969.

Both women were stigmatized. Margaret Hamilton's stigma was unduly placed on her, she was a genuinely nice woman. Judy Garland's silver screen stigma was also unduly placed on her. She had lived an exceedingly difficult life and suffered from the disease of addiction. Unfortunately she never did get into recovery. These two examples serve to demonstrate the deep danger of stigmatizing or stereotyping anyone. This is true if they are viewed in a good light or in a bad light.

Some families have a certain dysfunctional traits that they practice. It shows up in multiple patterns, but it all can be summated by saying that they stigmatize their members. A simpler example of this might be calling one child the "good one" and the other child the "bad one." Neither child should be labeled as such. The dynamic that plays out is that the good one has that role exclusively, leaving no room for siblings to ascend to that title. Additionally, if there is a good one, it seems to dysfunctionally necessitate the need for there to be a bad child. This bad child, who by reason of the stigmatization, can do nothing good, and all that this child does, good or bad, is automatically deemed to be bad. Other roles that people can be stereotyped into are numerous but can include such things as one is very capable and the other is incapable, one is ambitious and the other lazy.

The problems that arise from this are also many. The family may force the favored child to live up to superhuman standards. The disfavored child may feel their only way to be recognized or valued in the family is to live down to the low reputation forced on them. Sometimes the way this stigmatization is lived out is very subtle, other times it is talked about and enforced in very outright ways. In most cases the entire family picks up on it and lives it out. In many ways the stigma becomes something of a self-fulfilling prophecy that the family forces to come about in those person's lives. Many people's full potential in life has been lost due to these kinds of terrible practices. Breaking free of the stereotypes that the family has played into can be exceedingly difficult to do, if not impossible. If a person does escape it, they may be ostracized by their family for doing it and labeled as a troublemaker or a rebel.

As addicts now in recovery we are compelled to examine and re-examine our lives so that we can progress in our journey. When we find that we were stereotyped in some way, favorably or unfavorably in our family of origin or in any setting, we need to break free of it. Sometimes that means that we must live down an undeserved reputation by our consistent actions until everyone sees we aren't the person they thought we were. Other times we need to stand up for ourselves and shed light on the lies of stigmatization, so that everyone is made aware of the sickness they have been perpetuating on us. In highly rigid and dysfunctional settings there will be a lot of resistance made to changing the status quo. Regardless, for the sake of having a strong and healthy recovery in our lives, we need to push our agenda forward to be free from being branded, but we must always do this in appropriate ways.

For us as a people who love God, we can take heart because he has the solutions that we need to escape from our dysfunctional past. The Lord shows his love to us in countless ways. There are things that we can do to break free from stigmas. If this has affected us too severely we really should see a professionally licensed Christian counselor. We would also greatly benefit from getting spiritual care from a competent pastor who can counsel us, lay hands on us and pray for our deliverance from this evil generational curse.

Thank you Lord God for your never ending, never failing love that has sustained us in all the temptations and tests we have had to face. Free us from our sinful past, release us from the evil bonds that have constrained us. Liberate us from the stereotypes, the stigmas, the branding, and the generational curses that we have felt forced into living under. As your son was raised from the dead by the power of the Holy Spirit, so also raise us up from the bonds of death and destruction that have restrained us. Empower us to live as your children, holy and righteous, humble and with servant's hearts so that glory may be given to your almighty name. For the sake of your son, Jesus Christ, our Savior and Lord, we pray. Amen

Just Today Please

**Jesus said,
"Therefore do not be anxious about tomorrow,
for tomorrow will be anxious for itself.
Sufficient for the day is its own trouble.
Matthew 6:34**

Our recovery admonition of living *one day at a time* has its source in the Lord. Part of what keeps us in recovery is not having too much on our plates at one time. Having too much going on in our lives leads to overload and we become overwhelmed in maintaining our recovery lifestyle. If we have too much on our minds everyone knows that leads to too much stress and that can be a trigger for us as addicts. We need to live lives that have structure and definition which includes planning for the future, but our primary focus is one day at a time. We don't want to imagine a stressful week when we don't know what the week will actually be like. Equally true, we don't want to image an unrealistically easy week and then be letdown when it doesn't turn out so well for us. Yet again, we don't need to imagine too perfect a week and then think that we can somehow, because of it, we can get away with using again. Our minds will lie to us in that way, we know it because we have lied to ourselves in that exact way in the past and more than once at that.

Being fully present in the moment is a solid place to be. Dealing with the issues of the day and as best we can bring them to a successful resolution is all that we need to do right now. We will not need to needlessly add to our troubles with the dealings of another day. Keeping our minds on the present and not being distracted by what is irrelevant for now is to be our practice.

Gracious God in heaven, help us to focus on the day, this day, and just this day, so that we may live one day at a time. Grant to us the ability to trust you for all things and that in our covenant relationship we may please you by the faith that we hold in our hearts. Empower us for all that we will do and seek to accomplish before the sun sets and our day comes to completion. This we ask in the name of our blessed Lord Jesus Christ. Amen

Eyes Forward

**But one thing I do: forgetting what lies behind
and straining forward to what lies ahead,
I press on toward the goal for the prize of
the upward call of God in Christ Jesus.
Let those of us who are mature think this way.
Philippians 3:13-15**

In our addiction we lived for the moment with little forethought for our future. We lived to get high, get more drugs, and get high again. Our limited forward thinking was about getting more and if we thought too much about it we became anxious, so we got high to relieve that. We were in a vicious cycle that would not stop spinning for us or anyone, for any reason. Then we turned to God and asked for his help. He intervened in our lives and though the spinning cycle did not want to let us go, he is the Almighty and therefore he is more powerful than the drug's power over us. He freed us and brought us into recovery.

Early in our recovery we focused on not using. But there is an inherent problem with that. Focusing on what we are not going to do tends to make us anxious and gives us nothing to do as an alternative. Focusing on not doing drugs might have even made us more tempted to go back and start using again. So, soon enough we got busy with our lives and our focus began to switch from trying not to use, to focusing on being in recovery and doing those kind of activities. We got counseling, went to 12-step meetings, made new friends who were clean. We got busy at church in new ways, read our Bibles, prayed, read books and more. As the days passed, day by day, we became more comfortable with our new lifestyles. Our hunger to be in recovery, to grow and retake our lives back, to make amends where needed, all of it became especially important to us. And we learned to press onward and move forward.

Heavenly Father, by your grace you have saved us from ourselves and Satan's dominion. Thank you for your forgiveness, and for our freedom from the drugs that once enslaved us. Lead us in your ways and empower us to live with servant's heart for the sake of your son, Jesus Christ our Lord. Amen

Turning Our Lives Over to God

**After this many of his disciples turned
back and no longer walked with him.
So Jesus said to the twelve,
"Do you want to go away as well?"
Simon Peter answered him,
"Lord, to whom shall we go?
You have the words of eternal life,
and we have believed,
and have come to know,
that you are the Holy One of God."
John 6:66-69**

There was a time in Jesus' public ministry when some of his followers fell away. The Lord looked to those who remained and asked them about their intensions to see if they too would stop following him. The Apostle Peter responded by indicating that he had no other person to turn to because he believed Jesus alone had the words of true life, and that he was from God.

In our addiction we sought relief from our cares and troubles by using drugs. At first they offered us temporary refuge from our worries. Then their painful grip reached into the core of our being and would not let us go. The drugs became the worst of our troubles and still we used them even though they were offering only continually diminishing relief for our woes.

In our addiction we came to a point where we were ready to give up our bad habit. We turned to God and asked for help. We had reached a desperate place in our lives. This brought us to the place where we came to believe that God alone could and would restore us to sanity as described in step two. Then, as Peter confessed he would follow the Lord, we too made decisions to surrender the entirety of our lives over to God, as in step three. This was the beginning of our recovery, a recovery that would continue to unfold in our lives. Just as drugs had painfully gripped the core of our being, God now gently freed us from its wicked tentacles and softly but firmly carried us into lives of freedom and relief from our addictions.

Loving and gracious God, thank you for sending your son Jesus to suffer and die in our stead. You preserved us from a drug overdose and gave us life instead of death. In Jesus name we pray. Amen

Eureka

"We have found the Messiah"
John 1:41

In American history it was 1849 when the gold rush happened out in California in the Sierra Nevada mountains. The gold prospectors worked hard to find their fortunes in the mines they dug and in the streams they panned in. When they found gold they were ecstatic and danced about wildly and loudly exclaiming the word, "Eureka, eureka, eureka!" *Eureka* is a Greek word that means *found*. Fortunes were made by many in this gold rush, others died trying.

In addiction we thought we had found something special in drugs. They lifted us up and made us feel wonderful. Our problems seemed to just melt away and we were on top of the world. We thought we had really found something, just like those gold prospectors who shouted eureka. The truth was that we were more like those who died trying to find gold in a mine when it collapsed, or like those who drown in the streams where they panned for gold. Drugs had a powerful alure for us, but in the end they brought us destruction.

In recovery we found out how we had been tricked and let down by drugs and we realized that we had found the equivalent of fool's gold rather than the real thing. We began living clean and free because we found a new way of living. We suffered with the trials and temptations of going back to using, but we knew we had found the real thing. Eureka, because now life had some golden moments for us in recovery and we knew there were more, a lot more to come.

As disciples of our Lord Jesus Christ we need to know that Jesus' first disciples said, "Eureka" when they found him. We must not take for granted who our Lord is. As our Messiah, or the Christ, he is the one anointed by God in a very special way, so that he could also be the One who would save us from our sins and deliver us from our addictions. Praise be to God, eureka!

Jesus, Savior, Master, O how we love you, we were so unworthy and completely lost but still you came to us and rescued us from our sins and bondage to drug addiction. Lead and guide us, fill us with your love, make us into your disciples and keep us by the power of your Holy Spirit living in us. Amen

The Ups and Downs of Life

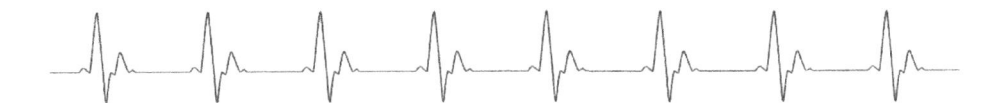

**For I have learned in whatever situation I am to be content.
I know how to be brought low, and I know how to abound.
In any and every circumstance, I have learned the secret
of facing plenty and hunger, abundance and need.
I can do all things through him who strengthens me.
Philippians 4:11-13**

We know about the ups and downs that come our way in life. Of course we like the high points that came our way, we hated the down times, who wouldn't? We need to know that these highs and lows are part of a normal life, just as the tracing of our heartbeats have ups and downs. As Christians we believe that we can avoid some of the troubles that can come our way by living devout lives for God. Equally true we believe that by living as Christians we can be blessed in this world. In reality, we need to understand and accept that there are no guarantees that things will turn out this way. We don't earn God's special favor by our devotion to him, neither do we automatically avoid troubles by the same token. There is a danger if we believe otherwise, it is called *destructive entitlement*.

What God does for us in our lives is that he promises to be with us in all that comes our way in life. In the high points we need to remember God and give him thanks for the blessings. In our troubles we need to look to God in prayer asking him to lighten the suffering, and to seek his strength in our lives to empower us to endure it while we remain faithful to him.

Thank you heavenly Father for your love and care for our lives. Keep us ever close to you and in the highs and lows of our lives remind us that your love for us is unchanging. Help us to grow and mature in our faith as we follow the example you have given us in your son. Through Christ our Lord we pray. Amen

Healthy Boundaries: Abraham

Now the LORD **said to Abram, "Go from your country and your kindred and your father's house to the land that I will show you. And I will make of you a great nation, and I will bless you and make your name great, so that you will be a blessing. I will bless those who bless you, and him who dishonors you I will curse, and in you all the families of the earth shall be blessed."**
Genesis 12:1-3

    Life was not so easy in Abraham's day. There were no government handouts for those in need, no social services that could aid you if you were down and out. Life was still very primitive and hard. Therefore, you stuck close to your family, and communities were very tight. It was incredibly risky to venture out on your own. There were dangers everywhere, you could be robbed, raped, kidnapped, sold into slavery, or murdered. It did not matter if you liked your family or the community you lived in, you were pretty much stuck with it.

    Our patriarch in the faith, Abraham, grew up in a pagan home. According to tradition his father made idols of false gods and sold them for a living. The religious practices of those who worshiped some of the idols included making child sacrifices. That alone tells us that their society had some very cruel and barbaric ways about them.

    The one and true living God revealed himself to Abraham and he came to believe in him. Then God called him to venture out, leaving his family behind and to become separated from them. The need for this was great because of the great perversity that was practiced everywhere. By separating himself and his own family from them he was able to preserve true faith in the one God from being corrupted by them.

    As Christians we are admonished to be in the world but not of the world.[117] In recovery this is doubly true for us. We must set and actively maintain our boundaries when it comes to our continuing recovery. To return to certain places where drugs were bought and sold or used is dangerous for us. It is best not to go there again because it can contribute to a relapse. To spend time with anyone still using is also very worrisome for us. It is a good idea to let them know we are no longer using and are in recovery. Maybe that will plant some seeds of hope in them. If they are high, make it a very short visit, if we visit with them at all. If they offer to sell drugs to us or get us high, run away without hesitation.

    When it comes to family members who are using drugs it gets a little more dicey. There is a saying, you can pick your friends but not your

---

[117] John 17:16

relatives. While that is true it doesn't say enough. We can choose if we will or will not spend time with relatives who are using. We can decide for ourselves if we will be around them and under what circumstances. If any given circumstances and contact with them puts us at risk for using, then the choice is clear and we must not be around them. To do otherwise puts us at risk for a relapse.

In recovery we not only gave up using, we gave up an entire lifestyle. In our lives of faith we have fellowship with likeminded people. Just as Abraham no longer associated with his pagan relatives, neither can we be around anyone, family or not, who is high or may still be using. Our lives depend on it, so we don't die like the children of those pagans did when their parents sacrificed them.

Gracious Lord and God in heaven, you have called us to have faith in you. Help us to live in this world without becoming intwined in its fallen nature and relapse into drug use again. Guard and shield us from all dangers especially those to which we are most vulnerable. Use us to witness to others who are still using and to implant the seeds of hope for recovery in their lives. Through Christ Jesus our Lord and Savior's name we pray. Amen

Stewards of the Mystery

**This is how one should regard us,
as servants of Christ and stewards of the mysteries of God.
Moreover, it is required of stewards that they be found faithful.
1 Corinthians 4:1-2**

In our addictions we were enslaved by a ruthless and impersonal master who held us in its concentration camp and had every intension of starving us and working us to our deaths. In our case there was no law that could be enacted to free us. It was impossible for us to escape and there was nothing that could be done by us to win or earn our freedom.

In recovery things changed. We were freed from our enslavement to drugs by our Savior who delivered us from addiction and brought us into his dominion and kingly reign. We were made to be servants to a new master, Christ our Lord. He loved us and gave himself over to death in order to purchase our redemption by shedding his blood. He loved us then and he loves us now. Though we are called his servants we enjoy the freedom of a new life because of him. We serve him in a love relationship.

He has made us free and given to us the secret of the mystery of his salvation that God had planned since the beginning of time. This is what angels and prophets had longed to know and understand. This secret we know and have lived, because we are saved from our sins and by his great salvation we have been freed from addiction to drugs too.

God has proved his greatness in our lives. What we could not do for ourselves, what no man or medicine could do, what was impossible for us, he has done. It was a problem greater than ourselves, it was a problem worthy of God. Drugs would have taken our lives but God gave over to death the life of his only son to deliver us.

Heavenly Father, with our whole being we give you thanks for delivering us from the dominion of death and drugs and for bringing us into the glorious kingdom of your beloved son, Jesus Christ our Lord. Praise be to your name, forever and forever. Amen

The Mount of Transfiguration

**Now about eight days after these sayings he took with him Peter and John and James and went up on the mountain to pray. And as he was praying, the appearance of his face was altered, and his clothing became dazzling white. And behold, two men were talking with him, Moses and Elijah, who appeared in glory and spoke of his departure, which he was about to accomplish at Jerusalem. Now Peter and those who were with him were heavy with sleep, but when they became fully awake they saw his glory and the two men who stood with him. And as the men were parting from him, Peter said to Jesus, "Master, it is good that we are here. Let us make three tents, one for you and one for Moses and one for Elijah"—not knowing what he said.
As he was saying these things, a cloud came and overshadowed them, and they were afraid as they entered the cloud. And a voice came out of the cloud, saying, "This is my Son, my Chosen One; listen to him!" And when the voice had spoken, Jesus was found alone. And they kept silent and told no one in those days anything of what they had seen.
Luke 9:28-36**

There was a day when Peter, James and John had an experience so fantastic that they never wanted it to end. Jesus had taken them up to a mountain top where he prayed. The three disciples looked on and to their absolute amazement Moses and the Prophet Elijah appeared in great glory. They were astounded by it. When these two visitors from heaven were leaving Peter got the notion to put up three tents so that Jesus, Moses, and Elijah could live there. This would prolong indefinitely this fantastic experience for them. That, however, wasn't God's will in this situation.

While the situation was totally amazing and glorious, we need to note what the Lord, Moses and Elijah were taking about. Though they appeared in glory their conversation was not what you might expect. Their conversation centered around the Lord's *departure*, or literally in the Greek, his exodus. The topic of their conversation was about something very terrible. What they were discussing was about our Lord's pending suffering and death on the cross for our sins.

What does this mean for us? There are some very wonderful things that we can experience in our lifetimes. The birth of a child, their first steps, or their first birthday. On and on the list can go with all the high points of a lifetime. Drugs mess all that up. Sometimes we were too wasted to be fully present to enjoy it. At other times the drugs put such a twist on our minds that the events seemed to be supernaturally bigger than actual life. It is in those cases that our altered perception works hard against us. Because of this occurrence when the drugs made an event seem greater than it actually was, it caused us to unrealistically expect too much out of life.

When we got into recovery our experiences in the real world, though they were true to life, might have seemed like a letdown or even a great disappointment. The use of drugs had reset our normal and healthy range of enjoyment in life to an unrealistically high standard. On drugs our highpoints in life were supersized into over the mountain top, soaring high above the clouds fantastic-galactic outer space experiences. Nothing could compare to them. Equally true our lows were far worse than the typical lows of an average life that didn't have the problem of addiction.

This phenomenon is called *anhedonia*.[118] Simply put, as addicts on drugs our mood swings went much higher and also much lower than what is the normal mood range of everyone else. When we got clean in our new normal range of emotions we got let down because things were not bigger than life for us anymore. When we experience this it could be a trigger to use again so that we could return to what we had become accustomed to.

On drugs we were out of touch with ourselves and our emotions. In recovery we needed to get in touch again with our normal range of emotions and come to appreciate them in the real world. Over time we do adjust. In the early days of our recovery we needed to be on guard that we were not tempted to relapse in the hopes of creating a false over the top experience for ourselves.

Heavenly Father, you hold in your hand for us many great experiences and revelations of your truth in the Bible. Excite our hearts and minds and let us live in anticipation of all that you have in store for our lives. This we ask in the name of Christ Jesus our Lord and Savior. Amen

---

[118] Theodule-Armand Ribot described this in 1896.

Alcohol is a Drug

**And do not get drunk with wine, for that is debauchery,
but be filled with the Spirit.
Ephesians 5:18**

In the ancient world alcohol was commonly referred to as spirits because of the intoxicating aromatic vapors it gave off. While alcohol is not a living spirit, it does have a poisonous spiritual quality. For the addict, or alcoholic, its use became a poisonous spirituality for us. It functioned like a demigod that demanded devotion from those addicted to it. Its demands for devotion may have begun in small ways, but in the end it demanded all to the sacrifice of the rest of our lives.

When we drank the alcohol was detoxified in the liver, eliminated in the kidneys, and metabolized throughout the body. When it was consumed in high enough quantities it was also eliminated by the lungs and exhaled as we breathed. Because of how it affected us physically, it was also able to adversely affect us spiritually. It was carried by the blood to every cell in our body including our brains. This meant that it also affected our behavior and our thinking. It affected us adversely in a spiritual way intermingling with the breath-of-life we have from God as well as our souls. It overrode things like the healthy boundaries we had practiced because it overrode our inhibitions. It caused us to act, think and behave in ways we would not have otherwise. In addiction it overpowered us completely.

In recovery our bodies start to heal from the adverse effects. However our minds, souls and spirits need help. Without help we remain sickened and behave as a dry drunk, meaning that we are still behaving like an alcoholic even though we are not intoxicated. By going to treatment, getting counseling, attending recovery meetings, and devoting ourselves to God, the diseases progress can be halted and we can live a healthier lifestyle.

Heavenly Father, we have wasted so many years drinking, being drunk and using drugs. We have missed so much of life, we have ruined so many relationships and destroyed what our lives could have been like. Forgive us and renew us. Restore our lives and lead us in sobriety so that we can live for your glory, through Jesus Christ our Lord. Amen

The Flip Flop

Woe to those who call evil good and good evil,
who put darkness for light
and light for darkness, who put bitter
for sweet and sweet for bitter!
Woe to those who are wise in their own eyes,
and shrewd in their own sight!
Woe to those who are heroes at drinking wine,
and valiant men in mixing strong drink,
who acquit the guilty for a bribe,
and deprive the innocent of his right!
Isaiah 5:20-23

There is a social dynamic that commonly happens in active addiction. It involves projection and passive aggression. Here is the situation where an addict not in recovery victimizes someone in some way. The victim then confronts them about their abusive behavior. The addict's response is to flip flop the situation. The active addict typically acts very offended and works in the conversation to try to make the person confronting them feel guilty for confronting their inappropriate actions. They try to take on the role of the victim and push the role of victimizer on the person they were abusive to. Commonly they also get somewhat dramatic, even to the point of overacting as well.

When this happens, it is best to call it for what it is. Be sensitive and compassionate. Remember that their heart is very tender though covered by a course and rough exterior. Be straight forward and forthright with them. Tell them what they are doing, and that you are not fooled by them. If the matter is of a more serious nature, come back to them with another person or two for support. Speak in clear, simple, black and white terms, calling the behavior exactly what it was.

Let them know what the consequences for their offense will be, as well the consequences for their trying to flip-flop the situation. Hold them fully accountable and let them know that you are doing it for their own good, that you are acting in love, which is now tough love. Let them know what they need to do to make amends for behavior and that once they do it, if they do it, they will be forgiven.

Heavenly Father, you have called us to be lights to the world of the truth and grace that you have revealed to us in the life of your son Jesus. Help us to help those in need of salvation and deliverance. Through Christ Jesus our Lord and Savior we ask this today. Amen

Overcoming the World

**Jesus said, "I have said these things to you,
that in me you may have peace.
In the world you will have tribulation.
But take heart; I have overcome the world."
John 16:33**

We know and have experienced the tribulation that is in the world. What we hadn't experienced in our addiction was the peace that only Jesus can provide. We wanted that kind of peace. We sought for it, longed for it, tried to get it from our drugs, all to no avail. It seemed like the more we desired it, the more distant it was to us. We hoped that in the absence of tribulation we could find peace, but that didn't happen for us. Because of our drug addiction it seemed that tribulation was not only unavoidable, we had it disproportionally in our lives. We were not willing to admit that our drug use and avoidance of responsibility was causing troubles for us. By our practices, we acted like we could make our troubles go away and also have peace just by using. In the end, peace had totally alluded us and our problems grew to overwhelming proportions.

When we got into recovery it was because we gave our lives in surrender to the care of God. We had no power of our own to quit using, but our Heavenly Father and his son, Jesus Christ, had almighty power. They were able to intervene in our lives and because they were stronger than the drugs grip on us they wrestled our lives free of that enslaving addiction. We gave up fighting and let the Lord fight for us. We found out in a big way what Jesus meant when he said he had overcome the world. Because our Lord has overcome the world and all of its temptations he is able to, as God's son, share his victory with us. We walked free from addiction and we were no longer overcome by the tribulation of this world. In our recovery we enjoyed the peace that Jesus promised to his disciples.

Dear Lord Jesus Christ, your promises to us mean everything. Because of them we have put our trust in you and now know the freedom of recovery from addiction. Thank you for sharing your victory with us so that we can live for you and bring glory to your name. Amen

I'm Not the Problem, They Are

**Why do you see the speck that is in your brother's eye,
but do not notice the log that is in your own eye?
Or how can you say to your brother,
'Let me take the speck out of your eye,'
when there is the log in your own eye?
You hypocrite, first take the
log out of your own eye,
and then you will see clearly
to take the speck out of
your brother's eye.
Matthew 7:3-5**

Drug use and addiction had a way of giving us two blind eyes that could not see what we ourselves were doing and our impact on others. Addiction also gave us better than 20/20 vision to see the faults of others, even if they didn't have any. In addiction we had great insight, but it was only into other people's problems, and not any of our own. As a result, our thoughts did not include the truth about our own issues of which we had many. Also, it skewed our conversations and the way we worded our sentences tended to be overloaded with projective personal pronouns like: *you*, *them*, and *they*. We came up dry when it came to including ourselves in these statements and we left out inclusive personal pronouns like: *we* and *us*. Because of this in our addiction and lack of recovery we could easily come across as judgmental and accusatory or even self-righteous. Because of our own woundedness we, in or out of recovery, took offense where none was intended or given.

The truth is that we are all sinners and deserving of God's judgement in our lives for what we have done. However, God in his love has brought forgiveness into our lives. In recovery our eyes were opened to the truth about our lives. Hopefully this was a gradual process that allowed us to have our eyes opened to the truth so we could adjust and correct our thinking. Then we could respond without being completely overwhelmed. We found stability in knowing that God loved us with such a great love that he gave his only son in death for our redemption from sin and addiction.

Heavenly Father, your love motivates and sustains us in all that we endure to achieve. Be with us in our hardship and rejoice with us in our progress, through Christ our Lord. Amen

Peel an Onion

**For who knows a person's thoughts
except the spirit of that person, which is in him?
1 Corinthians 2:11**

In recovery work there is a lot of growing that we need to do. Because of our addiction we had been exceptionally good at deceiving ourselves and we even became experts at denial. Now we needed to become introspective and take some serious looks at ourselves in the mirror. That can be very frightening. In recovery we know ourselves best when we become able to be honest with ourselves. In being honest we typically needed to look at some disturbing memories of what we had done and who we had become. We needed to become responsible for our actions and when appropriate, make amends with those we offended.

As Christians in recovery we have the greatest benefit there is, which is knowing that our sins have been forgiven us by God. It is not a matter of if they are forgiven, they are. This is true, not because of anything that we did, or will do. It is because this is the free gift of God to us. Embracing this truth can be very freeing. Knowing that our sins are wiped away might make us feel like even if the world ends we will be okay because we are square with God. We have his love and forgiveness. Having that great burden lifted from our shoulders is wonderful.

We also needed to be patient with ourselves, we have been sick and are getting better. As addicts we can be awfully hard on ourselves, to a fault and then some. We can reassure ourselves with the knowledge of God's love, forgiveness, acceptance, and care for us. Asking others for their forgiveness over what we did can also be very freeing. Even though it may start out as a difficult task we are motivated by God's love for us and them as well.

Heavenly Father, your love constrains us from sinning against you and your love motivates us to care for others who we may have harmed. By your Holy Spirit living in us lead and guide us into all truth and empower us to service as we live in the example of the life of your son Jesus Christ, in whose name we pray. Amen

I'm First

For by the grace given to me I say to everyone among you not to think of himself more highly than he ought to think, but to think with sober judgment, each according to the measure of faith that God has assigned. For as in one body we have many members, and the members do not all have the same function, so we, though many, are one body in Christ, and individually members one of another.
Romans 12:3-5

    Addiction can bring on some terrible changes in us. We might have been well mannered in our childhood. Using drugs changed all that. We became addicts and we were not the same courteous person anymore. The heart wanted what the heart wanted which meant we were first with no allowances for a second. We thought only of using and getting more. We were only able to talk about ourselves with others, our needs, and our interests. We took no consideration for anyone else and that offended them.

    In recovery we began to see what we had become. We compared ourselves with the person we had been. We saw how other addicts acted and could see a version of our worst self in them. As addicts in recovery we were hard on ourselves and needed to learn to take it easy. We learned to forgive ourselves and asked those we offended for forgiveness. We learned God was the one who could remove our character flaws and replace them with appropriate behavior. By God's grace we came to have the fruit of the Holy Spirit providing us with love, joy, peace, patience, kindness and goodness.[119] In recovery we found that we could enjoy our lives again and it made us feel good to be able to put others first because we had come to love our neighbors as ourselves again.

    Gracious loving God, you have redeemed us from the worst of ourselves and brought us in to the glorious kingdom of your son Jesus Christ. Thank you for setting our hearts right and putting your love in us. Praise to your name through Christ our eternal King. Amen

---

[119] Galatians 5:22-23

Guilt Not Shame

**If we claim to be without sin,
we deceive ourselves and the truth is not in us.
If we confess our sins, he is faithful and just and
will forgive us our sins and purify us from all unrighteousness.
1 John 1:8-9**

Shame tells us that we are worthless and without hope. It tells us that there is a fundamental problem with us and there is no way we can change or be helped to change. Shaming makes us feel berated, abused, and insulted. Shaming is what we do to a dog or a cat to train them, but it is never how we should treat others or allow ourselves to be treated that way. One of the worst things that we suffer from as addicts is shame, and shame is never a good thing. If someone speaks to us in a shaming tone we need to reject what they are saying to us. It may even mean that for our own good, we just walk away from them. If we shame ourselves with our self-talk or in our thinking we need to stop and learn a better way to get along with ourselves.

Shame in addiction is horrible. When we felt shamed we found that our only relief was to harden our hearts and get high. That lead to us shaming ourselves for getting high and on went the sick cycle of using. The healthy response in life is to feel guilt, not shame.

In recovery we strove to allow changes to come into our lives. We dealt with our issues with help from others. We learned to take responsibility for our actions because we felt guilt over how we had behaved. We found out that feeling shame was not something that we needed to experience anymore. We accepted that we were not perfect and never would be, and we became comfortable with that. We learned to feel comfortable with feeling guilty, that we could do something about. We accepted God's forgiveness for our sins and worked to make amends with those who we had offended as well.

Heavenly Father, thank you for forgiving us for our sins and giving us hope in our lives. Thank you for delivering us from a life of addiction and shame. Through Christ our Lord. Amen

The Structured Life of Discipline

Now there was a man in Jerusalem, whose name was Simeon, and this man was righteous and devout, waiting for the consolation of Israel, and the Holy Spirit was upon him. And it had been revealed to him by the Holy Spirit that he would not see death before he had seen the Lord's Christ.
Luke 2:25-26

Historically, two Christian groups, the Temperance Movement of the nineteenth century, and the Oxford Group of the early twentieth century, both discovered what our current 12-step groups promote. They believed that the principled lives that we live in recovery is what keeps us in recovery. The 12-steps, weekly meetings, living one day at a time, and easy does it among other things all work together to aid us in staying clean.

Dr. Bob and Bill W. adapted the work of the Oxford Group into a spiritually generic program and AA became the successful program that it is. What all of these programs had in common was their spiritual basis. They all believed that it was necessary to surrender to God and lead a godly life to get into recovery. They all promoted a lifestyle that had a specific structure to it, such as in the way our meetings are conducted with a certain amount of ritual-like formality. The basis from where these practices came from were Christian prayer and Bible study meetings. In AA things were made generic so that even an atheist could participate and get into recovery, God save their souls. The truth is that the steps simply promote how Christians should be living anyway. For these steps to work to help us in our recovery we must live them with great intentionality, purpose and follow through. All of the steps have Bible verses for their foundation.[120]

Heavenly Father, Lord Jesus Christ, keep us by thy grace both by day and by night. Let us rise in the mornings in confidence of your love and let us rest securely in our beds by night under the shadow of your protection. Amen

---

[120] See Appendix Two

Owning Our Own Feelings

Know this, my beloved brothers: let every person be quick to hear, slow to speak, slow to anger; for the anger of man does not produce the righteousness of God.
James 1:19-20

Perhaps it is a bad choice of words to say to someone, "You really make me angry." The question needs to be asked, and the mechanics of this needs to be better understood. How did they make us angry? Did they put their hand inside our brain and push some button that turned on our anger? The more accurate way to view situations like this is to say something about what they did that led to us being angry. It is more accurate to say, "When you are late to our appointments, I get angry" rather than to say, "You make me angry" when they are late." This way we are owning our anger, or whatever our emotional reaction is.

We are emotional people and we do have emotional reactions to the things that happen around us. If the things around us affect us in a specific way, we typically react in tandem. In all cases no one and nothing can actually create an emotion in us, we alone do that. It is very unhealthy to cast that ability on to others and then accuse them, or credit them with how we feel about it. They are responsible for their own actions and emotions, as are we.

When we were using, the drugs were able to take control of our emotions and make them more muted or make them exaggerated too. They could also create emotions in us which was a common reason for us to want to use them. In recovery our emotions could return to normal over time and then we needed to learn how to process them in healthy ways.

Heavenly Father because of your unstoppable love for us you sent your son to redeem us from all of our sins. In your love for us you sustain us and keep us in your love. Abide with us now and forever, leading and guiding us in all that we do and say, through Christ our Lord. Amen

Our Calling in Life

**Train up a child in the way he should go,
even when he is old he will not depart from it.
Proverbs 22:6**

This verse is telling us two things. First that we need to raise our children as Christians. They need to know who their Creator is, and that as sinners we need forgiveness through Jesus Christ. This text is also telling us that sometimes when a child is inclined towards a certain set of activities that they may very well go into a vocation related to their early interests. Therefore we should support them in it by enriching their lives and nurturing them in that direction. If your child is drawn toward transportation toys, trucks, trains, and airplanes, they may be headed towards a career in that field. If they are concerned with caring for a sick doll, band aids and patient comfort, maybe they will go into a health care field. This should be supported by their families as well. Alfred Adler, a prominent Christian psychiatrist in his day, said that the earlier a child knows the career field they want to go into the better.

We also need to know that whether we are working in a religious job or a secular job, they are both spiritual callings for vocation from God. Both are necessary unless there is something inherently sinful about the job. A religious position is no more special than a secular one. God knows that we need farmers to provide our daily bread. God forbid, but if we had to we could live without a pastor for a while but not the farmer.

In our recovery we need to see that our God given purpose in life is also being fulfilled in our careers. That alone is not the only thing God calls us to, we are also called to live active lives of faith in him, praying, studying his Word, and sharing in fellowship with his people too.

Loving Father in heaven, bless us in the callings you have appointed for us to serve in. Help us to serve in your creation and contribute to the good of all, through Christ our Lord. Amen

Spiritual Practices: Mediation

**"Be still, and know that I am God.
I will be exalted among the nations, I will be exalted in the earth!"
The Lord of hosts is with us; the God of Jacob is our fortress. Selah
Psalm 46:10-11**

Among the most beloved verses from the Bible is this one from Psalm 46, *"Be still, and know that I am God."* It is asking us to be still from all of our busy body activities and to physically rest from all motion. It is asking us to take time to quiet our minds and our souls from all distracting thoughts and feelings. It is asking us to commune with our Maker and to experience our relationship with God on a new and intimate level. In this meditation we are asked to fathom and consider the deeper and eternal things of God.

Prepare for this meditation in advance by eliminating all the noise in your room for thirty minutes. Let there be no TV or radio that you can hear. If there is noise from outside, go to another room where you can have as absolute silence as possible. Take a little time by reading from your Bible and begin your meditation by turning to Psalm 46 and reading it aloud in its entirety. Note that the word *Selah* appears three times in the psalm. This Hebrew word means to take a thoughtful pause and consider what you have just read before you go on reading. Verses 1-3 are about the uncertainty of the earth and how unstable a place it is. Verses 4-7 are about heaven and the city of Jerusalem. Verses 8-11 call us to meditate and to consider the greatness of God on the earth. In verse 10 we are invited to experience God on a personal level. At the end of reading this Psalm come back to verse eight and ponder it longer. If you have tension in your muscles look to God and let his Holy Spirit warm your body and bring rest to your tense muscles. Breathe and shrug your shoulders casting your burdens on him.

Lord, our God, you are almighty and you are holy. Before you we worship from our hearts and we praise you with our voices. Let your majesty be made know to all, for you alone are God and we are your people. We praise and adore you, thank and bless you, forever and ever into eternity. Through Christ our Lord we pray. Amen

Spiritual Practices: The Incense Ritual

**Let my prayer be counted as incense before you,
and the lifting up of my hands as the evening sacrifice!
Psalm 141:2**

Temple worship included burning incense twice a day. It was symbolic of the prayers of the people rising up to God. According to Jewish traditions in the Talmud and Mishna the Biblical record in Exodus 30 has only part of the ingredients listed for their incense recipe. The full recipe was held by the Avtians family. They held the secrets of an ingredient referred to as *Maaleh Ashan* that gave the incense the ability to rise up in a large single and undisturbed column until it reached the ceiling of the temple before it would disperse. Apparently, this was quite an entrancing sight to watch.

The priests were in charge of the rite of burning incense. So sought after was this responsibility that a priest could volunteer every day for a lifetime and never be selected by lot to do it. Having the lot falling on you and serving at the Altar of Incense was valued as an extremely high honor and sacred experience.

Burning incense can have an incredibly positive influence on our daily devotions and on our day in general. When done as a part of our life of faith we need to keep in mind that in the Bible the rising smoke is considered to be symbolic of our prayers and worship rising up to God and filling his nostrils. Because the aroma of the incense is sweet and pleasant it is pleasing to God. Incense can heighten our senses by stimulating our sense of smell. It can lift up our spirits, have a soothing effect on our minds and souls, and help us to concentrate and focus. By stimulating our sight and our sense of smell it adds a certain richness to our devotional time. As we watch its columns of smoke rise it gets our eyes looking heavenward. It creates a spiritual ambiance that is especially supportive of us living spiritual lives.

Heavenly Father, may you bless our devotional practices to you and enhance our relationship with you through them. For we long to bless you and honor you with all that we do. This we pray through Christ our Lord. Amen

The Complete Rebirth and Renewal of our Minds

I appeal to you therefore, brothers, by the mercies of God, to present your bodies as a living sacrifice, holy and acceptable to God, which is your spiritual worship. Do not be conformed to this world, but be transformed by the renewal of your mind, that by testing you may discern what is the will of God, what is good and acceptable and perfect.
Romans 12:1-2

In all of creation there are only a few species that are completely transformed physically from their birth into their adult forms. The frog, who is born as a tadpole is one. But the most complete transformation is a butterfly's. It begins life as an egg, becomes a caterpillar, becomes a chrysalis in the cocoon, and emerges as a butterfly. So complete are the changes that the position of its internal organs have even been relocated. This process of change from early life to mature life is called metamorphosis and in the case of the butterfly it is called complete metamorphosis.

In writing this text the Apostle Paul uses this same Greek word, *metamorphosis*, when he says we are to be "transformed" by the renewal of our minds. He is referring to what happens to us in our spiritual birth. In our lives there are times of slow and tedious change that are referred to as *micro-metamorphosis*, meaning small changes. At other times our lives are swept quickly along by the Holy Spirit and dramatic changes occur in us over a noticeably short period of time. These are called *macro-metamorphosis*, meaning big changes.

As addicts we do not need convincing that we aren't able to produce these kinds of changes in our lives. We could not quit, let alone become any kind of a saint by our own efforts. It is by the working of God's Spirit that we become the passive recipients of these miracles in our lives.

Heavenly Father, we are excited about all that you are doing in our lives. We are blessed to be transformed by you, we are relieved to know that you can remove our character defects from us and give us better ways to live by. In Jesus name we pray. Amen

Confessing Saving Faith

If you confess with your mouth that Jesus is Lord and believe in your heart that God raised him from the dead, you will be saved. For with the heart one believes and is justified, and with the mouth one confesses and is saved. For the Scripture says, "Everyone who believes in him will not be put to shame."
Romans 10:9-11

The ancient church fathers would call this Bible text a description of the *order of salvation*. Simply put, we get saved when we believe in our hearts and confess with our mouths that Jesus Christ is our Lord. Similarly, for us in addiction, when we admit aloud that we are addicted and cannot stop on our own, when we surrender ours wills and our lives over to the care of God then we can live free of drug use. It is no coincidence that this is a close parallel to how we come to be in recovery and how we get saved. In salvation we are delivered from our sins and made to be Christians. In the case of our addictions we are delivered from drug use and made to be in recovery.

Another thing that we should all know about is how faith comes about. There is that saying, seeing is believing. That one doesn't work in the case of the creation of Christian faith, at least not according to Saint Paul. He said, "faith comes from hearing, and hearing through the word of Christ."[121] Lost in translation is that Paul was referring to the spoken Word of Christ, spoken so that by hearing it faith is created in the receivers.

In recovery we share out loud in treatment, with our counselor and with those in our small group meetings. We share out loud with others in our 12-step meetings too. It is the process of saying out loud so we hear it and others hear it that our confession has a redeeming effect on us.

Heavenly Father, we believe in our hearts that Jesus is our Savior. We believe he is our Lord and has delivered us from our addictions. For this we bless and praise you, in his name. Amen

---

[121] Romans 10:17

Think or Don't Think About the Future

And Adam knew his wife again, and she bore a son and called his name Seth, for she said, "God has appointed for me another offspring instead of Abel, for Cain killed him." To Seth also a son was born, and he called his name Enosh. At that time people began to call upon the name of the Lord.
Genesis 4:25-26

With the birth of children into our lives there are certain triggers that get set into motion. For us it is a major life event and very stress filled. On the one hand, it can trigger a relapse; but on the other hand because pregnancy lasts nine months we have a long preparation period that allows us to put plenty of safeguards for ourselves in place.

If we are using, being pregnant can get us thinking about the baby's and our future. It can become a time when we take stock of our lives and we consider pursuing recovery. Women naturally think about the effects that drugs will have on the baby. Men think about providing a good home and having enough money. How we respond, to pursue recovery or continue using, is critical because of the coming of a child of ours into this world.

In the family of Adam and Eve they had been given a special child. Because Cain killed his brother Abel, he was disinherited. God brought Seth into their lives. That alone was not enough to trigger them to continue in the covenant though. It wasn't until Seth had a son that the people began to call on the Lord once more, which is a reference to resuming up the sacrifices again. Right or wrong, horrible events in our lives can lead us to forsaking our faith. They can also move us to greater faith. In recovery, in our desperation, we have to turn to God in faith. In our despair we reach out to get the help we need and renew ourselves in faith.

Heavenly Father, too often we have not looked to you as we should, we have tried to keep you at a distance in our lives. Forgive us and renew us in faith and teach us about who you truly are. Though Christ our Lord. Amen

The Routines We Thrive On

**To this he called you through our gospel, so that
you may obtain the glory of our Lord Jesus Christ.
So then, brothers, stand firm and hold to the
traditions that you were taught by us,
either by our spoken word
or by our letter.
2 Thessalonians 2:14-15**

Simply put, we thrive on habits which are a lot like the traditions that the Apostle Paul referred to. From as early as our conceptions we were exposed to routines that continued to repeat themselves with the greatest of regularity. Our lives revolve around the rising and setting of the sun. We organize ourselves around certain practices that make our lives go easier. In order to interact with others in productive ways, we have specific customs that we follow. We greet each other, share information, make inquiries, and set goals. Routines make our lives run better.

Good habits are hard to break, as is true of bad habits too. The good ones we tend to not give much thought to until they become a problem. Bad habits, such as cigarette smoking, we ignore until they become an issue for us. They cost a lot, they ruin our health, stink and are addictive. Our good habits and routines are helpful in leading a productive life. We go through them with little to no forethought, we only miss them if we forget to do them. They help us in countless ways.

In addiction our occasional use turned into routine use, which turned into a compulsion that we could not shake. It was a deeply rooted problem that was so much a part of us that we could not part with it. It was who we were. In recovery we needed God's intervention to have this terrible problem removed from us. We were still plagued with the temptation to use. For that we found we needed to practice some daily routines and habits to maintain our life of freedom from drug use.

By your grace, O Lord, we have come to live clean and free of drug use. By your daily blessings we are able to continue on in our lives clean and free. For this and all of your blessings we give you thanks and praise through our Lord Jesus Christ. Amen

The Spirit's Help

**Likewise the Spirit helps us in our weakness.
For we do not know what to pray for as we ought,
but the Spirit himself intercedes for us with groanings too
deep for words. And he who searches hearts knows what is
the mind of the Spirit, because the Spirit intercedes
for the saints according to the will of God.
Romans 8:26-27**

It was great reformer Martin Luther who explained that everything we do, even as Christians, falls short of God's glory. It is all imperfect and tainted with sin. Even when a preacher is in the pulpit and offering a great sermon, it falls short of what it should be by God's standards. Therefore, God's Spirit, the Holy Spirit, works with us, helping us, anointing our work, and making it effective. As Christians we can expect that the Spirit aids in us in life frequently, perhaps in all that we do.

In the example given, prayer and our weakness, we find that our imperfect prayer is aided by the Holy Spirit who joins with us, praying with us, in a certain way that as Paul describes it are *"groanings too deep for words."* The Holy Spirit takes our prayers to the throne of God and intercedes for us, according to God's perfect will. This should encourage us greatly, that when we pray we are not praying alone but in tandem with God's Holy Spirit. We need to take hope and have confidence that our prayers are most certainly being heard because of the Bible's promises.

O Lord our God, too often our prayers are few and infrequent. As addicts we know that our recovery is dependent on you supporting us. Forgive us for our failings, support us in our recovery day by day, and keep us in the palm of your almighty hand. In Jesus' name, our Lord and Savior we pray. Amen

Going Our Own Way

**In those days there was no king in Israel.
Everyone did what was right in his own eyes.
Judges 21:25**

In the ancient world there was this general understanding about God that continues on to this day. The belief was that you did not want God too close to you because if he got involved in your life he only messed things up. Therefore you thought about him occasionally, prayed to him on special occasions such as when you were in need but otherwise you kept him at a convenient distance from yourself.

The truth about God is actually just the opposite. We all know very well that God was the one who brought us into recovery, we could not have done it alone. We know too that he is the one who keeps us in recovery. In our devotions we are instructed to seek to know and to do his will in our lives. Knowing his will for our lives and being committed to fulfilling it is a great safeguard for us. If we were to keep him at a distance so we could do whatever we wanted we very well may fall into a relapse. Our own will wants what it wants and it doesn't really care about much else. If we were to go our own way it could be disastrous for us because that is exactly what we did and that lead to our addiction in the first place.

In recovery we need to have God close to us. We have a great need to trust that he is looking out for our best and will care for us in all that life brings our way. We should have learned for ourselves by now that we cannot and must not go our own way. Compromises like that tend to multiply and bring us to unsafe places. Often times God will help us to grow by putting a test before us. His goal for us is to get us to make the right decisions and succeed in the test. We cannot know the future and even when things seem impossible, we need to trust that God knows our future and he knows exactly how things will turn out.

God, you called us by name and brought us into salvation and recovery. Help us to grow in you and to trust you in all things. Through the name of Jesus we pray. Amen

Guilt and Shame

There is therefore now no condemnation for those who are in Christ Jesus. For the law of the Spirit of life has set you free in Christ Jesus from the law of sin and death.
Romans 8:1-2

One of the worst things that we suffer from as addicts is shame. Shame, which is always unhealthy, tells us that we are worthless and not reformable, therefore there is no hope for us. It says not only are our actions wrong and sinful, but we are by nature wrong, un-reformable and there is nothing anyone, including God, can do to help us. Closely related to this is that as addicts we often times suffer with a terrible self-image. Because of things that were said to us, attitudes that came out from others in our interactions with them, or things that were perpetrated upon us we have felt like there was something fundamentally wrong with us that cannot be fixed by God or anyone. We have been unaccepted and rejected by others, treated as unworthy, told we are un-loveable and treated with contempt by others. All these things are shame-based behaviors or attitudes and they contributed significantly to our personal sense of shame about ourselves.

Using drugs was one of the ways we tried to escape feeling shameful about ourselves. They seemed to erase our bad feelings of rejection and inadequacy, and they boosted our sense of being someone of value. However, when we came down from that high the illusions that the drugs created were gone and our sense of shame returned with a vengeance. This contributed to a cycle of feeling increasingly shameful and using drugs to escape it, only to feel more shame and then using drugs all the more.

God's answer for us on all these shame-based accusations against us is to make us righteous. As believers we have become acceptable to God because of the blood Jesus shed on the cross. Therefore we are acceptable to God because he has made us to be righteous. This is such a powerful thing in our lives that we can effectively sidestep the shame-based feelings that we have had towards ourselves, and those that come to us from others no matter who they are.

Heavenly Father, thank you for your forgiveness for our sins and making us worthy of being called your children. Thank you for accepting us for the sake of your son, Jesus Christ. Amen

Hot Potato

**Anxiety in a man's heart weighs him down,
but a good word makes him glad.
Proverbs 12:25**

There is a children's game call hot potato where they gather in a circle and toss a ball back and forth. They all wanted the ball to come to them, but then because they were pretending it was hot, they instantly sent the ball away so their hands did not get burned.

A similar thing happens in real life, only it is not a game played with a ball. It is when someone shares a highly charged piece of information with someone else. It might be a dirty piece of gossip or some other anxiety producing information. It causes the person to be anxious and in order to get out from under the distressing emotions that it created they had to tell it to someone else. As they tell their story, they transmit some of their anxiety along with it to the other person who then feels anxious too. If that is what they are doing with us then it is best to cut them off and not listen to them. In the case of gossip sharing they may even enjoy seeing others distressed by the news and be glad to cause someone else undo anxiety. If that is the case this person has some extremely sick practices in their life and may need to be confronted in a healthy way about what they are doing.

Sometimes there is very distressing news that needs to be shared, such as news about someone who has been in an accident or come down with an illness. Maybe we know the person, or our friend who is sharing just needs a listening ear to help them provided it is not gossip. In our recovery life we don't want to take part in a gossip mill. When it comes to legitimate anxious news that needs to be shared we have a resource that will help us immensely. We have the Lord on our side. As we are hearing the news we can pray and lift it up to God who is able to help us manage the anxiety it might be bringing to us. We can trust that God will care for us and the situation.

Lord God, you are Almighty. Be with us as we journey in this world, assuring us of your loving care and abiding presence in all things, through Christ our Lord. Amen

Generational Curses

For I the LORD your God am a jealous God, visiting the iniquity of the fathers on the children to the third and the fourth generation of those who hate me, but showing steadfast love to thousands of those who love me and keep my commandments.
Exodus 20:5-6

Suppose great grandpa was an addict who actively used for his entire life. He introduced his son, your grandpa, to drugs while he was a young teenager. That pattern repeated itself with your father who was an addict too. This went on until it stopped because you were the one who refused to use and follow in that generational pattern. All those men in all those generations really messed up their lives though. You were the one who worked to reverse the pattern, but because you were brought up in it, you still had your struggles. You dropped out of school, went from job to job. You had an anger problem like your father, you were mean to your wife and children, and on and on. Then your son also determined to never use or live like that. He still had some troubles in the world but they were not as severe as your troubles. Your son got some counseling, married well, and struggled to not live in the same pattern that had influence you. Now your grandson was also determined to not fall into the pattern of drug use and irresponsible living. He learned from the past generations and his life went along fairly well with very few problems and those that did occur were pretty well common to the average family.

Modern social scientists have found that family dysfunction and the ill-effects of drug use continue to take their toll for three to four generations even when there is a concerted effort to recover from them. This is consistent with what the Bible says about these things too. Many things get passed on in life from one generation to the next. They get passed on in active ways when a parent teaches a child how to do something. They get passed on when a child passively observes a parent living it out in their life. Some things even get passed on when the child is adopted out while it is only days old, suggesting somehow the negative behavior was passed on while the child was still in the womb.

Now imagine the same scenario except this time great grandpa goes to the pastor. In the pastor's office he confesses that he has been using and abusing. He admits that he is an addict, confesses to all his sin and repents. He begins to take his faith seriously, praying and reading his Bible, and living like a Christian. He asks his family's forgiveness for his abusive behavior. Then he brings his family to worship on Sunday regularly. His family notices the difference. His children, though they were adversely affected by his life, are very aware of the changes in his life and why they happened and they follow in his footsteps of living a life based on Christian faith. Consequently, the children do not take on his bad habits of using, dropping out of school, going from job to job, abusing their spouses and children and on and on. Such a scenario is entirely possible because as the Exodus text says, God shows his steadfast love to those who love and keep his commandment.

Heavenly Father, forgive our parents, grandparents, and great grandparents for their failings. Bring healing to all the members of our families and close relatives. Break the generational curses that have undermined us from having healthy relationships. Bring us into your love and lead us in recovery from all dysfunction and abuse. This we pray through Christ our Lord, who lives and reigns with you and the Holy Spirit, one God now and forever more. Amen

Healthy Communication: Speaking the Truth in Love

**Rather, speaking the truth in love,
we are to grow up in every way into him who is the head, into
Christ, from whom the whole body, joined and held together by every
joint with which it is equipped, when each part is working properly,
makes the body grow so that it builds itself up in love.
Ephesians 4:15-16**

There is a style of language that uses *"I"* statements that is especially heathy and can be used when difficult situations arise. We need to understand that we don't always hear correctly what someone said. In those cases, when we need to talk to them about what we think we heard, this style of speaking works well. Image you have heard someone say what sounded like, "…that brat is such a spoil sport." We might have believed they were talking about us. There are inherent problems with us going to them and saying, "Why did you call me a brat and a spoilsport?" Stating it this way is very accusatory and presumptive especially if we are mistaken about what we think our ears heard. The healthier way to go about resolving our concerns might be to say, *"Did I did hear correctly,* that you believe I am a brat and a spoilsport?" By wording it this way, we are leaving ourselves and the person we are talking with open to the possibility that we misheard them.

This is not to say that others are without fault. This is to say we are loaded with faults and if we need to speak to someone about an offense, we need to address them with the same love that God has shown us. In our recovery we need to prayerfully consider how we might approach them. We need to gingerly share with them what we experienced in objective terms such as *I think I might* have heard this and what it was that we heard. We can wait for their response about what they remember they said. Sometimes the two match pretty closely, but not always. By using "I" statements we are sharing what we experienced, rather than speaking as though we are absolutely correct.

Heavenly Father, grant to us that we may be as kind and gentle to others in life as you have been toward us. Help us to find healing in our woundedness and use us to bring healing to others as well. Through Christ our Lord we pray. Amen

We Have Today

**And God said, "Let there be lights in the expanse
of the heavens to separate the day from the night.
And let them be for signs and for seasons, and for days and years.
Genesis 1:14**

In recovery we give a lot of attention to the markers of time that pass. We recognize the time: 24 hours, 1 week, 30, 60, or 90 days, 6 months, 9 months, and the years. Recovery is hard work and to reward the time that passes is the least we can do for ourselves and for each other. At our meetings we applaud for those who have come up on their marks and we give them a recognition coin or maybe a key ring. Sometimes they share about their recovery journey and how they did it.

There is a reason for recognizing each other's recovery at these times. It goes back to Genesis and the days of creation. God gave the light of the sun and the moon to be signs to show the passage of time and the seasons. With the passing of the basic sign, which is one day, there was a beginning, and an ending and with it the fullness of the day passed and was complete. There is closure in its completion. The same is true with the passage of a week, a month, a season, and a year. There is a beginning, an ending, and with it the fullness of that time that has passed and it has come to completion. Closure comes with each unit of time and with closure there is an end to the time that has passed.

When the day of our last drug use had past we could say we were done and this falls in line with God's rhythm for his creation. With the close of that day there was closure on our using, together the two, the day and the using were done. With recovery the same is applicable too. We began our recovery journey on day one. It has a measurable beginning that continues day by day in rhythm with God's creation. Each day comes to its fullness at the end of the day. Then the days add up and at each mark of the time we have accumulated more and more days like the first. This adds up to stability in our recovery, day by day, one day at a time.

Heavenly Father, you have made the heavens and earth. You have given us new spiritual birth. Help us to live each day of our lives giving glory to you. Through Christ our Lord. Amen

Pox Christi

**Now may the Lord of peace himself give
you peace at all times in every way.
The Lord be with you all.
2 Thessalonians 3:16**

Back in the ancient world traveling could be an extremely dangerous thing. Travelers were always preyed upon by road bandits who would brutalize them and rob them of anything of value. With the rise of the Roman Empire there came a massive expansion of the road systems throughout their vast domain. Their legions worked to keep rebellions under foot. They also dealt swiftly and harshly with crime. As a result of this travelers in those days moved about with a certain amount of safety. Because of the empires influence, as one group of travelers came near to another group coming in their direction, they would exchange greetings saying, "Caesar is lord." This gave everyone a sense of peace and safety while out in the countryside. This peace that was enjoyed was renown. It was called the *Pox Romana*, meaning the *Peace of Rome*.

With the rise of Christianity things in the Empire were changing. Travelers passing others on the roads might still say, "Caesar is lord" but the response from Christians was to say, "No, Jesus is Lord." No doubt that ruffled more than a few feathers. As a result of the expansion of Christian faith the peace of the Lord was becoming renown and in the Latin language of the empire, this was called the *Pox Christi*, or the *Peace of Christ*.

Some of us used drugs because we had no peace. We were traumatized and discouraged. Our souls were restless and we were feeling down. We might have felt some kind of drug induced peace or tranquility when we were high but when we came down our true feelings were worse than when we began. It wasn't until we turned to God through Christ and found salvation for our sins and deliverance from our addictions that we came into the peace of Christ our Lord. Not that we had made peace with God, but because he made peace with us through his blood on the cross.

Heavenly Father, may your peace supernaturally be a strength to us in all that we do and everywhere we go. This we ask through Christ our Lord, the Prince of Peace. Amen

The Original Steps and The Oxford Group

For centuries the problems of alcoholism and drug addiction destroyed careers, marriages, families, and lives. It continued for the most part unabated until the early twentieth century. It was then that a Lutheran Pastor named Frank Buchman, and others with him formed up the Oxford Group. This was of course a Christian organization. Pastor Buchman believed that the root of all our personal problems were fear and selfishness, and he said that our problem is sin and faith in Jesus Christ is the only possible solution. He believed that God had a plan for our lives and all we needed to do was seek out his will and fulfill it in our lives.

He held as a personal belief that the solution to being overcome by fear and selfishness was to surrender his life over to God and live according to God's plan for our lives. He and the other members of the group strove to develop a Biblically based spiritual program to help themselves and others escape the grips of alcoholism. They believed in leading an intentional and active life of Christian faith. They worked to live this to the fullest degree believing that they were taking life-changing steps. There basic beliefs and practices included many elements that were incorporated into the Alcoholics Anonymous program, and later into the Narcotics Anonymous program. Here is a list of some of the spiritual practices they devoted themselves to:

- The admission that we are sinners before God. (Compares to Step 1)
- We must have change in our lives if we are to solve our personal problems. (Compares to Step 2)
- We admitted we needed to practice daily surrender and live under God's control, and not try to control our own lives. (Compares to Step 3)
- Be led by the Holy Spirit. (Compares to Step 3)
- Practicing personal introspection that included examining our own lives for sin. (Compares to Steps 4 and 10)
- Searched our thought life for self-deception and lies. (Compares to Step 4)
- Share with each other what our sins and temptations were in a one-on-one meeting. Practiced confession of those sins to God and another group member. (Compares to Step 5)
- Talked about Soul Surgery, or the cutting out of sin in our lives. (Compares to Steps 6 and 7)
- Practice restitution to all the people we had wronged. (Compares to Steps 8 and 9)

- Practice having a quiet time daily that would include Bible study, prayer and listening for God's instructions, and journaling. (Compares to Step 11)
- Looking to God for direction and work to live that out in our lives. (Compares to Step 11)
- Believe in conversion of our souls so that being born-of-the-Spirit takes place. Believe that we needed to share our message and practices with others as well. (Compares to Step 12)

Some of their spiritual principles were: *love, purity, honesty, and unselfishness* which compares to NA's spiritual principles of *honesty, open-mindedness, and willingness*. They met in their groups regularly and shared with each other about their lives. In the group process they found relief for their troubles, victory over temptation, hope, developed trust, and used this time to encourage others to share. They believed in leading a very intentional and active life of Christian faith. They worked to live this to the fullest degree believing that they were taking life changing steps. Members of the group had spiritual transformation that changed their lives as a result of their devotion to the message of the cross of Jesus Christ. Because of their dedication they had the spiritual experience of an awakening in their lives. They believed they needed to continue in their practices for the transformation to continue to unfold in their lives.

Gracious Father, by your intervening in our lives we have been and continue to be transformed from addicts to Christ-like men and women. Ever continue to work in our lives and help us to continue in our devotion to you. This we ask through Christ our Lord and Redeemer from addiction. Amen

The Logos of God

In the beginning was the Word,
and the Word was with God,
and the Word was God.
John 1:1

    A pastor once explained the nature of addiction based on this passage from the Gospel According to Saint John. This Word that occurs here in this text, is the New Testament Greek word *logos*. This word logos can mean many things. For example, it appears in the words: biology, sociology, and psychology. It is the *ology* suffix and it comes from that word logos. In those words, it means that it is their field of study and the standard by which we understand physical life, social life, and the human psyche. In Scriptural terms, as the pastor explained it, the logos Word of God is the organizing principle of all of creation.

    There is more John the Apostle wrote about this too. He said, "All things were made through him, and without him was not anything made that was made."[122] This means for us that we exist because of him. But there is more to it than that. Our lives were meant to be organized around him, after all, he is the Lord of creation.

    Our addiction tore us away from any chance we had at being devoted to God and made itself the central most thing in our lives. We were revolving around it and it truly was our lord and god. For this false god we gave up our principles and our values, and sacrificed ourselves on its unholy altar.

    In addiction our lives became organized, not around our Maker as they should have been, but around our drugs. We lived to use and used to live. Our lives centered around this and around getting and acquiring more drugs to get high on.

    What this means for us in addiction is that we can be delivered from active drug use. If God can, and he can, find the solution to the sins of the entire world, from all of time, for all the people who have lived and will ever live, then how much trouble is it for him to deliver us from our addictions?

Through him then let us continually
offer up a sacrifice of praise to God, that is,
the fruit of lips that acknowledge his name.
Hebrews 13:15

---

[122] John 1:3

Heavenly Father, may our lives become centered in you and anchored strongly so that we don't lose our way. May we seek always to serve you by knowing your will and fulfilling it daily in our lives. This we ask in the name of the one who died and rose again, Christ Jesus our Lord and Deliverer. Amen

Our Purpose in Redemption

**Everyone who is called by my name,
whom I created for my glory,
whom I formed and made.
Isaiah 43:7**

Philosophy Class 101 poses a question to those who wish to speculate. It goes like this, "What if an unstoppable object came into contact with an unmovable object? What would happen?" Students have thoughtfully considered, inquired, speculated, debated, and philosophized about that for years. The answer in short is that for it to be realistically considered and solved, it must first be practical, which this question fails to be.

The redemption of our souls have a complicated side to them too. We have sinned and fallen short of God's purpose for our lives. Our sin is not only an offence to God, by our sins we have broken his absolute Law that must be enforced. There is but one punishment, death. Each must die for their own sins. No one person can die for another's sins. Death to all who sin, death to all persons great and small, death for all sins if they be great or small, death is the final word. So, God's Law being absolute, it therefore unequivocally requires our death. God, being Almighty and absolute cannot simply forgo his own Law. It must be fulfilled. Yet, God loves us, made us in his own image and he is merciful and full of grace. He did not want to, but he had no choice but to enforce his Law because the requirement is unwaveringly unconditional. He cannot set aside his Law. It is as much about him and who he is, as it is a part of his Law.

In the case of our sin and consequential death there is a practical solution that God has provided for us. Prophets and scribes had searched the scriptures over for God's plan of salvation for centuries. They had slight glimpses of it. They hoped and longed for its coming, but no one but God alone knew how things would unfold. It is what we call a problem worthy of God, meaning the solution is beyond the possibility that a human might somehow reason it out for themselves or by chance accidentally stumble upon it.

Our heavenly Father's solution was this, to become a man himself, which he did in the life of his son Jesus of Nazareth. He was incarnated and born a human being. He is fully human and also, fully divine. As a human, he could die. As God he can do all things, such as die for everyone's sins, for all of time, past, present, and future. Once dead, as God, he cannot stay dead. So he was raised from the dead by the power of the Holy Spirit as was seen on Easter and the grave was left empty. On that day he presented himself alive to many of his followers and his disciples.

Our part in salvation is that we respond to God's gift of salvation in faith and receive our redemption. Our part in recovery is also that we turn to God and admit to our desperate helplessness. In both cases our Lord Jesus Christ saves us from our sins and delivers us into his kingdom's reign. In turn we serve God with our lives as was his purpose for us from the beginning of time.

Heavenly Father, you have done the impossible with the life of your son. You have made it possible for the sins of mankind to be forgiven us if we simply turn in repentance to you in faith and receive the Savior into our lives. By his redeeming death, you have also provided for our freedom from addiction. Grant us this day the grace we need to walk in your ways and live as your son has taught, in his name we pray. Amen

When the disciples heard this,
they were greatly astonished, saying,
"Who then can be saved?"
But Jesus looked at them and said,
"With man this is impossible,
but with God all things are possible."
Matthew 19:25-26

Saint Augustine

You have made us for yourself, O Lord, and our heart is restless until it rests in you.[123]

Saint Augustine wrote with great eloquence. His point is very appropriate. Beginning with the fruitless wanderings of the murderer Cain, restlessness has been a part of human life. Cain refused to share in the covenant and sacrifice a lamb for the atonement of his sin. Instead, he murdered the shepherd who kept the sheep, who was his brother Abel.

Restlessness continues to this day and it affects all of us from time to time. Sometimes it is due to a medical condition and therefore needs to be properly treated by a competent doctor. Sometimes it is due to the state of our heart. It could be due to our uncertainty over life, career, family, and so many things.

When we use drugs and develop an addiction while trying to manage our restlessness it is called self-medicating. This is never good. Any mediations we take must come from a physician who knows what he is doing. We must also, in our own best interests, inform our physician that we are addicts and that we will trust him not to prescribe any mediations that might put us at risk. Those medications that can treat our condition are meant to be a blessing from God and are not meant to be abused by us like a street drug.

In our spirituality we need to look to God for all that we need, including peace of mind, a restful heart, and a spiritual calm. Restlessness tells us something is unsettled in our lives and so we are fidgety. By faith in God we can find a peaceful rest and calm for our souls. With God we can be in a place where even though so much is wrong, our relationship with him is doing fine.

Heavenly Father, though so much in our world is worrisome, and our souls want to wander in restless anxiety, be with us and may your peace rule over us in all that we do. Through Christ our Lord. Amen

---

[123] Saint Augustine of Hippo, 354-430, Confessions 1.1.1.

I Know the Lord

"Behold, the days are coming, declares the Lord, when I will make a new covenant with the house of Israel and the house of Judah, ... For this is the covenant that I will make with the house of Israel after those days, declares the Lord: I will put my law within them, and I will write it on their hearts. And I will be their God, and they shall be my people. And no longer shall each one teach his neighbor and each his brother, saying, 'Know the Lord,' for they shall all know me, from the least of them to the greatest, declares the Lord. For I will forgive their iniquity, and I will remember their sin no more."
Jeremiah 31:31, 32-34

The covenant of the Old Testament under Moses was all about a relationship between God and his chosen people. A covenant is between people and families and it is all about relationships. In the Old Covenant the people did not necessarily come into having a close relationship with God. There was an emphasis on obedience and punishment for disobedience. There were six hundred and thirteen laws for them to obey and over two thousand admonitions to live by as well.

In the New Testament period there came a new covenant that was established. The emphasis is not on keeping the laws and obedience but on loving God and Jesus from our hearts. The emphasis is on having close loving relationships that are based on all that God has done for us in the life of his son beginning with his death for the forgiveness of our sins. Ours is a relationship where we more than willingly and with gratitude in our hearts want to serve God because he has loved us, cleansed us, given us new spiritual birth and new lives.

Dearest Father when we had gone astray you sent your son to find us. Though it cost him his life, Jesus died for our redemption from sin and was buried. By the power of your Holy Spirit you brought him back to life and now he is with you again. By your Holy Spirit breathe life into us and inspire us to serve you in all that we do. This we ask through Christ our Lord. Amen

Prayer Over Anxiety

**Do not be anxious about anything,
but in everything by prayer and supplication with thanksgiving
let your requests be made known to God.
Philippians 4:6**

It is easier said than done, to not be anxious. Trying to not be anxious without an alternative action to occupy ourselves with is next to impossible. Paul gives us something else to fill our lives with. Something to do instead of being anxious. He says pray. Pray and petition God with your requests and then give thanks to God as well.

We need to know something about the origin and meaning of the word *anxiety* and of what it means to be anxious. It literally means to be without air, specifically oxygen. It implies strongly that we are being choked. That is more than enough to make us feel anxious and worse, to be choked is a struggle of life or death.

In addiction we struggled with anxiety, overwhelming anxiety sometimes. True, our lives may have been at risk from an overdose. We may have been threatened by a dealer who wanted to get paid for what we owed him. We were also anxious because the lives we made for ourselves as addicts were ones with many perils in them. At times we felt threatened because we put our homes, our families and friends, our jobs, and even our marriage at risk by our addiction. As addicts we felt anxiety because we worried about where our next score was coming from. We lived on the outer edges of survival. We wanted to quit but couldn't quit. All of these factors produced anxiety in us and our only relief came from using again, which offered only temporary relief followed by a certain increase in our anxiety. Rather than continue in anxiety we are to pray daily, multiple times a day. Pray to God with the heart felt emotions that would otherwise overwhelm us.

Heavenly Father, hear our prayer and answer these requests we ask. We give over to your hands all things that cause us to be anxious. Strengthen us in our recovery and bring us into abundant life on earth. Through Christ our Lord. Amen

Natures: The Covenant of Our Baptism

What shall we say then?
Are we to continue in sin that grace may abound?
By no means! How can we who died to sin still live in it?
Do you not know that all of us who have been baptized
into Christ Jesus were baptized into his death?
We were buried therefore with him by baptism into death,
in order that, just as Christ was raised
from the dead by the glory of the Father,
we too might walk in newness of life.
Romans 6:1-4

    Maybe we have wondered about how our sinful nature is put to death? It is, of course, put to death on the cross. Also, how is it that we share now in Jesus' resurrection? This comes to pass in the waters of our baptism. As Paul wrote to the church in Rome saying in our baptism we were baptized into Jesus' death, into a watery grave and raised to newness of life, therefore through our baptisms we share in a death like his in this way. Therefore, we walk in newness of life. God's reputation was shown in him when he was raised from the dead after three days when he presented himself alive. We too, as we have shared in his death, will also share with him in his resurrection.

    In sharing in his death we have died to sin in our lives and are freed from it. Therefore, we don't have to live in it, which for us as addicts is wonderful. By his death and us being joined to it in the waters of our baptism he delivers us not only from our sinful life but also from our addictions. Being raised from death with him we are able to live in Christ which frees us to live to fulfill God's will in our lives. Our personal relationship with God was made possible by Jesus' life, death, and resurrection. We share in this through our baptismal covenant that God made with us.

    Heavenly Father, thank you for freeing us from our sinful lives and drug additions. You have raised us up with your son so that we can live for your glory. Ever empower us by the indwelling of your Holy Spirit, that your will may be fulfilled in our lives every day, day by day, through Christ Jesus our Lord who lives and reigns with you and the Holy Spirit. Amen

Doing Whatever it Takes to Be Clean

**Now great crowds accompanied him,
and [Jesus] turned and said to them,
"If anyone comes to me and does
not hate his own father and mother and wife and
children and brothers and sisters, yes,
and even his own life, he cannot be my disciple.
Whoever does not bear his own cross
and come after me cannot be my disciple.
Luke 14:25-27**

Many people confess faith in Christ but how many are his disciples? How many of us can say our lives are truly reflective of his teachings? As his disciples we are to be like our Lord's in that we adhere with devotion to what he taught. We adhere to his Word. The cost of being his disciple is clear. We need to hate, which would be better translated as *love less*, all our family members than the Lord. He needs to be first in our lives, even closer to us than our spouses if we are married.

As this applies to us, we need to love our Lord and separate ourselves from anyone who might compromise our relationship to him. That includes family and friends without exception. In the case of guarding our recovery, we can say that we need to truly hate those things that would compromise us, not the people who use, but the things that they do that would compromise us.

The danger they bring to us is something like this: We first compromise to be around people who are using. Then we compromise the compromise, which might mean that we allow ourselves to be around them when they are high. Then we compromise the compromise that we compromised, and we are around them when they have drugs on them. Maybe we are riding in a car with them and it gets pulled over. At that point we are in danger of breaking the law and facing jail time. And if they don't get pulled over, maybe they offer to get us high. Or, just out of calloused hearts they light-up in front of us, or maybe they are in our home when they do. We don't want to set ourselves up for trouble when we should have entirely avoided them in the first place.

Dearest Savior, lover of our souls, to you we yield our lives and our hearts. By your great sacrifice for us we have been made new and in you we are made complete. We love you. Amen

Covenant Relationships: The Covenant of Our Baptisms

**And Jesus came and said to them,
"All authority in heaven and on earth has been given to me.
Go therefore and make disciples of all nations,
baptizing them in the name of the Father and of the Son and of the
Holy Spirit, teaching them to observe all that I have commanded you.
And behold, I am with you always, to the end of the age."
Matthew 28:18-20**

In some churches, as you enter the sanctuary you pass by their baptismal fountain. It is situated there to show us and to be a reminder that we enter into membership in the church through our baptism. In the waters of our baptism much happens. We are washed clean of our sins. We are joined with our Lord in a watery grave and we are raised with him into newness of life as we share with him in a resurrection like his. In our baptism the blood of Christ is applied to us, granting us forgiveness through his death.

As addicts we shared in an unholy fellowship that began on the day we first got high. It was something of an initiation rite into a secret society. We were locked in and the bond of that toxic spirituality ruled in our lives. In our recovery as Christians we publicly confessed our faith and joined in the fellowship of the believers which is the church. Because we are in a covenant relationship with God all other bonds that would make their claim on our lives were broken by the unsurpassing power of God. If you haven't been baptized, take time this week to contact your pastor and meet with him about getting that done.

Heavenly Father, by your grace we are in recovery from our addictions. You have given your all to bring us out of darkness and into the light of your son's Kingdom on earth. Aid and guide us this day so that we may walk in fellowship with other believers and live to bring you glory for the great things you have done. This we ask through Christ Jesus our Lord and Savior who lives and reigns with you and the Holy Spirit, one God now and forever and ever. Amen

Covenant Relationships: Baptism and Putting on Christ

For as many of you as were baptized into Christ have put on Christ.
Galatians 3:27

We live in a covenant relationship with God our Father through our Lord Jesus Christ. The covenant relationship is entered into through faith and in faithfulness we need to be baptized. We need to remind ourselves often of our personal relationship with God. In it God has fully committed himself to us in the life of his son who he gave unto death for the forgiveness of our sins. For us as addicts that also means that he is fully committed to supporting us in our recovery.

In the days of the early church when a person was baptized it was typically done in a large fountain. As they entered the water they shed their outer robe and wore only a simple tunic. Then they were baptized under the water in the name of the Father, Son and Holy Spirit. As they came up out of the water the worship leaders put a bright white robe on them and told them that they were clothed in Christ. That robe was symbolic of Christ's own righteousness being given to them as a free gift to wear and the robe they had shed was seen as their unrighteousness being taken from them.

In our own baptisms our sins have been washed away and we were cleansed. In this there was a partnership that was formed. Christ in us, working in and through us, to lead us into the life that God has prepared for us to live.

Dearest God, when we were weak and helpless you came and rescued us from our sins and our addictions as well. You provided your strength for our weakness, deliverance for our bondage and freedom for our addiction. Now we pray that you would empower us to live our lives in a manner worthy of your grace and for your glory. In Christ's name we pray. Amen

But put on the Lord Jesus Christ,
and make no provision for the flesh, to gratify its desires.
Romans 13:14

Spiritual Character Traits: Maturity

**So Christ himself gave the apostles, the prophets, the evangelists, the pastors and teachers, to equip his people for works of service, so that the body of Christ may be built up until we all reach unity in the faith and in the knowledge of the Son of God and become mature, attaining to the whole measure of the fullness of Christ.
Ephesians 4:11-13**

In our own lives we move from infancy and complete dependency on our mothers to childhood and being somewhat independent. First, we crawl, then walk, and then we run. We learn to pick out our own clothes and dress ourselves. Later we move from adolescence to adulthood and many more things change. We get a job, earn and save money, we learn how to drive a car, we complete school. We make plans for our futures, including moving out of our parent's home and into our own. In this process we become less dependent on our parents and more self-reliant.

Spiritual maturity is not at all this way, rather it is just the opposite. In spiritual maturity we grow and become even more dependent on God. We realize more and more how much we have always needed to be entirely dependent on God right down to the very air we breathe.

Too often in our lives we are too busy to give attention to our spiritual growth. Sometimes we rely on our pastor to tell us on Sunday mornings the things that we need to know. We can be too dependent on him. We neglect reading and studying our own Bibles and learning more about the Scriptures by reading other Christian books intended for our growth and maturity.

The work of the ministry of the pastor and others in public ministry is there to help us to grow so that we can be doing the work of the ministry ourselves alongside our pastors. The pastor is not there to make us overly dependent on himself. Also true the maturity we gain and the growth we come into is not for us to function independently of our churches but to work alongside them.

Gracious God, help us to grow day by day and mature in all areas of our lives. As we grow help us to live in dependency on you and for your glory. In Christ's holy name. Amen

Mighty Because of the Lord

When I Am Weak, Then I Am Strong
2 Corinthians 4:10

Recovery is not possible without God. Recovery is not possible without admitting that we are addicts. It is not possible to recover without help from outside of ourselves. We can pledge all we want, we can muster up more resolve, we can summon all of our will-power, but this is all to no avail. As addicts we do what addicts do, we use, and we use to excess. Making a greater effort not to use falls short and sometimes leads us to using even more than before as the addiction progresses. Our addiction will naturally get worse over time. If we try harder, we might find some short-lived success, but this too will fail. All our efforts will fail, and the truth is our fortified efforts will likely make things worse as we spin into a downward spiral. The problem is us because we have this disease. We cannot contribute to our own recovery shy of first getting help from God and relying on his help for the full length of our lives for a sustained recovery.

It is when we as Christians confess our sins to one another then we can find help for all of our needs. When we admit we are addicted and cannot quit on our own, that we are weaker than the drug's power over us, then we can be helped. Anything short of that is not enough, it never has been enough and never will be enough. By admitting our weaknesses and that the drugs have power over us, then strength comes to us from outside of ourselves, it comes from God.

Unlike the way this world works, faith and recovery have their own way of operating. God, our Father, has made it this way. As Jesus said, "whoever exalts themselves will be humbled and who ever humbles themselves will be exalted."[124] So also, when we become humble and we admit our weakness over drugs and their strength over us, then we can receive the supernatural help that we need to recover.

God, we are addicts and cannot stop using on our own. You alone are our rock and our strength. By your grace alone can we live clean and free of drugs. In Jesus name. Amen

---

[124] Matthew 23:12

Spiritual Character Traits: Poor in Spirit

**Jesus said,
"Blessed are the poor in spirit, for theirs is the kingdom of heaven."
Matthew 5:3**

Jesus is talking about a spiritual state of being when he says *blessed*. Being blessed is a unique thing. Though externally it may resemble being happy, it is not the same as being happy. The word happy comes from the word *happenstance*, meaning that when our circumstances in life are favorable it makes us happy. When your circumstances are not so good, you are not so happy. Being blessed has nothing to do with that. Rather, to be blessed is to have a certain inner tranquility that is based entirely on our relationship with the Lord who always loves us, cares for, and keeps us.

What we need to remember about the poor in Jesus' day is that they were always seen reaching out with empty hands and asking for help. From that image we need to imagine ourselves as always reaching out to God with the great needs in our lives. We need to have a heart that is always looking for more from God even though we might be fully satisfied with our lives. We must learn to live, satisfied or not, as never having enough of the things of God, because there is a blessing in this.

In our spirituality there is always more for us. Becoming complacent is hazardous for any Christian and for us in recovery becoming complacent is outright dangerous. We need to daily walk with our Lord and grow in him. We can always go deeper, peel an onion, as the saying goes, there are lots of layers. The frontiers of our spiritual lives are virtually limitless. God always has more for us. Hidden to our minds and memories are countless landmines that could lead to our ruin. We must, our continuing recovery requires it, seek to heal from our past and find new strength daily for our walk.

Gracious God in heaven, you love us with an eternal love. You have promised to be with us always. Help us to always thirst for more of you in our lives. In Christ's name. Amen

Spiritual Character Traits: Mourning

**Jesus said,
"Blessed are those who mourn, for they shall be comforted."
Matthew 5:4**

In our drug use our emotions were all messed up. Some of us used to coverup difficult and traumatic emotions. Sometimes we were already numb to our emotions and we used just to have emotions even though they were generated by the drugs. The chemical effects of the drugs fouled up the chemistry of our brains which lead to a cycle of deep depression when we weren't high and unrealistic emotional highs when we got stoned. We were out of touch with our own emotional reactions and their connections to our memories and to our current circumstances. We had, for example, no idea that we were getting headaches, or knots in our stomachs because we were under duress over something from our past or present that was unresolved. Typically the emotions we did have were from our underreacting or overreacting to our current situation. We did not understand them. We were frightened of them and we did not know what to do with them.

Our Lord encourages us to embrace the emotions that come to us in our lives. We need to work through, not avoid or try to go around our emotions particularly those that have to do with the losses that we have gone through. For some of us that was the loss of our innocence at a young age because of sexual abuse. We may need to mourn over the loss of our lives as they should have been if it were not for our addiction to drugs. We may need help from our sponsor, our group, a licensed Christian counselor, or someone else to do this. There is a promise from the Lord that comes with this, Jesus says that we will be comforted in our mourning. God will give us comfort by his Holy Spirit to strengthen us and to aid us for the weight of the grief we need to face.

God in heaven, have mercy on us according to the love you have for your son. Bring us comfort for our mourning and in our distress. May we find peace and blessing in our relationships with you. Through your beloved son Jesus we pray. Amen

Spiritual Character Traits: Righteousness

**Jesus said, "Blessed are those who hunger
and thirst for righteousness,
for they shall be satisfied."
Matthew 5:6**

It began in the Garden of Eden with Adam and Eve immediately after the fall. It was like a dream that you were naked, everybody could see you, and there was nothing you could do about it. The man and his wife realized they were naked, and even though they were married it made them incredibly uncomfortable because things between them were not right. So, they invented clothing. That morning when they awoke, though naked, it did not occur to them that they were naked at all. Now, having sinned, nothing was right about it. What a monumental problem they had on their hands. So, what did they do about it? From their own resources, from the trees of the garden that they kept, they harvested and used those tough and resilient leaves of their fig trees and sewed them together into concealing garments in an attempt to make things right between them again. With those clothes donned they now regained their composure and sense of self before the other and things were right again between them because their private parts were masked. Or so they thought.

Things went along simply fine for them until the end of the day and God showed up. They again realized they were naked and hid from his presence behind the trees they kept. Something was again not right in their lives, not between the two of them, but between the two of them and God. That dream about being naked and not being able to do anything about it just turned into the worst nightmare of all time for all of mankind. Little did they know God had just the solution for them. He sacrificed an animal for the forgiveness of their sins and then he clothed them in garments of leather made from the sacrificed animal. Now things were right between the two of them and things were right with them and their Maker.

We need to know that the clothing that Adam and Eve made represented their self-righteous efforts at fixing their problems themselves. The problem was that it was a problem that only God could fix for them. The only right solution was when God supplied them with a righteousness that was not their own, but one that he gave to them that made things right again. Adam and Eve were anything but righteous and anything they did on their own was by default of themselves, hence it was self-righteousness. The clothing God supplied to them represented true righteousness. God's work made things right between them all.

What this means for us is a few things. Any attempt we make at becoming righteous is merely an extension of ourselves and therefore by definition it is self-righteousness, which is not righteousness at all. It was the Prophet Isaiah who said that our righteousness, our best holy and religious acts are like the most filthy garment a person could imagine wearing.[125]

    Jesus said we need to have a gnawing hunger and a nearly unquenchable thirst for righteousness. That is so that we don't settle for anything short of true righteousness to satisfy us. The mere appearance of it is not enough for us. We need righteousness that comes from God alone to satisfy our need for living a life of faith and that includes being in recovery, free and clean from all drug use. We cannot and must not settle for anything less, God save our souls.

    Heavenly Father, you sent your son to seek and save the lost. We were utterly lost and without a hope in this world. Your son found us and brought us home to you. You have made us your sons and daughters and, like the prodigal son who returned, you have dressed and clothed us in your son's righteous garments. For all that you have done and will do in our lives we give you eternal thanks and praise. In the name of Jesus Christ our Lord and Savior we pray. Amen

---

[125] Isaiah 64:6

Natures: Old Self – New Self

But now you must also rid yourselves of all such things as these: anger, rage, malice, slander, and filthy language from your lips. Do not lie to each other, since you have taken off your old self with its practices and have put on the new self, which is being renewed in knowledge in the image of its Creator.
Colossians 3:8-10

When we were born-of-the-Spirit a new life was begun within us. Our dear Heavenly Father imparted to us a new and holy life. Our old life was put to death on the cross with Jesus and just as he rose from the dead we too were raised up with him into new lives. What died for us was our old adamic and sinful selves along with our addiction.

Daily we need to practice dying to our old sinful selves and following diligently after Christ as his disciples. In sharing in Christ's death we are surrendering our lives to him. No longer do we live for ourselves and our lives are no longer our own to do with as we choose. This is the same for all Christians, or at least that is what we are called to. Those without addictions might not practice their faith as devout disciples, but because of our addiction we need to be very dedicated for the sake of our recovery. We need the structure and the intensity. We need to be very intentional about dying to self daily and following him and following him closely.

Our Lord, by his grace, extends to us his hand of fellowship so that we can have a close and personal walk with him. It is in the strength of this relationship that our recovery succeeds. Because we have fallen in love with Jesus, we would not want to act in any way, or do anything that would offend him or separate us from him, such is the nature of love.

Blessed Redeemer, you suffered greatly and died on the cross for us. You endured the shame and the pain because of your great love for each and every one of us. Deepen our love for you and fill our hearts to overflowing with that love. Amen

Spiritual Character Traits: Transcending Peace

**And the peace of God, which transcends all understanding,
will guard your hearts and your minds in Christ Jesus.
Philippians 4:7**

Transcendence, meaning to rise above something, is a matter of spirituality and faith. We alone cannot transcend much of anything, let alone something of significance; case in point, our addiction to drugs. It is through the blood of the eternal covenant and our relationship with God though our Savior Jesus Christ that we can have transcending peace in our lives. This is a peace that is stout, that is resilient and defies being wore down by both a constant barrage of harassment and by the assault of massively unsettling events in our lives. It is not that we are untouched by them or callous to them; we are deeply moved in every way by them. For us, we can carry their weight upon our shoulders but that is only because we are first upheld by the Lord.

God's son Jesus said he would not leave us as abandoned orphans, but he would send us the Holy Spirit to be near to us and to help us in all our needs.[126] We know that there are events in life that are overwhelming and that bring us to our knees. We live in a fallen world, and are subjected to the greatest of difficulties at times, even as faithful Christians. Nonetheless, when we put our trust in God, and pray without ceasing, we can experience him carrying us through.

Besides the obvious benefit of having transcending peace in our lives, we find that this peace has a shielding effect on us. As addicts we have been known to think in the worst of terms about minor difficulties. That is called *catastrophizing*. It is making a mountain out of a mole hill. God's transcending peace shields us from doing this. God's peace also guards us from overreacting to all kinds of worldly troubles. Thanks be to God who keeps us in his perfect peace!

Heavenly Father, you are our refuge and strong tower. In you we find ourselves. Let us live with transcending peace from you as we seek to do your will in our lives. In Jesus' name. Amen

---

[126] John 14:16-18

Spiritual Practices: Worshipping with Holy Hands

**I desire then that in every place the
men should pray lifting holy hands.
1 Timothy 2:8**

While holding up hands in worship is not universal to us all, there is a reason to encourage this practice among our ranks as addicts. We should do this if not in public worship, then at least in our private devotions. We have in the past yielded ourselves to the impersonal demigods of meth, heroin, marijuana, and other drugs. In our devotion to our addictions we raised our hands to hold a pipe or a joint to our mouth or used a hand to inject into our veins what we just cooked to get high.

In recovery lifting our hands up to worship God is a good thing to do, it is an act of righteousness. Think about it this way, if we are being robbed at gun point, we raise our hands up to show that we are not hostile toward the thief and that we are yielding to their will. It is an act of surrender. In raising our hands to God, we are showing him that we are yielding to him. We are showing honor to God and surrendering to him.

There is a benefit that we gain which is great in our own lives of recovery by raising our hands. When we physically show what is in our hearts the rest of our lives line up in obedience to God motivated by our love for him. Equally true, when we physically yield in surrender to God, we open the door for a resistant heart to follow our actions by willingly yielding to him. When we are tempted to yield our bodies to the use of drugs, using our hands in this way to worship God is perhaps the best way we can resist and overcome that temptation. Because addiction to drugs has had such a powerful grip on our lives, our recovery is dependent on countering that dependence with a greater, more powerful devotion to our God from whom our recovery comes.

Gracious God, heavenly Father, we worship and adore you. You have done so much for us in the life of your dear son. Receive our thanks and praise as we offer our gratitude to you. Because of your love for us our lives have been restored. Through Christ our Lord. Amen

Spiritual Promises

Bless the Lord, O my soul, and forget not all his benefits.
Psalm 103:2

One of the great things that comes with living lives in recovery are the promises we have from God our Father and our Lord Jesus Christ. The AA program offers similar promises and they are genuine. For us as Christians there are endless promises that have been made to us by God. They are there for all Christians in fact. By following our Lord we will have these promises at work in our lives. They will bring about in us a more positive outlook on life, a sense of security and a hope that cannot be quenched.

Jesus said that we will know the truth and the truth will set us free:

> So Jesus said to the Jews who had believed him, "If you abide in my word, you are truly my disciples, and you will know the truth, and the truth will set you free." John 8:31-32

Jesus said that we will have his joy in our lives:

> "These things I have spoken to you, that my joy may be in you, and that your joy may be full." John 15:11

Jesus said that we will have peace in our lives:

> "Peace I leave with you; my peace I give to you. Not as the world gives do I give to you. Let not your hearts be troubled, neither let them be afraid." John 14:27

Jesus said we will be accepted by him:

> "Whoever comes to me I will never cast out." John 6:37

Jesus said that our basic needs will be met so we will have no need to be anxious:

> "But seek first the kingdom of God and his righteousness, and all these things will be added to you." Matthew 6:33

Jesus said that our sins will be forgiven:

> "Truly, I say to you, all sins will be forgiven the children of man, and whatever blasphemies they utter." Mark 3:28

Jesus said we will have stability in our lives:

> "Everyone then who hears these words of mine and does them will be like a wise man who built his house on the rock. And the rain fell, and the floods came, and the winds blew and beat on that house, but it did not fall, because it had been founded on the rock. And everyone who hears these words of mine and does not do them will be like a foolish man who built his house on the sand. And the rain fell, and the floods came, and the winds blew and beat against that house, and it fell, and great was the fall of it." Matthew 7:24-27

Heavenly Father, thank you for sending your son Jesus to redeem us from all of our sins. Thank you that you have delivered us from our addictions and given us a better way to live. Lead us in the ways of your son that others may see what you have done for us and find hope in you just as we have. Through Christ our Lord we pray. Amen

The Occult V

For we do not wrestle against flesh and blood, but against the rulers, against the authorities, against the cosmic powers over this present darkness, against the spiritual forces of evil in the heavenly places.
Ephesians 6:12

There are so many versions of occult religions out there. In the witchcraft branches some say they are white witches, meaning that they are more benevolent because they are not casting evil spells. Others are black meaning that their practices allow them to do very evil things to others. There are the Satanists, those that are self-styled, the new agers, and an endless array of self-styled groups to which there is no end.

Categorically, they are all evil and need to be avoided like the black plague. Many may claim to be of a good nature. Others make it no secret, they are glad to reveal that they are spiritually evil such as the Satanists. Do not ever believe for one minute that any of them have any redeeming qualities or are good. They aren't and they don't. They will lie to us bold faced and with all assurances given, they will gladly lie to us and they will not regret it for even an instant. Universally they are deceived themselves and the god of this world has blinded their eyes to the truth. Do not associate with them.

If any of us have been involved in this kind of activity it is best to seek out competent spiritual care from a mature pastor who is experienced in these areas. This kind of problem needs the care of a spiritually mature person who is experienced in spiritual warfare and who can spiritually discern our needs.

Almighty and everlasting God, keep us under your watchful eyes. Guard and protect us from all evil. As your son Christ our Lord taught us to pray, deliver us from evil. Deliver us and every part of our lives from the dominion of Satan and cast out from us all evil influences. Bring us into the glorious Kingdom's reign of your son, Jesus Christ the righteous, in whose name we humbly pray. Amen

Where Are Your Accusers?

The scribes and the Pharisees brought a woman who had been caught in adultery, and placing her in the midst they said to him, "Teacher, this woman has been caught in the act of adultery. Now in the Law, Moses commanded us to stone such women. So what do you say?" This they said to test him, that they might have some charge to bring against him. Jesus bent down and wrote with his finger on the ground. And as they continued to ask him, he stood up and said to them, "Let him who is without sin among you be the first to throw a stone at her." And once more he bent down and wrote on the ground. But when they heard it, they went away one by one, beginning with the older ones, and Jesus was left alone with the woman standing before him. Jesus stood up and said to her, "Woman, where are they? Has no one condemned you?" She said, "No one, Lord." And Jesus said, "Neither do I condemn you; go, and from now on sin no more.
John 8:3-11

When we were using, deep down inside we knew that we were addicts, but it was our secret. When we were found out, by a spouse, a relative, employer, the police or someone else our hearts dropped down to our knees. We dreaded the moment that we had feared for so long. We froze, we denied it to them, we just moved on in life and forgot about it. None of us were ready for that moment to happen. Because we were still active in our addiction our reaction was anything but healthy. We knew that we were condemned and our sense of shame overwhelmed us.

This poor women was in a terrible circumstance. Everyone there was ready to kill her by heaving heavy rocks on her. They said that the Law of Moses commanded them to do it. Jesus put an end to that by uniquely reminding her accusers of their own sins. It is understood that what he was writing in the sand was the sins of those people who were accusing the women.

Our practice of one addict helping another is truly unprecedented. Because we have been there and done that, we need to take the lead by gently bringing the Word of hope that has nurtured us in our recovery to those tender hearts who still need help. Because we share in this struggle we are able to share with those not in recovery about the hope that we have found. Those without our struggle can never have the effectiveness that we possess.

Heavenly Father, you came to us through the life of your son and brought us the message of forgiveness for our sins. Though we had run from you in fear, you were so kind and pastoral with us. Now in our recoveries we are loving you and seeking to do your will in our lives. Bless and watch over us so that we may serve you with faithful and peaceable lives. This we ask through Christ our Lord, who lives and reigns with you and the Holy Spirit, one God now and forever. Amen

Healthy Boundaries: Bad Company

Do not be deceived: "Bad company ruins good morals."
1 Corinthians 15:33

    In recovery we frequently need to shore up our boundaries of where we go and who we associate with. When we were using neither we nor the crowd we were running with was in a good place. Sometimes our own family members were using drugs too. They may have even been the ones who introduced us to using drugs. When we got clean, in order to stay clean, there was a good reason to avoid those who used, especially if they were our own family members. Because we are addicts, we cannot simply say, "NO" and still be around others who are using. As addicts we aren't just testing fate, we are taking dangerous risks with our recovery. In fact, it is worse than that, we are flat out setting ourselves up for failure. Not only can't we use a little and quit, we have an exceedingly difficult time saying, "no" in the first place when temptation comes that close to us.

    It is a particularly good practice to project forward in our minds what it would take for us to stay clean and then work backwards. If we see ourselves using around certain people we definitely need to avoid them like black death. Certain places can be a problem for us, as well as certain times of the day, week, and year such as Friday nights or New Years.

    We have no obligation to be around anyone who is active in their addiction, though they may try to lure us in. We don't need to give them a reason, but if we choose to, we can tell them straight up that we believe they are high or will get high. We can offer our story to them and tell them we don't use anymore and we can offer them help for their own addiction. Most of all we need to uphold our recovery by practicing healthy boundaries.

    God in heaven, it is by your life-giving-spirit that we can live and move and breathe. Through your Holy Spirit living in us we are clean and free from our addictions that once enslaved us. We give you thanks for all that you have done for us. We give you praise for you are worthy of our worship. All glory in heaven and on earth is eternally yours, through Christ our Lord, who lives and reigns with you and the Holy Spirit, one God now and forever more. Amen

Spiritual Intimacy with God

To the choirmaster. A Psalm of David.
O LORD, you have searched me and known me!
You know when I sit down and when I rise up;
    you discern my thoughts from afar.
You search out my path and my lying down
    and are acquainted with all my ways.
Even before a word is on my tongue, behold,
    O LORD, you know it altogether.
You hem me in, behind and before,
    and lay your hand upon me.
Such knowledge is too wonderful for me;
    it is high; I cannot attain it.
Where shall I go from your Spirit?
Or where shall I flee from your presence?
If I ascend to heaven, you are there!
If I make my bed in Sheol, you are there!
If I take the wings of the morning
    and dwell in the uttermost parts of the sea,
    even there your hand shall lead me,
    and your right hand shall hold me.
If I say, "Surely the darkness shall cover me,
    and the light about me be night,"
even the darkness is not dark to you;
    the night is bright as the day,
    for darkness is as light with you.
For you formed my inward parts;
    you knitted me together in my mother's womb.
I praise you, for I am fearfully and wonderfully made.
Wonderful are your works; my soul knows it very well.
My frame was not hidden from you,
    when I was being made in secret,
    intricately woven in the depths of the earth.
Your eyes saw my unformed substance;
in your book were written, every one of them,
    the days that were formed for me,
    when as yet there was none of them.
How precious to me are your thoughts, O God!
    How vast is the sum of them!
If I would count them,
    they are more than the sand.
I awake, and I am still with you.

Search me, O God, and know my heart!
Try me and know my thoughts!
And see if there be any grievous way in me,
and lead me in the way everlasting!
Psalm 139:1-18, 23-24

This psalm was written to the choirmaster which tells us that it was meant to be sung in unison with many people. We don't know if David himself set it to music or if he wanted the choirmaster to do that for him. Apparently David's encounter with God was very inspiring to him and he felt it was so meaningful that he wanted to share it with others.

The heart of this song has incredible insight into just how close God is to us. In its beginning David comes to the realization that God is everywhere, which brings him to think about where he might try to go to escape from God's presence. He comes to see that from his inception God has been intimately involved in his life, including his very physical development in the womb. He realizes that he cannot escape his presence and then he welcomes God to be personal with him. He comes to have a sense of trust about God and in the end he opens his life up to him. He is wonderfully comfortable with being vulnerable with God.

In our own lives we came to see God more clearly with our growing faith in recovery. We may have in our childhood or youth come to have saving faith in Christ. We may have only come to have saving faith in Christ early in our recovery. In recovery we found that faith in God was not only necessary, it was absolutely necessary. It was also a time for questioning and examining what we believed. We found that we may have had some beliefs that were misconceptions. Like David we came into a deeper understanding of who God is and what he is like. The Bible is our best source for understanding who God is and what he is like. It is in the Bible that we learn about God's son Jesus, and it is in his life that we are able to best know who God is. In learning that God loves us and has done all to bring us into recovery we in return come to love him and desire to serve him.

Heavenly Father, like King David we are coming to understand more deeply about how close you are to us. We desire to grow closer to you and to know and love you more deeply too. Aid us in our lives so that we too may continue to live lives clean and free of drug use. Free us from all of the bondage that once ruled over us. Refine our lives in your love. Give us strength day by day to complete the race set before us. Fill us with the knowledge of your will and empower us to fulfill it in our daily lives. This we ask of you in the name of your precious son Jesus Christ who is our Lord and Savior. Amen

Healthy Boundaries: Codependency

**Then the mother of the sons of Zebedee came up to him with her sons, and kneeling before him she asked him for something. And he said to her, "What do you want?" She said to him, "Say that these two sons of mine are to sit, one at your right hand and one at your left, in your kingdom." Jesus answered, "You do not know what you are asking.
Matthew 20:20-22**

Codependency can appear in many ways and forms in the lives in all of us. If we are addicted we are automatically also codependent. This problem is simply described as having unhealthy relationships with others. In addiction it shows up when we seek others to enable and support us in our addiction or with our personal problems such as living irresponsibly. Years ago it was called co-addiction because the dysfunctional traits of the addict were supported by their family members or their friends. An example of this might be that an addict was too tired to go to work because of their using and their spouse called their boss and lied, reporting that they were too sick go into work. In a broader sense, it can include a wide range of dysfunctional relationship traits and having unhealthy interpersonal boundaries. As a rule it effects every addict and to varying degrees everyone in their family and potentially everyone they are close with.

In recovery this problem may get better, or it may just continue on indefinitely. With the cessation of drug use the problems may lighten up, but these patterns of having unhealthy ways of interacting and relating to others won't simply go away on their own. In these situations personal counseling, as well as marriage and family counseling is advisable. Fortunately for us as believers, we are empowered by God to change and learn new ways. Having had such a great debt of sin forgiven us, we are free to go to others and begin renewed and healthy relationships with them.

Heavenly Father, forgive us our wayward behaviors and how we used people including those we love the most. Give us servant's hearts to care for others and help us to never use others for our own selfish interests again. Heal the riffs that we had created and give us sound and healthy relationships with all people. In Jesus name. Amen

Switching Seats on the HMS Titanic

**And when he got into the boat, his disciples followed him.
And behold, there arose a great storm on the sea,
so that the boat was being swamped by the waves;
but he was asleep. And they went and woke him, saying,
"Save us, Lord; we are perishing." And he said to them,
"Why are you afraid, O you of little faith?"
Then he rose and rebuked the winds and the sea,
and there was a great calm. And the men marveled, saying,
"What sort of man is this, that even winds and sea obey him?"
Matthew 8:23-27**

She was a luxury steamer with a revolutionary design that was meant to prevent it from sinking. Even still, the HMS Titanic sank on April 15, 1912. More than 1,500 souls perished. It was a tragedy beyond words and because of that it is the thing that makes for a good movie. Everyone loves to see the drama, but of course no one wants to be in a real to life situation like that.

How often have we heard at a meeting from someone claiming to be clean from one drug like meth for many months, or even many years? Then as they continue to share we hear them say they are still using marijuana or another substance. That is not clean, that is using. They are not in recovery and there are no two ways about it. Yes, it is good they are off the one drug, but while they are using something else, they are not in recovery.

One senior gentleman put it this way at a meeting saying that is simply changing seats on the Titanic. Their ship is going down no matter where they are seated. The end of using in all of our lives is to either be completely clean, or it will be jails, institutions and finally, death. Do not be deceived.

God, help us to get clean, stay clean and to recover the lives that you have designed for us to live. Empower us by your Holy Spirit to live as your people, remove from us all of our character flaws, and let our lives reflect your glory everywhere we go. In Jesus name. Amen

What About Hate?

[Jesus said,] "You have heard that it was said, 'You shall love your neighbor and hate your enemy.' But I say to you, Love your enemies and pray for those who persecute you, so that you may be sons of your Father who is in heaven. For he makes his sun rise on the evil and on the good, and sends rain on the just and on the unjust."
Matthew 5:43-45

Back when we were high on drugs we were not in very close touch with our own thoughts and feelings. The drugs we used manipulated how our brains functioned and induced emotions in us that were not entirely our own. Worse, we did not really know how to properly respond to what we were feeling and thinking. We were a hodgepodge mess of emotions, thoughts, feelings, and beliefs that were contradictory and disrelated to each other. Because of the chemical effects of the drugs on us we were a mess.

Among our many emotions is the one called hate. It is neither a good nor bad emotion, but how we apply it to our lives can be either good or bad. For example, if someone were to lie to another person about us, it would be unhealthy to react by hating them. The healthy reaction is to hate what they have said rather than hating them. The dynamics behind not hating them is that this could be and most likely would be shame based, which is not at all healthy. They are a human being, and though what they have done is not good, it would not be right to hate them.

In living by this example we leave open the door in our relationship with them for things to be healed. By showing them that we don't hate them, though we do hate what they have done and said, we make it easier for them to make their amends with us. If we hate them they may feel they cannot change themselves and therefore there is no hope for the relationship to be made right.

Loving Heavenly Father, thank you for loving and caring for us. Thank you for showing us and leading us in better ways to live. Empower us to live as your children, and may others see in us your glorious power to transform us from the gutter-most to the uttermost. In Jesus name. Amen

Covenant Relationships: Married to Our Addiction

And the Two Shall Become One
Mark 10:8

We know that in marriage the couple are joined physically and the two become one flesh. It is a wonderful gift from God and the bonds that are formed in this way are extraordinarily strong. There is a unifying of their lifestyles, verbal agreements on how they want to live together, if they want to have children and how they will raise them, and what to do with their time together. It is a very holistic accord that takes place on every level of their lives, body, soul, and spirit.

With drug use there is a similar union that happens, albeit an unholy one. Whether the drugs are swallowed, lit up and inhaled, cut up and snorted, or cooked and injected they are taken into our bodies. It is as if the drugs are a person themselves and that person begins to take over our lives. This impersonal creature is completely selfish and it does not consider the consequences of its actions. It is a monster. These drugs that take over in our lives slowly, sometimes quickly, consumes all that we have worked for in life until it finally consumes all that we ourselves are. The bonds that it forms are very much like an unhealthy marriage, only a thousand times worse.

That is a very spiritual description of how the addiction works in our lives and of how addiction is a toxic form of spirituality. The addiction keeps us from the lives that God intended for us to have. This life is waiting for us when we enter into recovery. We need to remember that it was God who formed Adam and then later made Eve and united them in marriage. As believers we also need to remember how we, as the church, are the bride of Christ. As such, we will at the consummation of time be united with him in heaven where we will celebrate our union with him in a great heavenly marriage banquet. Our drug use was like an extramarital affair that did not and could not fulfill us, and it also kept us from being the bride of Christ.

Heavenly Father, you have made us for yourself and you desire to be in a covenant relationship with us. We know that you love us and are jealous for our devotion. We love you and we pray that we may be faithful to you all of our days, through Christ our Lord we pray. Amen

Spirituality: Detachment

**But whatever gain I had, I counted as loss for the sake of Christ. Indeed, I count everything as loss because of the surpassing worth of knowing Christ Jesus my Lord. For his sake I have suffered the loss of all things and count them as rubbish, in order that I may gain Christ and be found in him, not having a righteousness of my own that comes from the law, but that which comes through faith in Christ, the righteousness from God that depends on faith.
Philippians 3:7-9**

The day was in many of our lives when we had dropped out and detached to one degree or another from participating in society. Some of us stopped paying our bills, we drove without a license or without insurance, we dealt drugs for our income, we quit or lost our jobs. Some of us lived in someone's basement or garage, others among us were homeless. We had lost interest in being a member of our community unless it involved getting high. We were fugitives, living on the edge of society and on the edge of life itself.

In recovery we were changed by God. New life was breathed into us and we took on new ways of living. We were clean and like dry sponges soaking up water, we took in everything we needed to get underway in our new lifestyles. We were encouraged by others who were godsent to help us engage in life again as clean and free people. In our using days we were detached from life so that we could use; now we are detached from our old way of life. We also found a new sense of spiritual attachment in our recovery. We were able to focus on our lives from an eternal point of view. We could see how our relationship with Jesus Christ motivated us to have an entirely new set of values and interests.

Dearest Heavenly Father, you have freed us from drugs so that we can live for you. Help us this day so that we may walk in a manner worthy of our spiritual calling in you. Aid and guide us to live fully in the present as we grow in you, through Christ our Lord. Amen

Clean Mouths

**Let the words of my mouth and the meditation of my heart
be acceptable in your sight, O Lord, my rock and my redeemer.
Psalm 19:14**

  While Ecclesiastes says that there is a time for every matter under heaven, it does not endorse us to say just anything we want, namely swearing. On that matter, there are two concerns. First is the foul language, sometimes referred to as four-letter words. It is offensive to others, and if we are on the receiving end of it, it is offensive to us. Let the truth also be told, we have all sworn at one time or another, and more than once at that. On the one hand we need to live by our admonition, *easy does it*. On the other hand, and in keeping life practical maybe we can keep that language to more of a minimum. Beyond that, we should really refrain from directing it at others.

  There is also a type of swearing that involves invoking God's name. This is also not good, and we really should refrain from this kind of swearing altogether.[127] If we invoke God's name to damn something he will hear us when we call out his name and he will pay special attention to what we are saying. So, how foolish are we when we swear using his name while at that same moment we are ironically asking him to pay attention to us as we commit that grievous sin. God, the Lord, has given us his name so that we can call on him in prayer and in worship. As part of our recovery, in our gratefulness for all that he has done for us, let's not offend him in this way.

  Lord God, Creator of heaven and earth, we give you thanks for our recovery, which without your intervention in our lives would not be possible. We call on you to give you our worship and offer our prayers. We praise your holy and precious name, for you alone are worthy and glory is due your name. This we pray to you though Christ our Lord, who died and rose from the dead by the power of your Holy Spirit. Amen

---

[127] Exodus 20:7

Supernatural Help

For because he himself has suffered when tempted,
he is able to help those who are being tempted.
Hebrews 2:18

How many of us have come close to a relapse because we were tempted in one way or another? Virtually all of us, right? And what were our reasons? We were lonely and missed our friends or family members who still use? We wanted to make our problems go away even if it was only for a little while. We were having flashbacks to some traumatic memories and it was hard on us. We wanted to feel great again, just once. We were down and needed to lift up our emotions.

Our Lord has also suffered. He does know the depth of our sorrows. He was tempted in worse ways than we were and it was a worse enemy, it was the devil himself. Jesus was tempted to find quick, shortcut solutions to the difficulties he faced in his life. Jesus of Nazareth, the man, suffered and died rather than accept what looked like a quick and easy fix to his problems. He did not choose any shortcuts that would have undermined the work God sent him here to accomplish. He was tempted with turning stones into bread to satisfy his hunger. He was tempted to call on angels to bring him deliverance from the suffering he endured on the cross. He was spat on, mocked, reviled and he did not refuse to be mistreated.

Our Lord is fully able to understand where we are, feel what we feel, and suffer as we do. Because of this he is the perfect one to turn to. We can call on him, pray to him and receive from him the very help we need.

Savior, Lord, friend, Jesus hear our prayers. Help us to see that you suffered and died to redeem us from the grip of sin, death, the grave and drugs. We call upon your name and ask you to be with us in our weaknesses so that we may have your strength to endure our suffering and overcome the clutches of our addictions. You rose from the dead by the power of the Holy Spirit and we ask that you raise us up above our problems that we might live for you in all that we do. Amen

Wellness: Being Good Stewards of Our Bodies

**And his name—by faith in his name—has made this
man strong whom you see and know, and the faith that is through
Jesus has given the man this perfect health in the presence of you all.
Acts 3:16**

The ravages of our addiction robbed us of everything including our health. Many of us who used meth had damaged our teeth and many of us had damaged our hearts. We ate too much and became obese, or we ate too little and became malnourished. We failed to see a physician when we were ill. We did not go in for checkups. For some the damage done to our bodies from neglect became permanent. In some cases our health was restored once we got into recovery.

As people of faith we know from the Old Testament that the Law of Moses was genuinely concerned with the people's health. They had extensive public health requirements to prevent and stop the spread of illness. There were the kosher food requirements that worked to maintain a person's health and vitality. The first chapter of the Book of the Prophet Daniel also testifies to the great advantage of eating a healthy diet.

For us in our recoveries, we know that we needed to be restored not just in the soundness of our minds, but also in our bodies. From the stories of the Gospel we know that our Lord was genuinely concerned with the physical health of people everywhere. He healed all who were brought to him. Now, as we regain the lives that God has meant for us, we also need to be good stewards of our bodies. We need to eat a healthy diet, get our exercise, and manage our stress well.

Heavenly Father, restore our bodies to good health and aid us as we seek to live in healthy ways. Help us to maintain our physical strength and eat nutritiously. In Jesus' name. Amen

**Beloved, I pray that all may go well with you and
that you may be in good health, as it goes well with your soul.
3 John 2**

The Prodigal Son
Luke 15:11-32

And he said, "There was a man who had two sons. And the younger of them said to his father, 'Father, give me the share of property that is coming to me.' And he divided his property between them. Not many days later, the younger son gathered all he had and took a journey into a far country, and there he squandered his property in reckless living. And when he had spent everything, a severe famine arose in that country, and he began to be in need. So he went and hired himself out to one of the citizens of that country, who sent him into his fields to feed pigs. And he was longing to be fed with the pods that the pigs ate, and no one gave him anything. "But when he came to himself, he said, 'How many of my father's hired servants have more than enough bread, but I perish here with hunger! I will arise and go to my father, and I will say to him, "Father, I have sinned against heaven and before you. I am no longer worthy to be called your son. Treat me as one of your hired servants."' And he arose and came to his father. But while he was still a long way off, his father saw him and felt compassion, and ran and embraced him and kissed him. And the son said to him, 'Father, I have sinned against heaven and before you. I am no longer worthy to be called your son.' But the father said to his servants, 'Bring quickly the best robe, and put it on him, and put a ring on his hand, and shoes on his feet. And bring the fattened calf and kill it, and let us eat and celebrate. For this my son was dead, and is alive again; he was lost, and is found.' And they began to celebrate. "Now his older son was in the field, and as he came and drew near to the house, he heard music and dancing. And he called one of the servants and asked what these things meant. And he said to him, 'Your brother has come, and your father has killed the fattened calf, because he has received him back safe and sound.' But he was angry and refused to go in. His father came out and entreated him, but he answered his father, 'Look, these many years I have served you, and I never disobeyed your command, yet you never gave me a young goat, that I might celebrate with my friends. But when this son of yours came, who has devoured your property with prostitutes, you killed the fattened calf for him!' And he said to him, 'Son, you are always with me, and all that is mine is yours. It was fitting to celebrate and be glad, for this your brother was dead, and is alive; he was lost, and is found.'"

We truly were prodigal sons and daughters with our drug use. We went far astray from what our lives should have been like. Unlike the man in this story, we could not simply decide to change and return home. We needed God's intervention in our lives to quit using. We are grateful that

God is always willing to act in our best interests and bring us into recovery. When we decided to seek his aid in this way and we entered into recovery our heavenly Father treated us like the father in the story treated his son. We also felt like the son returning home, we felt like we were completely unworthy to be called God's son or daughter. God was not willing to treat us as anything less than his children, and beloved children at that.

  Heavenly Father, we are forever grateful that you have welcomed us home in such warm ways and blessed us by calling us your children. By your grace you have saved us and by your mighty right hand you have delivered us from our addictions. Keep us safely in your care and bring us through this day victorious in you. This we pray in Jesus' blessed name. Amen

It Is A Fearful Thing to Fall into The Hands of The Living God
Hebrew 10:31

As addicts it is obvious to us that we could not quit on our own. And, if it isn't obvious to everyone it will become clear before long. That is just one of the distinguishing characteristics of being an addict. The drugs have more power over us than our own self-restraint and wimpy will-power. Therefore, we needed to enlist the help of someone who was not only more powerful than ourselves, but also more powerful than the drugs power over us. This is God's place in our lives.

But the problem is that many, maybe even most of us, have been afraid of turning to him for help. We have sinned, we screwed up, we were in a terrible place in our lives and we knew it. Turning to the one person who could help us was what we needed to do. But there was another problem. As the Bible verse says, "It is a fearful thing to fall into the hands of the living God. Why is that so? The Scriptures say that we cannot see God's face and live.[128] Why is that so? Because if we see him, he sees us, and if he sees us, he needs to do something about our sin, which is to our death.[129] Now all that paints a very gloomy and doom filled future, or so it would seem. The story of our recovery doesn't end there, not at all. The Bible also says this:

**Therefore, since we have been justified by faith,
we have peace with God through our Lord Jesus Christ.
Through him we have also obtained access by
faith into this grace in which we stand,
and we rejoice in hope of the glory of God.
Romans 5:1-2**

It is by your grace O Lord that we have been redeemed not just from our sins but also from our addictions. May we walk this day according to your Word. In Jesus' name. Amen

---

[128] Exodus 33:20
[129] Romans 6:23

God Does ~~Not~~ Give Us More Than We Can Handle

**For we were so utterly burdened beyond our strength
that we despaired of life itself. Indeed, we felt that we had
received the sentence of death. But that was to make us
rely not on ourselves but on God who raises the dead.
2 Corinthians 1:8-9**

Sometimes there are these saying that are circulated among us and believed in by some that don't really ring true. This saying, that God will not give us more than we can handle, is one of them. It is not true for several reasons. Not everything that comes our way in life is directly orchestrated by God. While this statement might seem logical, agreeable, and desirable it is not supported by the Scriptures. Life's random and impersonal nature can bring us immeasurable tragedy. For us as Christians we can be treated very badly, even martyred for our faith. At times God intervenes and we escape great difficulties, at other times we must go through them. There is no clear Biblical reason why there is this disparity, but we know it exists.

As the Apostle Paul said, all the terrible burdens that he faced made him despair of his very life. Among other things he was imprisoned, suffered countless beatings with both whips and rods that brought him near to death, and three times the ship he was on was wrecked while at sea.[130] While some of us have suffered greatly too, as Christians we need to face life with the same practice that Paul employed. He relied on God because his circumstances forced him to.

In addiction we brought many difficulties on ourselves. In recovery we need to take responsibility for our actions. In some cases we need to make amends with others or face other consequences for our actions. By God's grace we are able to accept what life will bring us.

Dearest God, by your grace we are redeemed and delivered from our addictions. May we live in accordance with your will and flourish in life through your love. In Jesus' name. Amen

---

[130] 2 Corinthians 11:23-27

Maintenance in Recovery

With my whole heart I seek you;
let me not wander from your commandments!
I have stored up your word in my heart,
that I might not sin against you.
Blessed are you, O Lord; teach me your statutes!
Psalm 119:10-12

We live with a disease for which there is no cure. We also know that our disease can be arrested and its progression can be stopped by us getting ourselves into recovery. Our old and sinful nature may try to lie to us and tell us that we are healthy enough to use again on a limited basis. We should never believe a lie such as that. Once an addict, always an addict, only for us we are addicts in recovery.

There are things that we can always do, and should do, to strengthen our recovery. From the NA program the final three steps, 10, 11 and 12, are considered our maintenance steps. They tell us that we need to continue with our inventories and quickly admit when we are wrong. That we need to seek to know and do God's will. And, that we need to seek to carry the message to others while we practice our recovery in all that we do.

For us in spiritual recovery from addiction we need to add this practice to our lives. We need to saturate our lives with God's Word. This is especially true in the beginning when we are new to recovery. The Word of God has the special quality of being inspired by the Holy Spirit. As such it works on us to achieve God's will in our lives. By God's Word he created the heavens and the earth. By his Word he transformed us from sinners to saints and from addicts to addicts in recovery. By the power of his Word our old and sinful nature was put to death on the cross of our Lord as we are joined with him in his suffering and death. By his Word we are raised from death and given spiritual birth. By the power of his Word, all things are held together, including our lives lived in recovery.

Holy God, you have saved us and you keep and preserve us. Thank you for bringing us into recovery and making our new lives possible. In Jesus' precious name. Amen

Crisis: An Opportunity for Change

**At that time his voice shook the earth, but now he has promised, "Yet once more I will shake not only the earth but also the heavens." This phrase, "Yet once more," indicates the removal of things that are shaken—that is, things that have been made— in order that the things that cannot be shaken may remain. Therefore let us be grateful for receiving a kingdom that cannot be shaken, and thus let us offer to God acceptable worship, with reverence and awe, for our God is a consuming fire.
Hebrew 12:25-29**

It seems that in life God has designed things that will bring us to our knees in surrender to him. Never let these things bring us to reverting back into using again. We need to be on guard against these things pulling us down into old sinful nature behaviors, old addictive behavior and especially into the temptation to use again. Even though we may be feeling very overwhelmed, we are in a position to make some healthy changes in our lives. In our distress we are feeling like anything that we can do to lighten the load we will do. Anything that we can do that will prevent this from ever happening again, we will do it and we will do it now. The direction we need to take our lives during a crisis is one that is healthy, recovery oriented and for the better.

Doing whatever we need to do to maintain ourselves in recovery is vital for us. Continuing in our daily devotions, attending meetings, calling our sponsor, especially making time to see our counselor are even more necessary than ever given the circumstances. Equally true is the need to avoid those things that might bring us down into a relapse. Avoiding the old crowd, an old friend not in recovery, returning to our old stomping grounds or whatever it might be.

Heavenly Father, we are weak but you are strong to save us. We need you every day, every hour, every moment in our lives. Give to us your strength, remind us of your constant presence in our lives and uphold us in our recovery with your omnipotent right hand. In Jesus' name. Amen

Alcohol and the Bible

**Wine is a mocker, strong drink a brawler,
and whoever is led astray by it is not wise.
Proverbs 20:1**

If you were to do even a brief Bible study on the key words *wine* and *strong drink* you would soon find that there are apparent conflicting views on these beverages. In some references alcoholic beverages seem to be encouraged, and at other times alcohol is strongly opposed. In those ancient days they did recognize that alcohol could be a serious problem for some people; they did not know yet that alcoholism was a disease.

Yes, there were times when alcohol use was suggested. Yes, alcohol was abused and by some very prominent people such as Noah[131] and King Belshazzar of Babylon.[132] Yes, these people suffered significant consequences for their drinking. Alcohol use was specifically and strongly discouraged among rulers and kings.[133] The spiritual calling of priests prohibited them from drinking while serving in the temple.[134] The spiritual calling of a Nazarite required them to completely abstain from alcohol during the time when their vows of separation were in effect. They were also prohibited from even touching grapes.[135]

For us in recovery from drug use we know that we are cross addicted to all drugs including the drug alcohol. Spiritually our recovery program is much like that of the Nazarite who abstained entirely from alcohol.

Heavenly Father, help us to be ever mindful that we must abstain from all drugs of abuse no matter what they are. Aid us in recovery and transform our lives. In Christ's name. Amen

---

[131] Genesis 9:20-21
[132] Daniel 5
[133] Proverbs 31:4
[134] Leviticus 10:9
[135] Numbers 6:13-20

That's a Big IF

**If my people who are called by
my name humble themselves,
and pray and seek my face and
turn from their wicked ways,
then I will hear from heaven and
will forgive their sin and heal their land.
2 Chronicles 7:14**

What the history of the Bible reveals should come as no surprise to us. We have seen the same pattern in our lives, and it is not just regarding our drug addiction. We are fallen and sinful. Beginning with Adam and Eve who had it directly from God who told them, that fruit, don't eat it. How simple could it be? They were living in ideal conditions in the Garden. Still, they failed. Then God established the first covenant with them to atone for their sins. That worked until one of their sons decided not to share in it. We know how that turned out, Cain killed Abel and he got cursed from the ground. Then he was sentenced to be a restless wanderer on the face of the earth. Following that the world progressed from bad to worse until in the days of Noah when their every thought was inclined to do evil. God sent a great flood and washed those people away. Righteous Noah and his family alone were saved. Still, the world failed to follow after God.

Following this, God called Abraham to be the father of a great nation who would be his chosen people. Through his servant Moses he established a new covenant, gave them their tabernacle, and brought them into the promised land. As was true of the past, as was true of their present and as would continue to be true to this day, among God's people, who confess faith in him, there are reoccurring periods of following God and periods of falling away.

In the community of addicts we have our ups and downs. A good program includes a plan for what to if we relapse. The difference between those among us who relapse and those in recovery is that among those in recovery are included the ones who relapsed but then got back into the program one more time. For us the promise always remains, God is faithful and he will always receive us back.

Heavenly Father, by your grace you have saved us and by your grace you keep us. Thank you for your love which is there for us no matter what befalls us. In Jesus' name. Amen

Anxiety and Living One Day At a Time

**Jesus said,
"Therefore do not be anxious about tomorrow, for tomorrow will be anxious for itself. Sufficient for the day is its own trouble."
Matthew 6:34**

We have this saying, *one day at a time,* that we live by. It works to counter our anxiety and keep us in touch with the present rather than projecting what the future might hold for us. It is simple to understand. We should not add to today's stress because today's worries are about all we should need to handle. When we project into the future and wonder about what will happen that could add up to be a heavy burden in a hurry because the future is infinite. Worse, our imaginations can overload us with literally unlimited scenarios of what all could go wrong for us. The terrible emotion that this creates is called *anticipatory anxiety*. We don't need to do that to ourselves. In addiction or in recovery, no one should do that to themselves.

In recovery our rational minds return to us and we begin to think in healthy ways for ourselves again. We are no longer focused on using and acquiring more drugs. Having free time, meaning both time free of drugs and leisure time, gives us the opportunity to think about so much else. Yes, we do need to plan for our near future and our long-term futures. No, we do not need to fret about it and on a high-stress day we certainly don't want to add to our troubles with worrying. When we are stressing and feeling the pinch of anxiety we simply need to say to ourselves, *"Easy does it."* We need to train ourselves to relax when we hear ourselves saying that. We need to think it and say it out loud to ourselves and most of all learn to live by it.

Gracious and loving God, thank you for being there for us in our lives and in our recoveries. We are weak, but you are strong. We are but mortal men and women who must rely on you in all things. Teach us and speak to us, ever reminding us of what your beloved son has said to us, "do not be anxious about tomorrow, for tomorrow will be anxious for itself. Sufficient for the day is its own trouble." Help us to live one day at a time through Christ our Lord we pray. Amen

John Wesley's Covenant Prayer

**But as it is, Christ has obtained a ministry that is as much more excellent than the old as the covenant he mediates is better, since it is enacted on better promises.
Hebrews 8:6**

I am no longer my own, but thine.
Put me to what thou wilt, rank me with whom thou wilt.
Put me to doing, put me to suffering.
Let me be employed for thee or laid aside for thee,
exalted for thee or brought low for thee.
Let me be full, let me be empty.
Let me have all things, let me have nothing.
I freely and heartily yield all things
to thy pleasure and disposal.
And now, O glorious and blessed God,
Father, Son and Holy Spirit,
thou art mine, and I am thine.
So be it.
And the covenant which I have made on earth,
let it be ratified in heaven. Amen[136]

Wesley was a man of God who sought the Lord and earnestly desired to walk with God in all that he did. He was a priest in the Church of England who called upon believers to commit themselves to a life of holiness and the study of God's Word. While an accomplished Oxford scholar, he was devoted to his study of the Bible. It was by his work that England had their greatest ever spiritual revival and renewal of faith. He is credited with having had substantial influence in establishing the Wesleyan, Methodist and Nazarene churches.

---

[136] Source Unknown

The Seeds of Recovery

**Then the LORD put out his hand and touched my mouth.
And the LORD said to me,
"Behold, I have put my words in your mouth.
See, I have set you this day over nations and over kingdoms,
to pluck up and to break down, to destroy and to overthrow,
to build and to plant."
Jeremiah 1:9-10**

    Jeremiah was a very mighty prophet who was called by God to pluck up, break down, destroy, overthrow, build and plant. Two-thirds of his calling was to tear things down and the other third was to build things up. You might say that is what needs to happen in our lives especially early in our recovery. We have built up walls of resistance, believed in lies, acquired terrible habits, and lived in active addiction for some time. All that needs to be disassembled in our lives so that a healthier lifestyle can take its place.

    In recovery the blinding fog that had covered our minds lifted and truth brought light and life to us again. We began with small baby-steps. We returned to living clean and free. We took care of our personal hygiene, our work ethic returned, and our job performance improved. We confessed to our loved ones and our friends that we had been using drugs and we had not treated them very well because of it. We asked for their forgiveness and understanding. Life began to take on a new normalcy as we started going to our weekly meetings and practiced our daily devotions, living one day at a time.

    Heavenly Father, though we went far astray in our addiction you called us to your side and to lives of recovery. In surrendering our lives to you we ask that you remove from us all of our character defects and our terrible habits. We ask that you tear down our walls of resistance and remove from us the lies that we chose to believe in. Plant in us the seeds of your holy Word and cause them to take deep root in our lives. Lead us in the way that is everlasting through Christ Jesus our Lord and Savior. Amen

Spirituality: Transcendence

**For everyone who has been born of God overcomes the world.
And this is the victory that has overcome the world—our faith.
Who is it that overcomes the world except the one
who believes that Jesus is the Son of God?
1 John 5:4-5**

When we first used drugs we surrendered ourselves to them. Drugs were glad to take control of our lives. It was as if they had a personality of their own and it took over in our lives. We were defeated and from there it was downhill for us. Try as we might, we could not shake the drugs growing influence in our lives. Slowly, sometimes quickly, their influence progressed into absolute control over us. The drugs were greater in our lives than anything and consequently we were their slaves.

When we got into recovery, it was made possible only because someone greater than ourselves got involved with us. That was the Lord and when we turned our lives over to him our recovery began. The reason our recovery happened was that the Lord is greater than our measly willpower and he is greater than the hold that drugs had on us. Overcoming active addiction was possible because the Lord himself has overcome the world.[137]

It is never enough to simply find recovery one day in our lives. We need to daily surrender and die to self by picking up our own crosses and follow our Lord. We live day by day, one day at a time. Our recovery is not in our own hands, it is in God's hands and we need to pursue a close relationship with him every day for the rest of our lives.

Father in heaven, you came to us in the life of your son Jesus Christ. We are forever thankful for all that you have done for us and for restoring us to life after addiction took control of our lives. All praise and glory and honor and power belong to you. Amen

---

[137] John 16:33

We Are More Than Conquerors

**No, in all these things we are more than
conquerors through him who loved us.
For I am sure that neither death nor life,
nor angels nor rulers, nor things present
nor things to come, nor powers,
nor height nor depth,
nor anything else in all creation,
will be able to separate us from the
love of God in Christ Jesus our Lord.
Romans 8:37-39**

Our lives of recovery are dependent on our walk with the Lord. As the text says, it is through the Lord that we have become more than conquerors. We can relish in the victory that is ours, but we need to always give credit where credit is due. Let there be no doubts remaining in our own minds or in the things we say. We are in recovery because of what the Lord has done in our lives.

As Christians in addiction or recovery, in relapse or in abstinence, as he has promised the Lord is present with us.[138] We need to know that time and time again. Christian addicts in relapse testify that getting high again after recovery is not the same for them. It does not hold the same sense of elation or relief for them. Rather, they are quickly convicted by the Holy Spirit of their sins and feel so guilt ridden that there is no enjoyment in it for them anymore. This knowledge persuades us from falling back into our former way of life. Because of his promise to be with us always, we hold from this verse that we are securely held in God's powerful embrace. The advantage this gives us is that we do not need to worry about our strength failing. We can rest securely knowing that the Almighty upholds us by his omnipotent right hand.

Heavenly Father, thank you for your never-failing love for us, for holding us so secure, and for letting nothing come between us and you. We rest peacefully in your arms and take confidence not in our ability, but in your almighty power to sustain us in salvation and recovery. Through Christ our Lord, who lives and reigns with you and the Holy Spirit. Amen

---

[138] Hebrews 13:5

Relapse and Recovery

**Seek the Lord while he may be found; call upon him while he is near; let the wicked forsake his way, and the unrighteous man his thoughts; let him return to the Lord, that he may have compassion on him, and to our God, for he will abundantly pardon. For my thoughts are not your thoughts, neither are your ways my ways, declares the Lord. For as the heavens are higher than the earth, so are my ways higher than your ways and my thoughts than your thoughts. "For as the rain and the snow come down from heaven and do not return there but water the earth, making it bring forth and sprout, giving seed to the sower and bread to the eater, so shall my word be that goes out from my mouth; it shall not return to me empty, but it shall accomplish that which I purpose, and shall succeed in the thing for which I sent it.
Isaiah 55:6-11**

Having a relapse is not a taboo topic for us. We are human, perfection is not our goal but maturity is. We live and learn. Shaming ourselves for a relapse is never helpful but when it occurs it's time to get back into recovery. What then should we do? It is time to get back to going to our meetings, calling our sponsor, seeing our counselor, and moving forward into recovery again.

Once we are back on the track of recovery we need to review the reason we had a relapse in a non-judgmental way. We need to ask ourselves what were our triggers? Was it running into an old friend? Did we go somewhere that put us at risk? Was it a memory that surfaced that caused us distress? We need to think for ourselves and also ask this question, was I thinking nostalgically about using when I know that it was never a good thing back then?

Most of all we need to know and be reassured that when we return to the Lord in our recovery that he will abundantly pardon us and receive us with loving and open arms. As we confess our sins he will forgive and bless us.

Heavenly Father, forgive us for our sins and pardon us according to the favor that you bear for your son Jesus Christ. Renew us in your love and restore us by your grace. Amen

Bringing the Message to Those Who Need It the Most

**I have become all things to all people,
that by all means I might save some.
I do it all for the sake of the gospel,
that I may share with them in its blessings.
1 Corinthians 9:22-23**

As Christians it is our responsibility to share our faith. As addicts in recovery it is also our responsibility to share with other addicts about the hope that we have come into. We can speak about our difficulties and failings, and about the terrible effects that drugs have had on us. Along with that we must also share that we received help. Maybe we just started going to meetings and it worked for us. Maybe we went to outpatient treatment, maybe it was inpatient. Share the message we must, it is up to them how they will respond. Being nonjudgmental is essential. We know how hard they have already been on themselves, we don't need to add to it. Maybe we should carry with us a list of the meetings in our area to share. At the very least, plant a seed that will grow with the kindness bestowed on them as we shared. Nothing more needs to be said unless they open up to us.

Be prepared for the variety of reactions that can be given. Some will act very offended and deny that they have a problem or are even using. Others behave as if we are the offender for suggesting they are using, are addicted or that they need help. A few may even announce to others that we are the one with a problems in an attempt to get the focus off themselves and on to someone else. Regardless of their reactions, our sharing what our hope and faith have done for us in bringing us into recovery is something that we are called to do. It is God's will that we share the message.

Heavenly Father, by your grace we have been brought into recovery. Thank you for the fellowship of the meetings that we attend and the friends who are supportive of the program. Help us to reach out to others who need to enter into recovery and let us share with them about what you have done for us. Bless us in our journey and aid us in our time of need. This we ask through Christ our Lord. Amen

Maturity: Our Teenage Years

Remember also your Creator in the days of your youth, before the evil days come and the years draw near of which you will say, "I have no pleasure in them".
Ecclesiastes 12:1

Our teenage years are a special time of life. It is a time when we are rounding off our developmental years and putting the final touches on who we are becoming. It is a time when we are able to begin adult-like thinking, but are not yet there. It is a time of self-discovery, of finding out our likes and dislikes apart from our family's preset preferences that we were a part of. Adolescence is a time for stepping out in new and more independent ways, making new friends who are like-minded. Our youth can be a time for spiritual awakening also. It can be a time of coming into a faith that is adult-like in many ways, a faith that is ours by choice rather than just an inheritance from our parents.

With this new sense of freedom also comes new dangers. Drugs were frequently available to us in our youth. This was when many of us got started with our addiction. Instead of growing into our pre-adult years in a healthy and responsible way, we dropped out of that track. We withdrew into the underworld of using and not being engage in the world around us. We did not have a spiritual awakening with God, but we did have an enslaving encounter with drugs. That threw everything off track. Our development was arrested and we were frozen in time.

When we got clean, we found that we felt awkward in social settings. We were in the body of an older person with the social skills of a teenager. In recovery we found we had a lot of catching up to do. By going to our meetings and getting help from others where we needed it, we found that we could return to growing up again and becoming the person God had intended for us to be.

Heavenly Father, guide us in our immaturity and help us to grow into our lives as healthy, clean, and responsible people. Give us your grace to become mature adults and live in recovery. Through Jesus our Lord we pray. Amen

Step 1. We admitted that we were powerless over our addiction, that our lives had become unmanageable.

**For my iniquities have gone over my head;
like a heavy burden, they are too heavy for me.
Psalm 38:4**

It can be a rude awakening to come to admit that we were out of control with our drug use. We may have started out believing that we were in control of our using, but that didn't last. To have to finally admit to being out of control and powerless over it to ourselves is one thing, but to say this to someone else takes it to a whole new level. This realization and confession are the beginning of recovery if we keep working forward on it and work the rest of the steps.

With this admission to ourselves and others we opened the door to recovery. In it we were becoming honest and not continuing to believing in a lie and practicing self-deception. We might call it a *come to Jesus meeting*. While this step didn't require us to make this admission to anyone, it worked better if we did. At the 12-step meetings there was a round of introductions and while we had the option to pass without saying so much as our name but most of us shared our name and that we were addicted. Recovery works better in the open among our peers. Addiction works in secret; openness on our part counters this hold it has on us.

Addiction and using are not the only problems we faced. As the confession goes, our lives, commonly our whole lives, were unmanageable, which was a nice way of saying we were in crisis because of it. We can remember how our lives were suffering. We had problems in school or at work, with our family and our friends. Our finances were in trouble, we had bills stacking up, rent or the mortgage payment was overdue and sometimes is was months behind. The list of our troubles went on. Then we got help. We were forced by our circumstances to look beyond ourselves and we did in the next step, step two.

Heavenly Father, help us to never forget how desperate we were to get help. Help us to always remember how terrible our lives had become. May these memories be paired with your grace and motivate us to remain free and clean in recovery, through Christ Jesus our Lord. Amen

Step 2. We came to believe that a Power greater than ourselves could restore us to sanity.

**But to all who did receive him,
who believed in his name,
he gave the right to become children of God,
who were born,
not of blood nor of the will of the flesh
nor of the will of man, but of God.
John 1:12-13**

Faith is especially important in recovery. Having faith in God means that we put our trust in him. In step two we have already come to believe that we could not quit on our own and needed help. We had given up hope that someone else could influence us enough to get us to quit. It doesn't work that way. We cannot have recovery from addiction if we are doing it solely for our spouses or for our kids or anyone but ourselves. Our lives were crazy. We had invited drugs into our lives and they came in like a ragging storm. They may have only occupied the corner of a room in our lives but they expanded their territory and kept on going until the whole of our lives were in their power. Somehow we existed but we were a ghost of a person living in a shell that used to be our life. We needed outside help and we could no longer deny it.

We came to believe God could bring us into recovery. It wasn't in us to quit, we wanted to though. Faith in God was the answer and our desperation forced us to turn to him wholeheartedly. We were exhausted, frustrated and at our wits end. We needed supernatural help and only God could provide it.

In coming to believe that he could deliver us from active addiction we became for the first time or became again a person of faith. It was not just a simple acknowledgement of saying sure I believe there is a God out there. It was a personal desperation that we brought to him and it was a personal intervention that he worked in our lives. We grew tremendously in our experience with what God could do and we became comfortable in knowing that the balance of our recovery rested in his hands.

Heavenly Father, thank you for rescuing us from addiction and providing us with healthy lives. Help us always to trust and live for you, through Christ Jesus our Lord we pray. Amen

Step 3. We made a decision to turn our will and our lives over to the care of God as we understood Him.

**Then Jesus told his disciples, "If anyone would come after me, let him deny himself and take up his cross and follow me.
Matthew 16:24**

Recovery requires us to yield our lives fully over to the care of God. As Christians that means we surrender to the Lord our God, and his son Jesus Christ. As Christians we believe that the fullness of God dwelt in his son Jesus of Nazareth. We believe that through his life we have the most clear picture of who God our Father is. This is not unique to us as addicts. It is for all Christians to know and live by. For us as addicts though, what works best to support our recovery is that we live active lives of faith in a deliberate and intensive way. For us it is not a casual thing that we do but we are proactive in our faith on a daily basis so that we can remain drug free and clean for the rest of our lives because our sustained recovery depends on it.

In our Christian lives we also need to come to know God more personally all the time. We have the Holy Bible as the best source of knowledge about him. We have a personal relationship with him that is mediated by the son. In addiction it is likely, highly likely, that we had a lot of mistaken ideas about who God is and what he is like. This may have begun in childhood and in addiction they likely became very skewed from the truth. In recovery we need to go deep to see and experience for ourselves who our Father is and what he is like. We need to root out all misconceptions that we have of him because they are stumbling blocks that can be the source of a relapse. We need to be in a growing relationship with God and our true experiences with him will always be consistent with what the Bible says about him.

Heavenly Father, we look to you daily for all of our needs to be met. Most of all we thank you for the salvation of our souls. We thank you for the revelation of you through the life of your son, our Lord. Guide us all the days of our lives and keep us by your grace. This we ask through the name of our Lord Jesus Christ. Amen

Step 4. We made a searching and fearless moral inventory of ourselves.

Let us test and examine our ways, and return to the Lord!
Lamentations 3:40

As addicts we have a greatly developed sense of denial paired with an extensive web of lies that we believed. These two things are part of our network of false beliefs. Because of these step four is vital to our sustained recovery. In the beginning we might do this once or twice and think we have done a great job. However early in our recovery we were novices and we were just getting started. We were still learning how to peel back the surface layers and not realizing that we, like onions, have a lot of layers. We needed to go deeper. After some time we might be able to look back at those first few years and see how we did this step. Then we might see that we were only scratching at the surface of a problem so big that it goes to the very bedrock of our souls.

Too often we have heard ourselves and others say something like, "I have no idea what I did to offend them" or, "I don't know what I was thinking or how I was feeling about it." That was because we did not have particularly good skills at introspection and self-examination. Many of us may not have even known what those terms meant. We were cut off from our own thoughts and emotions. We needed to learn how to look deeply into our souls and recognize what we were feeling and thinking, and about how our actions were impacting others as well as our own lives.

In recovery we grew in the life skills that we desperately needed. Thankfully we found supportive meetings and friends. This helped us grow and complete a fourth step inventory of ourselves.

Heavenly Father, you know us extensively and we pray that you will strengthen us for the journey of looking at our lives in honesty and seeing ourselves in a true light. Help us in your mercy and grace to bear the difficulty of dealing with our past and all the pain and damage we have caused. Comfort us by your Holy Spirit so that we can boldly complete this step and progress forward from addiction to recovery one day at a time. This we ask in the name of your beloved son, Jesus Christ, our Savior and Lord. Amen

**Step 5. We admitted to God, to ourselves,
and to another human being the exact nature of our wrongs.**

**Therefore, confess your sins to one another and pray
for one another, that you may be healed.
The prayer of a righteous person has great power as it is working.
James 5:16**

This step is of course paired with step 4. With our inventory in hand, because we wrote it out, we need to make our confession. We cannot just keep it to ourselves. That would not be complete enough and would definitely hamper our recovery. Our confession could be made to any number of people, a clergyman, a friend in recovery, our counselor, a sponsor, or someone in recovery who has a gift for helping others do this. The person listening to our confession may ask us questions; we need to be prepared for that. They may want to do this to encourage our thoroughness, after all we are all masters at minimizing and denial. We need to trust this person which can be hard for many of us, having trust issues is common. Therefore, it also became a time for growing in trust with others.

For some of us it became a white-knuckle experience. It was hard to do but our confessor listened patiently, nonjudgmentally and was not shocked by anything we said which may have included some of the crimes we had committed along the way. For those of us who were in treatment, we had the opportunity to confess our fifth step to our counselor and also receive the blessing of their professional help. It may have been easy for some of us, hard for others, but the results were the same. We felt a great load lifted from our shoulders. We found it was easier to do than expected. We may have even been left with the feeling that we wanted to go deeper and do it again sometime soon. We also wanted to encourage others to do their fifth step too, knowing how much it could help them out.

Heavenly Father, thank you for your unconditional love for us. This helps and assures us of how much you care for us. Lead and guide us out of our addictive ways, and into the fullness of recovery, for the sake of your son Jesus Christ, who is Lord and Savior to us all. Amen

**Step 6. We were entirely ready to have
God remove all these defects of character.**

**Therefore, my beloved, as you have always obeyed, so now, not only as in my presence but much more in my absence, work out your own salvation with fear and trembling, for it is God who works in you, both to will and to work for his good pleasure.
Philippians 2:12-13**

We fell in love with drugs and what they did for us in the beginning. We felt great and we believed we were great when we were high. All that was an illusion that went on to become a nightmare. We were trapped by them, and they attacked our minds and did terrible things to us too. We became our own worst enemy and we could not shake it. We heard ourselves and saw ourselves say and do things that we could not believe. We were out of control. We would have happily given all that up, if only we could have. We were addicted and just to make matters worse we had become someone we despised. We could not stop using and we could not behave civilly.

When we got to this step it could not have been soon enough. We hated who we had become. We wished we could have stopped both the addiction and the behavior that came with it. We might have settled for stopping one or the other, but these things are two to a pair and they were intrinsically linked together.

In recovery we were overjoyed to be able to not use anymore. But then these addictive character flaws lingered on. We tried to be on guard for them, a lot of good that did though. We had forgotten how to be nice to others, how to trust them and treat them respectfully. We might not have realized how much of a problem we were when we were high. Now we were out of the fog and we saw ourselves more clearly. We felt uncomfortable in social settings for fear of how we might act or what we might say. We cried out to God in sorrow for the pain we had caused others. We cried out surrendering ourselves and pleading to our Maker to remake us so that we would not behave that way. God worked on us to transform us into the image of his son, day by day, one day at a time, one step at a time.

Father, have mercy on us and remove far from us all of our defects of character. We want to bring glory to your name by all that we say and do. Through Jesus Christ our Lord we pray. Amen

Step 7. We humbly asked Him to remove our shortcomings.

When the man saw that he did not prevail against Jacob, he touched his hip socket, and Jacob's hip was put out of joint as he wrestled with him. Then he said, "Let me go, for the day has broken." But Jacob said, "I will not let you go unless you bless me." And he said to him, "What is your name?" And he said, "Jacob." Then he said, "Your name shall no longer be called Jacob, but Israel, for you have striven with God and with men, and have prevailed."
Genesis 32:25-28

In the full chapter of Genesis thirty-two there is a story about Jacob, whose name means a *deceiver* or *trickster*, who wrestled with God all night long. As the sun began to rise it was apparent that there was no clear winner. Jacob had one objective, he wanted God's blessing, and he wanted it at any cost. There was a danger for him in this situation too. With the rising of the sun he would be able to see God's face. If that were to happen it would mean his death.[139] The reason for that is, if he or anyone sees God, God sees them. If God sees us, he sees our sin and he has to do something about it, which means our life is over, as "the wages of sin is death."[140]

Jacob was already an exceedingly rich man, he had a lot to live for. On the other hand he was tired of being a trickster, tired of the sins he had committed and he knew he could not change himself. God was his only hope for change. He wanted it so badly that he was willing to die in pursuit of it.

Does it seem strange that God would ask him his name? What God wanted from him was a confession of his sins, which were apparent in his name. With that confession he admitted to his sins and God blessed him with a new name, *Israel*, meaning one who walks with God.

Heavenly Father we long for our lives to be transformed from their lowly states into lives that reflect the greatness of your name. This we ask of you through Christ our Lord's name. Amen

---

[139] Exodus 33:20
[140] Romans 6:23

Step 8. We made a list of all persons we had harmed, and became willing to make amends to them all.

**Jesus said, "…if you are offering your gift at the altar and there remember that your brother has something against you…"
Matthew 5:23**

This one takes some doing. There is no need to rush through it either. We can mull it over in our heads for a while and let our memories come to the surface before we start writing things down. The process can be something of a mild shock for us. We have lived in denial and with lies in our heads for quite a while. We were using to avoiding guilt and shame by denying it, lying about it, and getting high to avoid it. As we allow our memories to come to the surface we don't want them to flood in only to overwhelm us and be triggered into a relapse. A relapse is not what we want to happen. So remember, easy does it, and one day at a time. As we break free of the unhealthy shame cycle and come to facing our guilt then we can do something positive about it.

At this point the only thing we need to do is make the list and become willing to make some amends. We can admit that we have hurt others. It is simply the truth. We can write it down, we can even keep the list in secret while we come to terms with it. Being thorough is vital, but remember, we don't have to do it all at once. There will be plenty of time to do this more than once over the course of our lifetimes. Start slow and easy. Make the list and if it is too much for now stop. Work on it more later, or take the list you have and move on to step nine. You can come back to step eight again later. As the list grows imagine for yourselves the great sense of freedom you will be gaining by doing this and following through on it. Just as God has forgiven us, so also others will offer us their forgiveness too. Much of our feelings of guilt will melt away as well.

Heaven Father, as you have forgiven us our sins through Christ our Lord, help us to prepare to find forgiveness from others for our sins against them. In humility we pray that you will strengthen us for this part of our recovery journeys and bring healing to all who we have harmed. This we ask through Christ our Lord who lives and reigns with you and the Holy Spirit. Amen

Step 9. We made direct amends to such people wherever possible, except when to do so would injure them or others.

**And Zacchaeus stood and said to the Lord,
"Behold, Lord, the half of my goods I give to the poor.
And if I have defrauded anyone of anything, I restore it fourfold."
And Jesus said to him, "Today salvation has come to this house,
since he also is a son of Abraham.
For the Son of Man came to seek and to save the lost."
Luke 19:8-10**

In our recovery we have come to realize that by our actions we have hurt others. In some cases it is significant damage that we have done. In order for us to continue to progress in our journey we need to do something about it. We may have taken advantage of others financially, said things that we shouldn't have, hurt them physically or done any number of hurtful things. These people live with the memories of having been wronged by us. For us we live with the memory of hurting them. This can feed into a dysfunctional and revolving cycle of shame for us that can haunt us relentlessly. That is dangerous for our recovery because it can easily lead to a relapse for us. In recovery we face the guilt of what we have done. In order to be freed from the guilt we need to, at the very least, go to them and confess our guilt, apologize, and ask for their forgiveness. In some cases we might need to offer to make some kind of restitution for the damage we did. Given the nature of our problems, there may be restraining orders that keep us from contacting someone directly as well as through a second party. We need to honor and respect the courts orders. To break them would be inconsistent with our recovery oriented lifestyles. If we are uncertain of what to do we can talk to our sponsor, our confessor from step five, a counselor or a trusted friend who is also in recovery.

Heavenly Father, you have forgiven us our sins against you through the redeeming death of your son. Help us as we seek to bring healing to those we have offended and hurt by our addiction. This we ask through Christ Jesus our Lord and Savior. Amen

**Step 10. We continued to take personal inventory
and when we were wrong promptly admitted it.**

**I acknowledged my sin to you, and I did not cover my iniquity;
I said, "I will confess my transgressions to the Lord,"
and you forgave the iniquity of my sin. Selah
Psalm 34:5**

Recovery happens in our lives because it is our new lifestyle. We made great inroads into this new way of life with the previous steps, and now that we have come this far, this is something we want to practice whenever the situation comes up. We found some of the steps were hard at first, but then as we completed them we also found great relief. As we progressed, our desire to use again lightened and our hunger for working the program grew. The shame cycle that we had fallen prey to no longer trapped us as before. We were able to experience guilt and process it in a healthy way by admitting to what we had done and asking forgiveness if that was called for. We could then say, "Ahh..., what a relief it is." We found joy in our newfound freedom to admit we weren't perfect, that we were making progress, and that was good enough.

In recovery we found through the steps that we could accept others for where they were in the program. We didn't need to take offense that they weren't perfect either. We saw ourselves in them as they admitted to mistakes they made just like us. We were okay with being imperfect, living in an imperfect and fallen world, and with other people who were imperfect.

We made a free and easy admission of being wrong and we were comfortable with it. Along with that we were okay with however people around us took that admission. They might be forgiving, they might take offense anyway. We had done our part. We were accountable for our actions and kept it no secret that we were human.

Gracious Father, thank you for caring for us and in your love redeeming us from our sins. We love you and your son and will live in your will all the days of our lives. For you reign in heaven above with your son, Jesus Christ in whose name we pray. Amen

Step 11. We sought through prayer and meditation to improve our conscious contact with God as we understood Him, praying only for knowledge of His will for us and the power to carry that out.

**Do not be conformed to this world,
but be transformed by the renewal of your mind,
that by testing you may discern what is the will of God,
what is good and acceptable and perfect.
Romans 12:2**

Adam and Eve had been first charged by God on the sixth day of creation to, "Be fruitful and multiply and fill the earth and subdue it, and have dominion over the fish of the sea and over the birds of the heavens and over every living thing that moves on the earth."[141] They were incorporated into God's work of creation so that they were not only part of what he created, but also part of the continuing work of maintaining what he had created. This is his will for us from the beginning of time, that we take an active role in his creation.

In living out step eleven in our lives we continue with practicing our daily devotions with an active prayer life that also includes prayers throughout the entire day. We also continue in meditative practices, focusing again on knowing and experiencing God's presence in our lives, and reading, studying, and meditating on his Word as well.

As our relationship with God grows strong, our lives take on new purpose and direction. In our spirituality we see in new ways how we are living out his will in our lives. From our academic careers to our jobs, our place in our families, our community, and in our churches we see that we are fulfilling our place in creation and living out God's will in our lives.

Heavenly Father, by your breath-of-life in us we have been given our lives and it is you who sustains our recoveries. We pray that you will reveal your will to us and aid us in living it out fully in our lives every day. This we ask through Christ our Lord. Amen

---

[141] Genesis 1:28

Step 12. Having had a spiritual awakening as a result of these steps, we tried to carry this message to addicts, and to practice these principles in all our affairs.

And a leper came to him, imploring him, and kneeling said to him, "If you will, you can make me clean." Moved with pity, he stretched out his hand and touched him and said to him, "I will; be clean." And immediately the leprosy left him, and he was made clean. And Jesus sternly charged him and sent him away at once, and said to him, "See that you say nothing to anyone, but go, show yourself to the priest and offer for your cleansing what Moses commanded, for a proof to them." But he went out and began to talk freely about it, and to spread the news, so that Jesus could no longer openly enter a town, but was out in desolate places, and people were coming to him from every quarter.
Mark 1:40-45

    Anonymity is quite common among addicts. It is up to us to decide if we are going to let others know about our addiction and recoveries or not. In secret we can tell someone we come across who we know or suspect is suffering from our affliction. For some of us who would like to do the work of an evangelist, our recovery testimony can be a way to share God's message of salvation too. We need to remember that with addiction there comes a blindness in the one who is using to what the drugs are doing to them. Along with that there are the lies that they also believe in. The blindness is a spiritual one and the lies are of the devil. What we share can save the life of someone who is suffering. It can prevent them from ending up in prison, or an institution, or dead. We need to remember how it was that we found out about the program of recovery. We need to remember what our lives might have been like if no one had given up their anonymity to share the message with us. With this mission to share the message we are called upon to carry on in our lives with all of the steps in motion at once. That is practicing them in all our affairs.

    Heavenly Father, we are grateful for all that you have restored to us by your grace. Your love for us compels us to live for you and your glory. Reveal your will to us daily and strengthen us for the journey, through Christ Jesus our Lord and our Savior from sin and addiction. Amen

The Doxology

**Now to him who is able to keep you from stumbling and to present you blameless before the presence of his glory with great joy, to the only God, our Savior, through Jesus Christ our Lord, be glory, majesty, dominion, and authority, before all time and now and forever. Amen.
Jude 24-25**

Appendix 1

The 12-steps of Narcotics Anonymous-
How It Works

If you want what we have to offer, and are willing to make the effort to get it, then you are ready to take certain steps. These are the principles that made our recovery possible.

1. We admitted that we were powerless over our addiction, that our lives had become unmanageable.
2. We came to believe that a Power greater than ourselves could restore us to sanity.
3. We made a decision to turn our will and our lives over to the care of God as we understood Him.
4. We made a searching and fearless moral inventory of ourselves.
5. We admitted to God, to ourselves, and to another human being the exact nature of our wrongs.
6. We were entirely ready to have God remove all these defects of character.
7. We humbly asked Him to remove our shortcomings.
8. We made a list of all persons we had harmed, and became willing to make amends to them all.
9. We made direct amends to such people wherever possible, except when to do so would injure them or others.
10. We continued to take personal inventory and when we were wrong promptly admitted it.
11. We sought through prayer and meditation to improve our conscious contact with God as we understood Him, praying only for knowledge of His will for us and the power to carry that out.
12. Having had a spiritual awakening as a result of these steps, we tried to carry this message to addicts, and to practice these principles in all our affairs.

This sounds like a big order, and we can't do it all at once. We didn't become addicted in one day, so remember—easy does it.

There is one thing more than anything else that will defeat us in our recovery; this is an attitude of indifference or intolerance toward spiritual principles. Three of these that are indispensable are honesty, open-mindedness, and willingness. With these we are well on our way.

We feel that our approach to the disease of addiction is completely realistic, for the therapeutic value of one addict helping another is without parallel. We feel that our way is practical, for one addict can best understand and help another addict. We believe that the sooner we face our problems within our society, in everyday living, just that much faster do we become acceptable, responsible, and productive members of that society.[142]

---

[142] Who, What, How and Why, White Booklet, Narcotics Anonymous World Services, Inc., 2000.

Appendix 2

Here are the 12-steps from Narcotics Anonymous with Bible references.

The 12-steps of Narcotics Anonymous- How It Works

1) We admitted that we were powerless over our addiction, that our lives had become unmanageable.

> For my iniquities have gone over my head; like a heavy burden, they are too heavy for me.
> Psalm 38:4

> For I do not understand my own actions. For I do not do what I want, but I do the very thing I hate. Now if I do what I do not want, I agree with the law, that it is good. So now it is no longer I who do it, but sin that dwells within me. For I know that nothing good dwells in me, that is, in my flesh. For I have the desire to do what is right, but not the ability to carry it out. For I do not do the good I want, but the evil I do not want is what I keep on doing.
> Romans 7:15-20

> For when I am weak, then I am strong.
> 2 Corinthians 12:10

2) We came to believe that a Power greater than ourselves could restore us to sanity.

> But to all who did receive him, who believed in his name, he gave the right to become children of God, who were born, not of blood nor of the will of the flesh nor of the will of man, but of God.
> John 1:12-13

> For it is God who works in you, both to will and to work for his good pleasure.
> Philippians 2:13

3) We made a decision to turn our will and our lives over to the care of God as we understood Him.

> But as for me and my house, we will serve the Lord.
> Joshua 24:15

> Then Jesus told his disciples, "If anyone would come after me, let him deny himself and take up his cross and follow me.
> Matthew 16:24

> I appeal to you therefore, brothers, by the mercies of God, to present your bodies as a living sacrifice, holy and acceptable to God, which is your spiritual worship.
> Romans 12:1

4) We made a searching and fearless moral inventory of ourselves.

> Search me, O God, and know my heart! Try me and know my thoughts! And see if there be any grievous way in me, and lead me in the way everlasting!
> Psalm 139:23-24

> Let us test and examine our ways, and return to the Lord!
> Lamentations 3:40

5) We admitted to God, to ourselves, and to another human being the exact nature of our wrongs.

> Therefore, confess your sins to one another and pray for one another, that you may be healed. The prayer of a righteous person has great power as it is working.
> James 5:16

> And no creature is hidden from his sight, but all are naked and exposed to the eyes of him to whom we must give account.
> Hebrews 4:13

6) We were entirely ready to have God remove all these defects of character.

> Search me, O God, and know my heart! Try me and know my thoughts! And see if there be any grievous way in me, and lead me in the way everlasting!
> Psalm 139:23-24

> Now the Lord is the Spirit, and where the Spirit of the Lord is, there is freedom. And we all, with unveiled face, beholding the glory of the Lord, are being transformed into the same image from one degree of glory to another. For this comes from the Lord who is the Spirit.
> 2 Corinthians 3:17-18

> Therefore, my beloved, as you have always obeyed, so now, not only as in my presence but much more in my absence, work out your own salvation with fear and trembling, for it is God who works in you, both to will and to work for his good pleasure.
> Philippians 2:12-13

7) We humbly asked Him to remove our shortcomings.

> When the man saw that he did not prevail against Jacob, he touched his hip socket, and Jacob's hip was put out of joint as he wrestled with him. Then he said, "Let me go, for the day has broken." But Jacob said, "I will not let you go unless you bless me." And he said to him, "What is your name?" And he said, "Jacob." Then he said, "Your name shall no longer be called Jacob, but Israel, for you have striven with God and with men, and have prevailed."
> Genesis 32:25-28

> Do not be conformed to this world, but be transformed by the renewal of your mind, that by testing you may discern what is the will of God, what is good and acceptable and perfect.
> Romans 12:2

> If we confess our sins, he is faithful and just to forgive us our sins and to cleanse us from all unrighteousness.
> 1 John 1:9

8) We made a list of all persons we had harmed, and became willing to make amends to them all.

> So if you are offering your gift at the altar and there remember that your brother has something against you, leave your gift there before the altar and go. First be reconciled to your brother, and then come and offer your gift.
> Matt. 5:23-24

9) We made direct amends to such people wherever possible, except when to do so would injure them or others.

> I will arise and go to my father, and I will say to him, "Father, I have sinned against heaven and before you. I am no longer worthy to be called your son. Treat me as one of your hired servants."
> Luke 15:18-19

> And Zacchaeus stood and said to the Lord, "Behold, Lord, the half of my goods I give to the poor. And if I have defrauded anyone of anything, I restore it fourfold." And Jesus said to him, "Today salvation has come to this house, since he also is a son of Abraham. For the Son of Man came to seek and to save the lost."
> Luke 19:8-10

> Repay no one evil for evil, but give thought to do what is honorable in the sight of all.
> Romans 12:17

10) We continued to take personal inventory and when we were wrong promptly admitted it.

> I acknowledged my sin to you, and I did not cover my iniquity; I said, "I will confess my transgressions to the Lord," and you forgave the iniquity of my sin. Selah
> Psalm 34:5

> Search me, O God, and know my heart! Try me and know my thoughts! And see if there be any grievous way in me, and lead me in the way everlasting!
> Psalm 139:23-24

11) We sought through prayer and meditation to improve our conscious contact with God as we understood Him, praying only for knowledge of His will for us and the power to carry that out.

> Jesus said to him, "I am the way, and the truth, and the life. No one comes to the Father except through me. If you had known me, you would have known my Father also. From now on you do know him and have seen him."
> John 14:6-7

> Do not be conformed to this world, but be transformed by the renewal of your mind, that by testing you may discern what is the will of God, what is good and acceptable and perfect.
> Romans 12:2

12) Having had a spiritual awakening as a result of these steps, we tried to carry this message to addicts, and to practice these principles in all our affairs.

> Come and hear, all you who fear God, and I will tell what he has done for my soul.
> Psalm 66:16

> And a leper came to him, imploring him, and kneeling said to him, "If you will, you can make me clean." Moved with pity, he stretched out his hand and touched him and said to him, "I will; be clean." And immediately the leprosy left him, and he was made clean. And Jesus sternly charged him and sent him away at once, and said to him, "See that you say nothing to anyone, but go, show yourself to the priest and offer for your cleansing what Moses commanded, for a proof to them." But he went out and began to talk freely about it, and to spread the news, so that Jesus could no longer openly enter a town, but was out in desolate places, and people were coming to him from every quarter.
> Mark 1:40-45

Made in the USA
Monee, IL
31 January 2024